NATIVE PLANTS FOR NORTHERN GARDENS

Viola species (Violets). A woodland ground cover

at the Minnesota Landscape Arboretum, in spring 1975.

Photograph: Merv Eisel.

NATIVE PLANTS FOR NORTHERN GARDENS

By Dr. Leon C. Snyder

Edited by Richard T. Isaacson
Bibliographer and Head Librarian,
Andersen Horticultural Library

Andersen Horticultural Library
University of Minnesota Libraries
Minnesota Landscape Arboretum

1991

PREFACE

Dr. Leon Snyder, upon his death in 1987, left this unpublished manuscript on using native plants in the landscape. The manuscript evidences a lifelong interest and work with these plants. The editor has generally left the manuscript as Dr. Snyder wrote it with the exception of rearranging it into a different chapter order. The editor also attempted to use as many of Dr. Snyder's slides to illustrate this work as possible. Noncredited photographs are assumed to be Dr. Snyder's work.

Leon C. Snyder was born in Shepherd, Michigan in 1908. He received his B.S. degree in 1931 and his Ph.D. degree in 1935, both from the University of Washington in Seattle.

Dr. Snyder joined the University of Minnesota staff in 1945 as an extension horticulturist. He was promoted to Head of the Department of Horticultural Science in 1953. In 1958 he was named Director of The Minnesota Landscape Arboretum. On April 1, 1970 he relinquished his duties as Head of the Department to devote full time to his work at the Arboretum.

Under Dr. Snyder's guidance, the Arboretum grew from modest beginnings to a major research and educational institution containing over 4,000 species and cultivars. Until the establishment of the Arboretum, little work had been done on the evaluation of woody ornamentals for severe northern climates. Dr. Snyder retired in 1976.

Dr. Snyder was awarded many awards and distinctions including the Gold Medal of the Men's Garden Clubs of America; the Medal of Honor of The Garden Club of America; the Norman Jay Colman Award, the highest honor for research in the nursery trade; the Liberty Hyde Bailey Award of the American Horticultural Society; and the Silver Medal Award of the National Council of State Garden Clubs.

Dr. Snyder wrote a weekly gardening column for the **Minneapolis Tribune** from 1966 to his death. He wrote five previously published gardening books: **Gardening in the Upper Midwest** (U. of Minnesota Press, 1978, revised 1985), **Trees and Shrubs for Northern Gardens** (U. of Minnesota Press, 1980), **How Does Your Garden Grow?** (WCCO, 1982), **Flowers for Northern Gardens** (U. of Minnesota Press, 1983), and co-authored **A Minnesota Gardener's Companion** (Minneapolis Tribune, 1981).

Jane McKinnon, then Extension Horticulturist at the University of Minnesota, in a memorial published in the October/November 1987 **Minnesota Horticulturist**, wrote: "He taught both in scientific words and with dirt-stained hands. From his pencil on a note pad came scholarly publications; with sharp pruning shears he showed students how skills are perfected...He encouraged, challenged, forgave, and never reminded students of failures. He saw promise in the most unlikely freshmen, and freely complimented successful graduates. He always credited good work from colleagues and pupils as well. He forgot disagreements and had no time for grudge or malice. By his own industry he shamed sluggards. With his immaculate rows of vegetables and carefully tended rose beds, for anyone to enjoy on a moment's notice, he sent visitors home to try harder at gardening. By his example, he created visions of soft lawns, gracious trees, and bright flowers for those needing inspiration and encouragement".

The editor wishes to express appreciation to the following individuals. Mrs. Leon (Vera) Snyder, and members of her family, who graciously contributed Dr. Snyder's manuscript to the Andersen Horticultural Library's publication fund. It was a generous gesture which enabled the library to publish this useful book. Also, the library gratefully acknowledges those individuals listed under contributors who enabled this publication to be published. Mr. Peter Olin, Director of The Minnesota Landscape Arboretum, and Susan Fitzgerald, Development Officer, gave generously of their time and expertise. Also, we acknowledge the typing skills of Peggy Hood, and the following people who contributed slides: Dr. Harold Pellett, Mervin Eisel, Dr. Anne M. Hanchek, Mike Zins, Bonnie E. Harper Lore, Darrel G. Morrison, and Douglas Owens-Pike. Also, Andersen Horticultural Library staff members, Nancy Allison, Evy Sand, Amy Owen, and Renee Jensen contributed much to the publication of this book.

The Andersen Horticultural Library's publication fund was established by former Governor Elmer Andersen and his wife Eleanor to publish books in the areas of Minnesota natural history, and needed horticultural monographs of which this book is an example. Through its publication fund, Andersen Horticultural Library has been able to share its research and its horticultural information with a worldwide audience. This is the sixth work published through this fund.

Dr. Snyder was our teacher, friend, and colleague. He spent many hours in research in Andersen Horticultural Library.

LIST OF MAJOR DONORS

Major support for this publication was provided by

a donation in memory of Janet and Arthur Hartwell,

Arboretum friends with a lifelong interest

in books and gardening.

The following have provided additional support:

William and Dorothy Fobes

Lawrence and Ronya Greenberg

Reuel and Peggy Harmon

Malcolm and Honey Pfunder

Ruth Bovey Stevens

Harold W. Sweatt Foundation

J. Kimball and Helen Whitney

Smilacina racemosa. Photograph taken in 1978 at
Sissinghurst Castle, the famous garden of Vita Sackville-West
in England.

TABLE OF CONTENTS

INTRODUCTION

Backyard garden and design of

Darrel G. Morrison in Madison Wisconsin.

Photograph: Darrel G. Morrison.

There are native plants having landscape value that are not now being grown by American gardeners. We often seem to place a greater value on plants imported from other countries than what we place on our native species. In my travels I have noticed that, for instance, Australians feature plants that are native in Europe and America. While in southern California, more Australian plants are used than one would see in gardens in Sydney or Melbourne.

Why do we seem to prefer introduced plants? There is no simple answer. Maybe we feel that a native plant is commonplace while something that is imported is extra special. Demonstratively, some of the most beautiful plants in the world are native American species. Who could deny that our sugar maple is more beautiful than a Norway maple, especially in the fall of the year? The same is true of our white ash and pin oak as compared with European species.

There are many positive reasons to consider native plants. One of the primary reasons is that native plants have the further advantage of being adapted, through centuries of growth, to our climatic conditions. They are also better able to resist the effects of our native insects and diseases. Another reason is maintained landscapes featuring native plants also blend into their natural surroundings better than those planted with introduced species.

This is not to say that introduced species do not have a place in landscaping. There is certainly a place for such plants as lilacs, daylilies, and Asiatic lilies. Perhaps the only place where one might wish to use native plants exclusively might be a summer home near a lake or in a forest campground. The purpose of this book is to acquaint us with the wealth of our native plant material and to show how these plants might be used in the landscape.

The first part of this book describes morphological characteristics that are useful in plant identification. Other chapters focus on cultural practices and plant propagation. The main chapters cover native plant material with brief descriptions of each genera and species, its use in the landscape, and cultural requirements. Many chapters in this section also have plant lists for specific purposes.

Plants described in this book are native to the area defined by the southern portions of Manitoba and western Ontario, and those portions of the United States from the western Dakotas to eastern Wisconsin, south to central Iowa. This area includes portions of the tall grass prairies, the deciduous hardwoods, and the coniferous forests. Plants described in this book are native within this region; however, a few species that are native contiguous to this area are included. The Colorado spruce and the white or concolor fir are examples.

Before discussing native plants, we must be aware of possible problems in growing native plants. Native plants have specific site requirements which must be met if the plants are to thrive under cultivation. The stemless lady's-slipper and our native blueberries grow only in acid soils and soon perish when planted in neutral or slightly alkaline soils. Our sugar maple is found in well-drained clay loam soils and is short-lived in sandy soils. In using native plants, one must be familiar with their native habitats and try to duplicate these conditions as nearly as possible. Generally, however, it is true that most natives can be more easily grown in our region than many of our favorite introduced plants.

It is also important to emphasize that many native plants should not be collected or dug from the wild. For many wild plants, only those grown in commercial nurseries should be purchased. In the discussion of individual species, those that should not be collected are identified.

United States Department of Agriculture map of
hardiness zones. Most of the area covered by this
book is zone 4 to 2.

Photograph: Mike Zins.

How Plants Get Their Names

Every plant has a scientific name and one or more common names. The scientific name of plants consists of the genus and species and is the same in all parts of the world. Unfortunately, nurseries and garden centers often list plants only by their common names. This causes the same plant to be sold under a different common name by different companies. Also, when scientific names are used, often only the genus is given with no reference to species. To make matters worse, the generic names are often obsolete. In this book, the scientific names used are those given in **Hortus Third**, a modern listing of all plants under cultivation in North America. An alphabetic listing of common names is given in the index with reference to their correct scientific name. Common names, unfortunately, can differ in different countries and even within the same country. A plant may even have several common names in the same locality. The common name lily can be found in dozens of different genera and even in different plant families. It would be most convenient if each genus had but one common name and each species had but one descriptive common name. An example might be oak for the genus **Quercus** and white oak for **Quercus alba**. Unfortunately, such simplicity is not characteristic for most common names. The use of the genus name as a part of the common name is a step in the right direction. Anemone, aster, chrysanthemum, clematis, delphinium, iris, geranium, lobelia, phlox, and verbena are familiar common names as well as being generic names. The confusion comes when a generic name is used for the common name for a plant of a different genus. Geranium is the common name for a familiar house plant and garden flower belonging to the genus **Pelargonium**. The generic name **Geranium** is used for a native woodland wild flower. Often the common name is the English translation of the genus name as in gentian for Gentiana, lily for Lilium, and violet for Viola. However, more often the common name bears no resemblance to the genus name.

It must be kept in mind that not all plants within a species are identical. Plants of a certain species growing within a particular geographic area will differ from plants of the same species in other parts of its natural range. Occasionally flower and fruit size and color differ from the typical species. Where these differences are reproduced from seed under natural conditions, a third name is added to the scientific name. These names are prefixed by var. (for botanical variety), f. (for forma), or subsp. (for subspecies). Examples are **Picea glauca** var. **densata** for a geographic variant of the white spruce occurring in the Black Hills of South Dakota, **Geranium maculatum** f. **albiflorum** for a variant with white flowers, and **Heliopsis helianthoides** subsp. **scabra** for a variant with scabrous stems and leaves. When to use the prefix var., f., or subsp. is not always clear to the layman. It is a decision best left to a trained plant taxonomist. (We are ignoring hybrids and cultivated varieties, or cultivars, in this discussion because they are not generally naturally occurring plants).

Plant families, which contain groups of genera having similar flower structures, are one of the most important parts of plant classification. With a little study and practice, one can learn to recognize certain plant families. For instance, in the RANUNCULACEAE (Buttercup Family), the flowers consist of a whorl of sepals, many stamens, and numerous carpels. Petals may or may not be present. Knowing the plant family also helps to provide proper growing conditions, since most plants in a family can have similar cultural requirements. In the ERICACEAE (Heath Family), acid soil is a requirement.

Plant Hardiness

Plants differ greatly in their hardiness or ability to grow and thrive in a given area. This hardiness is genetically determined. In general, in species that have a wide geographical distribution, plants grown from seeds collected from northern plants will be hardier than those from southern plants. There are several environmental factors that affect hardiness. Low winter temperatures are probably the most important. Important determinates also include when low temperatures occur and the length of these cold periods. A sudden drop in temperature in late fall, before the plants are fully hardened, often causes more injury than the same temperatures would cause later in the winter. The relative humidity of the air can also be a factor.

With herbaceous plants that die to the ground each fall, snow cover can be an important factor in preventing winter injury. Some herbaceous plants may actually be hardier in the far north where they receive a more dependable snow cover.

Native plants are less susceptible to winter injury than introduced species. Survival of the fittest has eliminated some that are not fully hardy. It is important, however, to plant certain native species under conditions similar to their native habitat. For instance, the native Canadian yew is found on north-facing slopes, under trees, or where the plants will be covered with winter snow. When planted in an exposed site where winter sun can reflect on the yew's evergreen foliage, winter burn can be a serious problem.

Hardiness Zones

Several hardiness zone maps are in use. Canada has its own zone maps. Arnold Arboretum has a zone map that has been used in some books and nursery catalogues. The zone map used in this book is the one published by the United States Department of Agriculture. This map is based on minimum winter temperatures, but does not take into account such factors as rainfall and soil type. The recommended hardiness zones are given for all woody species. Because of the effect of snow cover, hardiness zones are not given for herbaceous species. Herbaceous species described in this book should be hardy throughout the Upper Midwest with adequate snow cover.

We should recognize the effect of microclimates. It is sometimes possible to grow a certain species in a protected site in a zone north of the recommended zone. Likewise it may be inadvisable to plant a certain species in a very exposed site in a zone where it is recommended.

Metric System

In this book all measurements are given in the metric system. It will help to visualize an inch as equalling about two and a half centimeters and a meter as equalling a little over three feet (39 inches). In the metric system, 10 millimeters equals a centimeter, and 100 centimeters equals a meter.

MORPHOLOGICAL CHARACTERISTICS

Plants vary greatly in plant habit. Some are woody, others are herbaceous. Woody plants are either trees, shrubs, or vines. Vines have weak stems so they require some support. In nature, vines climb into trees or shrubs or cover walls, fences, and rocks. Some vines have special structures for climbing called tendrils to attach themselves to their support. Other vines wrap themselves around their support by spiral twining.

There is no sharp distinction between shrubs and trees. Usually trees have a single stem and are taller than shrubs which usually have multiple stems. However, often when a young tree is eaten to the ground by rabbits or deer, multiple stems grow up from the base and a clump tree results such as in our native canoe or paper birch. This effect can also, of course, be created by horticultural pruning. Trees differ greatly in form. Some are columnar, others have rounded crowns, and some have a pyramidal outline. Shrubs may also be low, creeping, mound-shaped, or upright.

Herbaceous plants are classified as annual, biennial, or perennial according to their longevity. Annuals bloom the first year from seed and then die after maturing their seeds. Biennials grow vegetatively the first year, flower and produce seed the second year, and then die after fruiting. Perennials live for more than two years. They die to the ground in the fall but come up from underground buds each spring. While some perennials flower the first year from seed, most do not flower until the second or third year. The form of herbaceous plants is as variable as trees and shrubs, and ranges from low, creeping plants to tall, upright plants.

Stem Morphology

Stems differ from roots by bearing leaves and developing buds in the axils of their leaves. Buds that grow in leaf axils develop into lateral branches. Some buds are completely vegetative, others develop both vegetative branches and flowers. Most stems develop above ground. Stems that creep along the surface of the soil are called runners or stolons.

However, a few stems develop underground. These can be distinguished from roots by the presence of leaf scars and buds. Underground stems that are elongated and spread horizontally are called rhizomes. These rhizomes may be fleshy as in iris or slender as in many of the grasses. A corm is a fleshy underground stem that is vertically oriented. They are often round in outline with scalelike leaves and terminal or axillary buds. The jack-in-the-pulpit is a familiar example. Bulbs are also underground stems with fleshy leaf bases attached to a short conical stem. In the tunicate bulb the leaf bases form concentric rings when seen in cross section. The onion is a familiar example. In scaly bulbs, the leaf bases are separate scales that attach to the conical stem. The lily is a good example. Tubers are fleshy underground storage organs with leaf scars and buds like a rhizome but usually shorter. Potatoes and Jerusalem artichokes are examples.

Some above ground stems are also modified. A thorn is a sharp, pointed stem outgrowth that serves as a protective device. Hawthorns and honey locusts are examples of plants with thorns. Tendrils are modified structures for climbing. They may originate from stems or leaves. The tendrils in the grape or in the Virginia creeper are of stem origin.

Root Morphology

We are less familiar with roots than we are with stems. They usually develop underground, although in moist climates aerial roots are not uncommon. Roots may be fleshy or fibrous. Some root systems have a large central root that grows straight down with smaller lateral roots. Such a root system is called a tap root. In most plants several roots of equal size grow out from the base of the stem and branch as they extend through the soil. Such a root system is termed fascicled. Root hairs are single-celled extensions of epidermal cells that develop just back of the growing tip. These root hairs increase the capacity of roots to absorb water and plant nutrients from the soil. Plants such as the oak or black walnut have tap roots which are more difficult to transplant than plants with fascicled roots. What few people realize is the extent of a plant's root system. Roots of an elm can spread for 20 or more meters from the base of the trunk. In transplanting a shrub or a tree of any size, most of the smaller feeding roots are cut off in digging. This is why smaller trees and shrubs are easier to transplant.

Leaf Morphology

The chief function of leaves is to manufacture food by the process of photosynthesis. Their green color is due to chlorophyll. Most leaves are flat and oriented so a maximum amount of leaf surface is exposed to the sun.

A typical leaf is made up of an expanded portion (the blade) and a stalk portion (the petiole). The petiole may be short, long, or entirely lacking in some leaves. In some plants the leaf base attaches directly to the stem. In others, notably the grasses, the leaf base forms a sheath that surrounds the stem. In some leaves a pair of leaflike bracts (stipules) are attached to the base of the petiole.

The arrangement of leaves on stems is a characteristic that is useful in plant identification. When one leaf occurs at a node the leaves are alternate and usually arranged in a spiral fashion. When two leaves occur at a node they are opposite, and when three of more leaves occur at a node they are whorled.

Leaf venation refers to the arrangement of the main veins. In pinnate venation, there is a central midrib with lateral veins that spread out from the midrib like a feather. In palmate venation, three or more prominent veins radiate out from near the base of the blade. In both pinnate and palmated venation lateral veins branch and run together to form a network which can be seen when the leaf is held up to the light. Another type of venation is when the veins run parallel to each other. Netted venation of the pinnate or palmate type occurs in dicotyledonous plants (plants with two seed leaves). Parallel venation occurs in monocotyledonous plants (plants with a single seed leaf).

Leaves may be simple or compound. A simple leaf has a blade that is in one piece. In a compound leaf, the leaf blade is divided into separate leaflets. To distinguish a leaflet of a compound leaf from a simple leaf, look for the bud that develops in the axil where the petiole joins the stem. There will be no buds in the axils of the leaflets.

Leaves can vary greatly in size and thickness. Some leaves, especially those that are pinnately compound or twice pinnately compound can be very large. In the Kentucky coffee tree a single leaf can be as much as 1 meter long and nearly as wide. In our native arborvitae, the leaves are scalelike and are less than a quarter of an inch long. Most

Asclepias tuberosa (Butterfly Weed). In bloom near Sherburne, Minnesota.

Photograph: Bonnie L. Harper Lore.

leaves are flat and quite thin, but in some desert plants the leaves are thick and succulent. Such leaves are adapted for water storage as well as for photosynthesis.

Leaves have various shapes which are quite uniform for each species and useful in recognizing plants.

Leaf margins are also uniform for a given species and useful in plant identification.

Flower Morphology

The flower is the least variable of the morphological characteristics and therefore is used in most plant identification systems. A typical flower has four sets of modified leaves, either spirally arranged or in whorls, which are attached to a short terminal swelling of the stem called the receptacle. The four sets of leaves are as follows:

Sepals. Lowest set of leaves, usually green but may be brightly colored and petallike. Collectively called the calyx.

Petals. Attached above the sepals, usually colored. Collectively the corolla.

Stamens. Located above the petals. Each stamen consists of a stalk portion (the filament) and two pollen-producing sacs (the anthers). The number of stamens in a flower varies from few to many. Collectively the stamens are called the androecium.

Carpels. Produced in the center of the flower. A single carpel or several united carpels develop into a pistil. A pistil is made up of a swollen base (the ovary), the neck portion (the style), and the terminal portion, usually sticky for the reception of pollen (the stigma). The carpels in a single flower are collectively called the gynoecium.

The stamens and carpels are the reproductive organs of the flower. Pollen grains from the anthers alight on the stigma and germinate to form a pollen tube that digests its way through the style into the ovary chamber. Each pollen tube finds its way to an ovule where sperm cells are discharged to fertilize the egg and endosperm nuclei. The fertilized egg develops into an embryo enclosed within a seed that develops from the ovule.

The floral parts may remain separate or they may fuse. The calyx or corolla made up of fused sepals or petals may be rotate, campanulate, funnelform, or salverform. Fused stamens are less common, but in the pea, mallow, and sunflower families, the filaments are fused to form a tube. The fusion of carpels to form a compound ovary is common.

Types of Flowers

Flowers differ in the placement of floral parts and in the presence or absence of parts. The following terms describe these differences.

Regular flower. Has radial symmetry. That is, any line cut vertically through the flower will divide it into two symmetrical halves. Example: rose.

Irregular flower. Asymmetrical in structure, so only one vertical line will divide it into two symmetrical halves. Example: pea.

Complete flower. Has all floral parts, sepals, petals, stamens, and carpels. Example: rose.

Incomplete flower. Lacks one or more floral parts. Examples: anemone with petals lacking and sepals petallike, and cottonwood with sepals and petals lacking and stamens and carpels produced in flowers on separate plants.

Perfect flower. Has both stamens and carpels and may or may not have sepals and petals. Examples: rose with all floral parts, and anemone with petals lacking.

Anemone quinquifolia (Wood Anemone). A good ground cover for shady places.

Photographed in the Cannon River Valley in Northfield, Minnesota.

Photograph: Bonnie L. Harper Lore.

Imperfect flower. Has either stamens or carpels but not both in the same flower. Sepals and petals may or may not be present. Examples: willow, birch.

Monoecious flowers. Imperfect flowers in which the staminate and pistillate flowers occur on the same plant. Example: birch.

Dioecious flowers. Imperfect flowers in which the staminate and pistillate flowers occur on separate plants. Examples: cottonwood, bittersweet.

Hypogynous flowers. The ovary (gynoecium) is above (hypo) the attachment of the other flower parts. Example: lily.

Perigynous flower. The calyx cup (hypanthium) grows up around the ovary but is not attached to it. Calyx lobes, petals, and stamens are attached to the rim of the hypanthium. Example : cherry.

Epigynous flower. The hypanthium fuses with the ovary, and calyx lobes, petals, and stamens appear to rise above the ovary. The ovary is said to be inferior. Examples: apple, evening primrose.

Types of Inflorescences

The inflorescence is the grouping of flowers in a flower cluster.

Spike. Flowers are borne sessile (without pedicels) on a vertical axis. Examples: turtlehead, wheat.

Raceme. Flowers on short pedicels along a vertical axis. Example: choke cherry.

Corymb. Flowers on pedicels of varying length on a vertical axis. The lower pedicels are longest, giving the inflorescence a flat-topped appearance. Example: geum.

Panicle. A branched inflorescence with the oldest flowers near the base. Examples: Ohio buckeye, meadow sweet.

Cyme. A branched inflorescence with the oldest flowers at the tip of the main stem and lateral branches. Examples: elderberry, phlox.

Solitary. A single flower on a stalk (peduncle). Examples: pasqueflower, trillium.

Head. Many sessile flowers on a flat or rounded stem tip. Examples: clover, sunflower.

Umbel. A cluster of pedicelled flowers arising from one point at the tip of the stem, with pedicels all of about the same length. Examples: onion, parsnip.

Compound umbel. A cluster of simple umbels. Example: golden Alexanders.

Fruit Morphology

Fruits develop from the ovary or ovaries of pollinated flowers. In some fruits, accessory flower parts become a part of the fruit. Fruits may be either dry or fleshy. The following fruit types are found in plants covered in this book:

Dry Dehiscent Fruits

These are fruits that split open at maturity to shed their seeds.

Legume (pod). Composed of a single carpel that splits along two sutures with seeds in a single row. Examples: peas, black locust.

Follicle. Composed of a single carpel that splits along one suture. Examples: milk weed, ninebark.

Capsule. Composed of more than one carpel, opening by pores near the tip or by longitudinal splitting starting at the top. Many-seeded. Examples: poppy, lily.

Silique. A special type of capsule found in the mustard family in which two valves separate from a thin, longitudinal partition on which the seeds are attached. Example: toothwort.

Alnus rugosa (Smooth Alder).

Dry Indehiscent Fruits

These are fruits that do not open to shed their seeds.

Achene. A one-seeded fruit enclosed by a thin ovary wall that is separate from the seed coat. Examples: anemone, clematis.

Caryopsis. A one-seeded fruit in which the ovary wall is fused with the seed coat. Example: Indian grass.

Samara. Similar to an achene but with a flat wing or wings to aid in dispersal. Examples: ash, maple.

Nut. A one-seeded fruit with a hard bony shell. Examples: walnut, hazelnut.

Nutlet. A small nut. Examples: birch, mertensia.

Fleshy Fruits

Berry. A many-seeded fruit with a thin pericarp. Examples: baneberry, honeysuckle.

Drupe. Usually a one-seeded fruit with a thin exocarp, a fleshy mesocarp, and a hard, stony endocarp. Examples: cherry, viburnum.

Pome. An accessory fruit in which the fleshy portion develops from the hypanthium that surrounds the many-seeded ovary (core). Examples: crabapple, mountain ash.

Accessory. A fruit in which the fleshy portion is the enlarged receptacle; the true fruits (achenes) being embedded in the surface. Example: strawberry.

Aggregate fruit. A fruit consisting of several ripened ovaries (drupelets) from a single flower. Examples: blackberry, raspberry.

Multiple: a fruit consisting of several ripened ovaries from separate flowers. Example: mulberry.

CULTURAL PRACTICES

SOIL IMPROVEMENT

Types of Soils

It is important to know the type of soil on your property so you can select the best plants for your garden. Some plants, like our native sugar maple, do best on a moisture retentive but well-drained clay loam soil. Our native red maple will thrive on sandy loam soils and even on wet soils. It is also important to know the soil pH or acidity. For instance, if your soil is acid you will be able to grow acid-loving plants with little difficulty.

Soils are classified as mineral or organic depending on their origin. Mineral soils are made up largely of rock particles resulting from the disintegration of rocks. Particle size can vary greatly. Sand is made up of visible rock particles ranging in size from .05 to 2.0 mm.; silt is composed of microscopic sized particles ranging from .002 to .05 mm. Clay particles are under .002 mm. and are visible only under a microscope.

A loam soil is a mixture of various sizes of rock particles plus varying amounts of organic matter. A sandy loam contains a high portion of sand particles, etc. Sandy loams are usually porous and droughty, and relatively low in plant nutrients. A clay loam is moisture retentive, often poorly drained, but relatively high in plant nutrients. A silt loam is in between.

Organic soils are those derived from decaying organic matter. Peat soils are the best example. Since peat soils are usually formed in low areas, there is a tendency for mineral soils to wash down and mix with the organic peat, especially around the edges of a peat area. Organic matter, formed by the decomposition of plant and animal remains, is also a constituent of most mineral soils.

Regardless of the type of soil in your garden, it can usually be improved by the addition of organic matter. Adding organic matter improves the texture and aeration of clay soils and increases the moisture and nutrient retention of sandy soils. Since organic matter is constantly being oxidized and used up, it is necessary to add it at frequent intervals for best results.

Making a Compost Pile

There are many ways to make compost. If you understand the principles involved you can adapt a method to your situation. In nature, raw materials such as grass roots, tree leaves, old logs, and stumps, etc. decay to form humus without the aid of man. All that

Tilia americana (Basswood). Nutlike fruits.

is required is moisture, the right temperature, air, and the right bacteria or microorganisms. However, gardeners can speed this process by composting.

The first step is to choose a suitable site and a container that is not unsightly. This can be a purchased compost bin, or can be constructed using treated or decay resistant lumber, or also concrete blocks. A pit dug in the soil will also make an excellent place for composting. If you have a secluded spot, a simple compost pile can be built above ground.

The materials to be composted are usually deposited in layers about one foot thick. Each layer is moistened and covered with a thin layer of soil or manure which contains the necessary bacteria. A little fertilizer, high in nitrogen, should be added to supply essential nutrients for the decay bacteria. About one pound per 100 square feet of surface should be added to each layer. As many layers can be added, as you like, depending on the depth of the container and the quantity of material to be composted. The top of the pile should have a shallow depression to catch rain water so it soaks in to keep the pile moist. The decomposition will proceed even faster if the pile is turned over every few months.

Where space permits, it is best to have two or three compost piles in different stages of decomposition so you will have usable compost as you need it. I have a wooded area screened from the rest of the yard where I have 3 such piles.

For those gardeners who do not wish to be bothered with a compost pile, many communities have a community composting program where leaves can be deposited in the fall. After composting, the compost is available at little or no cost to the home gardener.

Plant Nutrients

The soil is a reservoir of chemical elements, present in both insoluble and soluble forms. However, only those elements that are in solution in the soil water can enter the plant through its root hairs that penetrate between the soil particles.

At least 16 elements are known to be essential to plant growth. These are carbon (C), hydrogen (H), oxygen (O), nitrogen (N), phosphorus (P), potassium (K), calcium (Ca), magnesium (Mg), manganese (Mn), iron (Fe), sulfur (S), boron (B), zinc (Zn), copper (Cu), molybdenum (Mo), and vanadium (Va). Some of the elements that enter the plant by osmosis are not essential to growth. Aluminum (Al), silicon (Si), and sodium (Na) are examples.

Carbon, hydrogen, and oxygen are the elements used in photosynthesis. Carbon dioxide, a gas that makes up about .03 percent of the atmosphere, combines with water which enters the plant mainly through the roots to form simple sugars in the chlorophyll-bearing cells in the leaves and green stems in the presence of light. The chemical equation for this very important process is: $6CO_2 + 6H_2O + chlorophyll + light ---- C_6H_{12}O_6 + 6O_2$. The simple sugars are changed in the plant into cellulose, starches, fats, and by the addition of nitrogen into amino acids and proteins.

Nitrogen is a constituent of chlorophyll, protoplasm, and stored protein. It makes up 80 percent of the atmosphere, but gaseous nitrogen is not available to higher plants. Certain bacteria in the soil change nitrogen into ammonia and nitrates, in which form it is used in higher plants.

Phosphorus is needed for flowering and fruiting and is an essential constituent of certain plant proteins. It also hastens maturity and aids in carbohydrate movement in the plant. Phosphorus is present in rock phosphate, a natural component of mineral soils. The phosphorus in rock phosphate must be acted on by soil acids before it becomes soluble and available to plants.

Potassium plays a catalytic role in the movement of carbohydrates within the plant. It is associated with a strong root system and sturdy stems. It is usually present as potassium chloride or potassium sulfate in the soil.

Calcium serves as a cementing substance to hold plant cells together. It also aids in cell division. In the soil calcium neutralizes soil acidity and minimizes the toxic effects of excessive amounts of aluminum and iron. Calcium is a constituent of limestone.

Magnesium is a constituent of chlorophyll and aids in the movement of phosphorus within the plant. It is usually present as magnesium sulfate in the soil.

Iron and manganese are essential for chlorophyll synthesis, serving as a catalyst. They are present as salts in the soil. Iron is often present but in an insoluble form. This is particularly true in alkaline soils.

Sulfur is a constituent of certain plant proteins. Molybdenum acts as a catalyst in the reduction of nitrate nitrogen in protein synthesis. The exact role of the other essential elements is not so clearly understood.

The availability of essential plant elements is of primary concern to all gardeners. They may be present in an insoluble form and hence unavailable for plant growth. Managing the soil to assure a steady supply of available plant nutrients is most important. Adding organic matter to the soil, improving soil aeration, and in some cases the addition of fertilizers to the soil, are methods used to assure an adequate supply. Bacteria that fix gaseous nitrogen require a moist, well-aerated soil. In wet soils, these beneficial bacteria are replaced by denitrification bacteria that release gaseous nitrogen. Soil acids are needed to release available phosphorus from rock phosphate. As mentioned, iron is often present in alkaline soils, but unavailable because it is present in complex molecules too large to enter the plant. By acidifying the soil, the iron becomes available. Iron chelates are also used.

Fertilizers

In nature, most plants grow and thrive without the addition of artificial fertilizers. This is because plant and animal remains are returned to the soil, and as they decompose available plant nutrients are released. In our yards much of the top soil has been removed by construction of our homes. On farms, the harvesting of crops removes the essential elements. Under these conditions the addition of essential elements in the form of fertilizers is required. Even in soils that have never been farmed, the addition of fertilizers will often improve the growth of plants.

Fertilizers are either organic or inorganic depending on their origin. Sewage sludge, bone meal, blood meal, fish meal and emulsion, soybean meal, cottonseed meal, manures and composts are examples of organic fertilizers. They are often high in nitrogen but relatively low in other essential elements. Bone meal is an exception since it contains mostly phosphorous.

Inorganic fertilizers are manufactured usually from mineral deposits. Inorganic nitrogen is synthesized by converting gaseous nitrogen into the nitrate or ammonia form. Rock phosphate is converted to acid phosphates by the addition of sulfuric acid. Whether to use organic or inorganic fertilizers is a matter of personal preference. Organic gardeners claim special benefits from the use of organic fertilizer. Commercial farmers are equally enthusiastic about the use of inorganic fertilizers. Personally, I favor the use of both the inorganic and organic forms. I use as much organic matter as possible to improve soil structure but I also use inorganic fertilizers to supply essential nutrients at a reasonable price. Actually, plants cannot distinguish between nitrogen that has been synthetically converted into the nitrate form from the nitrate that is formed from decomposing organic matter. The same is true of the acid phosphate in commercial fertilizers as compared to the acid phosphate resulting from the treatment of rock phosphate by soil acids.

In buying fertilizers, one should look for the analysis which should be on the bag. Usually, only the percentages of nitrogen, the phosphorus in the form of phosphorus pentoxide, and potassium in the form of potassium oxide is given. A 10-10-10 fertilizer contains 10 percent each of nitrogen, phosphorus, and potash. The first number refers to the nitrogen, the second to the phosphorus, and the third to the potassium.

The analysis to use depends on the crop being grown. For lawns, trees, and shrubs, a fertilizer high in nitrogen such as a 10-8-6 or a 10-5-5 is best. For flowers and fruits a fertilizer high in phosphorus such as a 5-10-5 would be good. For root crops that store high amounts of starch use one high in potassium such as a 5-5-10. For general use, I find a 10-10-10 or a 12-12-12 quite satisfactory.

Minor elements are often present as impurities in commercial fertilizer. Some specialty fertilizers have the minor elements added. Some gardeners add epsom salts containing magnesium sulfate to soils with a deficiency of available iron.

For plants that require an acid soil, such as blueberries and azaleas, use a fertilizer that gives an acid reaction. Most garden centers will have a fertilizer to meet your requirements.

Fertilizer application should be timed to give the maximum benefit. In the spring, just as growth is starting, is a good time to apply fertilizer to trees and shrubs. In preparing the soil for spring planting it is a good idea to mix fertilizer with the soil. For some plants, a side dressing applied in late fall after growth stops is absorbed by roots and is available for early spring growth. This is particularly beneficial to lawns.

The amount of fertilizer to use varies with the analysis, the fertility of the soil, and the plants being grown. Too much fertilizer can do more harm than good. For many wild flowers, no fertilizer may be needed if you have provided the right conditions. If the plants have a good color and are making satisfactory growth, there is no need to fertilize. A safe rule when plants are not making satisfactory growth is to make the application based on the nitrogen content. An application that applies one pound of actual nitrogen per 1,000 square feet of soil surface is a safe application for most plants. For a 10-10-10 fertilizer this would be 10 pounds of fertilizer per 1,000 square feet. For a 5-10-10 fertilizer, apply 20 pounds, etc.

The method of application is also important. In applying fertilizer to a lawn or a vegetable or flower garden, a whirlwind spreader gives an even application with minimum of effort. For trees it is important to put the fertilizer where the tree roots can absorb it. Most of the feeding roots are under the "drip line" of the tree. Bore holes can be made at 60 cm. intervals in a circular band under the tips of the branches using a soil auger or crowbar. The number of holes will depend on the size of the tree. Measure the diameter of the tree about 30 cm. above the soil. For each cm. in diameter, make about 4 holes. For a tree that is 30 cm. in diameter, make about 120 holes. Make the holes 30 to 40 cm. deep and for a fertilizer containing 10 percent nitrogen, use about 100 grams or a small handful of the fertilizer for each hole. Water the fertilizer in and fill the holes with soil. For shrubs growing in cultivated soil, the fertilizer can be broadcast and worked into the soil.

Other methods of fertilizer application include liquid application to the soil and foliar feeding by including soluble fertilizers in a spray solution. Some gardeners inject the soluble fertilizer into the irrigation water. Fertilizer spikes are still another method of application.

Soil Preparation

Proper soil preparation is essential to success in gardening. Fall plowing is beneficial for heavy clay soils. Freezing and thawing during the winter tends to break the soil clods down and make it possible to prepare a seedbed earlier in the spring. For sandy loam soils there is little benefit from fall plowing, except that it sometimes exposes larvae of harmful insects to winter freezing. This reduces their number and makes control easier.

Rototilling is a popular method of soil preparation in small gardens. It is sometimes necessary to go over the area several times with a small rototiller. Spading is the method of soil preparation used in very small areas. Double spading will be beneficial in soils that have a very hard subsoil. Wherever possible, work organic matter into the soil.

Minimum tillage is practiced by some farmers and some organic gardeners. This is practical only where perennial weeds are under control and where mulches are used to control annual weeds. In minimum tillage, seeds or plants are planted in untilled soil and the surface mulched between the rows or plants to smother weeds and conserve moisture.

Echinacea purpurea (Purple Coneflower).

Used in a perennial border.

PLANT PROPAGATION

Many of our native plants are on the protected list and cannot be dug without a special permit. Fortunately, many of our native plants can be purchased from licensed nurseries. Others can be propagated either from seeds or by vegetative means. If digging plants not on the protected list in the wild, none should be dug without the permission of the property owner. It is much better to leave these plants in their native habitats so others can enjoy them in their native states, and also so these plants can propagate and increase natural populations.

Seed Propagation

Most of our native plants come true from seed. The seeds can be collected without injury to the parent plants or they can be purchased from seed companies specializing in native plants.

Seeds differ greatly in their longevity. Most seeds should be planted as soon as ripe. They may not germinate immediately but should come up eventually. Some can take several years to germinate. Such seeds have a built-in rest period or dormancy that must be satisfied before the seeds will germinate. This dormancy may be due to immature embryos or thick seed coats that do not absorb water. Stratification of such seeds in moist sand and subjecting them to low temperatures of about 40 degree F. for several months will improve germination. In some cases alternate periods of cold and warm temperatures are required. In nature this might take several years. By artificially regulating the temperature, the period for germination can be shortened. Storing seeds in plastic bags or glass vials in a refrigerator can provide the needed cold. Some seeds such as nuts should never be allowed to dry out.

Seeds can be started in individual flower pots, in shallow flats, or they can be sown directly in soil. A cold frame can be of real help in protecting young seedlings over the first winter. The medium for starting seed will vary depending on the kind of plant. For acid-loving plants use a mixture of acid peat and coarse sand. In starting seeds indoors under lights or in a greenhouse, it is best to use a sterile medium such as Jiffy Mix or some similar product which consists largely of pulverized peat and either vermiculite or fine perlite. For starting seeds outdoors or in a cold frame, a mixture of sand and leaf mold works well. The advantage of using a sterile medium is to check the spread of the damping-off fungi. These organisms are soil borne and attack small seedlings soon after germination causing them to wilt and topple over. Once the seedlings develop their first true leaves, they can be safely transplanted to a soil mixture.

Seedlings of most herbaceous plants can either be grown in individual containers until large enough to be planted in the garden, or they can be grown in rows in a cold frame. Plants in pots can be wintered in a cold frame if heavily mulched with leaves or straw. Woody plants are usually seeded directly in specially prepared seedbeds in a sandy loam soil. Shading with a lath shade may be necessary to protect the seedlings from the direct sun during the first summer. As soon as the seedlings are large enough, they should be transplanted into nursery rows allowing enough space for the seedling to grow to a size suitable for planting in their permanent location.

Propagation of Ferns by Spores

This is the natural method of propagation for most ferns. Spores are produced in sporangia that are clustered together in sori on the under surface of the leaf. In some ferns the spore-bearing leaves are modified and distinctly different from the vegetative leaves. The mature spores are discharged from the sporangia and light on moist soil. If conditions are favorable the spores germinate to form small, green, heart-shaped plants about the size of a fingernail, called prothallia. As the prothallia grow, rhizoids which function as roots grow down into the moist earth for water and plant nutrients. Antheridia (male structures that produce mobile sperm cells) and archegonia (female structures that produce a single egg cell) are produced on the under surface of the prothallia. When moisture is present, the sperm cells swim to the neck of the archegonia and enter to fertilize the egg. Each fertilized egg cell divides to produce a typical fern plant.

In nature the odds are against a spore ever developing into a prothallium that in turn produces a new fern plant. Man can improve the odds by providing ideal conditions.

To collect the spores, select leaves with well developed sori on the under surface. Lay these leaves on a sheet of glossy white paper with sori facing the paper. Cover the leaves with several sheets of newspaper or a blotter. This absorbent covering prevents the spores from being blown away and helps to remove moisture from the leaves. After a day or two, the spores will have been discharged and the covering paper and fern leaves can be removed, leaving the spores and chaff on the paper. By tilting the paper and tapping the under surface, the coarse chaff can be removed leaving only the spores. By creasing the paper the spores can be funneled into a glass vial. Cap the vial and label giving the name of the fern and the location where the fern was growing. The spores can be stored for a short period in a cool place.

The spores are usually sown on a specially prepared mixture. A good mixture can be prepared by mixing equal parts of screened sphagnum moss, leaf mold, good top soil, and building sand. Use 4 inch clay pots 3 1/2 inches deep. Put 2 inches of coarse sphagnum moss in the bottom and fill with above mixture, gently pressing to form a smooth surface. Bake the pots and mixture for one hour at 250 degrees F. to kill any

Geum triflorum (Prairie-smoke). In flower

at the McKnight Prairie of Carleton College

in Northfield, Minnesota.

Photographs: Bonnie L. Harper Lore.

organisms. Place the pots in a shallow pan of water and leave long enough for the pots and their contents to become saturated with water. Drain off excess water and you are ready to sow the spores. Scatter the spores evenly over the surface. Label each pot. Spores can be germinated in a north-facing window, but a bench in the basement under fluorescent lights is better. Use a tray filled to a depth of 2 inches with moist vermiculite. Sink the pots into the moist vermiculite half way to the rim. The pots can be covered with glass or they can be misted with water from time to time to keep the surface moist. If glass covers are used, guard against excessive condensation. The fluorescent lights should be mounted about 18 inches above the trays and be left on for 14 hours a day. The time for spore germination and the formation of the prothallia can vary greatly with the species. If growing conditions are favorable, the prothallia should be producing sperms and eggs in about 3 months time. Occasional gentle spraying of the prothallia will provide the moisture needed for the sperms to reach the eggs. Young sporophytic plants will soon appear. These young plants will be large enough to transplant to the garden at the end of the second year. Keep all plants carefully labeled as it is difficult to identify young fern plants.

Damping off fungi can be a problem. If damping off should occur, reduce the amount of water used and spray the plants with a good fungicide.

Vegetative Propagation

Quite often it is faster to propagate plants by vegetative means rather than by seeds. It also makes it possible to propagate selected strains that do not come true from seeds.

Division

Propagation by division is a simple method of increasing plants. The best time to divide plants is when they are dormant, either in early spring or fall. All plants, with fleshy roots, rhizomes, tubers, bulbs, or corms, should be divided in the fall. Plants with fibrous roots are best divided in the spring just as new growth is starting. Fall division should be done early enough to allow new roots to develop before the soil freezes. For most plants, September and early October is the best time for fall division.

If you need only a few plants, it is possible with a spade or trowel to remove a portion of an established clump without disturbing the rest of the plant. If you need a large number of plants, lift the entire plant, shake off the loose soil, and separate the clump into the desired number of divisions. In some plants, the division can be pulled apart by hand. In others, a sharp spade or knife will be needed. The divisions should not be allowed to dry out and they should be replanted as soon as possible. Fall planted divisions should be mulched the first winter to prevent heaving by alternate freezing and thawing early in the spring.

Cuttings

Many plants can be propagated from stem cuttings. Hardwood cuttings are taken in late fall, usually in November, from healthy current year's growth. Each cutting should be 15 to 20 cm. long with several buds. Make the cuts at a 45 degree angle using a sharp knife or pruning shears. Tie the cuttings in a bundle with the buds all pointing in the same direction. Label and store in a cool, moist place over winter at a temperature of 40 degrees F. The cuttings must be kept moist. Burying them in moist sawdust is a good practice. In the spring, as soon as the soil starts to warm up, the cuttings can be planted in a nursery row. Have the soil loose and insert the cuttings at an angle with the uppermost bud just even with the soil surface. Firm the soil over the cuttings and keep them moist. Roots will form from the basal callus and new stems will form from the upper buds. The percentage of rooting will be increased if the base of the cutting is dipped in a root promoting hormone before planting. If one has a greenhouse, the cuttings might be started in a bench in coarse sand during the winter. The rooted cuttings could then be potted and transplanted to the nursery as soon as the weather permits in the spring.

Softwood cuttings are taken from healthy plants that are actively growing, usually in late June or early July. Tip cuttings are usually used. Remove some of the basal leaves but leave 3 or 4 leaves at the tip. Stick the cuttings in the rooting medium. Sharp sand or perlite is a good sterile rooting media. For acid-loving plants use a mixture of sand and acid peat. The rooting medium and the air around the cuttings must be kept moist at all times until roots form. This is done in several ways. The best way is to use a misting system that operates on a time clock. The periods of misting need not be more than a few seconds with intervals of 10 to 15 minutes between mistings. Another method is to enclose the propagation area with clear plastic to check moisture loss. The cuttings can then be sprayed as needed to keep them from drying out. For just a few cuttings, I have used a wooden flat with window glass cut to just fit inside the flat to form the 4 walls. The corners are then taped to hold the glass in place. For a cover I use two pieces of window glass cut to just cover the frame. By separating the two sheets of glass, ventilation can be provided as needed. After the cuttings are rooted, the cover can be removed to accustom the plants to a drier atmosphere before potting. As with hardwood cuttings, growth-promoting hormones usually improve rooting.

A few plants can be started from root cuttings. The roots are cut into pieces about 10 cm. long and planted in flats of sterilized soil or a rooting medium such as is used for stem cuttings. The cuttings are usually planted horizontally in rows and covered with about 2.5 cm. of the rooting medium. The medium must be kept moist.

Layering

Propagation by layering is similar to propagation by cuttings except that the tip of the branch is still attached to the parent plant. Many of our native shrubs can be propagated by layering. Some, such as the red osier dogwood, spread using this method. In layering, simply bend a stem over and hold it down by placing soil over the stem with the tip sticking out. Roots will form from the covered portion of the stem. When this happens, the rooted portion can be severed from the parent plant and replanted in its permanent location. Rooting can often be improved by bruising the covered portion of the stem. Cutting a notch into the lower side of the stem is another practice to improve rooting. Mound layering is a modification in which the stems are bruised or notched just above the soil level. A mound of soil is then placed around the base of the shrub. Roots will form from the bruised portion of the stems and grow into the mound of soil. When rooted, the mound of soil is removed. Each stem, with roots at the base, can then be severed from the parent plant and planted.

Air layering is still another method of propagation. A diagonal cut is made about two thirds of the way through the stem, about a foot below the tip of the branch. A small pebble or solid object is placed in the slit to keep the two surfaces from growing back together. Moist sphagnum moss is placed around the cut and held in place with clear plastic which is tied above and below the cut. Roots will form and grow into the moist sphagnum. When well rooted, the tip can be cut off and planted just below the area where the roots have formed. The sphagnum must be kept moist.

Grafting and Budding

This method of propagation is commonly used in propagating named varieties of fruits, shade trees, and ornamental trees. It is not used very often with native plants except to propagate plants that differ from the typical species. You may spot a native tree that has particularly good bloom or fall color. To propagate this particular plant you may need to use grafting or budding if the species does not root well from cuttings or layering. The desired selection is usually grafted on a seedling root, preferably of the same species. Grafting is usually done in early spring before growth starts. Cuttings are taken from the desired tree while the tree is still dormant. These cuttings, called scions, are usually taken in November and stored in a cool, moist place at a temperature of about 40 degrees F. until spring. The graft can be made outdoors on seedlings that are in the soil or the seedlings can be dug and the graft made indoors. Cut the stem of the seedling, called the root stalk, at about the soil line. Make the cut at a slant using a sharp knife. Cut the scions about 15 cm. long. Shape the base of the scion to match the slant on the stock. Make a vertical cut in both the stock and the scion about a third of the distance back from the tip to the base of the slant. Fit the two pieces together so the cambium will be in contact on at least one side. Hold the scion in place by wrapping with rubberized electrician's tape. If the stock was dug, plant immediately or store for a few weeks in a cool, moist place before planting. If more than one bud on the scion sends up a vertical stem, remove the weaker ones allowing just one to grow. This will grow into a tree with the desired characteristics.

Budding is a type of grafting in which a single bud is used as the scion. Budding is usually done in August. The buds on the scion variety must be fully developed, and the

Impatiens capensis (Jewelweed).

bark on the stock variety must still be easily separated from the wood beneath. The bud is inserted on the north side of the seedling stock just above the soil level. Make a T-shaped cut through the bark of the stock. With the tip of the knife lift the bark to allow the insertion of the bud. The bud is removed from the scion variety with a portion of the bark attached. Any wood should be removed. Insert the bud into the slit and push downward. Make a clean cut above the bud to correspond with the top of the T. Use a rubber budding strip to hold the bud in place. The cambium of the stock and scion will unite. The following spring, just as the bud is opening, cut off the top of the seedling stock just above the bud. The bud will grow into a tree of the selected variety.

Tissue Culture

The commercial use of tissue culture in propagating plants is quite new. First applied to orchids, the technique is now used on a wide variety of both woody and herbaceous plants in laboratories across the country.

In this method, entire plants are grown from fragments of meristematic tissue on a nutrient agar under aseptic conditions. The technique requires an autoclave for sterilizing the growing medium, a germ-free room for transferring the bits of meristematic tissue to the flasks containing the agar and nutrients, and a lighted room maintained at the ideal temperature for the growth of the plants being propagated. It takes several months for plants to differentiate from the meristematic tissue. As soon as the plants are large enough and have developed roots, they are transferred to flower pots in a suitable growing medium and grown in greenhouses until large enough to be planted in a nursery. Growing plants from tissue culture is a practical way to produce plants rapidly and at a moderate cost.

Planting Techniques

Whether you grow your own plants or purchase them, the planting techniques are the same.

Spacing of plants should be determined by their mature size. Shrubs and trees are often planted too close together. They may look nice for a few years but they soon become crowded and small shrubs are smothered by larger ones. Study mature plants in your neighborhood and visualize the mature size of the plants as they will grow in your own yard. Most small, ornamental trees, such as flowering crabapples, will need at least 8 to 10 meters between trees. Large shrubs should be spaced 2 to 3 meters apart, medium shrubs 1 to 2 meters, and small shrubs about 1 meter. For flowers the spacing may not be quite so critical but money can be saved if the plants are properly spaced.

In planting trees and shrubs, it is important to make the planting hole sufficiently large to accommodate the root system without crowding. If you are planting bare root plants, every effort should be made to keep the roots moist. Unwrap the plants as soon as you receive them, and if the roots are the least bit dry, soak them in water before planting. The roots can be soaked overnight, but a few hours is sufficient. Avoid leaving them in water too long. If you take bare root plants into the garden to plant, cover the roots with a wet burlap to protect the roots while you dig the holes. Before planting, prune off any dead or broken roots. Reduce the tops by pruning to compensate for root loss. In pruning, consider the mature shape of the tree. Select scaffold branches to leave, and remove entire branches that may not be needed. Cut back the scaffold branches to an outward-pointing bud. Make clean cuts.

In making the hole, place the good topsoil in one pile and any subsoil in another. If the soil is poor, it may be best to discard the subsoil and bring in good topsoil from a nearby field or purchase some good topsoil. In pruning shrubs with multiple stems, it is best to prune back all stems to about 1/3 of their original length. Some nurseries may already have pruned the plants before shipping.

Place the plant in the hole. Spread out the roots. If the hole is too small, make the hole larger rather than bending the roots to fit into too small a hole. The planting depth should be no deeper than it was in the nursery. A shovel handle can be laid across the hole to determine the proper depth. Holding the plant in place, fill in around the roots with good topsoil. Firm the soil as you add it making certain that there are no air pockets around the roots. Leave a depression at the top for watering. Water the plants as soon as planted making certain that the water soaks in to the depth of the root system.

In planting balled and burlapped stock or container stock, make the hole slightly larger than the ball and just deep enough so the plant will be at the same level as it was growing in the nursery. Some pruning may be needed, but since the root system is not disturbed as much, less pruning will be required. Remove the containers and remove any ties that hold the burlap around the root ball. Put the plant in place and adjust for proper depth. Fill in around the ball using good topsoil and firm. Water as you would for a bare root tree or shrub.

For small herbaceous plants a simple method can be used. The same precautions should be used to keep the roots moist. Remove the plants from their containers. With a spade or trowel open a slit in the soil, put the root system in the slit, and remove the spade or trowel. Soil will fall around the roots. Firm the soil with your hands or feet. Water as soon after planting as possible. Some gardeners will use a weak fertilizer solution or starter solution instead of plain water.

Weed Control

Young trees and shrubs grow best if they do not have to complete with grass and weeds. This competition can be removed either by cultivation, or by mulching around individual trees or shrubs. Mulching is the preferred method as it eliminates root injury by cultivation, and the mulch conserves moisture. The mulch also serves to keep lawn mowers from injuring the bark of young trees and shrubs. The size of the mulched circle around individual trees varies with the size of the tree. Usually, a circle 1 to 2 meters in diameter is sufficient. For shrubs, in a border planting, the space between shrubs should be kept mulched until the shrubs grow together. The depth of the mulch should be from 5 to 10 cm. or deep enough to smother annual weeds. Since the mulch will gradually decompose, it will be necessary to replenish the mulch at least once a year. Wood chips make an excellent mulch. Sawdust, clean straw, and marsh hay are also used. To prevent mouse injury to young trees, it is a good practice to put a cylinder of quarter inch mesh hardware cloth around each tree. The cylinder should be large enough to allow for the growth of the tree.

Wild flowers and ferns in the woodland garden prefer a minimum of tillage for weed control. Mulching with leaf mold to smother weeds is the best method. If weeds do grow up through the mulch, they can be easily pulled out after a rain. Do not use chemicals for weed control since many wild flowers are quite sensitive to the use of chemicals.

In the flower border, shallow cultivation for weed control is the method most commonly used, but even here it is often better to pull the weeds than to hoe them out. Mulching can also reduce the need for weeding.

Pruning and Training

Pruning is both an art and a science that continues to baffle most gardeners. Some are afraid to prune for fear of removing the wrong branches. Others delight in cutting off branches regardless of the results. Unfortunately, we see more examples of poor pruning than of good. There are no simple guidelines that can be applied to all plants. One learns to be a good pruner by practice and by studying the growth habits of plants.

Reasons for Pruning

1. To improve the health and appearance of the plant. The removal of dead or diseased wood improves the appearance and may help to prevent the spread of disease.

2. To reduce wind damage. Narrow-angled crotches are weak and apt to split in a wind storm. Wide-angled crotches are strong and resist breakage. By removing one of the branches of a narrow-angled crotch when small, future splitting is eliminated.

3. To remove branches that will interfere with foot or vehicular traffic or power lines. These branches should be removed gradually as the tree grows. There is much less injury to the tree if these branches are removed while still small.

4. To limit the size of the plant. Ideally, plants should be selected that will not outgrow their allotted space, but this is seldom done. The size of the plant and its shape can be controlled by judicious pruning. Size control should start early in the development of the plant.

5. To improve flowering and fruiting. The largest, showiest flowers and fruits are produced on young branches that are from 2 to 4 years old. Old shrubs can be renovated by removing the oldest stems at ground level each spring. By pruning out the older branches in a flowering or fruiting tree, vigorous young branches will develop.

Pruning Tools

Pruning tools should be of high quality steel and should be kept sharp. Such tools cost more, but they enable you to do a better job of pruning and last longer than cheap ones. A pair of hand pruning shears is the most important tool. The type with a shearing action will make a cleaner cut than the anvil type in which a single blade cuts against a flat surface. When done at the right time, most pruning can be done with the hand shears. A pair of long-handled shears, called loppers, is useful for larger branches up to 4 cm. in diameter. Loppers are also useful in pruning shrubs where the cuts are made near the ground. For hedges, a pair of hedge shears will be needed. There are also electric and gasoline operated hedge trimmers on the market. For large branches, a pruning saw is needed.

When to Prune

There is an old adage that pruning can be done at any time that the shears are sharp. This is partly true but there is a best time for most plants. Shrubs and flowering trees that bloom on old wood should be pruned as soon as they finish flowering. Shrubs that bloom on new wood should be pruned early in the spring before growth starts. Most shade trees should be pruned during the winter months, preferably toward spring. Oaks, to prevent the spread of the oak wilt disease, should be pruned only when the temperature is below freezing. Trees that have a heavy sap flow in late winter or early spring, such as maples, birches, and ironwood, should be pruned after the leaves are fully open to avoid bleeding.

How to Prune

Knowing how to prune requires skill and experience. Each species has a different habit of growth and requires special pruning. Except where size must be limited, the goal of pruning is to enhance and preserve the natural form of the plant.

Two general types of pruning are practiced, tip pruning and renewal pruning. Tip pruning is done on clipped hedges, evergreens that are confined to a limited space, and on certain herbaceous plants to force basal branching. Hedge shears and power pruners are usually used for this type of pruning. A pruning knife is sometimes used on evergreens. In shaping a clipped or formal hedge, prune to encourage a wide base with the sides tapering upward to a narrow top. This allows light to reach the base of the hedge.

In renewal pruning, entire stems or branches are removed. With most shrubs, the oldest stems are cut near the ground. Do not remove more than a third of the stems at any one time. After removing the oldest stems, it may be necessary to do a little tip pruning to balance the shape of the shrub. Pruning trees consists of a thinning out of the branches to allow light to enter and favor vigorous new growth. It also entails the removal of one of the branches that constitute a narrow crotch and branches that cross each other or grow toward the center of the tree.

Make all cuts close to the main stem or larger branches. Never leave stubs. Wound dressings are sometimes used on wounds over 5 cm. in diameter. Orange shellac or a wound dressing such as Tree-Cote or grafting wax is safe to use. There is some question as to whether these wound dressings are necessary. A clean cut heals over quickly whether wound dressings are used or not.

Fraxinus quadrangulata (Blue Ash).

Pest Control

The need for pest control measures will be minimal where native plants are used. Avoid using plants that are known to have serious insect or disease problems. Our native paper or canoe birch is very susceptible to the bronze birch borer, an insect that can kill the tree. Our native river birch is highly resistant to this insect and is preferable where a birch is desired. The native prairie crab is very susceptible to cedar-apple rust and should not be planted in areas where red cedar trees are present. In describing the various native plants in this book, mention is made of serious insect and disease problems.

Most plants are susceptible to certain insects and diseases. The effect on the plant varies. In most cases the damage is not permanent and control measures are not required. Learn to recognize harmful insects and disease symptoms. Your County Agricultural Extension Office or your local nurseryman can help you in identifying the insect or disease problems.

Sanitation helps to control insects and diseases by eliminating over wintering habitats. Before using protective insecticides or fungicides, be sure of the identity of your problem and use recommended sprays. Store all chemicals in a frost-free and safe place. Be careful in applying the sprays and wash thoroughly after using. Since the recommended chemicals change from year to year, no chemicals are listed in this book. Your Agricultural Extension Office has recent publications on pest control chemicals. Your favorite garden center or nursery will have the needed chemicals. Always read the label to be sure that the chemical is recommended for your problem.

Winter Protection

Since only native materials are described in this book, little winter protection is needed. However, since the natural growing conditions may be altered, some winter protection may be required. In nature, most woodland wild flowers have a protective winter cover of tree leaves. If your site does not provide sufficient winter cover, a winter mulch will help. Certain evergreens, such as the native Canada yew, grow where they have a dependable snow cover or winter shade from trees or an overhanging cliff. Protecting this yew with a burlap shade will prevent winter burn. I have successfully grown and flowered the mountain laurel by bending the stems over in the fall and holding them down with a bent, stiff wire such as a croquet wicket and then covering the stems with evergreen branches.

KINDS OF GARDENS

The process of landscape design is too complex to describe in a short chapter. Please refer to other works on landscape design, such as the ones listed in this work's bibliography. In discussing the uses of individual plants in the last chapters in this book, references are made to where certain plants should be used. Just as there are various environmental situations in nature, one can create similar conditions in one's yard or possibly utilize them where they already exist. We will refer to woodland gardens, prairie gardens, rock gardens, bog gardens, flower borders, and fruit gardens in this work.

Woodland Gardens

Woodland gardens are created where trees already exist or where trees have been planted to create a woodland effect. There are two types of woodland gardens, the deciduous woodland and the coniferous woodland. The type of soil will usually determine the kind of woodland garden to create. Deciduous woods are typical of clay or sandy loam soils that are near neutral or slightly acid, while coniferous woods are usually found on sandy soils that are on the acid side. Plants used in each of these types of woodland gardens will be quite different. A study of plants growing in nature in each of these situations will prove helpful.

A woodland garden will be most attractive in the spring. Most of our woodland wild flowers come up early in the spring, make their vegetative growth, flower, and produce seeds before the leaves are fully open on the trees. This is particularly true in deciduous woodlands. Some plants, such as the Dutchman's breeches and Virginia blue bells, die to the ground after flowering and fruiting. Others remain green during the summer and fall. Ferns are especially desirable for summer greenery.

In creating a woodland garden, the first step is to develop trails. These trails should follow the contour of the land and lead to points of interest. Wood chips make an ideal surface for a woodland trail. They tend to smother unwanted vegetation and are easy to walk on. They do disintegrate and must be renewed from time to time.

The soil in the woodland garden should be high in organic matter for best results. The addition of leaf mold or compost is the best means of increasing organic matter. For acid-loving plants, acid peat moss can be used. Wild flowers should be planted along the trails with suitable backgrounds of shade tolerant shrubs or tall ferns. It is best to plant the wild flowers in groups to simulate natural colonies.

Prairie Gardens

There is a great deal of interest in the preservation of our native prairies. Unfortunately, we have few native prairies left. This scarcity of native prairies has stimulated an interest in creating artificial prairies by using native prairie plants. Except in areas of low rainfall, trees and shrubs are the dominant plant species. Prairies exist under such conditions, only because of frequent prairie fires that kill the trees and shrubs without destroying the true prairie plants.

In our University of Minnesota Landscape Arboretum, we have had some experience in establishing a prairie. Some 20 years ago, an area of about 15 acres was set aside for this purpose. The area had been in pasture and many introduced grasses, including quack grass, smooth brome, and reed canary grass were firmly established. These introduced species were first killed by using chemical herbicides such as Round-up. Three methods of establishing prairie plants were tried. Hay from a native prairie was cut and scattered over the surface. This hay contained viable seeds of certain prairie species. Soil, containing seeds of prairie plants, was dug from a native prairie that was being destroyed for a real estate development and scattered over a portion of the area. The third and probably the most effective method used was to collect seed of individual prairie plants and either seed them directly or first start them in a nursery and transplant them to the prairie. The area is burned over about every three years to keep woody species under control. One must have a permit to burn in most areas. Before starting a prairie project, check with the local fire marshal to see if such a permit can be obtained. It is possible in some areas to purchase seeds and plants of prairie species from specialized nurserymen who will also offer suggestions for establishing a prairie.

To be really successful, one should have a fairly large area, preferably at some distance from the house. One should also observe a native prairie at different times of the year to be sure that this is what you want. A prairie can be beautiful in the summer when the prairie grasses and flowers are in bloom, but much less attractive after the foliage is killed by frost in the fall.

Even if you do not have room for a sizable prairie, many of the prairie plants can be planted in the flower border. Blazing star or Kansas gayfeather, blanket flower, and butterfly weed are examples.

Rock And Wall Gardens

There are many examples of rocky hillsides in nature with attractive wild flowers growing among the rocks. Many gardeners attempt to develop a rock garden in their yards to provide the proper conditions for rock garden plants. Quite often, these efforts are rewarding, but more often than not the results are disappointing. To be successful, one must understand the ecology of rock garden plants. Most require a well-drained soil. The soil under the rocks is usually cool and moist and provides an ideal place for good root development. In building a rock garden, a natural slope is an advantage although successful rock gardens have been created on level soil by creating artificial mounds. The choice of rocks and their placement is important. Preferably the rocks should be from a local source. They should be placed so they appear natural. A rock garden is a place to grow rock garden plants and not a place to exhibit rock specimens. The soil for the rock garden should be specially prepared. If your soil is a heavy clay that is poorly drained, replace it with a sandy loam soil that is high in organic matter. An inch or two of fine pea gravel on the surface will assure surface drainage and aid in weed control.

A rock wall is a type of rock garden that can be used to terrace a slope. The spaces between the rocks can be planted with low rock garden plants to soften the effect of the wall. In building the wall, flat cut stone can be used for a formal effect or rounded field stones can be used if they are available. A dry wall is one in which no mortar is used to hold the wall together. A dry wall offers more opportunity to provide soil pockets for plantings.

Flower Borders

Cercis canadensis (Eastern Redbud). The seedlings propagated from the Minnesota Landscape Arboretum seem to be hardy in the Twin Cities area after the tree is established.

Photograph: Dr. Anne M. Hanchek.

Flower borders are usually located where they can be seen from the house. They are usually in full sun and located toward one side of the yard. To be most effective the flower border needs a suitable background. This background can be a picket fence, a hedge, or an informal planting of shrubs. The size of the border will depend on your gardening interests. Do not make the border larger than you are willing to care for. A curving border is more pleasing to the eye than one with straight sides. The depth of the border should be deep enough to use flowers of varying heights. Taller plants should be planted toward the back of the border with lower ones in front. Plants should be carefully chosen to provide bloom over as long a period as possible unless you are planning a seasonal border. If you are planning a flower border for a summer home, you will want to plan it so you will have continuous bloom during the period you will be living there. Success with a flower border comes only with experience. The more you can learn about the plants you use, the better your success will be.

Bog Gardens

Bog gardens are a highly specialized type of garden. They depend on continuously moist soil conditions. In nature, there are low areas that are kept continuously moist by springs or seepage. Usually the soil is high in organic matter because the lack of oxygen in the soil prevents the normal decomposition of organic matter. Roots of bog plants are usually shallow and develop often on mounds or hummocks. The soil is often acid, especially if sphagnum moss is present.

Artificial bogs can be created but a natural bog is preferable. To create an artificial bog, excavate the soil to a depth of from 45 to 60 cm. Line the opening with black plastic and fill with acid peat moss or a mixture of acid peat and compost. The soil must be kept moist. To establish certain bog plants it may be necessary to create small mounds to provide sufficient aeration for roots to get established.

Water Gardens

Water gardens may consist of a shallow pool or they can be quite complex with recirculating streams and waterfalls. Waterlilies and other aquatic plants can be grown in submerged tubs or in the mud at the bottom of the pond or stream.

Heliopsis helianthoides (Oxeye). Grown in a flower border.

Photograph: Dr. Anne M. Hanchek.

ORNAMENTAL TREES AND SHRUBS

Ilex verticillata (Winterberry). One of the

better shrubs to add winter color to the landscape.

Unless we visit parks or reserves that have maintained the diversity of native plant material our region enjoyed before European settlement, it is difficult for us to picture how our native landscape truly looked. Today when we see Juneberry and plums blooming in the spring, or the oranges, yellows, and reds of our brilliant fall foliage we can in our minds reconstruct what our landscapes must have been like. We can add major, year around interest to our landscapes by planting our native ornamental trees and shrubs. They are certainly the most prominent of our native plants.

When selecting trees and shrubs it should be kept in mind that they perform many functions in landscape design. Most people remember that they are decorative adding texture, color, and form to the landscape. But trees and shrubs also serve functional purposes to define space, help to screen and enclose, and provide canopy for shade and cooling.

The following lists will help select the trees and shrubs described in this chapter.

Plants with Good Fall Color

Acer pensylvanicum (yellow)
Acer spicatum (red)
Aesculus glabra (yellow)
Amelanchier species (red, yellow)
Betula species (yellow)
Carpinus caroliniana (orange to red)
Carya species (yellow)
Cercis canadensis (yellow)
Chionanthus virginicus (yellow)
Cladrastis lutea (orange to yellow)
Cornus racemosa (purple)
Cornus sericea (red)
Cotinus obovatus (bronze)
Dirca palustris (yellow)
Euonymus atropurpurea (red)
Hamamelis virginiana (yellow)
Larix laricina (yellow)
Morus rubra (yellow)
Ostrya virginiana (yellow)
Potentilla tridentata (red)
Prunus pensylvanica (orange to red)
Rhus species (orange to red)
Sorbus species (red to yellow)
Vaccinium species (red)
Viburnum species (red)

Plants with Showy Flowers

Aesculus glabra (pale yellow)
Amelanchier species (white)
Aronia species (white)
Catalpa speciosa (white)
Ceanothus species (white)
Cephalanthus occidentalis (white)
Cercis canadensis (pink)
Chionanthus virginicus (white)
Cladrastis lutea (white)
Cornus species (white)
Crataegus species (white)
Epigaea repens (pink)
Hamamelis virginiana (yellow)
Hydrangea arborescens (white)
Hypericum species (yellow)

Catalpa speciosa.

Kalmia species (white to purple)
Lonicera species (yellowish)
Mahonia repens (yellow)
Malus species (white to pink)
Potentilla species (yellow to red)
Prunus species (white to pink)
Ribes odoratum (yellow)
Robinia species (pink)
Rosa species (pink)
Rubus parviflorus (white)
Salix discolor (catkins)
Sambucus species (white)
Sorbus species (white)
Spiraea species (white)
Viburnum species (white)

Plants with Fragrant Flowers

Ceanothus americanus
Cephalanthus occidentalis
Chionanthus virginicus
Cladrastis lutea
Elaeagnus commutata
Epigaea repens
Malus species
Prunus species
Ribes odoratum
Robinia pseudoacacia
Rosa species

Plants with Colored Fruits
(often attractive to wildlife)

Acer spicatum (red samara)
Alnus rugosa (black cone)
Amelanchier species (red to black berry)
Arctostaphylos uva-ursi (red berry)
Aronia species (red to black pome)
Carpinus caroliniana (brown bract)
Carya species (brown nut)
Catalpa speciosa (brown capsule)
Chionanthus virginicus (blue drupe)
Cornus species (white to blue drupe)
Corylus species (brown nut)
Crataegus species (red pome)
Gaultheria species (white or red berry)
Ilex verticillata (red drupe)
Lonicera species (blue to red berry)
Mahonia repens (black berry)
Malus species (red pome)
Morus rubra (purple berry)
Ostrya virginica (brown bract)
Prunus species (yellow to purple)
Ptelea trifoliata (brown samara)
Rhamnus alnifolia (black drupe)
Rhus species (red drupe)
Ribes odoratum (black berry)
Rosa species (red hip)
Rubus parviflorus (red drupe)
Sambucus species (red to black drupe)
Shepherdia argentea (red berry)

Sorbus species (red pome)
Staphylea trifolia (brown capsule)
Symphoricarpos species (white or red berry)
Vaccinium species (blue or red berry)
Viburnum species (blue to red berry)

Plants with Edible Fruits

Amelanchier species
Carya species
Corylus species
Gaylussacia baccata
Prunus species
Rosa species
Sambucus species
Shepherdia argentea
Vaccinium species

Plants with Interesting Winter Bark

Acer pensylvanicum (striped)
Betula nigra (reddish-brown)
Betula papyrifera (white)
Carpinus caroliniana (gray)
Carya ovata (shaggy brown)
Cladrastis lutea (smooth gray)
Cornus racemosa (gray)
Cornus sericea (red)
Rhus typhina (velvety)

Ornamental Trees and Shrubs that Tolerate Some Shade
(check tolerance in description of use)

Acer pensylvanicum
Acer spicatum
Amelanchier species
Arctostaphylos uva-ursi
Betula nigra
Cornus alternifolia
Cornus racemosa
Diervilla lonicera
Dirca palustris
Epigaea repens
Gaultheria species
Hydrangea arborescens
Lonicera species
Mahonia repens
Nemopanthus mucronatus
Ostrya virginica
Prunus pensylvanica
Rubus parviflorus
Sambucus pubens
Viburnum species

Ornamental Trees and Shrubs that Tolerate Dry Soils

Arctostaphylos uva-ursi
Ceanothus species
Comptonia peregrina
Corylus colurna
Elaeagnus commutata

Betula nigra (River Birch).

Photograph: Merv Eisel.

Epigaea repens
Gaultheria procumbens
Gaylussacia baccata
Larix laricina
Prunus besseyi
Rhus species
Shepherdia species
Vaccinium angustifolium

Ornamental Trees and Shrubs that Tolerate Wet Soils

Alnus species
Aronia species
Betula nigra
Betula papyrifera
Cephalanthus occidentalis
Chamaedaphne calyculata
Cornus sericea
Dirca palustris
Gaultheria hispidula
Ilex verticillata
Kalmia poliifolia
Larix laricina
Nemopanthus mucronatus
Potentilla palustris
Rhamnus alnifolia
Salix species
Viburnum lentago
Viburnum trilobum

Ornamental Shrubs Used for Ground Covers

Arctostaphylos uva-ursi
Comptonia peregrina
Diervilla lonicera
Elaeagnus commutata
Epigaea repens
Gaultheria species
Mahonia repens
Potentilla tridentata
Rhus glabra
Rubus parviflorus
Symphoricarpos occidentalis
Symphoricarpos orbiculatus
Vaccinium angustifolium

Ornamental Trees and Shrubs Useful for Hedges and Screens

Amelanchier species
Carpinus caroliniana
Cornus species
Corylus species
Crataegus species
Elaeagnus commutata
Hamamelis virginiana
Hydrangea arborescens
Larix laricina
Malus species
Physocarpus opulifolius
Potentilla fruticosa
Prunus species

Rhus aromatica
Ribes odoratum
Salix species
Shepherdia argentea
Sorbus species
Viburnum species

Dioecious Ornamental Trees and Shrubs
(Requires both male and female plants to set fruit)

Chionanthus virginicus
Ilex verticillata
Nemopanthus mucronatus
Rhus species
Salix species
Shepherdia argentea

Acer (L.) (Maple)
ACERACEAE (Maple family)
DESCRIPTION: About 200 species of mostly deciduous trees and shrubs, native in the temperate regions; **bark** smooth or furrowed; **buds** opposite with 2 outer scales; **leaves** opposite, usually simple and palmately lobed, sometimes palmately or pinnately compound, rarely entire; **flowers** small, in clusters, racemes, panicles, or corymbs, commonly dioecious, 5-merous, rarely 4-merous; stamens 4 to 10, usually 8; styles and stigmas 2; **fruits** are paired long-winged samaras.

Acer pensylvanicum L. (Striped Maple, Pennsylvania Maple, Whistlewood, Moosewood). Hardy in shade in zone 4; small tree to 8 m. tall.
DESCRIPTION: A shade tolerant, small tree with green bark striped with white lines on young stems and branches, native in moist woods from Wisconsin to Nova Scotia, south to Georgia; **leaves** roundish-obovate, to 20 cm. across, 3-lobed at apex, subcordate at base, serrulate, lobes acuminate; **flowers** yellow, in pendulous racemes, in May and June; **fruits** are paired, 2.5 cm. long samaras, diverging at an obtuse angle.
USE AND CULTURE: Occasionally planted in the shade of other trees for its ornamental, striped bark. This species is subject to winter sun scald when grown in the open, so it needs protection from the sun and wind. This upright growing maple has attractive yellow fall color. Propagation is by seeds sown in the fall or in the spring following stratification. Transplanting of larger trees is moderately difficult.

Acer pensylvanicum. Samaras.

Photograph: Research Department of the Minnesota Landscape Arboretum.

Acer spicatum (Mountain Maple). Leaves and samaras at the Arboretum in 1977.

Acer spicatum Lam. (Mountain Maple). Hardy in all zones; shrub to 7 m. tall.
DESCRIPTION: Large shrub or small tree, native in cool, moist woods in acid soils from Saskatchewan to Newfoundland, south to Minnesota and Georgia; **leaves** simple, 3- to 5-lobed, to 12 cm. across, light green above, pubescent beneath, turning red in September; leaf lobes ovate, acuminate, coarsely and irregularly serrate; **flowers** greenish-yellow, in narrow, upright spikes, in May and June; **fruits** are paired 2 cm. long samaras that are yellow to red when mature, diverging at nearly right angles.
USE AND CULTURE: This shrubby, usually multi-stemmed maple makes a good border shrub or screen. Their bright red samaras in the spring are attractive. They are easy to grow in partial shade in acid soils. Propagation is by seeds sown in the fall or in the spring following stratification.

Aesculus L. (Buckeye, Horse Chestnut)
HIPPOCASTANACEAE (Horse Chestnut Family)
DESCRIPTION: Thirteen species of deciduous shrubs and trees, native in eastern North America, Europe, and Asia; **leaves** opposite, palmately compound; **flowers** white, yellow, pink, or red, in erect terminal panicles; calyx 5-lobed; petals 4 or 5; stamens 6 to 8; **fruit** a smooth, slightly scaly, or spiny capsule, enclosing a dark brown, shiny nut.

Aesculus glabra Willd. (Ohio Buckeye, Fetid Buckeye). Hardy in all zones; tree to 12 m. tall.

Aesculus glabra (Ohio Buckeye).

Photograph: Flowers by Dr. Snyder in 1978, full habit by Merv Eisel.

DESCRIPTION: A small to medium tree, native from Nebraska to Pennsylvania, south to Arkansas and Alabama; winter **buds** large, non-resinous; **leaves** palmately compound with 5 to 7 leaflets; leaflets oblong-obovate or elliptic-obovate, to 15 cm. long, acute or acuminate; **flowers** pale yellow or greenish-yellow, in panicles to 15 cm. long, in May; stamens exserted; **fruits** prickly when young, becoming smooth at maturity in September.
USE AND CULTURE: A long-lived tree for street or yard with showy flowers and golden yellow fall color. It is easy to grow in most soils. Nuts, which are poisonous, fall to the ground and are messy in the fall. Although poisonous, some consider the nuts good luck charms. Propagation is by seeds planted in the fall or in the spring following stratification. The seeds must never be allowed to dry out or they will not grow. Because the tree develops a tap root, it should be transplanted when young. Leaf scorch can be a problem in dry areas.

Alnus B. Ehrh. (Alder)
BETULACEAE (Birch Family)
DESCRIPTION: About 30 species of deciduous trees and shrubs, native in the northern hemisphere and in the Andes Mountains of South America; **leaves** simple, alternate, dentate; **flowers** monoecious, opening before the leaves in most species; staminate catkins elongated; pistillate catkins short, becoming woody with 5-lobed scales; **fruit** a small, winged nutlet.

Alnus crispa (Ait.) Pursh. (American Green Alder, Mountain Alder). Hardy in all zones; large shrub to 3 m. tall.
DESCRIPTION: Large shrub, native in bogs, lake shores, and cold, moist woods from Alaska to Labrador, south to Minnesota and North Carolina; **buds** sessile, covered by unequal, overlapping scales; **leaves** ovate, to 7.5 cm. long, rounded at base, aromatic when young; **fruiting** cones in clusters of 3 to 6.
USE AND CULTURE: Alders are easy to grow in any moist soil, although they are seldom thought to have ornamental value. The male catkins in late winter can add interest to the landscape. They are typically multi-stemmed and the foliage is usually termed coarse. Propagation is by seeds sown in the fall or by softwood cuttings. If conditions are favorable, plants self sow and seedlings may come up where they are not wanted. Alders are relatively short-lived in cultivated situations. They are well suited for use in land reclamation as they establish well in very poor soils. They also fix nitrogen so they are soil builders. As their roots can be invasive, do not plant near sewer or water pipes.

Alnus rugosa (Du Roi) K. Spreng. (Smooth Alder, Hazel Alder, Speckled Alder). Hardy in all zones; tall shrub to 8 m. tall.
DESCRIPTION: Tall shrubs or small trees, native in moist soils along streams and lake shores from Saskatchewan to Labrador, south to Iowa and Pennsylvania; **bark** dark brown; **stems** erect or ascending, usually in clumps; **leaf buds** stipitate, covered with 2 or 3 equal scales; **leaves** elliptic or obovate, to 10 cm. long, rounded or short-pointed at apex, cuneate at base; **flowers** staminate catkins to 10 cm. long, in April; **fruiting** cones 4 to 10 in a cluster, ovoid, to 2 cm. long.
USE AND CULTURE: The same use and culture as **Alnus crispa**.

Amelanchier Medic. (Juneberry, Sarviceberry,
Serviceberry, Shad, Shadbush, Sugarplum)
ROSACEAE (Rose Family)

DESCRIPTION: About 25 species of shrubs or small trees, native in the North
Temperate Zone; **leaves** alternate, dentate; **flowers** white, mostly in terminal racemes,
appearing before or with the leaves, in May; calyx tube bell-shaped, with 5 sepal lobes;
petals 5, often narrow; **fruit** a small, dark purple or black spherical pome.

Amelanchier alnifolia Nutt. (Saskatoon). Hardy in all zones; shrub to 6 m. tall.
DESCRIPTION: Stoloniferous shrub, native along the edges of woods, and along
stream banks from the Yukon to Ontario, south to Idaho and Nebraska; **leaves** truncate
at apex, to 5 cm. wide, coarsely serrate-dentate; **flowers** few, white, with petals to 1
cm. long, in May and early June; ovary tomentose above; **fruits** purple, to 1 cm. long,
ripening in July and August.
USE AND CULTURE: Juneberries are planted in shrub borders and in fruit plantings.
They are typical thicket growing shrubs and are easy to grow in any fertile soil that is
neutral to slightly acid. Propagation is by suckers or by seeds planted as soon as ripe
or in the spring following stratification. Some seedlings may not come up until the
second year. A number of named cultivars have been selected for their edible fruits
which make excellent preserves and pies. Birds love the fruits, so use a bird netting to
protect the fruit.

Amelanchier arborea (Michx.f.) Fern. (Downy Serviceberry). Hardy in all zones; tree
to 10 m. tall.
DESCRIPTION: A small clump tree, native in dry and rocky woods from Ontario to
New Brunswick, south to Oklahoma and Florida; **leaves** oblong-obovate, less than half
grown when the flowers open, densely pubescent beneath when young, becoming
glabrous at maturity; **flowers** showy, in pendulous racemes to 2 cm. across; **fruit** dark,
reddish-purple, tending to be dry and of poor quality.
USE AND CULTURE: The same as for **Amelanchier alnifolia** except fruit is of poorer
quality. The bark is silvery-gray with darker striping.

Amelanchier laevis Wieg. (Allegheny Serviceberry). Hardy in all zones; tree to 10 m.
tall.
DESCRIPTION: A small, upright clump tree, native along the edges of woods, on moist
hillsides, or in ravines from Ontario to Newfoundland, south to Kansas and Georgia;
leaves a maroon color in early spring, elliptic, ovate, ovate-oblong, or slightly obovate,
to 6 cm. long, glabrous, acuminate, turning orange-red in fall; **flowers** showy, in
nodding racemes, opening when leaves are half grown, in May; petals oblong, linear,
to 2 cm. long.
USE AND CULTURE: This is one of the best of the serviceberries to plant as an
ornamental tree. Train as a clump tree with multiple stems. Culture is the same as for
Amelanchier alnifolia.

Amelanchier stolonifera. Both taken by
Dr. Snyder in the 1970's.

Amelanchier stolonifera Wieg. (Running Serviceberry). Hardy in all zones; shrub to 2 m. tall.

DESCRIPTION: A stoloniferous shrub, native in acid, rocky outcroppings and in open, sandy areas from Ontario to Newfoundland, south to Minnesota and Virginia; **leaves** with 15 to 20 marginal teeth per inch, dull green above, elliptic to round, to 5 cm. long, sometimes bronze when young; **flowers** showy, in pubescent racemes, in early May; petals oblong, to 1 cm. long; ovary tomentose above; **fruits** black and juicy when ripe in July.

USE AND CULTURE: The same as for **Amelanchier alnifolia**.

Arctostaphylos Adans. (Bearberry, Manzanita)
ERICACEAE (Heath Family)

DESCRIPTION: About 50 species of evergreen, prostrate shrubs to small trees, native on acid soils, mostly in western North America, with two species circumboreal; **stems** crooked, red to brown; **leaves** alternate, simple, leathery; **flowers** white to pink, in terminal racemes or panicles; calyx 4- to 5-parted; corolla urceolate; stamens 10, anthers awned, opening by terminal pores; ovary superior; **fruit** a berrylike drupe, red to brown, smooth.

Arctostaphylos uva-ursi (L.) K. Spreng. (Common Bearberry, Kinnikinick, Bear's Grape, Bog Cranberry, Creashak, Mealberry, Mountain Box Sandberry). Hardy in all zones; evergreen to 15 cm. tall.

DESCRIPTION: Creeping evergreen shrub, native on acid, sandy, or rocky soil in pine or oak forests, circumboreal, south in North America to California and Virginia; **leaves** obovate to spatulate, to 2.5 cm. long, shiny, green; **flowers** white or pink in terminal racemes, in May and June; ovary glabrous; **fruits** red in September, persisting over winter.

USE AND CULTURE: In the right location, this evergreen shrub can serve as an excellent ground cover. Bearberry requires an acid, well-drained soil, in full sun or partial shade. Acid peat should be added to neutral soils. Snow cover can prevent desiccation from the winter sun. Propagation is by cuttings and seeds. Cuttings should be taken in July and rooted in a sand-peat mixture. Seeds have dormant embryos and impervious seed coats. Seeds should be soaked in sulfuric acid for 3 to 6 hours and stratified for 3 months at room temperature followed by 3 months at 40 degrees Fahrenheit. Plant seeds in early summer. Seeds should germinate the following spring. Layering is another method of propagation. Transplanting should be done carefully.

Aronia Medic. (Chokeberry)
ROSACEAE (Rose Family)

DESCRIPTION: Three species of low, deciduous shrubs, native in North America; **leaves** alternate, simple, finely serrate, short-petioled; **flowers** white or pink, in terminal cymes; calyx tube urceolate; sepals 5; petals 5, concave, spreading; styles 3 to 5, united at base; ovary inferior; **fruit** a berrylike pome.

Aronia arbutifolia (L.) Pers. (Chokeberry, Red Chokeberry). Hardy in zone 5, or sheltered areas of zone 4; shrub to 3 m. tall.

DESCRIPTION: Stoloniferous shrub, native in bogs, swamps, and wet woods, from Ontario to Nova Scotia, south to Texas and Michigan, most common in coastal areas; **leaves** broadly oblanceolate or wider, pointed, crenate-serrate, green and glabrous above, tomentose and pale green beneath, to 8 cm. long; **flowers** white, 2 to 25 in a cyme, to 1 cm. across, in May or early June; calyx tube tomentose; **fruits** red, to 6 mm. across.

USE AND CULTURE: It is grown for its red fruit which ripen in August. Plant in the shrub border, at the edge of moist woods, or at the edge of a swamp. Requires a moist soil. Propagation is by seeds planted in the spring. Seeds have an embryo dormancy and must be stratified over winter at a temperature of 40 degrees F.

Aronia melanocarpa (Michx.) Elliott. (Black Chokeberry). Hardy in all zones; shrub to 1.5 m. tall.

Arctostaphylos uva-ursi (Bearberry). 1972.

Aronia melanocarpa (Black Chokeberry). Photograph of flower and fruit taken at Arboretum.

DESCRIPTION: A branched shrub, native in swamps, low ground, or in open coniferous woods, in acid soils, from Minnesota to Newfoundland, south to Tennessee and South Carolina; **leaves** broadly oblanceolate, glabrous underneath; **flowers** white, 2 to 25 in cymes, to 1 cm. across, in May and early June; calyx tube glabrous; **fruits** black, to 8 mm. across.

USE AND CULTURE: Plant in the shrub border or in wildlife plantings as birds are fond of the fruits. Although the plants are native in acid soils, this shrub has done well at the Arboretum where the soil is nearly neutral. Propagation is the same as for **Aronia arbutifolia**. Black knot, a fungus disease, is common in native stands but has not been a problem in the Arboretum's plantings.

Betula L. (Birch)
BETULACEAE (Birch Family)

DESCRIPTION: About 50 species of deciduous, monoecious, trees and shrubs, native in moist soils in the northern hemisphere; **leaves** simple, alternate, dentate; **flowers** monoecious, borne in catkins; staminate catkins develop in the fall, mature in the spring; pistillate catkins become woody and conelike, with 3-lobed scales, shattering to disperse their seeds when ripe; **fruit** a 1-seeded nutlet.

Betula alleghaniensis Britt. (Gray Birch, Yellow Birch). Hardy in all zones; tree to 30 m. tall.

DESCRIPTION: A large tree with yellowish or silvery-gray bark that becomes reddish-brown on mature trees, native in rich, moist woods from Manitoba to Newfoundland, south to Iowa and Georgia; **leaves** ovate, to 12 cm. long; pistillate **cones**, oblong, to 2.5 cm. long.

USE AND CULTURE: A good tree for parks or spacious grounds. Also, this birch is a good lumber tree. It features peeling bark like many other birches. Plant in a rich, moist soil. Propagation is by seed sown as soon as ripe or in the spring following stratification. The seeds must not be allowed to dry out. Softwood cuttings can also be rooted under mist. This species is more resistant to the bronze birch borer than **Betula papyrifera**. It is moderately difficult to transplant.

Betula lutea - see **Betula alleghaniensis**.

Betula alleghaniensis (Yellow Birch).

Betula alleghaniensis (Yellow Birch). Fall color.

Betula papyrifera (Paper Birch). Bark.

Betula nigra L. (River Birch, Red Birch, Black Birch). Hardy in zone 4; tree to 20 m. tall.

DESCRIPTION: Graceful, spreading tree with reddish-brown or silvery-gray, papery bark, native along stream banks and bottom lands from Minnesota to Massachusetts, south to Kansas and Florida; **leaves** rhombic-ovate, to 7.5 cm. long, dark green above, whitish beneath; **fruit** pistillate cones, oblong-cylindrical, to 4 cm. long.

USE AND CULTURE: Plant as a specimen tree. A clump tree with 5 to 7 stems is most effective. Trees native to our area feature lighter tan bark than typical eastern species. Excellent near ponds where the soil is moist. This birch is highly resistant to the bronze birch borer and is being widely planted as a replacement for the highly susceptible **Betula papyrifera**. Although native only in moist soils, this species is surprisingly drought resistant. Propagation is the same as for **Betula alleghaniensis**. Trees tend to be chlorotic on heavy, poorly-drained soils with a high pH.

Betula papyrifera Marsh. (Canoe Birch, Paper Birch, White Birch). Hardy in all zones; to 25 m. tall.

DESCRIPTION: A graceful tree with white, papery bark that flakes off in strips, native in moist, sandy soils or on rocky, north-facing slopes, or along streams, lakes, and in swamps from Alaska to Labrador, south to Nebraska and Pennsylvania; **leaves** ovate, to 10 cm. long; acuminate at apex, cuneate or cordate at base, coarsely serrate; pistillate **cones**, cylindrical, to 5 cm. long.

USE AND CULTURE: Although frequently planted as a lawn specimen, it also is one of the trees that causes homeowners the most problems. It grows best where soils can remain cooler and more moist. These requirements are not found typically in most lawns. Plant only in moist soil that will not become compacted. The bronze birch borer gains entrance during periods of moisture stress, so it is advisable to water during dry periods. A clump tree is more attractive than trees with a single trunk. In nature, clump trees result from rabbits or deer eating the young seedlings. The same effect can be achieved by cutting young trees off just above the ground. Because of the borer problem, we are encouraging the planting of **Betula nigra** as a replacement for **Betula papyrifera**. Native Americans used the bark for canoes, receptacles for catching maple sap, drinking cups, and for covering teepees.

Carpinus L. (Hornbeam, Ironwood)
BETULACEAE (Birch Family)

DESCRIPTION: About 35 species of deciduous, monoecious trees or large shrubs, native in woods in the northern hemisphere; **bark** gray, scaly or smooth; **leaves** simple, alternate, dentate; **flowers** small, monoecious, in catkins; **fruit** a small achenelike nut subtended by a 3-lobed leafy bract.

Carpinus caroliniana T. Walt. (American Hornbeam, Blue Beech, Water Beech). Hardy in all zones; tree to 10 m. tall.

DESCRIPTION: Small, multiple-stemmed tree, native in moist woods from Minnesota to New England, south to Texas and Florida; **bark** gray, smooth, muscular; **leaves** ovate-oblong, to 10 cm. long with 10 to 14 pairs of pinnate veins, turning red in the fall; pistillate **catkins** to 10 cm. long, maturing in the fall.

USE AND CULTURE: This species should be planted more often. Plant as specimen trees or for screens. It is an easy plant to grow in any fertile soil. The hornbeam can be grown either as a single-stemmed tree or as a clump tree, and with age, this tree can be wide spreading. Because of its wide natural growing range, one can find it in gardens as far south as Florida or Texas. Often, its fall color is outstanding. Unfortunately, this species is not commonly available from nurseries, probably because the tree is difficult to transplant. It can be propagated from seeds, collected before fully ripe, and planted immediately. Mulch the seedbed in November. Do not remove the mulch in the spring until danger of frost is past. The seedbed should be kept moist.

Carya Nutt. (Hickory)
JUGLANDACEAE (Walnut Family)

DESCRIPTION: About 20 species of deciduous, monoecious nut trees, native in eastern North America, Central America, and eastern Asia; **twigs** with solid pith; **leaves** alternate, odd-pinnate; staminate **flowers** in drooping catkins; pistillate flowers in 2- to 10-flowered terminal racemes; **fruit** a drupe with stone or nut enclosed in thick, green husk that splits into 4 valves.

Carya cordiformis (Wagenh.) C. Koch. (Bitternut, Pignut, Swamp Hickory). Hardy in zone 3; tree to 25 m. tall.
Spreading tree, native in rich, moist woods from Minnesota to Quebec, south to Texas and Florida; **buds** yellow, elongated; **bark** smooth when young, becoming rough; **nut** almost globose, nearly smooth, very bitter.
USE AND CULTURE: This straight trunked, picturesque tree is sometimes planted as a lawn tree. It is best started with young seedlings as a deep tap root makes this and other hickories difficult to transplant. Propagation is by seeds sown as soon as ripe or in the spring following stratification. The nuts should not be allowed to dry out. A gall-forming insect can mar the beauty of this species.

Carya laciniosa (Michx.f.) Loud. (Shellbark Hickory, Big Shellbark). Hardy in zone 4; tree to 30 m. tall.
DESCRIPTION: Large tree, native in moist woods from Oklahoma to New York; **leaflets** 7 to 9, oblong-lanceolate, to 20 cm. long, pubescent beneath, turning yellow in fall; **nuts** nearly globose, compressed and angled, yellow or red.
USE AND CULTURE: Plant as a shade and nut tree. Nuts are of excellent quality. Although native south and east of the area covered in this book, this species has been fully hardy in the Twin Cities area. Culture is the same as for **Carya cordiformis**.

Carya ovata (Mill.) C. Koch. (Shagbark Hickory, Shellbark Hickory). Hardy in zone 4; tree to 30 m. tall.
DESCRIPTION: Large tree with shaggy bark that separates in long strips on mature trees; **leaflets** usually 5, elliptic, to 15 cm. long, turning yellow in the fall; **nuts** ellipsoid, slightly angled, white.
USE AND CULTURE: Plant for shade and for the edible nuts which have the best flavor of any of our native nuts. As its common name suggests, it is also prized in landscapes for its shaggy bark which comes off in large plates. The culture is the same as for **Carya cordiformis**.

Carpinus caroliniana (Blue Beech). Fruit taken in 1978.

Carya ovata (Shagbark Hickory). Bark.

Photograph: Hickory by Research Department of the Minnesota

Landscape Arboretum.

Catalpa Scop. (Catalpa, Catawba, Indian Bean)
BIGNONIACEAE (Bignonia Family)
DESCRIPTION: About 13 species of mostly deciduous trees, native in North American and eastern Asia; **leaves** opposite or sometimes whorled, simple, long-petioled; **flowers** white, pink, or yellow, showy, in terminal racemes or panicles; calyx 2-lipped; corolla campanulate, 2-lipped; stamens 2; **fruit** a long, slender capsule, separating into 3 valves; seeds with tuft of hairs at both ends.

Catalpa speciosa Warder ex Engelm. (Catawba, Cigar Tree, Hardy Catalpa, Indian Bean, Western Catalpa). Hardy in zone 4, trial in zone 3; tree to 25 m. tall.
DESCRIPTION: Pyramidal tree, native in bottom lands from Iowa to Indiana, south to Texas and Arkansas; **leaves** ovate to ovate-oblong, to 30 cm. long, long-acuminate, densely pubescent beneath, odorless; **flowers** white, spotted with brown, in panicles to 15 cm. long, in May and June; corolla to 6 cm. across.
USE AND CULTURE: Plant for shade and flowers on lawns and streets. It is an easy tree to grow in most soils. Propagation is by seeds sown in the spring or by hardwood cuttings. The flowers, although very showy, drop to the ground and can be messy as can the seed pods in the fall.

Ceanothus L. (Ceanothus, Redroot)
RHAMNACEAE (Buckthorn Family)
DESCRIPTION: About 55 species of deciduous or evergreen shrubs or small trees, native mostly in western North America, with a few in eastern North America; **leaves** simple, alternate, often 3-veined at the base; **flowers** small, blue or white, in showy umbels, racemes, or panicles, perfect, 5-merous; **fruit** a 3-lobed capsule.

Cephalanthus occidentalis (Buttonbush). Flowers photographed in 1977.

Ceanothus americanus L. (Mountainsweet, New Jersey Tea, Wild Snowball). Hardy in all zones; shrub to 1 m. tall.
DESCRIPTION: Deciduous, mound-shaped shrub, native in dry, open woods, usually on sandy or gravelly soil from Manitoba to Maine, south to Texas and Florida; **leaves** alternate, ovate, finely dentate, pubescent; **flowers** white, in June and July.
USE AND CULTURE: This mound-shaped, erect branched shrub is planted in border and foundation plantings. Dried fruiting branches are used in winter bouquets. Plants require a well-drained soil, preferably a sandy loam. Propagation is by seeds sown in the spring following stratification. Plant in flats in a mixture of 5 parts loam, 4 parts acid peat, and 3 parts sand. Mature plants do not transplant well. The leaves were used in making tea in pioneer days.

Ceanothus ovatus Desf. (Inland Ceanothus, Smaller Redroot). Hardy in all zones; shrub to 60 cm. tall.
DESCRIPTION: Deciduous, mound-shaped shrub native on rocky slopes and sandy prairies, often associated with jack pine from Manitoba to Quebec, south to Texas and Georgia; **leaves** alternate, oblong or elliptic, to 6 cm. long, dentate, glossy above, nearly glabrous; **flowers** white.
USE AND CULTURE: The same as for **Ceanothus americanus**. It is slightly shorter and less open in character than **Ceanothus americanus**.

Cephalanthus L. (Buttonbush)
RUBIACEAE (Madder Family)
DESCRIPTION: About 6 species of shrubs or small trees, native in moist soils in temperate North America, Asia, and Africa; **leaves** opposite or whorled, with small stipules; **flowers** small, in dense, globe-shaped heads; corolla tubular; styles long, exserted; **fruit** a nutlet.

Cephalanthus occidentalis L. (Buttonbush). Hardy in zone 3; shrub to 3 m. tall.
DESCRIPTION: Deciduous shrub, native in swamps and along streams from Minnesota to Nova Scotia, south to Texas and Florida; **leaves** opposite or in whorls, ovate to elliptic-lanceolate, to 15 cm. long, glossy above; **flowers** creamy-white, in long-peduncled heads to 2.5 cm. across, in June.
USE AND CULTURE: This shrub is seldom planted but is striking when in bloom. Its dark green, lustrous foliage is also attractive. Plant in moist soil near ponds or streams. Plants grow best in a rich, fertile soil that is constantly moist. It transplants well. Propagation is by seeds planted in the spring or by either hardwood or softwood cuttings. As this shrub ages, it can be renewed by cutting older canes close to the ground.

Cercis L. (Redbud, Judas Tree)
LEGUMINOSAE (Pea Family)
DESCRIPTION: Seven species of small, deciduous trees, native at the edges of woods in North America, southern Europe, and Asia; **leaves** alternate, simple, entire, palmately veined, on slender petioles; **flowers** pealike, pink to mauve or white, opening before

or with the leaves, clustered or in racemes; petals 5, the upper 3 smaller than the lower 2; stamens 10, separate; **fruit** a thin, flat legume.

Cercis canadensis L. (Eastern Redbud). Trial in zone 4; tree to 10 m. tall.
DESCRIPTION: A small, spreading tree, native in moist woods from Nebraska to Pennsylvania, south to Mexico and Florida; **leaves** broadly ovate to nearly orbicular, to 10 cm. across, usually cordate at base; **flowers** rosy-pink, rarely white, to 1.25 cm. long, borne in clusters; **fruits** to 8 cm. long.
USE AND CULTURE: Plant as an ornamental lawn tree or naturalize at the edges of woods. This species has not been reliably hardy in zone 4. One tree, growing at the Horticultural Research Center at The Minnesota Landscape Arboretum, is over 50 years old and blooms every year. Seedlings from this tree are now being grown by nurserymen and are on the market. Also there is a "Wisconsin strain" being sold in the trade that has also proven to be hardy. Anyone attempting to grow redbud should insure they select these hardier strains. Propagation is mainly by seeds. The seeds have a hard seed coat but germinate after soaking overnight in water that has been heated to boiling. Plants can also be propagated by layering and by stem cuttings.

Chamaedaphne Moench (Leatherleaf)
ERICACEAE (Heath Family)

DESCRIPTION: A single species of low, evergreen shrub, native in moist, sandy or peaty soils in northern Europe, northern Asia, and in North America; **leaves** alternate, simple **flowers** white, nodding, in one-sided, terminal leafy racemes; sepals 5; corolla urceolate; stamens 10; ovary superior; **fruit** a capsule.

Chamaedaphne calyculata (L.) Moench. (Leatherleaf, Cassandra). Hardy in all zones; shrub to 1.6 m. tall.
DESCRIPTION: **Leaves** elliptic to oblong-lanceolate, to 5 cm. long; rusty-scaly beneath; **flowers** white, to 6 mm. long, in racemes to 12 cm. long, in April and May.
USE AND CULTURE: This mound-shaped shrub can be planted in peaty soil in rock gardens or in natural or artificial bog gardens. Plants require an acid, peaty or sandy soil that is kept moist. Propagation is by seeds started in a sand-peat mixture and just barely covered or by cuttings or layers.

Chiogenes hispidula - see **Gaultheria hispidula**.

Chionanthus L. (Fringe Tree)
OLEACEAE (Olive Family)

DESCRIPTION: 3 or 4 species of deciduous, polygamodioecius trees and shrubs, native in eastern North America and eastern Asia; **leaves** opposite, simple, entire; **flowers** many, white, in showy panicles; petals 4, linear, united only at the base; **fruit** a dark blue drupe.

Chionanthus virginicus L. (Fringe Tree, Old-man's-beard). Hardy in zone 4; shrub to 5 m. tall.
DESCRIPTION: Large deciduous shrub or small tree, native in moist woods from Ohio to New Jersey, south to Texas and Florida; leaves oblong or obovate-oblong, to 20 cm. long; **flowers** functionally dioecious, the pistil of the fertile flowers much larger than in the sterile ones; **flowers** white, very fragrant, in panicles to 20 cm. long, in June; **drupes** dark blue, to 1.5 cm. long.
USE AND CULTURE: This very attractive species should be planted more than it is. It can be used as a border shrub or as a screen. The fringe tree, although an eastern species, has been fully hardy in my yard and in Arboretum plantings. As it blooms on year-old wood, prune only lightly, directly after it flowers in the spring. It is easy to grow in any well-drained soil. Propagation is by seeds, planted as soon as ripe or in the spring following stratification.

Cladrastis Raf. (Yellowwood)
LEGUMINOSAE (Peas Family)

DESCRIPTION: Four species of deciduous trees, native in sheltered locations in temperate parts of eastern North America and eastern Asia; **leaves** odd-pinnate; leaflets

Cercis canadensis (Eastern Redbud).

Chionanthus virginicus (Fringe Tree). Both photographs taken in 1978.

alternate; **flowers** white, pealike, in panicled racemes; stamens 10, nearly separate; **fruit** a thin, flat, dehiscent legume.

Cladrastis lutea (Michx.f.) C. Koch. (Virgilia, Yellowwood). Trial in zone 4; tree to 10 m. tall.
DESCRIPTION: Broad, spreading tree, native from Missouri to Kentucky, south to Alabama and Georgia; **bark** smooth; **leaflets** 7 to 11, ovate, to 10 cm. long; **flowers** white, fragrant, in pendent panicles, in June.
USE AND CULTURE: Plant as a lawn specimen in a sheltered location. This southern species is surprisingly hardy and has grown well in sheltered areas in the Arboretum and elsewhere in the Twin Cities area. Propagation is by seeds sown in the fall or spring following stratification. Seeds have a hard seed coat and germination is improved by soaking the seeds in water that has been heated to the boiling point. As with maples, pruning should not be done in the spring because the yellowwood will bleed sap excessively.

Comptonia L'Her. (Sweet Fern)
MYRICACEAE (Bayberry Family)

DESCRIPTION: A single species of deciduous, usually monoecious shrub, native in dry, sandy or peaty, acid soils in eastern North America; **leaves** alternate, narrow, pinnatifid, fragrant; staminate **flowers** in short catkins, with 4 stamens; pistillate flowers in heads; ovary 1-celled, subtended by 8 linear bracts; **fruit** an ovoid nutlet, borne in headlike clusters.

Comptonia peregrina (L.) J. Coult. (Sweet Fern). Hardy in all zones; shrub to 1 m. tall.
DESCRIPTION: Deciduous shrub, native in dry, sandy, acid soils, usually in association with jack pine from Manitoba to New Brunswick, south to Illinois and Virginia; **branchlets** pubescent; **leaves** linear-oblong, deeply pinnatifid, fernlike, to 10 cm. long; **flowers** monoecious, not showy; **nutlets** glabrous, brown, in clusters 1 cm. across.
USE AND CULTURE: This thicket-forming shrub is often planted on sandy banks for erosion control. Its dissected foliage is also pleasingly scented. Plants require an acid, well-drained soil. Propagation is by seeds and division. Established plants can be divided in the spring and replanted. Seeds should be planted as soon as ripe or in the spring following stratification.

Cornus L. (Dogwood, Cornel)
CORNACEAE (Dogwood Family)

DESCRIPTION: About 45 species of mostly deciduous shrubs or small trees, native in North America, Europe, Asia, and in Africa; **leaves** usually opposite, simple, entire; **flowers** white, greenish-white, or yellow, in terminal cymes, panicles, umbels, or heads, small, 4-merous, sometimes surrounded by an involucre of showy bracts; **fruit** a 2-seeded drupe.

Cladrastis lutea (Yellowwood).

Comptonia peregrina (Sweet Fern).

Cornus alternifolia L.f. (Pagoda Dogwood, Alternate-leaved Dogwood, Green Osier). Hardy in all zones; small tree to 8 m. tall.
DESCRIPTION: A small tree with whorled branches, native in woods and thickets from Manitoba to Newfoundland, south to Missouri and Georgia; **leaves** alternate, crowded toward the end of the branches, ovate to elliptic, to 12 cm. long; **flowers** small, creamy-white, in flat-topped cymes to 6 cm. across; **drupes** dark blue.
USE AND CULTURE: Plant as a specimen tree or use as a screen. Its decidedly horizontal growth habit makes this one of our best specimen small trees. Plants are of easy culture in full sun or in partial shade. It requires some protection from strong winds. Propagation is by seeds sown as soon as ripe or in the spring following stratification. Softwood cuttings can be rooted under intermittent mist. Layering is another method of propagation.

Cornus baileyi - see **Cornus sericea** forma **baileyi**.

Cornus racemosa Lam. (Gray Dogwood, Panicled Dogwood). Hardy in all zones; shrub to 4 m. tall.
DESCRIPTION: Stoloniferous shrubs with gray stems, native in open woods from Manitoba to Maine, south to Oklahoma and North Carolina; **leaves** lanceolate to ovate-lanceolate, to 10 cm. long, turning plum-colored in the fall; **flowers** white, in cymose panicles, in June; **drupes** white on red pedicels in September.
USE AND CULTURE: An excellent shrub for a screen or border planting. Although its white fruits are eaten by the birds by early fall, the red pedicles persist. This makes the gray dogwood with its gray stems and red pedicles very striking against winter snows. It has a suckering habit and can be renewed by early spring pruning of older canes. Its culture is the same as for **Cornus alternifolia**.

Cornus rugosa Lam. (Round-leaved Dogwood). Hardy in all zones; shrub to 3 m. tall.
DESCRIPTION: Shrub with green stems, blotched with purple, native in woods from Manitoba to Quebec, south to Iowa and West Virginia; **pith** white; **leaves** broadly ovate to orbicular, to 15 cm. long, pale and pubescent beneath; **flowers** white, in flat-topped cymes to 6 cm. across, in June; **drupes** blue in August.
USE AND CULTURE: This upright growing shrub can be planted along paths in woodland gardens. The culture is the same as for **Cornus alternifolia**. It is more difficult to transplant.

Cornus sericea L. (Red-osier Dogwood, American Dogwood). Hardy in all zones; shrub to 3 m. tall.
DESCRIPTION: Stoloniferous shrub, rooting where stems touch ground, native in woods and in swamps widely distributed throughout North America; young **stems** bright red, especially in late winter; pith white; **leaves** oblong-lanceolate to ovate, to 12 cm. long, papillose beneath; **flowers** white in cymes to 5 cm. across, in May and June; **drupes** white or blue in August.
USE AND CULTURE: An excellent shrub for wet soils and for screen plantings. The culture is the same as for **Cornus alternifolia**. This species and its cultivars are often planted for its colored twigs which provide winter interest.

Cornus alternifolia (Pagoda Dogwood). In full leaf.

Cornus racemosa (Gray Dogwood). White fruit.

Cornus sericea forma **baileyi** (J. Coult. ex W.H. Evans). Fosb.
DESCRIPTION: Similar to species except the under surface of leaves have curling hairs.

Cornus stolonifera - see **Cornus sericea**.

Corylus L. (Filbert, Hazel, Hazelnut)
BETULACEAE (Birch Family)
DESCRIPTION: About 10 species of deciduous, monoecious shrubs or small trees, native at the edge of woods, thickets, and in pastures in the North Temperate Zone; **leaves** alternate, generally ovate, doubly dentate; staminate **flowers** in drooping catkins; **fruit** a nut enclosed in a leafy involucre, borne in clusters at the end of branches.

Corylus americana Marsh. (American Filbert, American Hazelnut). Hardy in all zones; shrub to 3 m. tall.
DESCRIPTION: Deciduous shrub, native in thickets and pastures from Saskatchewan to Maine, south to Oklahoma and Georgia; **leaves** ovate, to 12 cm. long, pubescent beneath; staminate **flowers** form in the fall but do not shed their pollen until April or May; **fruit** in clusters of 2 to 6 with nuts enclosed in an involucre about twice as long as the nut and with irregular lobes.
USE AND CULTURE: Sometimes planted for a screen or for the edible nuts. Its early flowering catkins add spring interest. Plants grow well in most soils. Propagation is by seeds, suckers, layering, and by cuttings. Nuts should be planted in the fall as soon as ripe. The nuts are often infested by an insect that destroys them.

Corylus cornuta Marsh. (Beaked Filbert, Beaked Hazelnut). Hardy in all zones; shrub to 3 m. tall.
DESCRIPTION: Deciduous shrub, native in woods, thickets, and clearings from British Columbia to Newfoundland, south to Colorado and Georgia; **leaves** elliptic, ovate, or obovate, sometimes cordate at base, to 10 cm. long, pubescent on veins beneath; staminate **flowers** form in the fall but do not shed their pollen until April or May; **fruit** solitary or in pairs; involucres tubular, bristly, much contracted above nut to form a beak to 3 cm. long.
USE AND CULTURE: The same as for **Corylus americana**. It is drought-resistant.

Corylus rostrata - see **Corylus cornuta**.

Cotinus Mill. (Smoke Bush, Smoke Tree)
ANACARDIACEAE (Cashew Family)
DESCRIPTION: Three species of deciduous, polygamous shrubs or small trees, native in well-drained soils of low fertility in North America, Eurasia, and China; **leaves** simple; **flowers** small, in large loose, terminal panicles; pedicels of sterile flowers lengthening and clothed with spreading hairs; stamens 5; **fruit** a small, compressed drupe.

Cotinus americanus - see **Cotinus obovatus**.

Cotinus obovatus Raf. (American Smoke Tree, Chittamwood). Hardy in zone 4; tree to 10 m. tall.
DESCRIPTION: Small tree, native from Missouri to Tennessee, south to Texas and Alabama; **leaves** mostly obovate, to 15 cm. long, cuneate or tapering at base, brightly colored with orange to scarlet in fall; **flowers** small, in large panicles in June.
USE AND CULTURE: Plant toward the back of the shrub border or as a specimen tree. This southern species is surprisingly hardy and has done well in our Arboretum plantings. Propagation is by seeds, cuttings, or by layering. Seeds should be planted as soon as ripe or in the spring following stratification.

Crataegus L. (Hawthorn, Red Haw, Thorn Apple)
ROSACEAE (Rose Family)

Cornus racemosa (Gray Dogwood). Fall color.

DESCRIPTION: About 1000 species of mostly thorny, deciduous shrubs or small trees, often horizontally branched, native in sunny locations in calcareous or rich loamy soil in the North Temperate Zone; **leaves** alternate, dentate or lobed; **flowers** mostly white, rarely pink or red, in corymbs; **fruit** a small pome with 5 or fewer, 1-seeded nutlets.

Crataegus chrysocarpa Asche. (Fireberry Thorn, Round-leaved Thorn). Hardy in all zones; tree to 7 m. tall.
DESCRIPTION: A small, round-topped, much-branched tree, native from Saskatchewan to Newfoundland, south to New Mexico and Pennsylvania; **thorns** numerous, to 4 cm. long; **leaves** ovate to nearly orbicular, to 5 cm. long, serrate except near the base, with 3 to 4 pairs of triangular, lateral lobes; **flowers** white, to 1.25 cm. across, in villous corymbs; sepals serrate; stamens about 10; **pomes** yellow to red.
USE AND CULTURE: Plant as a lawn specimen or for a screen. They need a fertile, well-drained soil and full sun. Propagation is by seeds sown as soon as ripe or in the spring following stratification. It may take 2 years for the seeds to germinate. Transplant to their permanent location when seedlings are one year old because of the tap root. Cedar-hawthorn rust can be a problem. Ferbam or Zineb fungicides can be used to control the rust but it must be applied soon after petal fall. If these problems are controlled, the glossy green foliage is very attractive. It is sharply thorned, which can be useful in some landscape situations.

Crataegus crus-galli L. (Cockspur, Cockspur Thorn, Newcastle Thorn). Hardy in zone 4; tree to 10 m. tall.
DESCRIPTION: A broad, spreading tree, native from Michigan to Quebec, south to Kansas and North Carolina; **thorns** to 7.5 cm. long; **leaves** obovate, cuneate at base, rounded at apex, to 7.5 cm. long, glabrous, leathery dentate; **flowers** white, to 1.5 cm. across, in June; stamens 10 or fewer; **pomes** dull red, to 1.25 cm. long.
USE AND CULTURE: The same as for **Crataegus chrysocarpa**. This species is resistant to the cedar-hawthorn rust and with its glossy, dark green foliage it can be a highly desirable landscape tree. There is a thornless cultivar, 'Inermis', available from nurseries, which may be preferable in some landscape situations to the native species. This tree is tolerant of many urban environments.

Crataegus mollis (Torr. ex A. Gray) Scheele. (Downy Hawthorn). Hardy in zone 4; tree to 10 m. tall.
DESCRIPTION: Small tree, native in bottom lands, hillsides, and borders of woods from South Dakota to Ontario, south to Oklahoma and Alabama; **leaves** ovate or triangular, to 10 cm. long, sharply or coarsely serrate, usually with 4 or 5 pairs of lateral lobes, pubescent beneath; **flowers** white, to 2.5 cm. across, in tomentose corymbs; stamens about 20; **pomes** subglobose, to 2 cm. across, red.
USE AND CULTURE: The same as for **Crataegus chrysocarpa**. Its foliage is coarser than other hawthorns.

Crataegus punctata Jacq. (Dotted Hawthorn, White Thorn). Hardy in all zones; tree to 10 m. tall.
DESCRIPTION: Small, thorny tree, native in clearings and pastures from Minnesota to eastern Canada, south to Kansas and West Virginia; **leaves** mostly obovate, serrate above the middle, slightly lobed toward the apex, to 10 cm. long, pubescent beneath;

Crataegus punctata. As a woodland understory tree. Photograph taken in 1970.

Crataegus chrysocarpa. Flowers.

flowers white, in pubescent corymbs; stamens about 20, with red or yellow anthers; **pomes** dull red, to 2 cm. across.
USE AND CULTURE: The same as for **Crataegus chrysocarpa**. This species is very susceptible to cedar-hawthorn rust.

Crataegus succulenta Link. (Fleshy Hawthorn). Hardy in all zones; tree to 10 m. tall.
DESCRIPTION: Small tree with ascending, thorny branches, native in thickets and pastures from Manitoba to New England, south to Colorado and North Carolina; **leaves** elliptic to ovate, sharply serrate, leathery, lustrous, to 7.5 cm. long, with 4 or 5 pairs of shallow lobes; **flowers** white, with pink anthers, to 2 cm. across, in corymbs, in June; **pomes** bright red, subglobose, to 1.25 cm. across.
USE AND CULTURE: The same as for **Crataegus chrysocarpa**.

Dirca palustris (Leatherwood). In bud in spring showing excellent form.

Diervilla Mill. (Bush Honeysuckle)
CAPRIFOLIACEAE (Honeysuckle Family)
DESCRIPTION: Three species of small, deciduous shrubs, spreading by underground rhizomes, native in moist soils in eastern North America; **leaves** opposite, simple; **flowers** yellow, in small, leafless, axillary clusters or terminal cymes; calyx 5-lobed; corolla 2-lipped, 5-lobed; stamens 5, exserted; ovary inferior, 2-celled; **fruit** a slender, 2-valved capsule.

Diervilla lonicera Mill. (Dwarf Bush Honeysuckle). Hardy in all zones; shrub to 1.2 m. tall.
DESCRIPTION: A spreading, rhizomatous shrub, native in dry to moist woods, often in rocky soils from Saskatchewan to Newfoundland, south to Iowa and Georgia; **leaves** ovate to elliptic, to 10 cm. long, acuminate, petioled; new growth bronze; **flowers** pale yellow, becoming darker as they age, to 1.5 cm. long, in June and July.
USE AND CULTURE: Plant in shrub borders or as a ground cover on banks. This is an easy shrub to grow that can easily be increased by division. Space the plants about 60 cm. apart in early spring. By fall, the ground will be completely covered. Some root pruning may be required to keep this shrub from spreading, and some spring pruning is necessary on established plantings to promote new growth.

Dirca L. (Leatherwood)
THYMELAEACEAE (Mezereum Family)
DESCRIPTION: Two species of erect, deciduous shrubs, native in open woods in North America; **branches** flexible with tough fibrous bark; **leaves** alternate, entire; **flowers** yellow, in small, nearly sessile clusters, subtended by hairy bud scales, appearing before the leaves; **fruit** a small, red or green drupe.

Dirca palustris L. (Atlantic Leatherwood, Moosewood, Rope Bark, Wicopy). Hardy in all zones; shrub to 2 m. tall.
DESCRIPTION: Rounded shrub, native in rich woods from Minnesota to New Brunswick, south to Louisiana and Florida; **bud** scales sparsely hairy, very large as leaves and flowers unfold; **twigs** yellowish-green, jointed; **leaves** ovate to elliptic, to 8 cm. long, rounded at base, blunt at apex, entire; **flowers** yellow, tubular, in April; calyx tubular; petals none; stamens exserted; **fruit** a yellowish-green drupe, dropping as soon as ripe.
USE AND CULTURE: This is an excellent shrub for foundation or border plantings. Plants grow well in most any well-drained soil in full sun or in partial shade. It is tolerant of wet soils. Propagation is by seeds planted as soon as ripe. Volunteer seedlings can often be found under established shrubs. Plants require little or no pruning.

Elaeagnus L. (Elaeagnus)
ELAEAGNACEAE (Oleaster Family)
DESCRIPTION: About 40 species of mostly deciduous shrubs or small trees, native in well-drained soil in full sun in southern Europe, Asia, and North America; **leaves**

alternate, covered with minute, silvery or brown scales; **flowers** small, inconspicuous, perfect; **fruit** a drupe.

Elaeagnus commutata Bernh. (Silverberry). Hardy in all zones; shrub to 3 m. tall.
DESCRIPTION: Deciduous, stoloniferous shrub, native in dry, limestone soils from Alaska to Quebec, south to Utah and Nebraska; **leaves** silvery on both sides, ovate to ovate-lanceolate, to 10 cm. long, acute or obtuse, cuneate at base; **flowers** small, fragrant in small axillary clusters, in May and June; **drupes** silvery, on short pedicels, ripening in August.
USE AND CULTURE: Plant as a bank cover on roadside slopes. They are easy to grow in any well-drained soil. Its gray foliage makes it useful as an accent in the shrub border. Propagation is by spring division, hardwood stem cuttings, root cuttings, and by seeds sown as soon as ripe or in the spring following stratification. Suckering can be a problem when planted in a shrub border.

Epigaea L. (Ground Laurel)
ERICACEAE (Heath Family)
DESCRIPTION: Two species of creeping, evergreen shrubs, native in acid, sandy soil in partial shade in Japan and North America; **leaves** simple, alternate, leathery; **flowers** white to rose, fragrant, clustered toward the tips of the branches; sepals 5; corolla urceolate or salverform, hairy inside; stamens 10; ovary superior; **fruit** a many-seeded capsule.

Epigaea repens L. (Mayflower, Trailing Arbutus). Hardy in all zones; creeping shrub to 10 cm. tall.
DESCRIPTION: Hairy-stemmed, creeping shrub native in acid, sandy soils, usually under jack pines from Saskatchewan to Labrador, south to Minnesota and North Carolina; **leaves** oblong-ovate, ovate, or suborbicular, to 7.5 cm. long, cordate at base, rounded at apex, bright green, hairy; **flowers** white to pink, very fragrant, in April and May; corolla salverform with spreading lobe.
USE AND CULTURE: Plant as a ground cover in woodland wild flower gardens. Effective on the north side of stumps. Mature plants are difficult to transplant. It is best to start plants from seeds or from cuttings. Seeds are difficult to collect as the mature capsule forcibly discharges its seed as soon as ripe. Seeds should be sown as soon as ripe in an acid sand-peat mixture. It takes 3 years for seedlings to bloom. Cuttings should be taken just after bloom and rooted in an acid sand-peat mixture. Cuttings should be rooted by fall. The practice of moving mature plants should be discouraged as this plant is becoming rare and such transplants seldom grow.

Epigaea repens (Trailing Arbutus). Taken May 1953.

Euonymus atropurpurea (Burning Bush).

Taken in Dr. Snyder's yard.

Euonymus L. (Spindle Tree)
CELASTRACEAE (Staff-tree Family)
DESCRIPTION: About 170 species of deciduous or evergreen shrubs and trees, rarely creeping or climbing, native mostly in Asia, a few in North America, Europe, Africa, and Australia; **branches** usually 4-angled; **leaves** simple, mostly opposite, rarely alternate or whorled; **flowers** small, green or purple, in axillary cymes, 4- to 5-merous; **fruit** a 3- to 5-valved capsule; **seeds** enclosed in a scarlet or orange aril.

Euonymus atropurpurea Jacq. (Burning Bush, Wahoo). Hardy in all zones; shrub to 8 m. tall.
DESCRIPTION: Deciduous shrub or small tree, native in rich woods and thickets from Montana to Ontario, south to Alabama and Florida; **stems** obtusely 4-angled; **leaves** opposite, elliptic, to 12 cm. long, acuminate, finely serrate, turning yellow or red in fall; **flowers** small, 4-merous, purple, in June; **capsules** crimson with scarlet arils.
USE AND CULTURE: This tall native can be planted in shrub borders or at the edges of woods. The burning bush is of easy culture and is not planted as often as it should be. It likes a rich, moist soil high in organic matter. The fall color, which can be striking, is best if grown in full sun. Propagation is by seeds, hardwood cuttings, or layering. Seeds should be planted in the fall or in the spring following stratification.

Hamamelis virginiana (Witch Hazel). Fall flowers.

Photograph: Dr. Anne M. Hanchek.

Gaultheria L. (Wintergreen)
ERICACEAE (Heath Family)
DESCRIPTION: About 100 species of evergreen shrubs, rarely small trees, native in moist, sandy or peaty soils in woods, widespread in North and South America, Asia, and Australia; **leaves** alternate, rarely opposite, simple; **flowers** pink or white, solitary, or in racemes or panicles; calyx 5-parted; corolla urceolate or campanulate, rarely tubular; stamens 8 to 10 with awned anthers; ovary superior; **fruit** a capsule enclosed by a fleshy, bright-colored calyx.

Gaultheria hispidula (L.) Muhlenb. ex Bigel. (Maidenhair Berry, Moxie Plum, Creeping Snowberry). Hardy in all zones; trailing shrub to 12 cm. tall.
DESCRIPTION: Trailing, mat-forming, semi-herbaceous, evergreen shrub, native in acid bogs or wet woods, often on logs, from British Columbia to Newfoundland, south to Minnesota and North Carolina; **leaves** ovate, to 1 cm. long, revolute, bristly beneath; **flowers** white, bell-shaped, less than 5 mm. long, in May and June; **fruits** white, berrylike.
USE AND CULTURE: Plant as a ground cover in acid soil in shade. This is a difficult plant to grow. It does best in a specially prepared soil consisting of a mixture of coarse sand, rotted pine logs, and sphagnum peat. Keep plants constantly moist. Propagation is by spring division or by cuttings taken in May and rooted in a sand-peat mixture.

Gaultheria procumbens L. (Checkerberry, Ivry-leaves, Mountain Tea, Teaberry, Wintergreen). Hardy in all zones; evergreen shrub to 15 cm. tall.
DESCRIPTION: Plants creeping, native in acid, sandy soils in dry or moist woods, occasionally on hummocks in peat bogs from Manitoba to Newfoundland, south to Alabama and Georgia; **leaves** elliptic to narrowing obovate, to 5 cm. long, bristly serrate, shiny above; young leaves with a minty flavor; **flowers** solitary, nodding, white, to 7 mm. long, in July and August; **fruits** scarlet, with a minty flavor, remaining on plants over winter.
USE AND CULTURE: Plant as a ground cover in wild flower gardens or in rock gardens. Young leaves are used to make a mint-flavored tea. Berries are also tasty with a minty flavor. Plant in an acid, sandy soil or in a soil that has been specially prepared by adding sand, acid peat, and rotted pine or oak sawdust. Propagation is by spring division, cuttings taken in July and rooted in a sand-peat mixture, or by seeds planted as soon as ripe. Germination is often poor.

Gaylussacia HBK. (Huckleberry)
ERICACEAE (Heath Family)
DESCRIPTION: About 40 species of shrubs, native in North and South America; **leaves** alternate, simple; **flowers** white, pink, or red, in axillary racemes; calyx 5-lobed; corolla urceolate, campanulate, or tubular; stamens 10; ovary inferior, 10-celled; **fruit** a berrylike drupe.

Gaylussacia baccata (Wagenh.) C. Koch. (Black Huckleberry). Hardy in all zones; shrub to 1 m. tall.
DESCRIPTION: Deciduous shrub with branches sticky when young, native in dry or moist woods and clearings, in acid, sandy soils from Saskatchewan to Newfoundland, south to Minnesota and Georgia; **leaves** elliptic to oblong-lanceolate, to 5 cm. long, entire, resinous on both surfaces; **flowers** red, in dense, drooping racemes, to 2.5 cm. long; **fruits** black, glossy, edible.
USE AND CULTURE: Plant in shrub borders or grow in fruit gardens for its edible fruit. Plants grow best in an acid, sandy soil. Propagation is by seeds, layers, or cuttings. Seeds should be sown in the fall or in the spring following stratification. Cuttings should be taken in July and rooted in a sand-peat mixture.

Hamamelis L. (Witch Hazel)
HAMAMELIDACEAE (Witch Hazel Family)
DESCRIPTION: Six species of deciduous shrubs or small trees, native in moist woods in north temperate regions in eastern North America and eastern Asia; **leaves** alternate,

simple, dentate; **flowers** small, in axillary clusters, appearing in the fall or late winter; calyx 4-parted; corolla of 4 strap-shaped petals; stamens 4; staminodes 4; **fruit** a capsule.

Hamamelis virginiana L. (Witch Hazel). Hardy in zone 3; shrub to 5 m. tall.
DESCRIPTION: A shrub or small tree, native in low rich soils or on rocky banks of streams from Minnesota to New England, south to Missouri and Georgia; **leaves** obovate, coarsely dentate, to 15 cm.; **flowers** golden-yellow, in October and November; calyx lobes dull, brownish-yellow inside, to 2 cm. long; **fruits** ripen in fall of second year.
USE AND CULTURE: Plant in shrub borders or as a screen. Witch hazels feature yellow blossoms which curiously bloom in October in our area. The flowers can actually blend in with the yellow fall foliage color. They are easy to grow in most soils. Propagation is by seeds or layering. It takes 2 years for seeds to germinate.

Hydrangea L. (Hydrangea)
SAXIFRAGACEAE (Saxifrage Family)
DESCRIPTION: About 20 species of erect or climbing, deciduous or evergreen shrubs, native in moist soils in North and South America and in eastern Asia; **leaves** opposite, entire or serrate, rarely pinnately lobed; **flowers** white, pink, or blue, in terminal, compound, rounded, or pyramidal panicles; fertile flowers small, perfect; sterile flowers often present, showy, consisting of 3 to 5 conspicuous petallike sepals, usually marginal or replacing the fertile flowers completely; **fruit** a dehiscent capsule.

Hydrangea arborescens L. (Hills-of-snow, Seven Bark, Wild Hydrangea). Hardy in zone 3; shrub to 1.2 m. tall.
DESCRIPTION: Much branched shrub, native in dry to moist, rocky woods and hillsides from Ontario, south to Oklahoma and Georgia; **leaves** ovate, to 15 cm. long, pubescent beneath, serrate, acuminate at apex; **flowers** white, in flattened or convex inflorescences, in June and July, all small and fertile or with showy, sterile flowers around the margins, rarely all sterile in named cultivars such as 'Annabelle'.
USE AND CULTURE: Plant in foundation plantings, shrub borders, or for informal hedges. Hydrangeas are easy to grow in most soils. Without snow cover, this hydrangea often kills to the ground, but in this species this actually promotes better bloom. Some shade is tolerated, but bloom is best in full sun. Propagation is largely by spring division or by cuttings. The species can be propagated by seeds but named cultivars must be vegetatively reproduced.

Hydrangea arborescens (Hills-of-snow). In 1973.

Hypericum kalmianum. Flowers in 1977.

Hypericum L. (St. John's-wort)
HYPERICACEAE (St. John's-wort Family)
DESCRIPTION: About 300 species of herbs, shrubs, or subshrubs, native in temperate regions; **stems** sometimes winged or angled; **leaves** evergreen or deciduous, opposite, entire, often black-dotted or with translucent dots; **flowers** yellow; sepals and petals 5; stamens many, separate or in 3 to 5 bundles, showy; **fruit** a capsule, rarely a berry.

Hypericum kalmianum L. (Kalm's St. John's-wort). Hardy in zone 4; shrub to 60 cm. tall.
DESCRIPTION: Semi-evergreen shrub, native in rocky soils from Wisconsin to Quebec, south to Indiana and Ohio; **leaves** semi-evergreen, oblong-linear or oblanceolate, to 6 cm. long; **flowers** yellow, to 2.5 cm. scross, in few-flowered cymes, in July and August; styles 5.
USE AND CULTURE: Plant as a foreground shrub or in rock gardens. Plants are easy to grow in any well-drained soil that is near neutral. Propagation is by seeds or by softwood cuttings rooted under mist. Tips of this shrub may die back. If this happens, prune back to live wood in early spring. The plant blooms on new wood so winter injury, if it occurs, is not serious.

Hypericum prolificum L. (Broombrush, Shrubby St. John's-wort). Hardy in zone 4; shrub to 1.5 m. tall.

DESCRIPTION: Branched shrub, native in dry, rocky soils from Minnesota to Ontario, south to Louisiana and Georgia; **leaves** narrowly oblong, to 7.5 cm. long; **flowers** yellow, to 2 cm. across, in cymes, from July to September.

USE AND CULTURE: Plant in shrub borders. The culture is the same as for **Hypericum kalmianum**.

Ilex L. (Holly)
AQUIFOLIACEAE (Holly Family)

DESCRIPTION: About 400 species of dioecious or polygamodioecious trees and shrubs, often evergreen; native in temperate and tropical regions of North and South America and Asia; **leaves** alternate, short-petioled, often thick, leathery, and evergreen with margins entire, dentate, or spiny; **flowers** small, solitary in leaf axils, in fascicles, or cymes, usually on short pedicels; calyx 4- to 6-parted, persistent; corolla white or green, rotate, with petals separate or united at base; stamens alternating with the petals; ovary superior capped by a lobed stigma; **fruit** a berrylike drupe, globular, black or red.

Ilex verticillata (L.) A. Gray. (Black Alder, Common Winterberry, Winterberry). Hardy in all zones; shrub to 3 m. tall.

DESCRIPTION: Deciduous shrub, native in acid swamps and wet woods from Minnesota to Newfoundland, south to Texas and Georgia; **leaves** dull green to moderately glossy above, lanceolate to obovate or elliptic, to 10 cm. long, serrate, cuneate at base; **flowers** dioecious, 5- to 7-merous, in May and June; **fruit** a red berrylike drupe, in October.

USE AND CULTURE: Plant in shrub borders. The red fruits, which are borne close to the twigs, stay on well into the winter, making winterberry one of the best shrubs for winter interest. Plants require a moist soil that is slightly acid. Propagation is by seed or hardwood cuttings. Seeds should be stratified and planted in the spring. It may take 2 to 3 years for complete germination. Since the sexes are separate, it is best to plant several seedlings to be sure of getting both staminate and pistillate plants.

Kalmia L. (American Laurel, Laurel)
ERICACEAE (Heath Family)

DESCRIPTION: About 6 species of evergreen shrubs, native in acid, peaty or sandy soils in North America; **leaves** alternate, opposite, or whorled, simple, entire, leathery; **flowers** white, pink, or purple, in lateral or terminal corymbs or umbels, rarely solitary; calyx 5-lobed; corolla broadly campanulate to somewhat funnelform with 10 pouches in which the anthers are held until they forcibly discharge their pollen; ovary superior; **fruit** a 5-celled capsule.

Kalmia latifolia L. (Calico Bush, Ivybush, Mountain Laurel, Spoonwood). Hardy in zone 5; shrub to 3 m. tall.

DESCRIPTION: Evergreen shrub, native in acid, well-drained soils high in organic matter from Ontario to Maine, south to Louisiana and Florida; **leaves** mostly alternate, rarely opposite or in 3's, elliptic, to 12 cm. long; **flowers** rose to white with purple markings, in terminal, glandular-pubescent corymbs, in May and June.

USE AND CULTURE: This eastern species is sometimes planted for its showy flowers. Plant in a sheltered, open area in the wild flower garden. Plants must have an acid soil rich in organic matter. Winter injury is the main problem when grown north of zone 5. By bending the plant over in early November and holding it down with wire loops and then covering it with evergreen boughs, I have had no difficulty in growing this delightful plant and in getting it to bloom. Propagation is by seeds, by cuttings, and layering. Seeds must have light to germinate. Plant them shallow in an acid sand-peat mixture.

Kalmia poliifolia Wangenb. (Bog Kalmia, Bog Laurel, Pale Laurel). Hardy in all zones; shrub to 60 cm. tall.

DESCRIPTION: A straggling shrub, native in acid peat bogs from Alaska to Labrador, south to California and Pennsylvania; **leaves** opposite or in 3's, nearly sessile, lanceolate to linear, to 4 cm. long, revolute, glossy green above, glaucous-white beneath; **flowers** rose-purple, to 1.25 cm. across, in glabrous terminal corymbs, in May and June.

USE AND CULTURE: Plant in a natural or artificial acid bog. Established plants are difficult to transplant. Young plants should be started from seeds or rooted cuttings. Plant seeds as soon as ripe in an acid sand-peat mixture.

Larix Mill. (Larch, Tamarack)
PINACEAE (Pine Family)

DESCRIPTION: About 10 species of deciduous, cone-bearing trees, native in moist soils in cooler parts of the northern hemisphere; **branches** spreading or ascending from a central trunk; **leaves** short, linear, spirally arranged on terminal shoots or clustered in a tuft or fascicle of 20 to 30 on short spurs, bright green, turning a golden-yellow in October; staminate **cones** solitary, globe-shaped on sides of twigs in early spring; pistillate cones with narrow, often brightly colored bracts, persistent; **seeds** winged, two produced on each scale, maturing first year.

Larix laricina (Du Roi) C. Koch. (American Larch, Black Larch, Hackmatack, Tamarack). Hardy in all zones; tree to 25 m. tall.
DESCRIPTION: Upright trees, native in swamps in northern parts of North America, south to Minnesota and Pennsylvania; **branchlets** glabrous, often glaucous, reddish-yellow; **leaves** to 4 cm. long, obtuse, bluish-green, turning yellow in October; pistillate **cones** to 2 cm. long with shiny, glabrous scales, maturing first year but persisting on the trees.
USE AND CULTURE: This deciduous conifer can be used as a lawn tree or as a screen. Tamaracks add interest to the landscape in the spring when its deciduous, lacy, pale green foliage is attractive and in the fall when it turns a dull yellow. Although native in swamps, it is surprisingly drought resistant and can be grown in most soils. Propagation is by seeds sown in the fall or in the spring following stratification. A winter mulch should be applied over the seedbed to prevent alternate freezing and thawing. The wood is very durable and is used for fence posts and for raspberry stakes.

Lonicera L. (Honeysuckle)
CAPRIFOLIACEAE (Honeysuckle Family)

DESCRIPTION: Over 150 species of mostly deciduous shrubs or woody vines, native in the northern hemisphere; **leaves** opposite, simple; **flowers** small to large, often in axillary pairs subtended by 2 bracts and 4 bractlets, or in sessile whorls at the tips of branches; calyx 4- to 5-toothed; corolla 4- to 5-lobed; stamens 5; ovary inferior; **fruit** a berry.

Lonicera canadensis Bartr. (Fly Honeysuckle). Hardy in all zones; shrub to 2 m. tall.
DESCRIPTION: Straggling shrub, native in cool, moist woods, rarely in swamps from Saskatchewan to Nova Scotia, south to Minnesota and North Carolina; **leaves** ovate or elliptic, to 7.5 cm. long, ciliate; **flowers** yellow or tinged red, in pairs, to 2 cm. long, in May; **fruit** a red berry.
USE AND CULTURE: Plant in shrub borders or naturalize at the edges of woods. Plants are easy to grow in any good garden soil either in full sun or in partial shade. Propagation is by seeds or by softwood cuttings. Seeds should be planted in the fall and the seedbed should be mulched over winter, or the seeds can be stratified and planted in the spring. Softwood cuttings should be rooted in sand under intermittent mist.

Larix laricina (Tamarack). Top panorama of trees in the fall taken in October, 1981 in Hayward, Wisconsin. Side photograph of habit taken in 1977.

Lonicera dioica L. (Limber Honeysuckle). Hardy in all zones; vining shrub to 3 m. tall.

DESCRIPTION: Twining vine or straggling shrub, native in moist woods and thickets from Minnesota to Quebec, south to Iowa and North Carolina; **stems** often twining; **leaves** elliptic or oblong, to 7.5 cm. long, glaucous beneath, upper pair united at base; **flowers** in whorls, green or yellow, 2-lipped, to 1.25 cm. long, in May and June; style usually glabrous; **fruit** a red berry.

USE AND CULTURE: The same as for **Lonicera canadensis**.

Lonicera dioica var. **glaucescens** - see **Lonicera glaucescens**.

Lonicera glaucescens (Rydb.) Rydb. (Donald Honeysuckle). Hardy in all zones; vining shrub to 3 m. tall.

DESCRIPTION: Twining vine or straggling shrub, native in moist woods and thickets from British Columbia to Quebec, south to Kansas and Virginia; **leaves** elliptic to oblong, pubescent beneath; **flowers** in whorls, green or yellow, 2-lipped, to 2 cm. long, in May and June; style usually pubescent; **fruit** a red berry.

USE AND CULTURE: The same as for **Lonicera canadensis**. This species is considered by some authors to be a variety of **Lonicera dioica**. It differs mainly in the pubescence on the under surface of the leaves, and on the styles.

Lonicera oblongifolia (J. Goldie) Hook. (Swamp Fly Honeysuckle). Hardy in all zones; shrub to 1.5 m. tall.

DESCRIPTION: Shrub, native in bogs and swampy thickets from Manitoba to New Brunswick, south to Minnesota and Pennsylvania; **leaves** oblong, to 7.5 cm. long, gray-pubescent beneath; **flowers** yellowish-white, in pairs, 2-lipped, to 1.25 cm. long, in May and June; **fruit** a red berry.

USE AND CULTURE: The same as for **Lonicera canadensis**.

Lonicera villosa (Michx.) R.& S. (Fly Honeysuckle, Mountain Fly Honeysuckle, Waterberry). Hardy in all zones; shrub to 1 m. tall.

DESCRIPTION: Shrub, native in swamps and wet woods from Canada south to Minnesota and Pennsylvania; **leaves** oval to oblong, to 8 cm. long, usually widest above the middle, hairy beneath; **flowers** yellow, gibbous at base, to 1.5 cm. long, pubescent, in May and June; **fruit** a blue berry.

USE AND CULTURE: The same as for **Lonicera canadensis**.

Mahonia Nutt. (Holly Grape, Mahonia, Oregon Grape)
BERBERIDACEAE (Barberry Family)

DESCRIPTION: Over 100 species of evergreen shrubs, native in moist woods in Asia, and North and Central America; **leaves** alternate, odd-pinnate; leaflets leathery, mostly spiny-toothed; **flowers** yellow, in often fascicled racemes or in panicles; sepals in 3 series, petals in 2 series; stamens 6; ovary 1-celled; **fruit** a blue or black berry with a bloom.

Mahonia repens. In flower in 1978.

Malus ioensis. In flower in 1979.

Mahonia repens (Lindl.) G. Don. (Creeping Mahonia). Hardy in zone 4 with snow protection; shrub to .5 m. tall.
DESCRIPTION: Stoloniferous evergreen shrub, native in coniferous woods from Washington to North Dakota, south to Utah and Colorado; **leaves** with 5 to 7 leaflets; leaflets ovate, rounded at apex, with wavy margins and 5 to 9 spines; **flowers** yellow, in fascicled racemes, in late May; **berries** glabrous, black with a bluish bloom.
USE AND CULTURE: Plant as a ground cover. Plant on north-facing slopes or where the plants will receive a dependable snow cover. Propagation is by division or by seeds sown as soon as ripe or in the spring following stratification.

Malus Mill. (Apple)
ROSACEAE (Rose Family)
DESCRIPTION: About 25 species of small, much-branched, deciduous trees, native in the North Temperate Zone; winter **buds** pubescent; **leaves** alternate, simple, with acute marginal teeth; **flowers** showy, in small clusters; sepal lobes and petals typically 5; stamens numerous, attached to the calyx disc; **fruit** a pome without stone cells.

Malus coronaria (L.) Mill. (American Crabapple, Garland Crab, Sweet-scented Crab, Wild Crab, Wild Sweet Crab). Hardy in zone 4; tree to 10 m. tall.
DESCRIPTION: Small tree, native in woods and thickets from Ontario south to Missouri and North Carolina; **leaves** ovate to lanceolate-ovate, with cordate base; **flowers** showy, white to pink, fragrant, in late May and early June; anthers pink or salmon-colored; **pomes** to 2.5 cm. across.
USE AND CULTURE: Plant as an ornamental lawn tree. Plants grow well in any moisture retentive, well-drained soil. Trees may be short-lived on sandy soils. Propagation is by seeds or by grafting. Seeds are usually planted in the spring following stratification. Double flowering forms must be grafted. Trees are very susceptible to cedar-apple rust, a disease that can mar the beauty of the foliage and cause early defoliation. Many named varieties of crabs have more disease resistance.

Malus ioensis (A. Wood) Britt. (Prairie Crabapple, Wild Crab). Hardy in zone 3; tree to 10 m. tall.
DESCRIPTION: Small tree, native at the edges of woods and in thickets from Minnesota to Wisconsin, south to Oklahoma and Missouri; **leaves** oblong-ovate, short-acute, serrate, sometimes with lateral lobes, tomentose beneath, to 10 cm. long; **flowers** white to pink, fragrant, to 5 cm. across, in late May and early June; **pomes** about 2.5 cm. across on slender pedicels.
USE AND CULTURE: The same as for **Malus coronaria**. The silvery-gray bark adds winter interest.

Morus L. (Mulberry)
MORACEAE (Mulberry Family)
DESCRIPTION: About 10 species of deciduous, monoecious trees, native in North and South America, Africa, and Asia; **leaves** alternate, simple, often irregularly lobed,

Ostrya virginiana (Ironwood). In flower and fruit.

usually crenate to dentate-serrate; **flowers** small, monoecious, in drooping catkins; **fruit** a juicy syncarp, resembling a blackberry.

Morus rubra L. (American Mulberry, Red Mulberry). Trial in zone 4; tree to 15 m. tall.
DESCRIPTION: Tree, native in rich bottom lands from South Dakota to Vermont, south to Texas and Florida; **leaves** ovate, to 12 cm. long, sharply dentate, occasionally unequally lobed, rough above; male **flowers** in catkins to 5 cm. long, in May; pistillate catkins to 2.5 cm. long; **fruits** dark purple, to 3 cm. long, ripening in July.
USE AND CULTURE: Although weedy, it is sometimes planted as a lawn tree. It is also planted for its edible fruit for wildlife. This species has been short-lived in Arboretum plantings. Propagation is by seeds sown in the spring following stratification.

Nemopanthus Raf. (Mountain Holly)
AQUIFOLIACEAE (Holly Family)
DESCRIPTION: A single species of polygamodioecious, deciduous shrub, native in eastern North America; **leaves** alternate, simple, oblong-ovate, mucronate, entire or slightly dentate, glabrous; **flowers** inconspicuous, axillary, solitary or few in a cluster, 4- to 5-merous; calyx lacking or early deciduous; petals separate; **fruit** a drupe.

Nemopanthus mucronatus (L.) Trel. (Catberry, Mountain Holly). Hardy in all zones; shrub to 3 m. tall.
DESCRIPTION: Stoloniferous shrub, native in damp woods, thickets, and swamps from Minnesota to Newfoundland, south to Illinois and Virginia; **branches** purplish when young, becoming ashy-gray; **leaves** thin, to 4 cm. long, bluish-green, turning yellow in the fall; **flowers** on pedicels to 2.5 cm. long; **fruits** dark red, subglobose, to 1.5 cm. across, showy in September and October.
USE AND CULTURE: This thicket-forming shrub can be planted in shrub borders or naturalized at the edges of woods. It is a close relative to American hollies. These plants require an acid, moist soil. Propagation is by seeds or softwood cuttings. Seeds should be stratified and planted in the spring. Due to immature embryos it make take several years for seeds to germinate.

Ostrya Scop. (Hop Hornbeam)
BETULACEAE (Birch Family)
DESCRIPTION: About 10 species of deciduous, monoecious trees, native in woods in the northern hemisphere; **leaves** alternate, simple, dentate; staminate **flowers** in slender, drooping catkins; pistillate flowers in erect catkins; **fruit** a nutlet enclosed in a bladderlike green involucre in hoplike clusters.

Ostrya virginiana (Mill.) C. Koch. (American Hop Hornbeam, Ironwood, Leverwood). Hardy in all zones; tree to 20 m. tall.
DESCRIPTION: Medium-sized deciduous tree, native in woods from Minnesota to Nova Scotia, south to Texas and Florida; **bark** dark brown, finely furrowed; **leaves** mostly subcordate; petioles short, with stalked glands, sharply and often doubly serrate; **nutlets** fusiform, smooth at apex.
USE AND CULTURE: Plant as a shade or as a specimen tree. This species can be grown with a single stem or as a clump tree. In nature the trees often grow in clumps with numerous stems. Deer and rabbits eat the young seedlings causing a proliferation of several stems from the base. The same effect can be created by pruning young seedlings back nearly to the ground. It is one of our most trouble-free natives and should be planted more. Plants grow best in a fertile, clay loam soil either in full sun or light shade. Propagation is by seeds sown in the fall and mulched over winter, or planted in the spring following stratification. It is relatively difficult to transplant and is also intolerant of salt so should not be used as a street tree.

Physocarpus (Camb.) Maxim. (Ninebark)
ROSACEAE (Rose Family)
DESCRIPTION: About 10 species of deciduous shrubs with exfoliating bark, native in North America and Asia; **leaves** alternate, petioled, simple, dentate or palmately

lobed; **flowers** white or pink, in umbellike corymbs; sepals and petals 5; stamens 20 to 40, inserted on calyx disc, **fruit** an inflated follicle.

Physocarpus opulifolius (L.) Maxim. (Common Ninebark). Hardy in all zones; shrub to 3 m. tall.
DESCRIPTION: Tall shrub with shredding bark, native along lake shores, river banks, and in thickets from Hudson Bay to Quebec, south to Minnesota and South Carolina; **leaves** rounded, somewhat 3-lobed, or subcordate, to 7.5 cm. long, truncate or rounded at base, acute at apex; **flowers** small, white to pink, to 6 mm. across, in flat-topped clusters, in June and July; **follicles** usually 3, glabrous.
USE AND CULTURE: Plant in shrub borders or use as a screen. They are easy to grow in most soils. Regular maintainance pruning greatly affects the landscape potential of this adaptable shrub. Propagation is by seeds or by cuttings. Seeds should be planted in the fall and mulched over winter, or planted in the spring following stratification.
VARIETIES: var. **intermedius** (Rydb.) B.L. Robinson. (Dwarf Ninebark). A western variety with smaller leaves and follicles that are hairy. It grows to a height of 1.5 m. This variety is superior to the species for foundation plantings.

Potentilla L. (Cinquefoil, Five-finger)
ROSACEAE (Rose Family)
DESCRIPTION: About 500 species of mostly annual or perennial herbs, rarely shrubs, native in temperate regions; **leaves** alternate, pinnately or palmately compound; **flowers** yellow, white, or red, perfect, solitary or in cymes; sepals 5, alternating with bractlets; petals 5, showy; stamens many; pistils many; **fruit** an achene.

Potentilla fruticosa L. (Golden Hardhack, Shrubby Cinquefoil, Widdy). Hardy in all zones; shrub to 1 m. tall.
DESCRIPTION: Small deciduous shrub, native in north temperate regions, circumpolar, south to Iowa in North America; **leaves** pinnate; leaflets mostly 5, ovate to oblong-lanceolate, acute, entire, with revolute margins, to 2 cm. long; **flowers** yellow, rarely white, in terminal cymes, from June to September; sepals triangular-ovate; bractlets narrow; petals rounded.
USE AND CULTURE: Widely planted in shrub borders, foundation plantings, and for informal hedges. There are many named cultivars and these are readily available from nurseries and garden centers. Plants grow well in most soils. Propagation is by seeds or cuttings. Cuttings are taken in July and rooted in sand under mist. The old seed heads persist over winter and these should be cut back in early spring.

Prunus nigra 'Princess Kay'. Habit and flowers pictured at the Arboretum .

Potentilla palustris (L.) Scop. (Marsh Cinquefoil, Marsh Five-finger). Hardy in all zones; perennial to 45 cm. tall.
DESCRIPTION: Decumbent perennial with ascending stems, native in swamps from Canada south to Iowa and New Jersey; **leaflets** 5 to 7, to 6 cm. long, sharply and coarsely serrate, more or less hairy beneath; **flowers** red to purple, to 3 cm. across, in loose cymes, from June to August; petals ovate-lanceolate, acuminate; sepals longer than the petals.
USE AND CULTURE: Plant in low, wet soil near a pond or stream. Plants can be grown in any soil that is kept moist, either in full sun or partial shade. Propagation is by division or by seeds.

Potentilla tridentata Ait. (Three-toothed Cinquefoil, Wineleaf Cinquefoil). Hardy in all zones; perennial to 25 cm. tall.
DESCRIPTION: Rhizomatous perennial, native along rocky or gravelly lake shores from Minnesota to Greenland, south to Iowa and Georgia; **leaflets** 3, palmate, leathery, more or less evergreen, cuneate-oblong, 3- to 5-toothed at apex, nearly glabrous, turning wine-colored in the fall; **flowers** white, in stiff cymes, from June to August.
USE AND CULTURE: Plant as a ground cover or in a rock garden. Plants grow well in any well-drained soil. Propagation is chiefly by division in early spring. Seeds can be planted as soon as ripe.

Prunus L. (Cherry, Peach, Plum)
ROSACEAE (Rose Family)

Prunus pensylvanica (Pin Cherry). In fruit in 1977.

Prunus virginiana (Chokecherry). In fruit in 1971.

DESCRIPTION: About 400 species of trees and shrubs, native in the northern hemisphere; **leaves** alternate, simple, mostly deciduous, serrate, often with glands along the base of the petioles; **flowers** white or pink; sepals and petals 5; stamens many, inserted on the calyx tube along with the petals; pistils 1 with 1 or 2 ovules; **fruit** a drupe.

Prunus americana Marsh. (American Plum, August Plum, Goose Plum, Hog Plum, Sloe, Wild Plum). Hardy in all zones; tree to 6 m. tall.
DESCRIPTION: Coarse shrub or small tree with shaggy bark, native in thickets along roadsides and streams, from Manitoba to New England, south to New Mexico and Florida; **branchlets** often thorny; **leaves** obovate to lanceolate-ovate, acuminate, sharply serrate, to 10 cm. long; **flowers** white, to 2.5 cm. across, in late April or early May; **fruit** yellow to red, to 2 cm. in diameter, with a flattened pit.
USE AND CULTURE: Plant for wildlife or for the edible fruits used in making jellies and preserves. When in bloom, the fragrance of these plants transform our spring landscapes. These shrubs are easy to grow in any well-drained soil. Propagation is by suckers or by seeds sown in the early spring following stratification. Plants sucker freely and soon form a thicket.

Prunus besseyi L.H. Bailey. (Sand Cherry, Western Sand Cherry). Hardy in all zones; shrub to 2 m. tall.
DESCRIPTION: A low bushy shrub with prostrate branches, native from Manitoba south to Colorado and Minnesota; **leaves** lanceolate, to 5 cm. long, leathery, dentate; **flowers** small, white, in May; **fruit** purple-black, sweet-astringent, with a rounded pit.
USE AND CULTURE: Plant for wildlife. Fruits sometimes used for making jellies and preserves. The culture is the same as for **Prunus americana.**

Prunus nigra Ait. (Canada Plum, Wild Plum). Hardy in all zones; tree to 5 m. tall.
DESCRIPTION: Small tree, often thorny, native in thickets from Manitoba to Quebec, south to Louisiana and Georgia; **leaves** elliptic to obovate, to 10 cm. long, with gland-tipped teeth and 2 glands near the base of the petiole; **flowers** white, turning to pink, to 3 cm. across, in May; sepals glandular-serrate; stamens tinged pink; **drupes** red or yellow, subglobose, to 2.5 cm. long.
USE AND CULTURE: The same as for **Prunus americana**. A double-flowered selection has been named 'Princess Kay'.

Prunus pensylvanica L.f. (Bird Cherry, Fire Cherry, Pin Cherry, Wild Red Cherry). Hardy in all zones; tree to 10 m. tall.
DESCRIPTION: Upright tree, native in woods, thickets, and clearings from British Columbia to Labrador, south to Iowa and North Carolina; **leaves** oblong-lanceolate to narrow-ovate, thin, gradually acute to acuminate, sharply serrate; **flowers** white, opening with the leaves, in late April or early May, to 1.25 cm. across, in umbels or corymbs; **fruits** globose, light red, to 6 mm. across, with thin, acid flesh.
USE AND CULTURE: Plant as a screen or for wildlife. Fruits make a clear, tart jelly. Although relatively short-lived, it features handsome mahogany bark, attractive red berries, and good fall color. The culture is the same as for **Prunus americana.**

Prunus serotina J.F. Ehrh. (Black Cherry, Rum Cherry, Whiskey Cherry, Wild Black Cherry). Hardy in all zones; tree to 25 m. tall.
DESCRIPTION: Large tree with deeply furrowed, nearly black bark, native in hardwood forests from North Dakota to Nova Scotia, south to Texas and Florida; **leaves** lanceolate-oblong to oblong-ovate, acuminate to acute, crenate-serrate, to 15 cm. long, shiny above; **flowers** white, small, in drooping racemes, in early June; calyx persistent in fruit; **fruits** globose, red to purple-black, sweet to bitter.
USE AND CULTURE: This large growing, trouble-free tree is planted in parks and as a lawn tree on large estates. The culture is the same as for **Prunus americana**. Fruits can be messy when they drop to the ground.

Prunus virginiana L. (Chokecherry). Hardy in all zones; shrub to 10 m. tall.
DESCRIPTION: Shrub or small tree, native in thickets, on lake shores, and borders of woods from Saskatchewan to Newfoundland, south to Kansas and North Carolina;

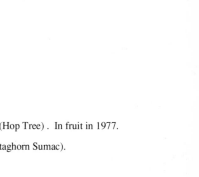

leaves elliptic to obovate, short-acuminate, sharply serrulate, glabrous, to 10 cm. long; **flowers** white, 8 mm. across, in dense racemes, in May; **fruits** red to almost purple, acid, astringent, to 8 mm. across.

USE AND CULTURE: Plant for wildlife at the edges of woods. Fruits often harvested for jelly. The culture is the same as for **Prunus americana**. It suckers heavily.

Ptelea trifoliata (Hop Tree) . In fruit in 1977.

Rhus typhina (Staghorn Sumac).

Ptelea L. (Hop Tree, Shrubby Trefoil)
RUTACEAE (Rue Family)

DESCRIPTION: Three species of polygamous trees or shrubs, native in shaded woods in North America; **leaves** alternate, usually with 3 leaflets that are glandular-dotted and aromatic; **flowers** small, greenish-white in cymose panicles; sepals, petals, and stamens 4 or 5; **fruit** an orbicular, oblong, or cordate samara with reticulate wings.

Ptelea trifoliata L. (Common Hop Tree, Stinking Ash, Water Ash). Hardy in zone 4; tree to 8 m. tall.

DESCRIPTION: Shrub or small tree, native in thickets with alluvial soil and on rocky slopes in moist soil from Ontario to Quebec, south to Texas and Florida; **bark** chestnut-brown; **leaflets** ovate, elliptic-ovate, or obovate, to 10 cm. long, dark green above; **flowers** inconspicuous, in May and June; filaments hirsute; ovary glabrous; **samara** orbicular, to 2.5 cm. across.

USE AND CULTURE: This trouble-free tree or large shurb can be planted at edges of woods. Plants are easy to grow in any moist soil. Propagation is by seeds sown either in the fall or in the spring following stratification. Plants can also be propagated by layering.

Rhamnus L. (Buckthorn)
RHAMNACEAE (Buckthorn Family)

DESCRIPTION: About 150 species of mostly deciduous shrubs or small trees, native mostly in north temperate regions, a few in Brazil and South Africa; **leaves** alternate or subopposite, pinnately veined with prominent veins showing on the under surface; **flowers** small, green, in axillary clusters, umbels, or racemes; **fruit** a berrylike drupe.

Rhamnus alnifolia L'Her. (Dwarf Alder). Hardy in all zones; shrub to 1 m. tall.

DESCRIPTION: Low shrub, native in swamps, woods, and marshes from British Columbia to Newfoundland, south to Nebraska and Pennsylvania; **leaves** ovate, to 10 cm. long, dentate, with 6 to 8 pairs of veins; **flowers** small, in axillary clusters, in May and June; **drupes** black.

USE AND CULTURE: Plant in shrub borders. Plants require a moist soil. Propagation is by seeds sown as soon as ripe or in the spring following stratification. Soaking seeds for about 20 minutes in sulfuric acid helps to break down the impermeable seed coats. Birds often distribute the seeds. Passing through a bird's digestive tract has the same effect as the acid soak.

Rhus L. (Sumac)
ANACARDIACEAE (Cashew Family)

DESCRIPTION: About 150 species of usually dioecious shrubs, small trees, or rarely woody vines with a milky or aromatic juice, native in temperate or subtropical regions;

leaves simple, with 3 leaflets, or pinnate; **flowers** small, usually dioecious, in upright or drooping panicles; stamens 5; ovary 1-celled; styles 3; **fruit** a small, 1-seeded drupe.

Rhus aromatica Ait. (Fragrant Sumac). Hardy in zone 4; shrub to 1 m. tall.
DESCRIPTION: Mound-shaped shrub, native on dry, rocky slopes from Minnesota to Ontario, south to Texas and Florida; **leaves** with 3 leaflets, aromatic; leaflets ovate, to 7.5 cm. long, coarsely dentate; **flowers** yellow, in clustered spikes, appearing before the leaves, in late April or early May; **drupes** red, hairy.
USE AND CULTURE: Plant in shrub borders, informal hedges, or naturalize at the edges of woods. Plants require a well-drained soil. The foliage turns red in the fall. Propagation is by seeds, root cuttings, or by layering. Seeds should be sown as soon as ripe or in the spring following stratification. Soaking the seeds for 20 minutes in sulfuric acid improves germination.

Rhus glabra L. (Scarlet Sumac, Smooth Sumac, Upland Sumac, Vinegar Sumac). Hardy in all zones; shrub to 3 m. tall.
DESCRIPTION: Glabrous shrub, native on dry or rocky hillsides from British Columbia to Maine, south to Arizona and Florida; **leaves** pinnate with 11 to 31 leaflets; leaflets oblong-lanceolate, to 12 cm. long, dentate, turning red in the fall; **flowers** green, in dense, upright panicles, in June and July; **drupes** scarlet, hairy, in dense panicles.
USE AND CULTURE: Plant as a ground cover on steep slopes to prevent erosion. The culture is the same as for **Rhus aromatica**.

Rhus trilobata Nutt. (Skunkbush, Skunkbush Sumac). Hardy in zone 3; shrub to 3 m. tall.
DESCRIPTION: Ill-smelling shrub, native in dry, sandy soils from North Dakota to New York, south to Mexico and Texas; **leaflets** 3, ovate, to 2.5 cm. long, usually coarsely dentate, **flowers** green, in clustered spikes, in May when the leaves are fully developed; **drupes** red, hairy.
USE AND CULTURE: The same as for **Rhus aromatica**. This species is very similar to **Rhus aromatica**, differing in the smaller leaves, the time of bloom, and its more upright growth habit. The foliage is ill smelling but scarcely resembles a skunk as the common name suggests.

Rhus typhina L. (Staghorn Sumac, Velvet Sumac, Virginian Sumac). Hardy in all zones; shrub to 8 m. tall.
DESCRIPTION: Shrub or small tree, native from Minnesota to Quebec, south to Iowa and North Carolina; **twigs** densely pubescent; **leaves** pinnate with 11 to 31 leaflets; leaflets oblong-lanceolate, dentate to serrate, to 12 cm. long, turning red in the fall; **flowers** green, in dense, terminal panicles, in June; **drupes** red, hairy.
USE AND CULTURE: The same as for **Rhus glabra**. The velvety twigs add seasonal interest. This species is an important source of tannin.

Ribes L. (Currant, Gooseberry)
SAXIFRAGACEAE (Saxifrage Family)

DESCRIPTION: About 150 species of low deciduous shrubs, native in north temperate regions; **stems** with or without prickles; **leaves** alternate, often clustered, palmately veined and lobed; **flowers** small, in racemes or solitary, mostly perfect, rarely dioecious, 5-merous; ovary inferior, 1-celled; **fruit** a berry.

Ribes odoratum H. Wendl. (Buffalo Currant, Clove Currant, Flowering Currant, Golden Currant, Missouri Currant). Hardy in all zones; shrub to 2 m. tall.
DESCRIPTION: Upright shrub, native on cliffs and rocky hillsides from North Dakota and Minnesota, south to Texas and Florida; **stems** without prickles; **leaves** broadly cuneate to orbicular, to 5 cm. long, deeply 3-to 5-lobed; **flowers** yellow, salverform, fragrant with the odor of cloves, in 5- to 10-flowered racemes, borne on pubescent pedicels, in May; **berries** black, rarely yellow, glabrous.
USE AND CULTURE: Plant in shrub borders, use as informal hedges, or naturalize at the edges of woods. Plants are easy to grow in most well-drained soils. Propagation is by seeds or by cuttings. Seeds should be sown as soon as ripe or in the spring following stratification.

Rhus glabra (Smooth Sumac). Pinnate leaf in 1977.

Ribes odoratum (Clove Currant). In 1978 at the

St. Paul Campus, University of Minnesota.

Robinia L. (Locust)
LEGUMINOSAE (Pea Family)
DESCRIPTION: About 20 species of deciduous trees and shrubs, native in North America; **leaves** odd-pinnate, with pairs of short stipular spines; **flowers** white or purple, in pendent racemes, showy, pealike, with keel petals united at base; **fruit** an elongate, flat legume.

Robinia hispida L. (Bristly Locust, Moss Locust, Mossy Locust, Rose Acacia). Hardy in zone 3; shrub to 2 m. tall.
DESCRIPTION: Stoloniferous shrub, native in well-drained soils in mountainous woods from Kentucky to Virginia, south to Alabama and Georgia, naturalized as far north as Minnesota; young **branches** with bristly hairs; **leaflets** in 3 to 6 pairs, oblong to nearly orbicular, to 3 cm. long, glabrous; **flowers** rose or pale purple, to 2.5 cm. long, in May and June; **legumes** hispid, to 7.5 cm. long.
USE AND CULTURE: Sometimes planted as an ornamental in the shrub border. Plants grow well in well-drained, sandy soils. Because suckers can come up some distance from the parent plant, it is seldom used in the landscape. Propagation is by seeds, suckers, and root cuttings. Seeds have impermeable seed coats and should be scarified by filing, treatment with sulfuric acid, or by soaking in hot water. Seeds are usually planted in the spring.

Robinia pseudoacacia L. (Black Locust, False Acacia, Yellow Locust). Hardy in zone 3; tree to 20 m. tall.
DESCRIPTION: Open spreading trees, native in deciduous woods and thickets from Indiana to Pennsylvania, south to Oklahoma and Georgia, naturalized as far west as Minnesota; **branches** bristly with stipular spines; **leaflets** up to 19, elliptic to ovate-obtuse, to 4 cm. long; **flowers** white, in dense racemes to 20 cm. long, fragrant, in late May or early June; **legumes** to 10 cm. long, reddish-brown, persisting over winter on trees.
USE AND CULTURE: The same as for **Robinia hispida**. This large, spreading tree is very susceptible to the locust borer, an insect that can shorten the life of the tree.

Rosa L. (Brier, Rose)
ROSACEAE (Rose Family)
DESCRIPTION: Over 100 species of mostly prickly shrubs or woody vines that trail on the ground, native in temperate parts of the northern hemisphere; **stems** mostly covered by prickles and spines; **leaves** alternate, mostly odd-pinnate, with stipules adnate to the petioles; **flowers** showy, solitary or in corymbs or panicles; sepals and petals 5; petals and stamens inserted on a disc at the edge of the calyx tube; pistils numerous, borne on the inside of the deep hypanthium; **fruit** a fleshy hip containing many hairy achenes.

Robinia hispida (Rose Acacia). In bloom in June 1979.

Rosa arkansana (Prairie Wild Rose).

Rosa woodsii (Wood's Rose).

Photographs: Research Department of the Minnesota Landscape Arboretum.

Rosa acicularis Lindl. (Prickly Rose). Hardy in all zones; shrub to 1 m. tall.

DESCRIPTION: A densely bristly shrub, native mostly in regions of coniferous forests from Alaska to New Brunswick, south to New Mexico and West Virginia, also in Siberia; **leaflets** 3 to 7, ovate to elliptic, to 5 cm. long, serrate; stipules glandular-ciliate; **flowers** solitary, dark red, fragrant, to 5 cm. across, in June; **hips** pear-shaped; to 1.25 cm. long.

USE AND CULTURE: Plant in shrub borders. Plants grow well in any well-drained soil that is slightly acid and high in organic matter. Propagation is by seeds or division. Seeds should be sown in the fall as soon as ripe or in the spring following stratification.

Rosa arkansana T. Porter. (Prairie Wild Rose). Hardy in all zones; shrub to 50 cm. tall.

DESCRIPTION: Spiny shrub, native from Alberta to New York, south to Texas and Virginia; **leaflets** 9 to 11, sharply serrate, to 5 cm. long; **flowers** bright red, to 2.5 cm. across, in June; **hips** globose, bright red, to 1.25 cm. in diameter.

USE AND CULTURE: The same as for **Rosa acicularis**.

VARIETIES: var. **suffulta** (Greene.) Cockerell. This variety differs from the species in having woolly pubescence on the petioles and under surface of the leaves. More common on prairies. This variety has a tendency toward repeat bloom.

Rosa blanda Ait. (Meadow Rose, Smooth Wild Rose). Hardy in all zones; shrub to 2 m. tall.

DESCRIPTION: Shrubs with nearly smooth stems, native at the edges of woods and on prairies from Manitoba to Newfoundland, south to Missouri and Pennsylvania; **leaflets** 5 to 7, elliptic to obovate, finely pubescent beneath, simply serrate, to 6 cm. long; **flowers** pink, mostly solitary, to 5 cm. across, in late May and June; **hips** red, round to 1 cm. across.

USE AND CULTURE: The same as for **Rosa acicularis**.

Rosa carolina L. (Pasture Rose). Hardy in all zones; shrub to 1 m. tall.

DESCRIPTION: Shrubs with slender branches and many prickles, native from Minnesota to Nova Scotia, south to Texas and Florida; **leaflets** 5 to 9, elliptic to lanceolate-ovate or narrow-obovate, rather dull above, to 4 cm. long, coarsely serrate; **flowers** rose, mostly solitary, to 5 cm. across, in June; **hips** red, subglobose, to 8 mm. in diameter.

USE AND CULTURE: The same as for **Rosa acicularis**.

Rosa macounii - see **Rosa woodsii**

Rosa setigera Michx. (Climbing Rose, Prairie Rose). Hardy in zone 4; vine to 2 m. long.

DESCRIPTION: Climbing or sprawling vine with remote, broad-based prickles, native from Kansas to Ontario, south to Texas and Florida; **leaflets** 3 to 5, to 10 cm. long, serrate, the under surface gray-green and hairy on veins; **flowers** several, rose fading to white, to 7.5 cm. across; sepals reflexed, deciduous; **hips** small, brownish-green.

USE AND CULTURE: The same as for **Rosa acicularis**.

Rosa woodsii Lindl. (Wood's Rose). Hardy in zone 4; shrub to 2 m. tall.

DESCRIPTION: Shrub with straight or curved bristles, native from British Columbia to Minnesota, south to Arizona and Nebraska; **leaflets** 5 to 7, obovate to oblong-obovate, to 3 cm. long, simply serrate; **flowers** pink, rarely white, 1 to 3, to 4 cm. across, in June; **hips** red.

USE AND CULTURE: The same as for **Rosa acicularis**.

Rubus L. (Bramble, Blackberry, Raspberry)
ROSACEAE (Rose Family)

DESCRIPTION: About 250 species of mostly woody shrubs with perennial roots and biennial stems, native mostly in the northern hemisphere; **stems** often spiny or prickly; **leaves** alternate, simple or compound; **flowers** white, pink, or rose, solitary or clustered, typical of the rose family; **fruit** an aggregate of small drupelets.

Rubus parviflorus (Thimbleberry). Taken in June 1984

in Port Wing, Wisconsin.

Salix discolor (Pussy Willow).

Rubus parviflorus Nutt. (Salmonberry, Thimbleberry). Hardy in all zones; shrub to 2 m. tall.
DESCRIPTION: Low shrubs, native in moist soil in open woods from Alaska to Ontario, south to New Mexico and Florida; **leaves** simple, round to reniform, to 20 cm. wide, shallowly 5-lobed with lobes serrate, acute; **flowers** white, in few-flowered cymes, to 5 cm. across; sepals with long, caudate tips; petals elliptic-obovate; **fruits** edible, red, to 2 cm. across, pubescent.
USE AND CULTURE: Plant as a ground cover for naturalizing in open woods. Plants are easy to grow in most soils. Propagation is by seeds or division. Seed may be planted in the fall or in the spring following stratification.

Salix L. (Osier, Willow)
SALICACEAE (Willow Family)

DESCRIPTION: About 300 species of dioecious shrubs or trees, native mostly in the cooler parts of the northern hemisphere; stem **buds** with a single bud scale; **leaves** alternate, mostly lanceolate; **flowers** small, borne in dense catkins; **fruit** a small capsule; seeds covered with hair or down.

Salix amygdaloides Anderss. (Peach-leaved Willow). Hardy in all zones; tree to 20 m. tall.
DESCRIPTION: Deciduous tree with dark brown ridged bark, native along streams and in low, moist soils from British Columbia to Quebec, south to Oklahoma and New York; **branchlets** glabrous, green or reddish-brown; **leaves** lanceolate to ovate-lanceolate, to 12 cm. long, dark green above, whitish beneath, serrate, short-acuminate; petioles slender, to 3 cm. long; **catkins** on leafy branchlets, in May; staminate catkins to 5 cm. long; pistillate catkins to 10 cm. long.
USE AND CULTURE: Plant as a lawn tree or for a screen. Plants grow well in any moist soil of good fertility. Propagation is by seeds or by hardwood cuttings. Seeds should be sown as soon as ripe. Do not cover seeds with soil but keep the surface moist until seedlings are well established.

Salix discolor Muhlenb. (Large Pussy Willow, Pussy Willow). Hardy in all zones; shrub to 7 m. tall.
DESCRIPTION: Large shrub or small tree, native along streams or in swamps from Alberta to Labrador, south to Missouri and Maryland; **leaves** oblong, to 10 cm. long, wavy-dentate to nearly entire, glaucous beneath; **flowers** in showy catkins appearing in late March or April.
USE AND CULTURE: Plant in shrub borders or for a screen. It is one of the harbingers of spring. The culture is the same as for **Salix amygdaloides**.

Salix lucida Muhlenb. (Shining Willow). Hardy in all zones; shrub to 6 m. tall.
DESCRIPTION: Large shrub or small tree, native along streams, roadside ditches, and moist meadows from Saskatchewan to Newfoundland, south to Nebraska and Virginia; **branchlets** chestnut-brown, glossy, glabrous; **leaves** ovate-lanceolate or lanceolate, to

12 cm. long, finely dentate, glossy on both surfaces, paler beneath; **catkins** appearing in May with the leaves.
USE AND CULTURE: The same as for **Salix discolor**.

Salix nigra Marsh. (Black Willow). Hardy in all zones; tree to 20 m. tall.
DESCRIPTION: Tree, native on stream banks and lake shores from Minnesota to New Brunswick, south to Texas and Florida; **bark** dark brown to black, rough and flaky; **branchlets** yellow; **leaves** lanceolate, to 12 cm. long; finely dentate, pale green beneath; **catkins** appearing in May with the leaves.
USE AND CULTURE: The same as for **Salix amygdaloides.**

Sambucus L. (Elder, Elderberry)
CAPRIFOLIACEAE (Honeysuckle Family)
DESCRIPTION: About 20 species of shrubs or small trees with pithy stems, native in rich, moist soils in north temperate and tropical regions; **leaves** opposite, odd-pinnate with dentate leaflets; **flowers** small, white, in terminal cymes or panicles, usually 5-merous; corolla rotate; ovary inferior 3- to 5-celled; **fruit** a small, berrylike drupe with 3 to 5 nutlets.

Sambucus canadensis L. (American Elder, Sweet Elder). Hardy in all zones; shrub to 3 m. tall.
DESCRIPTION: Stoloniferous shrub with white pith, native from Manitoba to Nova Scotia, south to Texas and Florida; **leaflets** usually 7, elliptic or lanceolate, to 15 cm. long; **flowers** white, in umbellike cymes to 25 cm. across, in June; **drupes** purple-black, edible, ripening in August and September.
USE AND CULTURE: Plant in shrub borders. Fruits are used in pies and in jellies. Both flowers and fruit add landscape interest. Plants are easy to grow in any moist, fertile soil. In the landscape, elderberries require routine pruning. Propagation is by seeds, cuttings, and suckers. Seed should be planted as soon as ripe or in the spring following stratification. Space plants 2 m. apart.

Sambucus pubens Michx. (American Red Elder, Red-berried Elder, Stinking Elder). Hardy in all zones; shrub to 4 m. tall.
DESCRIPTION: Tall shrub with reddish-brown pith, native on rocky banks, in ravines, and open woods from Alaska to Newfoundland, south to Colorado and Georgia; **leaflets** 5 to 7, oblong, to 10 cm. long; **flowers** white, in a rather loose, pyramidal cyme to 10 cm. long, in April and May; **drupes** red, in June and July.
USE AND CULTURE: The same as for **Sambucus canadensis**. It tolerates more shade.

Shepherdia Nutt. (Buffalo Berry)
ELAEAGNACEAE (Oleaster Family)
DESCRIPTION: Three species of dioecious, deciduous shrubs or small trees, native in dry, rocky soils in North America; **leaves** opposite, simple; **flowers** dioecious, small, yellow; **fruit** a drupelike berry.

Shepherdia argentea (Pursh.) Nutt. (Buffalo Berry, Silver Buffalo Berry). Hardy in all zones; shrub to 6 m. tall.

Sambucus canadensis (American Elder). In flower and fruit.

DESCRIPTION: Thorny shrub, native along dry streams, coulees, and on steep slopes from Alberta to Manitoba, south to New Mexico and Kansas; **leaves** oblong, silvery on both surfaces; **flowers** yellow, in May and June; **fruits** red, or rarely yellow, about 6 mm. in diameter, in August.

USE AND CULTURE: Plant in shrub borders or as a screen. The berries and fine-textured, silvery foliage add landscape interest. Berries are used for jellies and for wildlife. Plants are easy to grow in any well-drained soil. Propagation is by seeds sown as soon as ripe or in the spring following stratification. As these plants are dioecious, plant several seedlings to be sure of getting fruiting plants since the fruits are more colorful than the flowers.

Shepherdia canadensis (L.) Nutt. (Buffalo Berry, Canadian Buffalo Berry, Soapberry). Hardy in all zones; shrub to 2 m. tall.

DESCRIPTION: Spreading, thornless shrub, native on rocky and sandy soils from Alaska to Newfoundland, south to South Dakota and Illinois; **leaves** ovate or elliptic, green and nearly glabrous above, silvery and scurfy with brown scales below; **flowers** yellow, in short spikes borne in leaf axils, in April and May; **fruits** yellow, insipid, ripening in July and August.

USE AND CULTURE: The same as for **Shepherdia argentea**

Sorbus L. (Mountain Ash)
ROSACEAE (Rose Family)

DESCRIPTION: About 85 species of deciduous trees, native in the northern hemisphere; **leaves** alternate, simple or pinnate; **flowers** white, in terminal corymbs, sepals and petals 5; stamens 15 to 20; carpels 2 to 5, more or less united, each 2-ovuled; **fruit** a small pome with 2 to 5 cells.

Sorbus americana Marsh. (American Mountain Ash, Dogberry, Missey-moosey, Roundwood). Hardy in all zones; tree to 10 m. tall.

DESCRIPTION: Small tree or large shrub, native in moist woods from Minnesota to Newfoundland, south to Illinois and North Carolina; **leaves** odd-pinnate; leaflets 11 to 17, narrow-lanceolate, to 10 cm. long, sharply serrate, gray-green beneath; **flowers** white, to 6 mm. across, in dense corymbs to 15 cm. across, in May and June; **pomes** bright red, to 6 mm. in diameter.

Shepherdia argentea (Buffalo Berry).

Sorbus decora (Showy Mountain Ash).

USE AND CULTURE: Plant as a specimen lawn tree or in screen plantings. Plants prefer a moist but well-drained soil. Propagation is mostly by seeds sown as soon as ripe or in the spring following stratification. Propagation by layering is also possible. Seeds are scattered by birds and volunteer seedlings can often be found. The mountain ashes are susceptible to fire blight and winter sun scald and may be short-lived under cultivation.

Sorbus decora (Sarg.) C.K. Schneid. (Showy Mountain Ash). Hardy in all zones; tree to 10 m. tall.

DESCRIPTION: Small tree, native in moist, often rocky woods from Manitoba to Labrador, south to Iowa and Ohio; **leaves** odd-pinnate; leaflets 11 to 17, elliptic to lanceolate-ovate, to 7.5 cm. long, blunt or sharp-pointed, sparsely pubescent beneath; **flowers** white, to 1 cm. across, in pubescent inflorescences to 10 cm. across, in May and June; **pomes** red, to 10 mm. in diameter, in September.

USE AND CULTURE: The same as for **Sorbus americana**.

Spiraea L. (Bridal-wreath, Spirea)
ROSACEAE (Rose Family)

DESCRIPTION: About 100 species of deciduous shrubs, native in moist soil and sunny locations in the northern hemisphere; **leaves** alternate, simple, sometimes pinnately lobed; **flowers** white, pink, or red, small but showy, in umbellike racemes, corymbs, or panicles; sepals and petals 5; stamens many; pistils usually 5, distinct; **fruit** a dehiscent follicle.

Spiraea alba Du Roi. (Meadowsweet). Hardy in all zones; shrub to 2 m. tall.

DESCRIPTION: Erect shrub, native in low, wet soils from Saskatchewan to Quebec, south to Missouri and North Carolina; **stems** yellowish-brown; **leaves** lanceolate-

Staphylea trifolia (American Bladdernut). In flower and fruit.

oblong, to 7.5 cm. long, finely serrate; **flowers** white, in dense panicles, from June to August.

USE AND CULTURE: These thicket-forming shrubs prefer a moist, slightly acid soil in full sun. Propagation is by seeds sown as soon as ripe, by cuttings taken in July, and by layering.

Spiraea tomentosa L. (Hardhack, Steeplebush). Hardy in all zones; shrub to 1.2 m. tall.
DESCRIPTION: Upright shrub, native in swamps and meadows from Minnesota to Nova Scotia, south to Arkansas and North Carolina; **stems** brown-tomentose; **leaves** yellow-tomentose beneath, ovate or oblong, serrate, to 7.5 cm. long; **flowers** purple-rose, crowded in short, spikelike racemes, from July to September.
USE AND CULTURE: The same as for **Spiraea alba**. Weedier than most spireas.

Staphylea L. (Bladdernut)
STAPHYLEACEAE (Bladdernut Family)

DESCRIPTION: About 10 species of shrubs or small trees, native in moist, rich woods in temperate regions of the northern hemisphere; **leaves** opposite, compound, serrulate; **flowers** white, in terminal panicles, perfect, 5-merous; bell-shaped; **fruit** an inflated capsule.

Staphylea trifolia L. (American Bladdernut). Hardy in all zones; small tree to 5 m. tall.
DESCRIPTION: Upright small tree, native in moist thickets, ravines, and wooded slopes from Minnesota to Quebec, south to Oklahoma and Georgia; **leaflets** 3, elliptic or ovate, to 7.5 cm. long, acuminate; **flowers** white, bell-shaped, to 8 mm. long, in nodding panicles to 5 cm. long, in May; **fruits** bladdery, 3-lobed, to 5 cm. long, maturing in August.
USE AND CULTURE: This lovely native tree should be planted more often. Plant in shrub borders or as a specimen tree. The inflated pods are unusual. Plants are easy to grow in moist soil. Propagation is by seeds sown as soon as ripe or in the spring following stratification, and by suckers, layers, or cuttings taken in July.

Symphoricarpos Duh. (Snowberry, Wolfberry)
CAPRIFOLIACEAE (Honeysuckle Family)

DESCRIPTION: About 16 species of deciduous shrubs, native in North America and China; **leaves** opposite, simple; **flowers** white or pink, in clusters or spikes; calyx 4- to 5-lobed; corolla campanulate or tubular, 4- to 5-lobed; **fruit** a 2-seeded berry.

Symphoricarpos albus (L.) S. Blake. (Snowberry, Waxberry). Hardy in all zones; shrub to 1 m. tall.
DESCRIPTION: Deciduous shrub, native in dry or rocky woods from Alaska to the Gaspe Peninsula in Quebec, south to Minnesota and Pennsylvania; **leaves** elliptic, to 5 cm. long, sometimes lobed on young branches, pubescent beneath; **flowers** pink, campanulate, to 6 mm. long, in June; **berries** snow white, in August and September.
USE AND CULTURE: Plant in shrub borders. It is planted in the landscape for its white berries. Plants require a well-drained soil. Propagation is by seeds, cuttings, or division. Seeds must have both warm and cold stratification to germinate. Store for 3

Symphoricarpos orbiculatus (Coralberry). In fruit in October 1977.

months at 86 degrees F. before fall planting, or for 3 months at 86 degrees F. followed by winter stratification at 40 degrees F. for spring planting.
VARIETIES: var. **laevigatus** (Fernald) Blake. (Snowberry). Taller than the species and native in British Columbia and Washington as well as in the eastern states. This variety is planted more often than the species.

Symphoricarpos occidentalis Hook. (Wolfberry). Hardy in all zones; shrub to 1.5 m. tall.
DESCRIPTION: Suckering shrub, native in dry soil from British Columbia to Michigan, south to Kansas and Illinois; **leaves** elliptic to ovate, to 7.5 cm. long, gray-pubescent beneath; **flowers** pink, campanulate, to 6 mm. long, in June and July; stamens and styles exserted; **berries** dull white, turning brown.
USE AND CULTURE: Plant on banks for erosion control. Its culture is the same as for **Symphoricarpos albus**.

Symphoricarpos orbiculatus Moench. (Coralberry, Indian Currant). Native in zone 3; shrub to 1 m. tall.
DESCRIPTION: Deciduous shrub, native in open woods and thickets from South Dakota to New York, south to Texas and Florida; **leaves** elliptic to ovate, to 6 cm. long, glaucous and usually pubescent beneath; **flowers** white, campanulate, to 5 mm. long, in July and August; **berries** coral-red, to 6 mm. long, in September and October.
USE AND CULTURE: Plant on slopes for erosion control. The coral-red berries add interest to naturalized areas. Its culture is the same as for **Symphoricarpos albus**.

Vaccinium angustifolium (Lowbush Blueberry).

Photograph: Mr. Arvid Lund

Vaccinium L. (Bilberry, Blueberry,
Cranberry, Huckleberry)
ERICACEAE (Heath Family)
DESCRIPTION: About 450 species of deciduous or evergreen shrubs, native to acid soils that are peaty or sandy in the northern hemisphere, mostly in North America and in eastern Asia; **stems** upright or stoloniferous; **leaves** simple, alternate, often brightly colored in the fall; **flowers** white, green, red, or purple, solitary or in racemes or clustered; calyx 4- to 5-lobed; corolla urceolate, campanulate, or cylindrical; stamens 8 or 10 with anthers opening by a terminal pore; ovary inferior; **fruit** a many-seeded berry with a persistent calyx.

Vaccinium angustifolium Ait. (Late Sweet Blueberry, Lowbush Blueberry, Low Sweet Blueberry, Sweet-hurts). Hardy in all zones; shrub to 30 cm. tall.
DESCRIPTION: Deciduous, stoloniferous shrub, native in acid, sandy soils or in bogs from Manitoba to Newfoundland, south to Minnesota and Virginia; **leaves** lanceolate, to 2 cm. long, serrulate with bristle-tipped teeth, bright green, glabrous, turning red in the fall; **flowers** white or tinged pink, in small cluster; **berries** blue, rarely black, glaucous, to 1 cm. in diameter.
USE AND CULTURE: Sometimes planted as a ground cover and for the edible fruit. Plants require an acid soil in full sun for best results. It is necessary for this ground cover to be mowed or burned to keep it renewed. Propagation is by seeds and by division. Seeds should be sown as soon as ripe or in the spring following stratification.

Viburnum rafinesquianum (Downy Arrowwood).

In flower in June 1978.

Seedlings are easy to transplant. Cuttings can also be rooted. The fruit is usually gathered from wild stands.

Vaccinium vitis-idaea var. **minus** Lodd. (Lingen, Lingenberry, Lingonberry, Mountain Cranberry, Rock Cranberry). Hardy in all zones; shrub to 30 cm. tall.
DESCRIPTION: Evergreen shrub, native circumboreal, growing as far south in North America as northern Minnesota and Massachusetts, also in northern Europe; **leaves** obovate, to 3 cm. long, leathery, dark green and glossy above, glandular-dotted beneath; **flowers** white or pink, in drooping racemes, in June; corolla campanulate, to 6 mm. long; **berries** red, to 1 cm. in diameter, tart.
USE AND CULTURE: The same as for **Vaccinium angustifolium**, however it doesn't need as much pruning, or renewal.

Viburnum L. (Arrowwood, Viburnum)
CAPRIFOLIACEAE (Honeysuckle Family)
DESCRIPTION: About 225 species of upright shrubs or small trees, native in North America, Europe, and Asia; **leaves** opposite, simple, mostly deciduous; **flowers** small, white or pink, in showy terminal panicles or in umbrellalike cymes; calyx 5-toothed; corolla rotate to campanulate or tubular, 5-lobed; in a few species the marginal flowers may be sterile with enlarged corolla lobes; stamens 5; ovary inferior; **fruit** a 1-celled drupe.

Viburnum lentago L. (Black Haw, Cowberry, Nannyberry, Nanny Plum, Sheepberry, Sweetberry, Sweet Viburnum, Tea Plant, Wild Raisin). Hardy in all zones; shrub to 8 m. tall.
DESCRIPTION: Large shrub or small tree, native in rich woods and along streams from Manitoba to Quebec, south to Missouri and Georgia; **leaves** ovate, to 10 cm. long, finely dentate; **flowers** white, in sessile cymes to 12 cm. across, in May and June; **drupes** blue-black, in September and October.
USE AND CULTURE: Plant toward the back of shrub borders or use for a screen. Plants grow best in a moist, fertile, loam soil either in full sun or in partial shade. It does sucker. Plants can be propagated by cuttings, layering, or seeds. Seeds should be planted as soon as ripe. They may take several years to germinate. Germination can be speeded by warm followed by cold stratification. Powdery mildew often attacks the foliage in the fall. This is unsightly but seldom weakens the plants.

Viburnum rafinesquianum Schult. (Downy Arrowwood, Downy-leaved Arrowwood). Hardy in all zones; shrub to 2 m. tall.
DESCRIPTION: Deciduous shrub, native on dry slopes and in open woods from Manitoba to Quebec, south to Missouri and Georgia; **leaves** ovate, to 7.5 cm. long, coarsely dentate, densely pubescent on under surface; **flowers** white, in dense short-peduncled cymes, in May and June; corolla rotate; **drupes** bluish-black, ripening in September.
USE AND CULTURE: The same as for **Viburnum lentago**. Useful where a lower growing viburnum is desired.

Viburnum trilobum Marsh. (American Highbush Cranberry, Crampbark, Cranberry Bush, Grouseberry, Pimbina, Squawbush, Summerberry, Tree Cranberry). Hardy in all zones; shrub to 4 m. tall.

DESCRIPTION: Deciduous shrub, native in cool woods and thickets from British Columbia to Quebec, south to Iowa and Pennsylvania; **leaves** broad-ovate, to 12 cm. long, 3-lobed and coarsely dentate; petioles with a broad groove and small glands; **flowers** white, in short-peduncled cymes to 10 cm. across, in May and June; marginal flowers sterile and showy; corolla rotate; anthers yellow; **drupes** scarlet, in September.
USE AND CULTURE: The same as for **Viburnum lentago**. It usually has good fall color and the fruit persists in the landscape into late winter.

Viburnum trilobum (American Highbush Cranberry). Fall color

in October 1977. Fruit in September 1968.

SHADE TREES

Acer saccharum (Sugar Maple).

Shade trees are among the most important landscape features to select. Ultimate growing height, type of soil, and moisture level should be carefully considered. The following lists will help in the selection of shade trees.

Native Shade Trees for Good Fall Color

Acer rubrum (red to yellow)
Acer saccharum (red to yellow)
Carya species (yellow)
Fraxinus americana (yellow to purple)
Fraxinus nigra (yellow)
Fraxinus pennsylvanica (yellow)
Fraxinus quadrangulata (yellow)
Populus species (yellow)
Quercus alba (purple)
Quercus coccinea (scarlet)
Quercus palustris (red)

Native Shade Trees with Edible Fruits
(often attractive to wildlife)

Carya species (brown nut)
Castanea dentata (brown nut)
Fagus grandifolia (brown nut)
Juglans species (nut)

Native Shade Trees with Interesting Bark

Acer rubrum (gray)
Carya ovata (shaggy brown)
Populus tremuloides (yellow)

Native Shade Trees that Tolerate Dry Soil

Acer negundo
Celtis occidentalis
Fraxinus pennsylvanica
Gleditsia triacanthos

Native Shade Trees that Tolerate Wet Soil

Acer rubrum
Fraxinus nigra
Populus species
Quercus bicolor

Native Shade Trees Useful for Shelterbelts and Windbreaks

Acer negundo
Fraxinus pennsylvanica
Populus deltoides

Dioecious Native Shade Trees
(Require both male and female plants to set fruit)

Acer negundo
Acer rubrum
Fraxinus americana
Fraxinus nigra
Fraxinus pennsylvanica
Gymnocladus dioica

Populus species

Acer rubrum (Red Maple). Foliage taken in Deerfield Massachusetts in 1980.

Gymnocladus dioica (Kentucky Coffee Tree).

In Boerner Botanic Garden in 1977.

Photograph: Mike Zins.

Acer (L.) (Maple)
ACERACEAE (Maple family)

DESCRIPTION: About 200 species of mostly deciduous trees and shrubs, native in the temperate regions; **bark** smooth or furrowed; **buds** opposite with 2 outer scales; **leaves** opposite, usually simple and palmately lobed, sometimes palmately or pinnately compound, rarely entire; **flowers** small, in clusters, racemes, panicles, or corymbs, commonly dioecious, 5-merous, rarely 4-merous; stamens 4 to 10, usually 8; styles and stigmas 2; **fruits** are paired long-winged samaras.

Acer negundo L. (Box Elder, Ash-leaved Maple, Manitoba Maple). Hardy in all zones; medium tree to 20 m. tall.

DESCRIPTION: An irregular, spreading tree native from Saskatchewan to New England, south to Guatemala and Florida; **leaves** pinnately compound with 3 to 5 leaflets; leaflets ovate, coarsely serrate, with the terminal leaflet often 3-lobed; **flowers** dioecious, without petals, appearing before the leaves, in May, yellowish-green; staminate flowers in pendulous corymbs; pistillate flowers in pendulous racemes; **fruits** are paired, 4 cm. long samaras, diverging at an acute angle.

USE AND CULTURE: Because of its drought resistance, the box elder is often planted in Manitoba and the Dakotas as a shade and boulevard tree and for shelterbelts. One of the box elder's virtues is its fast growth rate. It is rather a brittle tree, so pruning is necessary to remove branches injured by winds. Where moisture is adequate there are better trees to plant. The box elder bug, harbored by box elders, can be a nuisance. Propagation is by seeds planted in the fall or in the spring following stratification.

Acer nigrum - see **Acer saccharum** subsp. **nigrum**

Acer rubrum L. (Red Maple, Scarlet Maple, Soft Maple, Swamp Maple). Hardy in zone 3; tree to 15 m. tall.

DESCRIPTION: Medium tree, native in swamps and moist woods from Minnesota to Newfoundland, south to Texas and Florida; **leaves** 3- to 5-lobed, to 15 cm. across, more or less cordate, lustrous green above, silvery beneath, turning yellow or red in fall, lobes triangular-ovate, short-acuminate, unequally crenate-serrate; **flowers** mostly dioecious, red, appearing before the leaves, in late March or early April, produced in short, dense clusters; **fruits** are paired 2.5 cm. long samaras, bright red when young, turning brown.

USE AND CULTURE: Widely planted as boulevard and shade trees. The red maple prefers a lightly acid soil. As it is native in swamps it will tolerate wet soils although it will also grow on sandy soils if given enough water. Do not plant on alkaline soils. It is weaker-wooded than the sugar maple, so pruning of storm-damaged limbs is often necessary. Propagation is by seeds sown as soon as ripe or by grafting or budding. Since fall color is variable, it is advisable to select trees in the fall when they are at their peak of fall color (seed propagation will bring variable results). Due to its wide geographic distribution, plant only northern strains. 'Northwood' is a selection recently introduced by the University of Minnesota and is available at nurseries. It has a strong branching habit and good fall color.

Acer saccharinum L. (Silver Maple, River Maple, Soft Maple, White Maple). Hardy in zone 3; tree to 25 m. tall.

DESCRIPTION: Large tree, native along river banks and in bottom lands from Minnesota to Quebec, south to Oklahoma and Florida; **leaves** 5-lobed, to 15 cm. across, with deeply and doubly serrated lobes, bright green above, silvery-white beneath; **flowers** unisexual, without petals, mostly pink, in short clusters, in late March and April; **fruits** are paired 6 cm. long samaras, diverging at right angles, maturing in early summer.

USE AND CULTURE: Because of its fast growth, this species is often planted as a shade or boulevard tree, especially in new real estate developments. However, because it grows to be a very large tree, it soon becomes too large for a small yard. Branches are also brittle and often break in storms. Heavy pruning can cause soft growth which

Acer saccharum (Sugar Maple). Fall color.

Acer saccharinum (Silver Maple). Leaves.

Photograph: Merv Eisel.

makes the tree more susceptible to storm damage. It is also a shallow rooted tree, causing lawn and bedding plant problems many feet away from the trunk. It would be best if the silver maple were planted only in parks or on spacious grounds away from buildings. Silver maples can be grown on most soils. Propagation is by seeds sown as soon as they are ripe. A few cultivars with cut leaves are on the market. 'Beebe Cutleaf Weeping' has deeply cut leaves and drooping branches, and 'Silver Queen' is a seedless selection. Both are available at nurseries. Named cultivars are propagated by budding.

Acer saccharum Marsh. (Sugar Maple, Hard Maple, Rock Maple). Hardy in zone 3; tree to 20 m. tall.
DESCRIPTION: A large tree with deeply furrowed bark, native in well-drained, clay loam soils from Minnesota to Nova Scotia, south to Texas and Florida; **leaves** 3- to 5-lobed, to 15 cm. across, usually with narrow and deep rounded sinuses, cordate at base, with acuminate lobes that are sparingly and coarsely dentate, turning yellow or scarlet in the fall; **flowers** in umbels, appearing in April or May just as the leaf buds start to open, without petals, greenish- to creamy-yellow; **fruits** are paired 4 cm. long samaras, ripening in fall.
USE AND CULTURE: The sugar maple is an excellent boulevard and shade tree where the soil is a well-drained clay loam. However, it is short-lived on sandy soils. It also dislikes compacted soils and should not be planted where there is heavy foot traffic. Like the red maple, trees purchased at a nursery should be selected in the fall when at their peak of fall color. Propagation is by seeds planted in the fall or in the spring following stratification. Because sugar maples bleed badly when pruned in late winter, it is best to delay pruning until after the leaves are fully opened in the spring. Maple syrup is made from this species.
Acer saccharum subsp. **nigrum** (Michx.) Desmarais. (Black Maple). Similar to the species except for its darker bark and its 3-lobed leaves that droop along the sides. This subspecies is sometimes incorrectly given specific rank.

Carya Nutt. (Hickory)
JUGLANDACEAE (Walnut Family)

DESCRIPTION: About 20 species of deciduous, monoecious nut trees, native in eastern North America, Central America, and eastern Asia; **twigs** with solid pith; **leaves** alternate, odd-pinnate; staminate **flowers** in drooping catkins; pistillate flowers in 2- to 10-flowered terminal racemes; **fruit** a drupe with stone or nut enclosed in thick, green husk that splits into 4 valves.

Carya cordiformis (Wagenh.) C. Koch. (Bitternut, Pignut, Swamp Hickory). Hardy in zone 3; tree to 25 m. tall.
DESCRIPTION: Spreading tree, native in rich, moist woods from Minnesota to Quebec, south to Texas and Florida; **buds** yellow, elongated; **bark** smooth when young, becoming rough; **nut** almost globose, nearly smooth, very bitter.
USE AND CULTURE: Sometimes used as a shade tree. It is best started with young seedlings as a deep taproot makes this and other hickories difficult to transplant. A gall-forming insect can mar the beauty of this species. Propagation is by seeds sown as

soon as ripe or in the spring following stratification. The nuts should not be allowed to dry out.

Carya laciniosa (Michx.f.) Loud. (Shellbark Hickory, Big Shellbark). Hardy in zone 4; tree to 30 m. tall.
DESCRIPTION: Large tree, native in moist woods from Oklahoma to New York; **leaflets** 7 to 9, oblong-lanceolate, to 20 cm. long, pubescent beneath, turning yellow in fall; **nuts** nearly globose, compressed and angled, yellow or red.
USE AND CULTURE: Plant as a shade and nut tree. Nuts are of excellent quality. Although native south and east of the area covered in this book, this species has been fully hardy in the Twin Cities area. Culture is the same as for **Carya cordiformis**.

Carya ovata (Mill.) C. Koch. (Shagbark Hickory, Shellbark Hickory). Hardy in zone 4; tree to 30 m. tall.
DESCRIPTION: Large tree with shaggy bark that separates in long strips on mature trees; **leaflets** usually 5, elliptic, to 15 cm. long, turning yellow in the fall; **nuts** ellipsoid, slightly angled, white.
USE AND CULTURE: Plant for shade and for the edible nuts which have the best flavor of any of our native nuts. The large dark green foliage turns yellow in the fall. The foliage and husks can cause litter. The culture is the same as for **Carya cordiformis**.

Castanea Mill. (Chestnut)
FAGACEAE (Beech Family)

DESCRIPTION: About 12 species of deciduous trees and shrubs, native in north temperate regions; **leaves** alternate, oblong or lanceolate, sharply dentate; **flowers** small, monoecious; staminate flowers in catkins; pistillate flowers at the base of the staminate catkins or in separate leaf axils; **fruit** made up of 1 to 7 brown nuts enclosed in a prickly, dehiscent bur.

Castanea dentata (Marsh.) Borkh. (American Chestnut). Hardy in zone 4; tree to 25 m. tall.
DESCRIPTION: Large, monoecious tree, native in moist woods from Michigan to Maine, south to Arkansas and Virginia; **leaves** to 25 cm. long, tapering toward the base, coarsely dentate, glabrous beneath; **flowers** small, monoecious, in June; staminate flowers in long catkins; **fruit** usually with 2 or 3 brown nuts in a bristly bur.
USE AND CULTURE: Sometimes planted as a shade tree or for its edible nuts. The chestnut blight has all but eliminated this species from its native range. A number of American chestnuts have been planted in the Upper Midwest area. So far, many of these have escaped the disease, probably because of their isolation. A Chestnut Foundation has been formed with the goal of developing a disease-resistant chestnut by hybridizing the American chestnut with the Chinese chestnut (**Castanea mollissima**). Trees planted at the Arboretum in a clay loam soil are doing well. Propagation is by seeds sown in the fall or in the spring following stratification. Do not allow the nuts to dry out.

Catalpa Scop. (Catalpa, Catawba, Indian Bean)
BIGNONIACEAE (Bignonia Family)

DESCRIPTION: About 13 species of mostly deciduous trees, native in North American and eastern Asia; **leaves** opposite or sometimes whorled, simple, long-petioled; **flowers** white, pink, or yellow, showy, in terminal racemes or panicles; calyx 2-lipped; corolla campanulate, 2-lipped; stamens 2; **fruit** a long, slender capsule, separating into 3 valves; seeds with tuft of hairs at both ends.

Catalpa speciosa Warder ex Engelm. (Catawba, Cigar Tree, Hardy Catalpa, Indian Bean, Western Catalpa). Hardy in zone 4, trial in zone 3; tree to 25 m. tall.
DESCRIPTION: Pyramidal tree, native in bottom lands from Iowa to Indiana, south to Texas and Arkansas; **leaves** ovate to ovate-oblong, to 30 cm. long, long-acuminate, densely pubescent beneath, odorless; **flowers** white, spotted with brown, in panicles to 15 cm. long, in May and June; corolla to 6 cm. across.
USE AND CULTURE: Plant as a street or lawn tree for its shade and flowers. It is an easy tree to grow in most soils. Propagation is by seeds sown in the spring or by

Celtis occidentalis (Hackberry). In flower at the Horticultural Research Center at the Arboretum in May 1979.

hardwood cuttings. The flowers, although very showy, drop to the ground and can be messy, as can the seed pods in the fall.

Celtis L. (Hackberry, Nettle Tree, Sugarberry)
ULMACEAE (Elm Family)

DESCRIPTION: About 70 species of mostly deciduous trees, rarely shrubs, native mostly in the northern hemisphere; **leaves** alternate, simple, asymmetrical at base, 3- to 5-veined, entire or serrate, rough above; **flowers** inconspicuous, monoecious or polygamous; staminate flowers in small clusters near the base of the twigs; pistillate flowers solitary or sometimes in pairs in the upper leaf axils; calyx deeply 5-parted; **fruit** a drupe with a thin, sweet pulp and a hard stone.

Celtis occidentalis L. (Hackberry, Nettle Tree, Sugarberry). Hardy in zone 3; tree to 30 m. tall.
DESCRIPTION: Large deciduous trees, native in deciduous woods and on bottom lands from Manitoba to Quebec, south to Oklahoma and Florida; **leaves** ovate, to 12 cm. long, dentate, green above, paler beneath, with unequal base; **flowers** inconspicuous, in May; **fruit** orange-red to dark purple, with thin, sweet, edible coat.
USE AND CULTURE: Plant as a street or lawn tree. This is a hardy, drought resistant tree that grows well in most soils. It is many times described as the best substitute for the American elm in the midwest. It is considered to be a difficult tree to transplant. Start with small seedlings or transplant with a ball of soil. Propagation is by seeds sown as soon as ripe or in the spring following stratification. A nipple gall on the leaves can mar the tree's beauty and the insects can also be a nuisance when they emerge in the fall. A witches broom disease often produces clusters of small twigs in the tops of the trees. These problems seldom shorten the life of the tree.

Fagus L. (Beech)
FAGACEAE (Beech Family)

DESCRIPTION: About 10 species of large, deciduous, monoecious trees with smooth, light gray bark, native in loamy limestone soils in the North Temperate Zone; **leaves** alternate, dentate; staminate **flowers** in drooping heads; **fruit** consisting of 1 or 2 brown, 3-angled nuts, enclosed in a prickly involucre.

Fagus americana - see **Fagus grandifolia**.

Fagus grandifolia J.F. Ehrh. (American Beech). Hardy in cool, moist sites in zone 4; tree to 25 m. tall.
DESCRIPTION: Large tree with smooth, gray bark, native in moist woods from Michigan to Nova Scotia, south to Texas and Florida; **leaves** ovate-oblong, to 12 cm. long, glabrate, short-petioled, turning yellow in October.
USE AND CULTURE: Plant as a shade tree in moist, protected sites. This is not a tree for the open prairies or exposed sites. A north facing slope is best. Surface roots can cause maintenance problems. Propagation is mainly by seed sown in the fall or in the spring following stratification. The seeds should never be allowed to dry out. The nuts are of excellent quality and often are gathered where the trees are native.

Fagus grandifolia (American Beech). Fall color in October 1977.

Fraxinus americana (White Ash). Fall Color.

Photograph: Merv Eisel.

Fraxinus nigra (Black Ash).

Photograph: Research Department of the Minnesota Landscape Arboretum.

Fraxinus L. (Ash)
OLEACEAE (Olive Family)

DESCRIPTION: About 65 species of trees, native in moist soils from the North Temperate Zone to the tropics; **leaves** opposite, mostly pinnate, usually deciduous; **flowers** small, not showy, perfect or imperfect, in panicles, opening before the leaves; calyx 4-lobed or irregularly dissected, or lacking; petals 2 to 6 or lacking; stamens 2; **fruit** a 1-seeded, winged samara.

Fraxinus americana L. (White Ash). Hardy in zone 3; tree to 30 m. tall.
DESCRIPTION: Large deciduous tree, native in rich woods from Minnesota to Nova Scotia, south to Texas and Florida; **leaflets** 5 to 9, to 15 cm. long, glaucous beneath, turning purple in the fall; **flowers** dioecious, appearing before the leaves, in May; petals 0; staminate flowers with 2 stamens, in loose panicles; pistillate flowers in loose panicles with conspicuous bracts with the calyx obscurely lobed and persistent; **samaras** linear-oblong, to 5 cm. long.
USE AND CULTURE: Plant for shade or as a street tree. Plants grow best in a fertile, well-drained loam soil. Propagation is by seeds sown as soon as ripe or in the spring following stratification. Plant dormant trees in early spring. This species is easily recognized in the fall when the leaves turn purple.

Fraxinus nigra Marsh. (Black Ash). Hardy in all zones; tree to 25 m. tall.
DESCRIPTION: Deciduous tree, native in low, swampy soils from Manitoba to Newfoundland, south to Arkansas and Virginia; **leaflets** 7 to 11, to 12 cm. long, rusty-tomentose at base; **flowers** small, polygamodioecious, in compact panicles, appearing before the leaves, in May; calyx and corolla lacking; pistillate flowers with rudimentary stamens; **samaras** oblong, to 4 cm. long, winged at base, rounded or emarginate at the apex.
USE AND CULTURE: Same as for **Fraxinus americana**. It is tolerant of wet soils.

Fraxinus pennsylvanica Marsh. (Green Ash, Red Ash). Hardy in all zones; tree to 20 m. tall.
DESCRIPTION: Deciduous tree, native in moist woods and bottom lands from Saskatchewan to Maine, south to Texas and Florida; **leaflets** 5 to 9, to 15 cm. long, pubescent beneath, turning yellow in the fall; **flowers** dioecious, appearing before the leaves, in May; calyx present in pistillate flowers, persisting; corolla lacking; staminate flowers in short, crowded panicles with 2 stamens per flower; **samaras** narrowly fusiform, winged near the base, to 6 cm. long.
USE AND CULTURE: Same as for **Fraxinus americana**. Plants are quite drought resistant. Several named cultivars of this species have been introduced that are superior to the species.

Fraxinus quadrangulata Michx. (Blue Ash). Hardy in zone 4; tree to 15 m. tall.
DESCRIPTION: Medium-sized tree, native in moist woods from Wisconsin to New York, south to Arkansas and Alabama; **leaflets** 7 to 11, to 12 cm. long, dark green,

turning yellow late in the fall; **flowers** perfect, appearing before the leaves, in May; sepals and petals lacking; **samaras** oblong, winged at base, to 5 cm. long.
USE AND CULTURE: Same as for **Fraxinus americana**. Its high-branching nature makes this a suitable street tree. This species is doing well in the Arboretum.

Gleditsia L. (Honey Locust)
LEGUMINOSAE (Pea Family)
DESCRIPTION: About 12 species of deciduous trees, usually armed with stout branched spines, native worldwide; **leaves** alternate, odd-pinnate or 2-pinnate; leaflets crenulate; **flowers** small, green, in spikelike racemes; sepals and petals 3 to 5; stamens 6 to 10; **fruit** a flat legume, slowly dehiscent or indehiscent.

Gleditsia triacanthos L. (Honey Locust, Honeyshuck, Sweet Locust). Hardy in zone 4; tree to 20 m. tall.
DESCRIPTION: Medium to large trees with flattened, 3-pronged spines to 10 cm. long, native in rich woods in the eastern states as far west as Nebraska; **leaves** odd-pinnate and 2-pinnate on the same tree; leaflets to 2 cm. long; **flowers** small, green, in racemes to 7 cm. long, in May and June; **legumes** flat, to 40 cm. long, twisted.
USE AND CULTURE: A good tree to plant for shade and for a street tree, as the compound leaves provide open shade. Trees can be grown in most soils. Propagation of the species is largely by seeds. However, because seed pods can be a litter problem, named, thornless cultivars are propagated by grafting or budding on seedling roots. Seeds have a hard, impermeable seed coat and should be soaked in hot water at 190 degrees Fahrenheit until the water cools. Soaking in sulfuric acid for 1 to 2 hours will also break down the seed coat. The major problem with honey locust is that it is susceptible to cytospora canker which can kill affected trees. The fungus enters through pruning wounds. Honey locust wood is hard and decay resistant, so the trees are often grown for fence posts.

Gymnocladus Lam. (Coffee Tree)
LEGUMINOSAE (Pea Family)
DESCRIPTION: Three species of deciduous, dioecious or polygamous trees with stout branches, native in eastern North America and eastern Asia; **leaves** 2-pinnate; leaflets entire; **flowers** in terminal, loose panicles, 5-merous, greenish-white; stamens 3 to 10; **fruit** an oblong, thick, flat legume.

Gymnocladus dioica (L.) C. Koch. (Chicot, Nicker Tree, Kentucky Coffee Tree). Hardy in zone 4; tree to 25 m. tall.
DESCRIPTION: A large tree with deeply-fissured gray bark, native in rich soil, mostly in river bottoms from South Dakota to New York, south to Arkansas and Tennessee; **leaves** large, to 90 cm. long, 2-pinnate; pinnae in 3 to 7 pairs, larger terminal ones with 3 to 7 pairs of ovate, acute leaflets, to 7.5 cm. long; new leaves in early spring a pinkish color; **flowers** in racemes, in June; racemes containing pistillate flowers to 25 cm. long; racemes containing staminate flowers denser, to 10 cm. long; **fruit** a persistent, reddish-brown legume, to 25 cm. long.
USE AND CULTURE: Kentucky coffee trees make excellent shade trees. The trees are easy to grow and are free from insect and disease problems. The large, 2-pinnate leaves, deeply-furrowed bark, and stout branches make this an interesting tree to grow. It is slow growing, especially when first planted. If one objects to the seed pods, plant a staminate tree. Propagation is by seeds or cuttings. Seeds have an impermeable seed coat and should be either filed or soaked in water for 24 hours followed by sulfuric acid for 2 hours. The seeds were used as a coffee substitute.

Juglans L. (Walnut)
JUGLANDACEAE (Walnut Family)
DESCRIPTION: About 20 species of deciduous, monoecious trees, native in North and South America and Eurasia; **pith** chambered; **leaves** large, aromatic, odd-pinnate; staminate **flowers** in drooping catkins borne on year old wood; pistillate flowers borne on new wood; **fruit** a drupelike, deeply furrowed nut enclosed by a thick husk.

Juglans cinerea L. (Butternut, White Walnut). Hardy in zone 3; tree to 20 m. tall.

Fraxinus pennsylvanica (Green Ash). Fall color

Photograph: Merv Eisel.

Juglans nigra (Black Walnut). At the Horticultural

Research Center at the Arboretum.

Photograph: Research Department of the Minnesota Landscape Arboretum.

Gymnocladus dioica (Kentucky Coffee Tree). Attractive bark.

DESCRIPTION: Large tree with widespreading branches, native in rich woods and fertile bottom lands from Minnesota to New Brunswick, south to Kansas and Georgia; **bark** deeply ridged, dark brown or gray; **leaves** with 11 to 19 leaflets; leaflets oblong-lanceolate, to 12 cm. long, round or cordate at base, acuminate at apex, serrate, pubescent and glandular beneath; staminate **flowers** in catkins to 8 cm. long, in June; pistillate flowers in 5- to 8-flowered spikes; **fruit** ovoid-oblong, to 7.5 cm. long, sticky-pubescent; nut thick-shelled with 8 prominent ridges.

USE AND CULTURE: Plant for shade and for the edible nuts. Walnuts grow best in a rich, moist soil. Propagation is by seeds either sown in the fall or in the spring following stratification. Do not allow the nuts to become dry. Because of the tap root, it is best to sow nuts where trees are to grow. If they must be transplanted it is best to move the seedlings when they are small. Root pruning at a depth of 30 cm. helps to develop lateral roots.

Juglans nigra L. (Black Walnut). Hardy in zone 4; tree to 25 m. tall.
DESCRIPTION: Large tree, native in rich woods and bottom lands from Ontario to Massachusetts, south to Texas and Florida; **leaves** with 15 to 23 leaflets; leaflets ovate-oblong, to 12 cm. long, pubescent beneath; staminate **flowers** in catkins to 12 cm. long, in June; stamens 20 to 30; pistillate flowers in clusters of 2 to 3; **fruits** globose to slightly pear-shaped, to 5 cm. across, pubescent; nuts ovoid and pointed, thick-shelled and deeply furrowed.
USE AND CULTURE: The same as for **Juglans cinerea**. The nuts, although difficult to crack, are prized for culinary purposes. Caution should be used in including black walnut in mixed plantings, as its roots give off a substance that is toxic to some plants.

Magnolia L. (Magnolia)
MAGNOLIACEAE (Magnolia Family)
DESCRIPTION: About 85 species of deciduous or evergreen trees and shrubs, native in moist woods in Asia, and North and Central America; **leaves** alternate, entire, often leathery; **flowers** large, showy, solitary, and terminal; sepals 3, petallike; petals 6 to 23, white, pink, purple, or yellow; stamens many; **fruit** of many separate carpels congested into a conelike structure; **seeds** often red or orange, suspended by a thread.

Magnolia acuminata (L.) L. (Cucumber Tree). Hardy in zone 4; tree to 20 m. tall.
DESCRIPTION: Pyramidal tree, native in moist woods from Illinois to New York, south to Georgia; **branches** smooth or slightly hairy, red-brown, shiny; **bark** dark brown, becoming furrowed; **buds** hairy; **leaves** elliptic or ovate to oblong-ovate, to 24 cm. long, short-acuminate, rounded or acute at the base; soft-hairy and light green on under surface; **flowers** campanulate, to 8 cm. across, in May; petals obovate-oblong, greenish-yellow; sepals lanceolate, much smaller than the petals, soon reflexed; **fruits** ovoid to oblong, to 8 cm. long, ripening in September.
USE AND CULTURE: This eastern species is surprisingly hardy. Plant as an ornamental shade tree. Its large, deep green leaves provide dense shade. Plant in the spring using freshly dug plants. Plants dug in the fall and stored seldom grow.

Magnolia tripetala L. (Umbrella Magnolia, Umbrella-tree). Hardy in zone 4; tree to 10 m. tall.
DESCRIPTION: Tree, native in moist woods from Pennsylvania to Mississippi and Alabama; **leaves** oblong-obovate, to 60 cm. long, pale green and pubescent beneath, tapering at base; **flowers** appearing with the leaves, white, of unpleasant odor, to 25 cm. across, in June; **fruits** rose-colored, to 10 cm. long.
USE AND CULTURE: The same as for **Magnolia acuminata**.

Magnolia tripetala (Umbrella Magnolia). In flower in June 1966.

Magnolia acuminata (Cucumber Tree).

Platanus L. (Buttonwood, Plane, Plane Tree, Sycamore)
PLATANACEAE (Plane Tree Family)
DESCRIPTION: About 6 species of large, deciduous trees with bark shredding in thin plates giving a spotted appearance to the trunk, native in North America and Asia; **leaves** alternate, large, palmately lobed, with conspicuous stipules and long petioles with swollen bases that cover the axillary buds; **flowers** small, monoecious, in dense, globular heads on nodding peduncles; sepals, petals when present, stamens, and pistils 3 to 8; **fruit** a 1-seeded nutlet, many in dense rounded heads.

Plantanus occidentalis L. (American Plane Tree, Buttonball, Buttonwood, Eastern Sycamore). Trial in zone 4; tree to 30 m. tall.
DESCRIPTION: Trees with broad open heads, native in moist alluvial soil from Iowa to Ontario, south to Texas and Florida; **leaves** palmately 3- to 5-lobed, to 25 cm. across with lobes broader than long, sinuate-dentate; **fruiting** heads solitary, glabrous, 2.5 cm. across.
USE AND CULTURE: Trees have been of borderline hardiness but there are several good sized trees growing in the Twin Cities. Plant as a street or lawn tree. The trees must have a moist, rich soil. Its exfoliating bark can provide landscape interest. Propagation is by seeds planted in the spring following winter stratification. Seeds should be covered with a quarter inch of sawdust.

Populus L. (Aspen, Cottonwood, Poplar)
SALICACEAE (Willow Family)
DESCRIPTION: About 40 species of deciduous trees, native in the northern hemisphere; **leaves** alternate, simple, with petioles that are often flattened sideways; **flowers** small, dioecious, in drooping catkins, appearing before the leaves; **fruit** a capsule; seeds surrounded by copious hairs.

Populus balsamifera L. (Balsam Poplar, Hackmatack, Tacamahac). Hardy in all zones; tree to 25 m. tall.
DESCRIPTION: Tree with sticky, resinous winter buds that appear varnished, native along streams and in swamps, often intermixed with conifers from Alaska to Labrador, south to Colorado and New England; **bark** gray or green, rough with age; **leaves** ovate to ovate-lanceolate, to 12 cm. long, rather thin but firm, glabrous, whitish beneath.
USE AND CULTURE: Plant as a specimen tree for large areas. Plants are easy to grow in most soils. Propagation is by seeds sown as soon as ripe. Seeds should not be covered but soil must be kept moist until seedlings are up. Plants can also be started from hardwood cuttings.

Populus deltoides (Cottonwood). Fall color in September 1977.

Populus tremuloides (Quaking Aspen). October 1977.

Populus deltoides Bartr. ex Marsh. (Cottonwood, Necklace Poplar). Hardy in all zones; tree to 30 m. tall.
DESCRIPTION: Fast growing tree with a broad crown, native in bottom lands and lake shores from Manitoba to Quebec, south to Texas and Florida; **bark** at first smooth and grayish-green, becoming dark gray and prominently ridged with age; **leaves** ovate, to 18 cm. long, truncate or cordate at base, glossy above.
USE AND CULTURE: The same as for **Populus balsamifera**. Trees grow very fast and get very large. This species should not be planted on small properties or near buildings. The hairy seeds (cotton) can be a nuisance.

Populus grandidentata Michx. (Large-toothed Aspen). Hardy in all zones; tree to 20 m. tall.
DESCRIPTION: Tree with smooth, yellowish-green bark, native in deciduous woods from Ontario to Nova Scotia, south to Missouri and Georgia; **leaves** ovate, to 10 cm. long, truncate or cuneate at base, coarsely dentate, white-tomentose beneath when young, becoming glabrous.
USE AND CULTURE: The same as for **Populus balsamifera**.

Populus tremuloides Michx. (Quaking Aspen, Trembling Aspen). Hardy in all zones; tree to 20 m. tall.
DESCRIPTION: Tree with smooth, greenish-white bark, native and common on logged or burnt-over areas from Alaska to Labrador, south to Arizona and Maryland; **leaves** ovate to orbicular, to 7.5 cm. long, truncate at base, finely dentate; petioles flattened sideways causing the leaves to quiver in the breeze.
USE AND CULTURE: The same as for **Populus balsamifera**. Aspen's foliage turns an attractive yellow in the fall. They are best grown in groups or drifts for landscape effect. The bark is the principal food of beaver.

Quercus L. (Oak)
FAGACEAE (Beech Family)
DESCRIPTION: About 450 species of monoecious, deciduous, rarely evergreen trees, native in north temperate regions and in the mountains of the tropics; **leaves** alternate, pinnately veined, dentate, serrate, or pinnately lobed, rarely entire; staminate **flowers** small, in drooping catkins; pistillate flowers in 1- to many-flowered spikes; **fruit** an acorn, a nut enclosed or surrounded at base by a cuplike involucre.

Quercus alba L. (White Oak). Hardy in zone 3; tree to 20 m. tall.
DESCRIPTION: Large, deciduous, tap-rooted tree, native in deciduous woods from Minnesota to Maine, south to Texas and Florida; **bark** pale gray, scaly but not deeply fissured; **leaves** obovate, to 22 cm. long, with 5 to 9 obtuse lobes, whitish beneath; involucral cup covering the basal one fourth of the **acorn**.
USE AND CULTURE: Plant as a lawn or street tree. The white oak's distinctive, massive branch habit and shaggy bark makes this a distinctive shade tree. The reddish-purple fall color is also distinctive. These trees are easy to grow in any well-drained soil. Propagation is by seeds sown as soon as ripe or in the spring following stratification. As with most nuts, the acorns must not be allowed to become dry. The

Quercus bicolor (Swamp White Oak). Foliage in August 1977.

white oak often hybridizes with the bur oak. The white oak is reported to be slow growing but in good soil the growth is comparable to other shade trees.

Quercus bicolor Willd. (Swamp White Oak). Hardy in zone 4; tree to 20 m. tall.
DESCRIPTION: Deciduous tree, native in moist bottom lands and in swamps from Minnesota to Quebec, south to Oklahoma and Georgia; **bark** grayish-brown, scaly; **leaves** obovate, to 15 cm. long, coarsely toothed or lobed, dark green above, whitish-tomentose beneath; involucral cup enclosing lower one third of the **acorn**.
USE AND CULTURE: The same as for **Quercus alba**. This species is surprisingly hardy on upland soils. The fall color is brown. Being native in swamps, it does not develop a tap root, which is characteristic of most oaks. It is tolerant of wetter soils than other oaks.

Quercus borealis - see **Quercus rubra**.

Quercus coccinea Muenchh. (Scarlet Oak). Hardy in zone 4; tree to 20 m. tall.
DESCRIPTION: Deciduous, tap-rooted tree, native in dry, sandy, acid soils from Wisconsin to Maine, south to Oklahoma and Georgia; **bark** gray, inner bark with a reddish tinge; **leaves** oblong to elliptic, to 15 cm. long, with 7 to 9 deeply cut, pointed lobes, bright green, turning scarlet in the fall; involucral cup covering basal one third of the **acorn**.
USE AND CULTURE: The same as for **Quercus alba** except it grows best in an acid, sandy soil.

Quercus ellipsoidalis E.J. Hill. (Hill's Oak, Jack Oak, Northern Pin Oak). Hardy in zone 3; tree to 20 m. tall.
DESCRIPTION: Deciduous tree, native in acid, sandy soil from Manitoba to Michigan, south to Iowa; **bark** gray, lightly fissured; **leaves** elliptic, to 12 cm. long, with deep, narrow lobes with pointed teeth; involucral cup covering basal one third to one half of the **acorn**.
USE AND CULTURE: The same as for **Quercus coccinea**. Leaves have a good red color in the fall. Susceptible to oak wilt (see **Quercus rubra**).

Quercus palustris (Pin Oak). Foliage with frost.

Quercus macrocarpa Michx. (Bur Oak, Mossy-cup Oak). Hardy in all zones; tree to 20 m. tall.
DESCRIPTION: Deciduous tree with sturdy branches, native from Manitoba to Nova Scotia, south to Texas and Pennsylvania; **bark** brown, scaly and deeply furrowed; **leaves** obovate, to 25 cm. long, pinnately bluntly lobed with broad terminal lobe, grayish-pubescent beneath; involucral cup burlike, covering basal one half of the **acorn**.
USE AND CULTURE: This species is seldom planted but native trees should be preserved. The culture is the same as for **Quercus alba**. The fall color is brown.

Quercus palustris Muenchh. (Eastern Pin Oak, Pin Oak, Spanish Oak). Hardy in zone 4; tree to 20 m. tall.
DESCRIPTION: Pyramidal deciduous trees, native in acid soils from Iowa to Massachusetts, south to Kansas and Delaware; mature **branches** drooping; **leaves** elliptic, to 12 cm. long, with 5 to 7 oblong, dentate, pointed lobes, bright green, turning red in the fall; involucral cup covering basal one third of **acorn**.
USE AND CULTURE: This is the most commonly planted oak. Plant for shade or for a street tree. The culture is the same as for **Quercus alba**. Leaves will turn yellow in neutral or alkaline soils due to unavailable iron.

Quercus rubra L. (Northern Red Oak, Red Oak). Hardy in zone 3; tree to 25 m. tall.
DESCRIPTION: Large deciduous tree with spreading branches, native in upland woods from Minnesota to Quebec, south to Oklahoma and Georgia; **bark** grayish-brown, deeply fissured with broad flat-topped ridges; **leaves** oblong, to 22 cm. long, with 7 to 11, pointed lobes cut half way to the midrib, paler beneath, turning red in the fall; involucral cup covering basal one third of the **acorn**.
USE AND CULTURE: Seldom planted. Native trees are worth saving. The culture is the same as for **Quercus alba**. This species is very susceptible to oak wilt, a disease that spreads from tree to tree through the roots. Because of oak wilt, do not prune during April, May, or June.

Tilia L. (Basswood, Lime Tree, Linden, Whitewood)
TILIACEAE (Linden Family)
DESCRIPTION: About 30 species of deciduous trees, native in temperate regions of the northern hemisphere; **leaves** alternate, 2-ranked, slender-petioled, usually abruptly acuminate, cordate or truncate; **flowers** yellow or white, fragrant, mostly in drooping cymes with peduncle united for half its length to a large bract; sepals and petals 5; stamens many, separate or in fascicles; **fruits** nutlike, globose, 1- to 3-seeded.

Quercus macrocarpa (Bur Oak).

Tilia americana (Basswood). Leaf, August 16, 1977.

Tilia americana L. (American Linden, Basswood, Whitewood). Hardy in all zones; tree to 40 m. tall.
DESCRIPTION: Large tree with deeply furrowed bark, native from Manitoba to Quebec, south to Texas and Alabama; **leaves** broadly ovate, to 20 cm. long, coarsely serrate; **flowers** in 6- to 15-flowered cymes, pendulous, in July; staminodes present; **fruits** with stellate pubescence, to 1 cm. across.
USE AND CULTURE: Plant as a lawn or street tree. Trees are easy to grow in most soils. Pruning is necessary for correct early development and to eliminate basal sprouts. Propagation is by seeds sown as soon as ripe or in the spring following stratification. The seeds have a hard seed coat and germination is improved by first soaking the seeds in sulfuric acid. It may take several years for germination.

Ulmus L. (Elm)
ULMACEAE (Elm Family)
DESCRIPTION: About 18 species of mostly deciduous trees, native in the temperate regions of North America, Europe, and Asia; **leaves** alternate, simple, dentate, usually asymmetrical at base; **flowers** small, perfect, usually appearing before the leaves, rarely in autumn; **fruit** a flat, 1-seeded samara with a membranous wing surrounding the nutlet, usually notched at the apex.

Ulmus americana L. (American Elm, Water Elm, White Elm). Hardy in all zones; tree to 30 m. tall.
DESCRIPTION: Large spreading tree, native mostly on bottom lands from Manitoba to Newfoundland, south to Texas and Florida; **leaves** ovate, to 12 cm. long; **flowers** on slender drooping pedicels, in April; **samaras** deeply notched and with ciliate margins.
USE AND CULTURE: Once widely planted as a shade and street tree. Seedlings frequently volunteer and can be transplanted. Many of our American elm trees have died from the Dutch elm disease. This species is now seldom planted for fear the trees will be killed by the disease. Efforts are being made to breed resistant strains.

Ulmus fulva - see **Ulmus rubra**.

Ulmus rubra Muhlenb. (Red Elm, Slippery Elm). Hardy in all zones; tree to 20 m. tall.
DESCRIPTION: Large tree, native in rich soils along river banks and lake shores from North Dakota to Quebec, south to Texas and Florida; inner **bark** mucilaginous, winter **buds** rusty-pubescent with reddish hairs; **leaves** large, to 20 cm. long, obovate or broadly oblong, acuminate, coarsely serrate, very rough above, pubescent below; **samaras** orbicular or elliptic, not ciliate on wing margins.
USE AND CULTURE: The same as for **Ulmus americana**.

Ulmus thomasii Sarg. (Cork Elm, Rock Elm). Hardy in all zones; tree to 20 m. tall.
DESCRIPTION: Columnar tree, native in rich river bottoms from Minnesota to Quebec, south to Nebraska and Kentucky; **branches** very corky; **bark** dark gray and deeply ridged; **leaves** large, to 15 cm. long, elliptic to oblong-obovate, acute, coarsely serrate, glabrous or nearly so above, pubescent beneath; **samaras** notched, pubescent.
USE AND CULTURE: The same as for **Ulmus americana**.

Tilia americana (Basswood). Two normal growth habits, as a single trunk specimen and with multi-stems.

EVERGREENS

Pinus ponderosa var. scopulorum (Rocky Mountain Yellow Pine
or Ponderosa Pine). January 11, 1983.

Evergreens dominate the landscape in many of the northernmost areas of our region. Because of our longer winters they are valued for providing the landscape with winter interest.

Evergreens with Interesting Bark

Pinus resinosa

Evergreens Useful as Ground Covers

Juniperus communis
Juniperus horizontalis

Evergreens Used as Screens or Windbreaks

Juniperus scopulorum
Juniperus virginiana
Picea glauca
Picea mariana
Pinus banksiana
Pinus ponderosa var. scopulorum
Pseudotsuga menziesii var. glauca
Thuja occidentalis
Tsuga canadensis

Evergreens that Tolerate Wet Soils

Picea mariana
Thuja occidentalis

Evergreens that Tolerate Dry Soils

Juniperus species
Pinus banksiana

Shade Tolerant Evergreens

Taxus canadensis
Tsuga canadensis

Abies concolor (White Fir). Needles in winter.

Abies balsamea (Balsam Fir). In October 1963.

Abies concolor (White Fir). In September 1963.

Abies Mill. (Fir)
PINACEAE (Pine Family)

Description: About 40 species of coniferous evergreen trees of conical shape native to the cooler parts of the North Temperate Zone; **leaves** flat, needlelike, usually glossy above and with a white band below, leaving a smooth scar on the stem when they drop; **flowers** monoecious, in cones; staminate cones very small, formed in the axils of last year's leaves, shedding their pollen in spring; pistillate cones erect, along the sides of the uppermost branches, maturing their seeds the first year; cones disintegrating after the seeds are dispersed; **seeds** winged.

Abies balsamea (L.) Mill. (Balsam Fir, Fir Balsam). Hardy in all zones; pyramidal tree to 15 m. tall.

DESCRIPTION: Upright tree of narrow pyramidal form, native from Manitoba to Labrador, south to Iowa and West Virginia; **branchlets** pubescent with soft grayish hairs; **bark** smooth on young trees, becoming grooved, with irregular, reddish-brown scaly plates on mature trees; **leaves** blunt or slightly notched at apex, up to 2.5 cm. long, dark green above, resinous; staminate **cones** yellow, in May; pistillate cones violet-purple when young, becoming grayish-brown and resinous at maturity, to 10 cm. long.

USE AND CULTURE: An attractive ornamental tree when young, but may lose branches and become unattractive and spare of foliage as it matures. Commonly grown for Christmas trees. Trees grow best in a slightly acid, moisture retentive soil but will grow in soils that are neutral. Propagation is by seeds sown in the fall or in the spring following stratification. Plants can also be grown from cuttings taken in March.

Abies concolor (Gord.) Lindl. (White Fir, Concolor Fir). Hardy in zone 4; pyramidal tree to 15 m. tall.

DESCRIPTION: Dense conical tree, native at higher elevations from Colorado to Mexico; **branchlets** yellowish-green; **bark** gray, deeply fissured and scaly on mature trees; **leaves** bluish-green above, rounded at apex, to 7 cm. long; pistillate **cones** to 12 cm. long, green or purple at maturity.

USE AND CULTURE: One of the most beautiful of the evergreen conifers for a lawn specimen. With its bluish cast, it is reminiscent of the blue spruce although not as stiff in texture and appearance. It does not need as moist a soil as the balsam fir. Trees may be slow to become established, but with maturity reach a very large size. Propagation is the same as for balsam fir. Some pruning may be required to shape young trees. White fir is not tolerant of pollution.

Juniperus L. (Juniper, Savin)
CUPRESSACEAE (Cypress Family)

DESCRIPTION: About 70 species of coniferous, evergreen trees or shrubs, native in sunny, well-drained soils in cool regions of the world; **leaves** needlelike or scalelike, commonly appressed on old branches, spreading on new growth; staminate **flowers** in yellow, catkinlike cones; pistillate **cones** berrylike with 3 to 8 fleshy scales; seeds not winged.

Juniperus communis L. (Common Juniper, Prostrate Juniper). Hardy in all zones; shrub or small tree of variable height.

DESCRIPTION: Erect or prostrate shrubs or small trees, native in sandy soils on steep bluffs, river bottoms, and swamp margins in North America and Eurasia; **stems** often prostrate or arching to form vase-shaped shrubs to 1 m. tall in North America; tree forms are found in Eurasia; **leaves** ternate, all linear, spreading and sharp-pointed, concave with a single white band above, jointed at base, often boat-shaped; pistillate **cones** berrylike, blue or black, to 1 cm. across, fleshy and aromatic.

USE AND CULTURE: Plant for a coarse ground cover on slopes. They are easy to grow in any well-drained soil in full sun. Common juniper is relatively tolerant of salt so it is often planted near roads. Propagation is by seeds sown in the fall or in the spring following cold stratification. Seeds have an embryo dormancy and it may take several years for all the seeds to germinate. Plants can also be grown from cuttings rooted in sand. The dried fruit of some juniper species are used to flavor gin.

Juniperus horizontalis.

Juniperus virginiana (Red Cedar). In September 1977.

Juniperus horizontalis Moench. (Creeping Cedar, Creeping Juniper, Creeping Savin).
Hardy in all zones; evergreen shrub to 30 cm. tall.
DESCRIPTION: Procumbent shrub with long, trailing branches, native in mostly sandy
soils from Alaska to Nova Scotia, south to Colorado and New Jersey; **branches**
ascending, forming a mat; **leaves** opposite, scalelike, entire, acute or apiculate, typically
bluish-green; pistillate **cones** berrylike, blue-black, glaucous, to 8 mm. across.
USE AND CULTURE: Plant for a ground cover in rock gardens and on sunny slopes.
The culture is the same as for **Juniperus communis**. It is also tolerant of salt. This is
a variable species with many named cultivars.

Juniperus scopulorum Sarg. (Colorado Red Cedar, Rocky Mountain Juniper). Hardy
in zone 3; tree to 10 m. tall.
DESCRIPTION: Pyramidal tree, native from British Columbia to North Dakota, south
to Arizona and Texas; **leaves** scalelike, green or bluish-green, often glaucous, scarcely
overlapping; pistillate **cones** berrylike, bluish-black, glaucous, to 6 mm. in diameter,
maturing the second year.
USE AND CULTURE: This popular juniper is widely planted for foundation plantings
and for screens. The foliage is more sparse than with some junipers, so it gives this
species a more open character. It is tolerant of dry conditions and also of salt. Many
named cultivars are usually preferred over the species, and feature distinctive colora-
tion. Plants should be moved with a ball of soil either in the spring or the fall. When
used in foundation plantings, annual shearing is required to control the size. It
propagates relatively easily by cuttings.

Juniperus virginiana L. (Red Cedar, Savin). Hardy in all zones; tree to 20 m. tall.
DESCRIPTION: Upright tree with a broad conical head, native in dry, calcareous soils
from Canada, south to Mississippi and Georgia; **leaves** of two types; juvenile leaves
linear, acicular, pungent, opposite or ternate; adult leaves scalelike, opposite, strongly
overlapping, acute, entire, turning reddish in the fall; pistillate **cones** a dark, purplish-
blue color, glaucous, to 6 mm. across, maturing the first year.
USE AND CULTURE: Commonly planted for screen plantings and on highway slopes.
The culture is the same as for **Juniperus scopulorum**. This is the alternate host for
cedar-apple rust and should not be planted near apple trees.

Larix laricina - see listing under ornamental trees and shrubs.

Picea A. Dietr. (Spruce)
PINACEAE (Pine Family)
DESCRIPTION: About 45 species of monoecious, coniferous, evergreen trees of
conical form, native in cooler parts of the northern hemisphere; **leaves** linear, 4-angled
or compressed, with persistent leaf bases; staminate **flowers** in catkinlike cones;
pistillate **cones** woody, pendulous.

Picea glauca (Moench) Voss. (Cat Spruce, White Spruce). Hardy in all zones; tree to
20 m. tall.

Picea glauca (White Spruce).

Pinus banksiana (Jack Pine). In April 1971

at the Minnesota Landscape Arboretum.

DESCRIPTION: Conical tree with spreading branches native in calcareous soils across Canada, south into the northern United States; **leaves** 4-angled, sharp-pointed, to 2 cm. long, bluish-green, glaucous, with an unpleasant odor when crushed; pistillate **cones** to 5 cm. long.

USE AND CULTURE: Plant as a lawn specimen or for a screen. Also planted in windbreaks. Plants are easy to grow in most soils. Propagation is by seeds sown in the fall in sandy seedbeds. Seedlings must be shaded the first year; two year seedlings are transplanted to a nursery row. Landscape plants should be moved with a ball of soil either in the spring or fall.

VARIETIES: var. **densata** Bailey (Black Hills Spruce). Denser and more drought resistant than the species. Widely planted in landscaping. Often listed as the cultivar 'Densata'.

Picea mariana (Mill.) BSP. (Black Spruce, Bog Spruce, Double Spruce). Hardy in all zones; tree to 15 m. tall.

DESCRIPTION: Narrow trees with drooping branches, forming a narrow, spirelike top, native mostly in swamps and bogs from Alaska to Newfoundland, south to Minnesota and Virginia; **leaves** 4-angled, to 1.5 cm. long, bluntly pointed, dark green with glaucous stripes on the upper surface, pleasantly aromatic in odor and taste; pistillate **cones** to 3.5 cm. long, on sharply recurved stalks, persisting on branches for many years.

USE AND CULTURE: The same as for **Picea glauca**. Although native in swamps, this species is fairly drought tolerant and grows well under cultivation.

Picea pungens Engelm. (Colorado Blue Spruce, Colorado Spruce). Hardy in zone 3; tree to 20 m. tall.

DESCRIPTION: Conical tree, native from Utah to Wyoming, south to Colorado; **leaves** quadrangular, usually curved, very stiff and sharp-pointed, unpleasant smelling when crushed, to 3 cm. long, green to blue, glaucous; pistillate **cones** sessile or short-stalked, oblong-cylindrical, to 7 cm. long.

USE AND CULTURE: Plant as a specimen tree in the lawn. It has the same culture as **Picea glauca**. Bluish strains are common and a number of named cultivars are on the market.

Pinus L. (Pine)
PINACEAE (Pine Family)

DESCRIPTION: About 90 species of tall coniferous, evergreen, monoecious trees, native in full sun in the northern hemisphere; **leaves** needle-shaped, usually borne in fascicles of 2 to 5, rarely solitary; staminate **cones** catkinlike, clustered; pistillate cones cylindrical to globose; cone scales woody, persistent; seeds 2 per scale.

Pinus banksiana Lamb. (Gray Pine, Jack Pine, Scrub Pine). Hardy in all zones; tree to 20 m. tall.

DESCRIPTION: Pyramidal tree with furrowed dark brown bark, native in acid, sandy soils of low fertility from Manitoba to Nova Scotia, south to Minnesota and New York;

leaves to 4 cm. long, in fascicles of 2, stiff and twisted, bright or dark green, flat; pistillate **cones** conic-oblong, to 5 cm. long.

USE AND CULTURE: Plant in windbreaks and for screen plantings. Plants thrive in acid, sandy soils of low fertility. Propagation is by seeds sown late in the fall or in early spring in a sandy soil. Seedlings should be shaded the first year. Small plants can be moved bare root but larger plants should be moved with a ball of soil.

Pinus ponderosa var. **scopulorum** Engelm. (Rocky Mountain Yellow Pine). Hardy in all zones; tree to 20 m. tall.
DESCRIPTION: Round-headed tree, native in the Rocky Mountain states as far east as South Dakota; branches usually drooping; **leaves** in fascicles of 2 or 3, to 15 cm. long, dark green; pistillate **cones** ovoid-oblong, to 7.5 cm. long.
USE AND CULTURE: Plant as lawn specimen or for a screen. Commonly planted in shelterbelts. Plants prefer a well-drained clay loam soil. Propagation and culture are the same as for **Pinus banksiana**.

Pinus resinosa Ait. (Norway Pine, Red Pine). Hardy in all zones; trees to 20 m. tall.
DESCRIPTION: Trees with straight trunks and a reddish-brown bark forming broad flat scales, native in sandy, acid soils from Manitoba to Newfoundland, south to Minnesota and Pennsylvania; **branches** whorled, horizontal on young trees; **leaves** in fascicles of 2, to 15 cm. long, flexible, glossy, semi-circular in cross section; pistillate **cones** conic-ovoid, to 6 cm. long, ripening the second year.
USE AND CULTURE: The same as for **Pinus banksiana**. Norway pine has attractive reddish-brown bark when mature. It is more difficult than most pines to transplant.

Pinus strobus L. (Eastern White Pine, White Pine). Hardy in all zones; tree to 25 m. tall.
DESCRIPTION: Large trees with straight trunks, native in well-drained, sandy loam soils from Manitoba to Newfoundland, south to Iowa and Georgia; **branches** whorled, ascending on mature trees; **leaves** needlelike, soft, in fascicles of 5, to 12 cm. long, bluish-green, triangular in cross section; pistillate **cones** cylindrical, to 15 cm. long, dark brown, maturing second year.
USE AND CULTURE: The same as for **Pinus banksiana**. Its leaf texture is finer than other pines. This species is susceptible to the white pine blister rust. Do not plant near currants or gooseberries, the alternate host for this disease. It is also intolerant of urban conditions and susceptible to salt damage, so do not plant near roads.

Pinus strobus (White Pine). At Horticultural Research Center of the Arboretum.

Pseudotsuga menziesii var. glauca (Rocky Mountain Douglas Fir)

Pseudotsuga Carriere. (Douglas Fir)
PINACEAE (Pine Family)
DESCRIPTION: About 5 species of coniferous evergreens with pointed, scaly buds, native in western North America and Asia; **leaves** flat, linear, with 2 white bands beneath; staminate cones borne in axils of year-old leaves; pistillate **cones** terminal or axillary, drooping at maturity, with conspicuous, 3-cleft bracts between the scales, maturing the first year; seeds winged.

Pseudotsuga menziesii var. **glauca** (Beissn.) Franco. (Rocky Mountain Douglas Fir). Hardy in zone 4; tree to 20 m. tall.
DESCRIPTION: Columnar tree, native in the Rocky Mountains from Montana to Colorado; **leaves** to 3 cm. long, blunt, bluish-green; pistillate **cones** to 8 cm. long with reflexed bracts.
USE AND CULTURE: Plant as a lawn specimen or as a screen. Plants grow well in most soils. This evergreen is a relatively fast growing tree. As it withstands shearing, it can be formed into a shaped hedge or screen. Plant only the Rocky Mountain variety. This is one of the best evergreens to plant where it is hardy. The species, which is the dominant timber tree in the Pacific Northwest, is not hardy in this area. Propagation is by seeds planted in the spring following stratification. As with most pines and firs, the Douglas fir does not propagate easily by cuttings.

Taxus L. (Yew)
TAXACEAE (Yew Family)

Taxus canadensis (American Yew).

Photograph: Merv Eisel.

Thuja occidentalis (Arborvitae).

DESCRIPTION: About 8 species of monoecious or dioecious, evergreen trees or shrubs, native in the northern hemisphere; **leaves** spirally arranged but twisted to appear 2-ranked, linear, dark green above, paler or yellow beneath; staminate **flowers** solitary, sessile, surrounded at base by perianthlike bud scales from which projects a short axis earing 4 to 12 peltate stamens; pistillate flowers usually solitary, borne on a stout peduncle consisting of a terminal ovule with several basal bracts; **fruit** a bony seed enclosed by a fleshy scarlet aril.

Taxus canadensis Marsh. (American Yew, Ground Hemlock). Hardy in all zones; shrub to 2 m. tall.
DESCRIPTION: Low spreading shrub with scaly winter buds, native in shady woods from Manitoba to Newfoundland, south to Iowa and Virginia; **leaves** linear, short-petioled, to 4 cm. long, dark yellowish-green above, abruptly pointed, with revolute margins; **flowers** as in genus; **fruits** bright red, nearly globose, to 1.25 cm. in diameter.
USE AND CULTURE: Use for naturalizing in shady locations. Plants prefer a slightly acid soil in shade. Propagation is by cuttings or by seeds sown as soon as ripe or in the spring following warm and cold stratification. Plants must be protected from the winter sun.

Thuja L. (Arborvitae)
CUPRESSACEAE (Cypress Family)
DESCRIPTION: Five species of coniferous, evergreen trees, native in North America and eastern Asia; **branchlets** flattened in a horizontal plane; **leaves** scalelike or needlelike when young, 4-ranked; **flowers** monoecious; staminate cones globose, with 3 pairs of stamens; pistillate **cones** erect, ovoid-oblong, small, with 8 to 20 thin, leathery scales; seeds winged.

Thuja occidentalis L. (American Arborvitae, White Cedar). Hardy in all zones; tree to 10 m. tall.
DESCRIPTION: Upright, evergreen tree, native in moist, calcareous soils from Saskatchewan to Nova Scotia, south to Minnesota and North Carolina; **leaves** dark green above, yellowish-green beneath, glandular; pistillate **cones** to 1.25 cm. long, with scales in 4 or 5 pairs.
USE AND CULTURE: Plant as a specimen tree or use as a screen or windbreak. Plants are easy to grow in any moisture-retentive soil. Propagation is by seeds or cuttings. Young plants can be planted bare root in the spring. Larger plants should be moved with a ball of soil. There are numerous named cultivars on the market, which are planted more often than the species.

Tsuga Carriere. (Hemlock, Hemlock Spruce)
PINACEAE (Pine Family)
DESCRIPTION: About 10 species of monoecious evergreen trees, native in North America and eastern Asia; **branches** slender, spreading or often drooping; **leaves** linear, flat, blunt, short-petioled, with 2 white bands beneath, leaving a jagged base when they fall; staminate **cones** small, axillary; pistillate cones small, with woody scales, maturing first year.

Tsuga canadensis (L.) Carriere. (Canada Hemlock). Hardy in all zones; tree to 30 m. tall.

DESCRIPTION: Upright tree, native from Minnesota to Nova Scotia, south to Delaware; **leaves** 1 cm. long, finely dentate, obtuse to acute; pistillate **cones** to 2 cm. long, stalked.

USE AND CULTURE: Plant as a specimen lawn tree or for a screen or hedge in more protected areas. Plants require a fertile, well-drained soil. Propagation is largely by seeds sown in the spring following stratification. Eastern strains are susceptible to winter burn. Trees grown from native Minnesota trees are more resistant to winter burn. Vines are used in the landscape to soften structures, provide screening, and to add vertical interest. Most vines need adequate support and regular pruning to do well in the landscape. Many vines grow quickly. The following lists provide vines for specific purposes:

Tsuga canadensis (Canada Hemlock). Young specimens in

Des Moines, Iowa. Mature forest tree in Mille Lacs, Minnesota.

VINES

Parthenocissus quinquefolia (Virginia Creeper). In October 1978.

Vines for Ground Cover

Clematis occidentalis
Menispermum canadense
Parthenocissus inserta
Parthenocissus quinquefolia
Smilax species

Vines for Trellis or Fence

Aristolochia durior
Celastrus scandens
Clematis pitcheri
Clematis virginiana
Echinocystis lobata
Lonicera species
Parthenocissus species
Vitis riparia

Vines that Tolerate Shade

Adlumia fungosa
Aristolochia durior
Lonicera species
Menispermum canadense
Parthenocissus species
Smilax species

Vines Having Colored Fruits

Celastrus scandens (red)
Vitis riparia (bluish-black)

Adlumia Raf. (Allegheny Vine, Mountain-fringe)
FUMARIACEAE (Fumitory Family)
DESCRIPTION: A single species of an herbaceous, biennial vine, native in eastern North America; **leaves** alternate, 3- to 4- pinnate; **flowers** narrow, heart-shaped, perfect, in axillary panicles; sepals 2, scalelike, falling early; petals 4, united and persistent, enclosing stamens and pistil; stamens 6, united at base and adhering to the petals, dividing into 2 bundles of 3 stamens each; **fruit** a few-seeded capsule.

Adlumia fungosa (Ait.) Greene ex BSP. (Allegheny Vine, Mountain-fringe, Climbing Fumitory). Hardy in zone 3; vine to 3 m. long.
DESCRIPTION: A biennial vine, climbing by petioles, native on wooded slopes from Minnesota to Quebec, south to Tennessee and North Carolina; **leaves** delicate, fernlike, mostly basal the first year, alternate on the climbing stems the second year, pinnately-ternately compound, to 25 cm. long near the base, smaller above; **flowers** pearly-pink, in drooping, axillary panicles to 10 cm. long, from June to frost; **fruit** an oblong capsule.
USE AND CULTURE: Grown in wooded wild flower gardens for its delicate, fernlike foliage and attractive flowers. Requires a rich, moist soil and shade. Some support is needed or it can be planted where it will trail over stumps or logs. Propagation is by seeds sown as soon as ripe. Once established, volunteer seedlings are often sufficient to maintain the planting.

Apios Medic. (Groundnut, Wild Bean)
LEGUMINOSAE (Pea Family)

Celastrus scandens (Bittersweet). Scrambling over shrubs.

DESCRIPTION: 8 to 10 species of tuberous, twining, herbaceous, perennial vines, native in North America and Asia; **leaves** alternate, pinnately compound; **flowers** pealike, in short racemes; stamens 10, 9 united, 1 separate; **fruit** a long, flat legume.

Apios americana Medic. (Groundnut, Potato Bean, Wild Bean). Hardy in all zones; perennial vine to 2.5 m. long.
DESCRIPTION: Perennial vine, native in moist woods and thickets from Canada south to Texas and Florida; **tubers** formed in strings on the roots; **leaves** with 5 to 7 leaflets; leaflets ovate-lanceolate, to 7.5 cm. long; **flowers** brownish-purple, fragrant, pealike, in axillary clusters.
USE AND CULTURE: These vines are grown for their edible tubers. They are also used for covering stumps in a wild flower garden. These plants like a rich, moist soil high in organic matter. Propagation is by division of tubers in fall or early spring. It is also propagated by seeds sown in the spring.

Apios tuberosa - see **Apios americana**.

Aristolochia L. (Birthwort)
ARISTOLOCHIACEAE (Birthwort Family)
DESCRIPTION: About 200 species of mostly tropical climbing shrubs or perennial herbs; **leaves** simple, often cordate, petioled; **flowers** solitary, clustered, or in racemes on axillary peduncles; calyx corollalike, tubular, irregular; tube bent, often constricted at mouth; stamens 6; ovary inferior; **fruit** a capsule.

Aristolochia durior J. Hill. (Dutchman's-pipe, Pipe Vine). Hardy in zone 4; vine to 10 m. long.
DESCRIPTION: A deciduous woody climber, native in rich, moist woods from Kansas to Pennsylvania, south to Georgia; **leaves** usually opposite, reniform-orbicular, to 30 cm. long; **flowers** mostly solitary, axillary, on pedicels to 5 cm. long with a bract below the center, in May; calyx greenish-yellow, with a u-shaped tube to 7.5 cm. long, glabrous, 3-lobed, brownish-purple, shaped like an old-time pipe with a flare at the top; **fruit** capsules cylindrical, to 7.5 cm. long.
USE AND CULTURE: A dense, coarse textured vine needing sturdy support used to cover porches or fences. It needs a soil high in organic matter that is neutral or slightly acid. Light shade is preferred but the vine will grow in full sun. Propagation is by seeds sown as soon as ripe.

Aristolochia macrophylla - see **Aristolochia durior**.

Celastrus L. (Bittersweet, Shrubby Bittersweet)
CELASTRACEAE (Staff-tree Family)
DESCRIPTION: About 30 species of usually twining polygamous shrubs or vines, native in North and South America, eastern Asia, and Madagascar; **leaves** alternate, simple; **flowers** small, green, yellow, or white, in axillary or terminal cymes, racemes,

or panicles, 5-merous; **fruit** an orange or yellow capsule, opening to expose a fleshy, orange, red, or yellow aril which encloses the seeds.

Celastrus scandens L. (American Bittersweet, Climbing Bittersweet, False Bittersweet, Shrubby Bittersweet, Staff Vine, Waxwork). Hardy in all zones; vine to 8 m. long.

DESCRIPTION: Climbing woody vine, native in thickets and along rivers from Manitoba to Quebec, south to Oklahoma and Georgia; **leaves** ovate-lanceolate, to 10 cm. long, dentate, turning golden-yellow in the fall; **flowers** mostly dioecious, rarely polygamous, in racemes or panicles to 10 cm. long; **fruit** a yellow capsule, opening to expose a scarlet to crimson aril, in September.

USE AND CULTURE: Widely planted for its colorful fruits that are harvested for winter bouquets. The American bittersweet is easy to grow in most soils. It climbs by twining and a sturdy trellis or fence is needed to support its weight. Since most plants are dioecious, plant several to be sure of getting both pistillate and staminate plants. Propagation is by stem or root cuttings, by layering, and by seeds sown as soon as ripe or in the spring following stratification. Seeds germinate best in a mixture of sand and sawdust. Keep vines away from trees and shrubs as the vines can strangle and kill young trees.

Clematis L. (Clematis, Leather Flower,
Vase Vine, Virgin's Bower)
RANUNCULACEAE (Buttercup Family)

DESCRIPTION: Over 200 species of perennial herbs or woody vines, native in the North Temperate Zone; **leaves** opposite, simple or compound; **flowers** solitary or in panicles, usually showy, urceolate, campanulate, or saucer-shaped; sepals petallike; petals lacking; stamens many; **fruit** an achene, usually with a feathery style.

Clematis occidentalis (Hornem.) DC. (Mountain Clematis, Purple Clematis). Hardy in all zones; trailing perennial to 15 cm. tall.

DESCRIPTION: A trailing woody vine, native on rocky slopes and open woods from Manitoba to Quebec, south to Iowa and New Jersey; **leaves** ternate; leaflets lanceolate-ovate to triangular or nearly round; **flowers** solitary, blue-purple, nodding, on long peduncles, in May and June; sepals 4, divergent, prominently veined, to 5 cm. long; stamen filaments flat, petallike; **achenes** with plumose styles.

USE AND CULTURE: Plant in rock gardens or use as a ground cover. Plants will grow in most soils. Propagation is by seeds sown in the fall or in the spring following stratification. Cuttings taken in July root when planted under intermittent mist.

Clematis pitcheri Torr. & A. Gray. (Leather Flower). Hardy in zone 4; climbing vine to 3 m. tall.

DESCRIPTION: A high-climbing pubescent vine, native from Nebraska to Indiana, south to Texas and Tennessee; **leaves** pinnate; leaflets 3 to 9, ovate or subcordate, entire or 3-lobed; **flowers** solitary, dull purple, campanulate, to 2.5 cm. long, from June to August; **achenes** with styles to 2.5 cm. long.

USE AND CULTURE: Use to cover fences and trellises. Culture is the same as for **Clematis occidentalis**.

Clematis virginiana (Virgin's Bower). Flowers in August 1977.

Fruit in March 1991.

Photograph: Douglas Owens-Pike.

Echinocystis lobata. In August 1977.

Clematis verticillaris - see **Clematis occidentalis**.

Clematis virginiana L. (Devil's-darning-needle, Leather Flower, Virgin's Bower, Woodbine). Hardy in all zones; vine to 6 m. long.
DESCRIPTION: Vigorous vine, native in woods and thickets from Manitoba to Nova Scotia, south to Kansas and Georgia; **leaves** compound; leaflets 3, ovate, acuminate, incised, with few teeth; **flowers** creamy-white, numerous in corymblike panciles, in June and July; sepals 1 cm. long; **achenes** with plumose styles to 4 cm. long.
USE AND CULTURE: Used for covering fences or stumps. Same as for **Clematis occidentalis**.

Echinocystis Torr. & A. Gray. (Balsam Apple, Wild Cucumber)
CUCURBITACEAE (Gourd Family)
DESCRIPTION: A single species of annual, tendril-bearing vines, native in southern Canada and the United States; **leaves** 3- to 5-lobed; **flowers** monoecious; staminate flowers in peduncled, axillary panicles; calyx with 6 bristlelike lobes; corolla with 6 slender lobes; stamens 3 with filaments and anthers united; pistillate flowers solitary or paired, in the same leaf axils as the staminate flowers; ovary 2-celled; **fruit** a papery, inflated, spiny pod, bursting irregularly at apex.

Echinocystis lobata (Michx.) Torr. & A. Gray. (Balsam Apple, Wild Cucumber). Hardy in all zones; annual to 7 m. long.
DESCRIPTION: Annual vine, native in bottom lands, thickets, and waste ground, often found growing on fences and over shrubs from Saskatchewan to New Brunswick, south to Texas and Florida; **leaves** thin, light green, shaped like an English ivy leaf; tendrils branched; **flowers** greenish-white, from July to September; corolla lobes to 6 mm. long; **fruit** ellipsoid or globose, inflated, covered with spines, to 5 cm. long.
USE AND CULTURE: Plant along fences for a screen. These plants grow well in any moist soil. Plant seeds in late May where the plants are to grow. Plants self sow once established.

Lonicera L. (Honeysuckle)
CAPRIFOLIACEAE (Honeysuckle Family)
DESCRIPTION: Over 150 species of mostly deciduous shrubs or woody vines, native in the northern hemisphere; **leaves** opposite, simple; **flowers** small to large, often in axillary pairs subtended by 2 bracts and 4 bractlets, or in sessile whorls at the tips of branches; calyx 4- to 5-toothed; corolla 4- to 5-lobed; stamens 5; ovary inferior; **fruit** a berry.

Lonicera hirsuta Eat. (Hairy Honeysuckle). Hardy in all zones; climbing vine to 3 m. long.
DESCRIPTION: Climbing vine, native in moist woods from Saskatchewan to Quebec, south to Nebraska and Pennsylvania; **leaves** elliptic, to 10 cm. long with upper leaves united at base, hairy on the under surface; **flowers** orange-yellow, 2-lipped, to 2.5 cm. long, in May and June; **fruit** a red berry.
USE AND CULTURE: Plant by a trellis or use to cover a fence. They are easy to grow in any good garden soil either in full sun or in partial shade. Propagation is by seeds or by softwood cuttings. Seeds should be planted in the fall and the seedbed should be mulched over winter, or the seeds can be stratified and planted in the spring. Softwood cuttings should be rooted in sand under intermittent mist.

Lonicera prolifera (Kirchn.) Rehd. (Grape Honeysuckle). Hardy in all zones; climbing vine to 4 m. long.
DESCRIPTION: Climbing vine, native in moist woods and thickets from Minnesota to Ontario, south to Kansas and Tennessee; **leaves** elliptic or oblong, to 10 cm. long, very glaucous; upper leaves united at base; **flowers** in whorls, pale yellow, marked with purple, 2-lipped, to 2.5 cm. long, in May and June; **fruit** a red berry.
USE AND CULTURE: The culture and use is the same as for **Lonicera hirsuta**.

Lonicera sempervirens L. (Coral Honeysuckle, Trumpet Honeysuckle). Hardy in sheltered locations in zone 4; vine to 6 m. long.

DESCRIPTION: Climbing deciduous vine, sometimes evergreen in the south, native in woods and thickets from Nebraska to Maine, south to Texas and Florida; **leaves** ovate to oblong, to 7.5 cm. long, glaucous beneath; upper leaves united at base; **flowers** orange-scarlet, yellow inside, to 5 cm. long, produced in spikes, from June to frost; **fruit** a red berry.
USE AND CULTURE: The culture and use is the same as for **Lonicera hirsuta**.

Menispermum L. (Moonseed)
MENISPERMACEAE (Moonseed Family)
DESCRIPTION: Two species of dioecious, woody, twining vines, native in eastern North America and Asia; **leaves** alternate, peltate; **flowers** small, in racemes or panicles, white or yellow; sepals 4 to 10; petals 6 to 9; pistillate flowers with 6 to 12 staminodes and 2 to 4 ovaries; staminate flowers with 12 to 24 stamens; **fruit** a subglobose drupe.

Menispermum canadense L. (Moonseed, Yellow Parilla). Hardy in all zones; vine to 4 m. long.
DESCRIPTION: Trailing vine, native in woods and thickets and along streams from Manitoba to Quebec, south to Oklahoma and Georgia; **stems** slightly pubescent; **leaves** circular-ovate, to 20 cm. wide, entire or shallowly lobed, mostly peltate near the margin; petioles long and slender; **flowers** greenish-white, in loose panicles, in June; **drupes** oblong, black, glaucous; seeds crescent-shaped.
USE AND CULTURE: Plant as a ground cover in wild flower gardens. It has attractive, dark green foliage and is trouble-free. Plants like a moist, humus-rich soil in shade. Propagation is by division either in the fall or spring, by seed, or cuttings. Seeds should be sown as soon as ripe. Softwood cuttings taken in July can be rooted under mist.

Parthenocissus Planch. (Woodbine)
VITACEAE (Grape Family)
DESCRIPTION: About 15 species of woody vines, climbing by tendrils that are often tipped by suckerlike discs, native in temperate regions of North America and Asia; **leaves** alternate, unlobed or palmately lobed, or palmately compound; **flowers** small, green, in compound cymes, 5-merous; **fruit** a blue or blue-black berry.

Parthenocissus inserta (A. Kern.) Fritsch. (Thicket Creeper). Hardy in all zones; vine to 5 m. long.
DESCRIPTION: Creeping or climbing vine, native in moist woods from Manitoba to Quebec, south to Texas and Indiana; **tendrils** lack suckerlike discs; **leaves** with 5 to 7 leaflets; leaflets elliptic to oblong, 5 to 12 cm. long, acuminate, usually wedge-shaped at base, coarsely and sharply serrate, dark green and shiny above, glabrous, turning red in the fall; **flowers** in dichotomously branched cymes on peduncles to 7 cm. long, in June and July; **fruits** bluish-black, usually with a bloom, to 8 mm. across.
USE AND CULTURE: Plant as a ground cover in woodland gardens or use on fences and arbors. These plants are easy to grow in any well-drained soil. Propagation is by division, layers, and seed. Plant seeds in fall or in spring following stratification. This species is seldom sold by nurseries. It is very similar to **Parthenocissus quinquefolia**, differing in not having suckerlike discs on the tendrils.

Parthenocissus quinquefolia (L.) Planch. (American Ivy, Five-leaved Ivy, Virginia Creeper, Woodbine). Hardy in all zones; vine to 10 m. long.
DESCRIPTION: High-climbing vine with adhesive, disc-tipped tendrils, native in woods, thickets, and rocky banks from Minnesota to Maine, south to Texas and Florida; **leaflets** 5, elliptic-ovate, to 15 cm. long, coarsely dentate turning red in fall; **flowers** small, in paniclelike cymes, in June; **berries** bluish-black, to 1 cm. across.
USE AND CULTURE: The same as for **Parthenocissus inserta**. Having adhesivelike discs, it will climb stone and brick. It usually has good red fall foliage color.

Parthenocissus vitacea - see **Parthenocissus inserta**

Menispermum canadense (Moonseed).
Photograph: Research Department of the Minnesota Landscape Arboretum.

Parthenocissus quinquefolia (Virginia Creeper).

Vitis riparia (River-bank Grape). Fall foliage in September 1977. Fruit in August 1979.

Smilax L. (Catbrier, Greenbrier)
LILIACEAE (Lily Family)
DESCRIPTION: About 200 species of dioecious, woody or herbaceous vines, climbing by paired stipular tendrils, native in moist woods in temperate and tropical regions; underground **stems** rhizomatous or tuberous; stems climbing or sprawling, sometimes prickly; **leaves** alternate, the lower reduced to scales; **flowers** dioecious, small, in axillary umbels; perianth segments 6, separate; stamens 6, emerging from base of perianth segments; **fruit** a berry.

Smilax herbacea L. (Carion Flower, Jacob's-ladder). Hardy in all zones; vines to 2 m. tall.
DESCRIPTION: Spineless perennial vine, native in moist woods from Ontario to Quebec, south to Wyoming and Georgia; **leaves** oblong-ovate to round, to 12 cm. long, glabrous beneath; **flowers** small, in May and June; **berries** black.
USE AND CULTURE: Plant in wild flower gardens. Plants are easy to grow in humus-rich soil in partial shade. Propagation is by seeds sown as soon as ripe. Space plants 45 cm. apart.

Smilax hispida Muhlenb. (Bristly Greenbrier, Hagbrier, Hellfetter). Hardy in all zones; woody vine to 3 m. long.
DESCRIPTION: High-climbing deciduous vine, native from Ontario to Connecticut, south to Texas and Virginia; **stems** prickly; **leaves** ovate to round, to 12 cm. long, serrulate, prominently veined, sharply pointed or acuminate; **flowers** small, in May and June; **berries** black, to 6 mm. in diameter.
USE AND CULTURE: The same as for **Smilax herbacea**.

Vitis L. (Grape)
VITACEAE (Grape Family)
DESCRIPTION: About 40 species of tendril-climbing vines, native in north temperate regions; **stems** with brown pith and shreddy bark; tendrils simple or branched, often coiled; **leaves** simple, palmately lobed and veined; **flowers** small, in narrow panicles, usually perfect but sometimes dioecious; petals united at apex, separate at base, early deciduous; **fruit** a globose to ovoid berry.

Vitis riparia Michx. (Frost Grape, River-bank Grape). Hardy in all zones; vine to 10 m. long.
DESCRIPTION: A vigorous, woody climber, native on river banks and in rich woods, often climbing in tall trees from Montana to Nova Scotia, south to Texas and Tennessee; **leaves** to 15 cm. long with acuminate lobes; **flowers** fragrant, in clusters to 15 cm. long, in May and June; **berries** small, glaucous, nearly black, acid.
USE AND CULTURE: Often planted to cover fences and arbors. Sometimes planted for the fruits that are prized for jellies. Plants grow well in most soils. Propagation is by seeds or hardwood cuttings. Seeds should be planted in the spring following stratification. Cuttings are usually taken while the plant is still dormant, stored in a cool, moist place, and planted in spring.

PERENNIALS, BIENNIALS, AND ANNUALS

Sanguinaria canadensis (Bloodroot).

Perennials, biennials, and annuals make up the largest grouping of native plants in this region. Most people rely on these plants for seasonal color, texture, and interest. The following lists will help in their selection:

Plants for Seasonal Interest:

Spring

Achillea millefolium var. lanulosa
Actaea species
Aletris farinosa
Andromeda glaucophylla
Antennaria species
Aquilegia canadensis
Arisaema species
Arnica cordifolia
Aruncus dioicus
Astragalus species
Baptisia australis
Camassia species
Caulophyllum thalictroides
Chimaphila species
Claytonia species
Clintonia borealis
Collinsonia canadensis
Coptis groenlandica
Cornus canadensis
Corydalis species
Delphinium species
Dentaria species
Desmodium canadense
Dicentra species
Disporum species
Erigeron species
Erythronium species
Fragaria vesca (flower & fruit)
Galium boreale
Gaultheria species
Geranium maculatum
Geum species (flower & fruit)
Gillenia trifoliata
Goodyera pubescens
Hedyotis species
Helianthemum canadense
Hepatica species
Hydrastis canadensis
Ipomoea leptophylla
Iris species
Isopyrum biternatum
Jeffersonia diphylla
Leucocrinum montanum
Lilium species
Linnaea borealis
Linum species
Lithospermum species
Lobelia spicata
Lupinus perennis
Maianthemum canadense
Medeola virginica
Mertensia species
Mitella species

Clintonia borealis (Bluebead Lily)

Orchis species
Oxytropis campestris
Pedicularis canadensis
Penstemon species
Phlox divaricata
Phlox pilosa
Podophyllum peltatum
Polemonium reptans
Polygala paucifolia
Polygonatum commutatum
Psoralea esculenta
Salvia azurea
Sanguinaria canadensis
Saxifraga virginiensis
Senecio aureus
Silene virginica
Sisyrinchium species
Smilacina species
Sphaeralcea coccinea
Stylophorum diphyllum
Talinum parviflorum
Thalictrum species
Tradescantia virginiana
Trientalis borealis
Trillium species
Triosteum perfoliatum
Uvularia species
Vicia americana
Viola species
Waldsteinia fragarioides
Yucca glauca

Summer

Actaea species (fruits)
Agastache species
Aletris farinosa
Allium species
Anemone virginiana
Apocynum androsaemifolium
Aralia hispida
Arnica cordifolia
Asclepias species
Callirhoe species
Campanula species
Cassia species
Caulophyllum thalictroides
Chelone species
Chrysopsis villosa
Cimicifuga species
Coreopsis species
Corydalis species
Coryphantha vivipara
Crotalaria sagittalis
Dicentra eximia
Echinacea species
Elymus glaucus
Epilobium angustifolium
Eupatorium species
Euphorbia species
Eustoma grandiflorum

Dentaria laciniata. In flower in May 1978.

Filipendula rubra
Gaillardia species
Galium boreale
Gentiana species
Gentianella amarella
Gillenia trifoliata
Goodyera pubescens
Grindelia squarrosa
Habenaria species
Helenium autumnale
Helianthus species
Heliopsis helianthoides
Heracleum sphondylium ssp. montanum
Hibiscus species
Impatiens species
Ipomopsis rubra
Lathyrus species
Liatris species
Lilium species
Linum species
Lobelia cardinalis
Lobelia siphilitica
Lysimachia species
Lythrum alatum
Machaeranthera tanacetifolia
Mentzelia decapetala
Mertensia paniculata
Mimulus species
Mitchella repens (fruit)
Monarda species
Moneses uniflora
Oenothera species
Opuntia species
Panax species
Pedicularis lanceolata
Penstemon species
Phlox paniculata
Physostegia virginiana
Phytolacca americana (flowers & fruit)
Pyrola species
Ratibida species
Rudbeckia species
Ruellia humilis
Salvia azurea
Saxifraga species
Scutellaria species
Silene stellata
Silphium species
Solidago canadensis
Stachys species
Streptopus species (fruit)
Talinum parviflorum
Thermopsis caroliniana
Tradescantia virginiana
Triodanis perfoliata
Vernonia species
Veronicastrum virginicum
Yucca glauca

Fall

Actaea species (fruit)
Agastache species
Anaphalis margaritacea
Aralia species (fruit)
Asclepias species (flower & fruit)
Aster species
Caulophyllum thalictroides (fruit)
Clintonia borealis (fruit)
Cornus canadensis (fruit)
Epilobium angustifolium
Helianthus species
Heliopsis helianthoides
Hibiscus species
Impatiens species
Liatris species
Linum species
Lobelia cardinalis
Lobelia siphilitica
Machaeranthera tanacetifolia
Mentzelia decapetala
Mitchella repens (fruit)
Physostegia virginiana
Phytolacca americana (fruit)
Polygonatum species (fruit)
Solidago canadensis
Vernonia species
Veronicastrum virginicum

Plants for Rock Gardens

Achillea millefolium var. lanulosa
Aletris farinosa
Allium species
Andromeda glaucophylla
Anemone caroliniana
Anemone nuttalliana
Anemonella thalictroides
Antennaria species
Asarum canadense
Astragalus species
Callirhoe species
Camassia quamash
Campanula rotundifolia
Claytonia species
Corydalis species
Coryphantha vivipara
Dentaria species
Dicentra eximia
Dodecatheon meadia
Erigeron species
Eustoma grandiflorum
Gaultheria procumbens
Gentiana affinis
Geum triflorum
Goodyera pubescens
Hedyotis species
Helianthemum canadense
Hepatica species
Heuchera species
Hypoxis hirsuta
Iris species

Leucocrinum montanum
Linnaea borealis
Linum species
Lithospermum species
Mitella species
Oenothera species
Opuntia species
Orchis species
Oxalis violacea
Pedicularis species
Penstemon species
Phlox divaricata
Phlox pilosa
Polemonium reptans
Potentilla tridentata
Primula mistassinica
Pyrola species
Ruellia humilis
Sanguinaria canadensis
Saxifraga species
Sisyrinchium species
Talinum parviflorum
Tiarella cordifolia
Townsendia exscapa
Trillium nivale
Viola pedata
Waldsteinia fragarioides
Yucca glauca

Plants Suitable for Ground Covers

Achillea millefolium var. lanulosa
Anemone quinquefolia
Antennaria species
Aralia nudicaulis
Asarum canadense
Cornus canadensis
Dentaria species
Epigaea repens
Fragaria vesca
Gaultheria species
Iris species
Mitella species
Oenothera fruticosa
Podophyllum peltatum
Potentilla tridentata
Tiarella cordifolia
Trientalis borealis
Vicia americana
Viola species
Waldsteinia fragarioides

Plants that Tolerate or Prefer Shade

Actaea species
Anemone quinquefolia
Apocynum androsaemifolium
Aquilegia canadensis
Aralia species
Arisaema species
Aruncus dioicus

Asarum canadense
Camassia scilloides
Campanula americana
Claytonia species
Collinsonia canadensis
Coptis groenlandica
Cornus canadensis
Cypripedium species
Delphinium species
Dicentra species
Disporum species
Epigaea repens
Erythronium species
Galium boreale
Gaultheria hispidula
Geranium maculatum
Gillenia trifoliata
Habenaria species
Hepatica species
Heuchera species
Hydrastis canadensis
Impatiens species
Iris cristata
Isopyrum biternatum
Jeffersonia diphylla
Lobelia cardinalis
Maianthemum canadense
Medeola virginica
Mertensia species
Orchis species
Panax species
Podophyllum peltatum
Polygonatum species
Sanguinaria canadensis
Silene species
Smilacina species
Streptopus species
Stylophorum diphyllum
Thalictrum species
Tiarella cordifolia
Tradescantia virginiana
Trillium species
Triosteum perfoliatum
Uvularia species
Veronicastrum virginicum
Vicia americana
Viola species
Waldsteinia fragarioides

Plants that Tolerate Wet Soils
(see also chapter on bog plants)

Anemone quinquefolia
Arisaema dracontium
Asclepias incarnata
Clintonia borealis
Coptis groenlandica
Dentaria species
Eupatorium species
Gentiana andrewsii
Geum rivale

Habenaria species
Heracleum sphondylium ssp. montanum
Impatiens species
Iris versicolor
Lysimachia species
Lythrum alatum
Mimulus species

Plants that Tolerate or Prefer Acid Soils

Aletris farinosa
Andromeda glaucophylla
Callirhoe species
Caulophyllum thalictroides
Chelone species
Chimaphila species
Cimicifuga species
Claytonia species
Clintonia borealis
Coptis groenlandica
Cornus canadensis
Cypripedium species
Dodecatheon meadia
Epigaea repens
Epilobium angustifolium
Fragaria vesca
Gaultheria species
Geranium maculatum
Gillenia trifoliata
Goodyera pubescens
Habenaria species
Heuchera species
Hypoxis hirsuta
Iris cristata
Jeffersonia diphylla
Linnaea borealis
Lobelia species
Lupinus perennis
Maianthemum canadense
Medeola virginica
Mertensia virginica
Mitchella repens
Mitella species
Monarda didyma
Moneses uniflora
Orchis species
Oxalis violacea
Phlox divaricata
Phlox pilosa
Podophyllum peltatum
Polemonium reptans
Polygala paucifolia
Polygonatum species
Pyrola species
Ruellia humilis
Scutellaria species
Talinum parviflorum
Thalictrum dioicum
Tiarella cordifolia
Trientalis borealis
Trillium undulatum

Triosteum perfoliatum
Uvularia perfoliata
Viola pedata
Waldsteinia fragarioides

Achillea L. (Yarrow)
COMPOSITAE (Sunflower Family)
Anthemis Tribe

DESCRIPTION: Nearly 100 species of aromatic perennial herbs native mostly in the North Temperate Zone of the Old World; **leaves** alternate or in basal rosettes, simple and toothed or pinnately dissected; **flower** heads small, mostly numerous in corymbs; involucral bracts in several rows, dry and often scarious on margins; receptacle flat to conical, scaly; flowers pink, white, or yellow; ray flowers pistillate or lacking; disc flowers tubular, perfect; **fruits** are strongly compressed, glabrous achenes.

Achillea lanulosa - see **Achillea millefolium** var. **lanulosa**

Achillea millefolium var. **lanulosa** (Nutt.) Piper. (Common Yarrow). Hardy in all zones; perennial to 45 cm. tall.
DESCRIPTION: Aromatic, nearly cespitose perennial, native from the Yukon to Quebec, south to California and Oklahoma; **leaves** linear-lanceolate, gray, woolly, mostly basal; **flowers** heads numerous, forming a convex corymb, from June to August; involucral bracts with straw-colored to light brown margins; flowers white.
USE AND CULTURE: Yarrow's dark green, finely cut foliage is attractive when used in the rock garden. It can also be used as a ground cover on hot, dry slopes. Plants thrive in almost any soil in full sun. Propagation is by seeds or by division in the spring. Yarrow can spread so care should be taken where it is planted.

Actaea L. (Baneberry, Cohosh, Necklaceweed)
RANUNCULACEAE (Buttercup Family)

DESCRIPTION: Eight species of erect, perennial herbs, native in rich, moist woods in the North Temperate Zone; **leaves** large, compound; **flowers** small, white, in terminal racemes; sepals 4 or 5, petallike, falling early; petals 4 to 10, small, flat, spatulate, clawed; stamens many; pistils 1; **fruit** a glossy berry.

Actaea alba - see **Actaea pachypoda**.

Actaea pachypoda Elliott. (White Baneberry, White Cohosh, Doll's-eyes). Hardy in all zones; perennial to 60 cm. tall.
DESCRIPTION: Upright perennial, native in deciduous woods from Minnesota to Newfoundland, south to Missouri and Georgia; **leaves** ternately compound; leaflets finely cut with pointed teeth; **flowers** white, in oblong, terminal racemes, in May and June; petals truncate at apex; **fruits** are white (rarely red) berries borne on a thick, red pedicel; stigma persists on the berry giving a doll's eye appearance.

Achillea millefolium var. lanulosa (Yarrow).

Actaea rubra (Red Baneberry). In fruit.

Actaea rubra (Red Baneberry). In flower.

Photograph: Mr. Arvid Lund.

USE AND CULTURE: Planted in shady wild flower gardens. Plants require a rich soil high in organic matter with a pH between 6 and 7. Berries are poisonous, so do not plant where children can reach them. Propagation is by seeds sown as soon as ripe or by division in early spring or fall. It takes 3 years to produce fruiting plants from seeds. One of the few attractive perennials in August.

Actaea rubra (Ait.) Willd. (Red Baneberry, Snakeberry). Hardy in all zones; perennial to 60 cm. tall.
DESCRIPTION: Upright, bushy perennial, native in rich woods and thickets from Manitoba to Nova Scotia, south to Nebraska and Pennsylvania; **leaves** ternate; leaflets ovate, dentate to cleft or incised, downy along the veins on the undersurface; **flowers** white, in upright racemes, in May and June; pedicels slender, about 1 cm. long; petals spatulate; **fruits** are red (rarely white) berries.
USE AND CULTURE: Same as for **Actaea pachypoda**.

Agastache Clayt. ex Gronov. (Giant Hyssop)
LABIATAE (Mint Family)
DESCRIPTION: About 30 species of coarse, perennial herbs, native in North America and Asia; **stems** square; **leaves** opposite, petioled, serrate; **flowers** small, in many-flowered verticillasters arranged in interrupted terminal spikes; calyx tubular, 15-veined, 5-toothed; corolla 2-lipped, upper lip erect, 2-lobed, lower lip 3-lobed, the middle lobe crenate; stamens 4, exserted; **fruit** a nutlet borne in 4's.

Agastache foeniculum (Pursh) O. Kuntze. (Anise Hyssop, Blue Giant Hyssop, Fennel Giant Hyssop, Fragrant Giant Hyssop). Hardy in all zones; perennial to 1 m. tall.
DESCRIPTION: A coarse glabrescent perennial, native in dry woods and on prairies from Alberta to Quebec, south to Colorado and Iowa; **leaves** ovate, to 7.5 cm. long, serrate, whitish beneath; **flowers** blue, in cylindrical, bracted spikes to 10 cm. long, from June to September; bracts large, ovate, acuminate, often tinged purple; calyx teeth acute; corolla to 8 mm. long.

Agastache foeniculum (Anise Hyssop).

Allium cernuum (Wild Onion).

Photograph: Mr. Arvid Lund

Allium cernuum (Wild Onion)

Photograph: Dr. Anne M. Hanchek.

USE AND CULTURE: Plant in back of flower border or in wild flower garden. Dried leaves of this plant are used for making a tea and for seasoning. It is also planted as a honey plant. Easy to grow either in full sun or in partial shade. Propagation is by seeds or by division in spring.

Agastache nepetoides (L.) O. Kuntze. (Yellow Giant Hyssop). Hardy in all zones; perennial to 1.5 m. tall.
DESCRIPTION: Tall, glabrous perennial, native in open woods from Ontario to Quebec, south to Kansas and Georgia; **leaves** ovate, to 12 cm. long, acute, coarsely crenate; **flowers** yellowish-green, in bracted spikes to 12 cm. long, in August and September; calyx teeth ovate, obtuse; floral bracts ovate, acute.
USE AND CULTURE: Same as for **Agastache foeniculum**.

Aletris L. (Colicroot, Star Grass)
LILIACEAE (Lily Family)
DESCRIPTION: About 10 species of perennial, fibrous-rooted herbs, native in eastern North America and eastern Asia; **leaves** basal, grasslike, from a short, thick rhizome; **flowers** white or yellow, in erect, spikelike racemes; perianth 6-lobed; stamens 6; **fruit** a capsule.

Aletris farinosa . (Colicroot, Star Grass, Agueroot, Crow Corn, Unicorn Root). Hardy in zone 3; 1 m. tall, 60 cm. wide.
DESCRIPTION: A grasslike perennial, native in sandy or peaty soils in open woods or barrens from Minnesota to Maine, south to Texas and Florida; **leaves** pale yellowish-green, to 15 cm. long, firm, resembling those of a miniature yucca; **flowers** white, tubular, from May to August; perianth segments covered with small projections suggesting "mealiness"; **fruit** a short capsule.
USE AND CULTURE: Can be grown in either a wild flower garden or rock garden. Requires an acid soil either in full sun or light shade. Propagation is by seeds or division in the spring or early fall.

Allium L. (Onion)
AMARYLLIDACEAE (Amaryllis Family)
DESCRIPTION: About 400 species of strongly odorous, rhizomatous or bulbous, perennial herbs, native in the northern hemisphere; **leaves** narrow, sheathing, solid or hollow, flat to cylindrical; **flowers** small, borne in few- to many-flowered umbels terminal on a scape and subtended by a spathe; perianth segments 6; stamens 6; ovary superior; **fruit** a capsule.

Allium cernuum Roth. (Wild Onion, Nodding Onion, Lady's Leek). Hardy in all zones; perennial to 50 cm. tall.
DESCRIPTION: Bulbous perennial, native in sandy or gravelly soil in open woods and prairies from British Columbia to New York, south to California and Georgia; **bulb** coat membranous; **leaves** linear, flat; **flowers** white or rose lavender with a pinkish cast in many-flowered, nodding umbels, in July and August; stamens and styles exserted; ovary 6-crested.
USE AND CULTURE: Used in rock gardens and prairies. Grows best on a well-drained soil that is neutral or slightly acid. Plant in colonies in full sun for best landscape effect. Propagation is by seeds or by division of the bulbs in fall.

Allium stellatum Ker. (Prairie Onion). Hardy in all zones; perennial to 45 cm. tall.
DESCRIPTION: A bulbous perennial, native in prairies and on open, rocky slopes; **bulbs** elongated with membranous coats; **leaves** linear and flat; **flowers** lavender-pink, in many-flowered umbels that face upward, from July to September; stamens and styles exserted.
USE AND CULTURE: Same as for **Allium cernuum**.

Amsonia Walt. (Amsonia, Bluestar).
APOCYNACEAE (Dogbane Family)
DESCRIPTION: About 20 species of perennial herbs with milky sap, native in North America and eastern Asia; **leaves** simple, alternate or more or less whorled, entire;

flowers regular, 5-merous, in terminal cymes; corolla salverform, villous inside, with spreading ovate to lanceolate lobes; stamens borne above center of corolla lobes; **fruits** a pair of cylindrical follicles.

Amsonia tabernaemontana Walt. (Amsonia, Blue Dogbane, Bluestar). Hardy in zone 3; perennial to 1 m. tall.
DESCRIPTION: Bushy perennial, native in moist woods from Missouri to New Jersey, south to Texas and Florida; **leaves** willowlike, alternate, dull green, ovate to oblong-elliptic, or lanceolate, glaucous beneath, petioled; **flowers** light blue, in short cymes, scarcely longer than the leaves, from April to July; calyx glabrous; corolla with tube 1 cm. long and with lobes slightly longer than the tube and starlike; **fruits** erect, acuminate, glabrous follicles.
USE AND CULTURE: Used in flower borders and wild flower gardens. It is a long-lived perennial of easy culture in either full sun or partial shade. Grows best if the soil is kept moist. Propagation is by seeds sown as soon as ripe or by division of the roots in early spring. It usually takes 3 years to get blooming-sized plants from seeds.

Anaphalis DC. (Everlasting, Life-everlasting)
COMPOSITAE (Sunflower Family)
Inula Tribe

DESCRIPTION: About 35 species of dioecious or polygamodioecious gray- or white-woolly perennial herbs, native in Europe, Asia, and North America; **stems** leafy; **leaves** simple, alternate, entire; **flower** heads discoid, small, in corymbs; involucral bracts stiff, dry, white or gray; flowers all tubular, yellow; **fruit** an oblong-ovate achene; pappus of capillary bristles.

Anaphalis margaritacea (L.) Benth. ex Hook.f. (Pearly Everlasting). Hardy in all zones; perennial to 45 cm. tall.
DESCRIPTION: A white-tomentose perennial herb, native in disturbed soils along roadsides in northern North America and eastern Asia; **leaves** willowlike, linear-lanceolate to lanceolate, sessile, to 10 cm. long, white-tomentose, often green above; **flower** heads many, to 6 mm. across, in August and September; involucral bracts pearly white; disc flowers yellow.
USE AND CULTURE: Used in flower borders and grown for dried flower arrangements. To use for dried flowers, cut when yellow centers show in flowers heads and hang upside down to dry. These plants are easy to grow in most soils. Propagation is by seeds or division. Grows best in full sun.

Andromeda L. (Bog Rosemary)
ERICACEAE (Heath Family)

DESCRIPTION: Two species of low, evergreen shrubs, native in North America, Europe, and Asia; **leaves** alternate, simple, with revolute margins, leathery; **flowers** pink to white, nodding, in terminal umbels; sepals 5; corolla urceolate; stamens 10, with awned anthers; ovary superior; **fruit** a capsule.

Amsonia tabernaemontana. In flower (above).

Anaphalis margaritacea (Pearly Everlasting). In flower in Hayward, Wisconsin. (left).

Andromeda glaucophylla Link. (Bog Rosemary). Hardy in all zones; shrub to 75 cm. tall.

DESCRIPTION: Glaucous evergreen shrub, native in bogs and edges of ponds throughout coniferous forests from Manitoba to Labrador, south to Minnesota and West Virginia; **leaves** linear to oblong, to 6 cm. long, white-puberulent beneath, revolute, green above; **flowers** white, in small umbellike clusters; **fruit** a short, glaucous capsule.

USE AND CULTURE: Used in rock gardens and bog gardens. It requires an acid, peaty soil that is kept moist. Propagation is by seeds sown as soon as ripe or in the spring following stratification, or by softwood cuttings.

Anemone L. (Anemone, Lily-of-the-field, Windflower)
RANUNCULACEAE (Buttercup Family).

DESCRIPTION: About 120 species of perennial herbs, native in the North Temperate Zone, often in high mountains; **leaves** more or less divided or dissected, or even compound; stem leaves forming an involucre below the flowers; **flowers** mostly showy, solitary; sepals yellow, white, rose, red, purple, or violet; petals 0; stamens many; pistils many; **fruit** an achene with a long plumose style.

Anemone caroliniana Walt. (Carolina Anemone). Hardy in zone 4; perennial to 30 cm. tall.

DESCRIPTION: Perennial with tuberous rhizomes, native on dry prairies and barrens from South Dakota to Indiana, south to Texas and Georgia; **leaves** ternate or 3-parted, with lobed segments, petioled; involucral leaves sessile; **flowers** solitary, erect, purple, red, or white, to 4 cm. across, in April and May; sepals 10 to 20, hairy underneath.

USE AND CULTURE: Used in rock gardens or prairie plantings. Requires full sun and a well-drained soil. Propagation is by seeds sown as soon as ripe and by fall division of rhizomes.

Anemone cylindrica A. Gray. (Long-headed Anemone, Sheep's Wool, Thimbleweed). Hardy in all zones; perennial to 90 cm. tall.

DESCRIPTION: Erect perennial, native in sandy soil in open woods and thickets from British Columbia to Maine, south to Arizona and New Jersey; basal **leaves** few, long-petioled, deeply 5-parted with rhombic segments; involucral leaves similar; **flowers** 2 to 6 on erect peduncles to 25 cm. long, greenish-white, to 2 cm. across, from May to July; **fruit** achenes woolly, in cylindrical, thimblelike heads.

USE AND CULTURE: Used in prairie plantings or wild flower gardens. It is of easy culture in any well-drained soil in full sun or partial shade. Propagation is by seed sown as soon as ripe or by division in spring.

Anemone nuttalliana DC. (Pasqueflower, Prairie-smoke, Hartshorn Plant, Lion's-beard, Wild Crocus). Hardy in all zones; perennial to 20 cm. tall.

DESCRIPTION: Tap-rooted perennial, native in rocky or sandy soils on prairies from Alaska to Wisconsin, south to Texas; differing from the European species, **Anemone patens**, in the basal leaves which develop before the flowers; **leaves** mostly basal, deeply cut into linear lobes; **flowers** solitary, lavender-blue, in April and early May; sepals hairy; **fruit** achenes, elongated with hairy styles.

USE AND CULTURE: It is an excellent rock garden plant when planted in a well-drained sandy soil. Seeds planted as soon as ripe will produce plants that bloom the third year. Plants can also be produced from root cuttings planted in a mixture of sand and peat. Mature plants are difficult to transplant because of the deep tap roots.

Anemone quinquefolia L. (Windflower, Wood Anemone). Hardy in all zones; perennial to 15 cm. tall.

DESCRIPTION: Rhizomatous, spreading perennial, native in open, moist woods, on stream banks, and in moist meadows from Manitoba to Quebec, south to Iowa and Georgia; a single basal **leaf** with 3 to 5 leaflets; leaflets rhombic, coarsely dentate; involucral leaves similar but smaller; **flowers** solitary, white, in May and June; sepals 4 to 9, white tinged pink or crimson, to 25 cm. long; stamens 30 or more.

USE AND CULTURE: It is an easy ground cover for shady, moist areas. Propagation is by division or seeds. Plant divisions either in early spring or fall with the rhizomes

Anemone nuttalliana (Pasqueflower).

Anemonella thalictroides (Rue Anemone)

about 2.5 cm. deep. Space the plants about 30 cm. apart. Seeds are sown as soon as they are ripe.

Anemone riparia Fern. (Thimbleweed). Hardy in all zones; perennial to 1 m. tall.
DESCRIPTION: Upright perennial, native on rocky ledges and along stream banks from British Columbia to Newfoundland, south to Minnesota and New York; **stems** 1 to 4, more or less hairy; basal **leaves** 3- to 5-parted, with deeply cleft segments; involucral leaves with 3 divisions; **flowers** white, on long peduncles, in clusters of 1 to 10, in May and June; central flower without an involucre, lateral ones with involucres; sepals 4 to 6, white, rarely red, to 2 cm. long; **fruit** achenes in round to oval heads.
USE AND CULTURE: Same as for **Anemone cylindrica**.

Anemone virginiana L. (Thimbleweed). Hardy in all zones; perennial to 45 cm. tall.
DESCRIPTION: A loosely villous perennial, native in rocky woodlands from North Dakota to Nova Scotia, south to Kansas and Georgia; basal **leaves** long-petioled, deeply 3- to 5-parted, then toothed or incised; involucral leaves similar; **flowers** 1 to 3 on upright peduncles, white to greenish-white, to 4 cm. across, from June to August.
USE AND CULTURE: Same as for **Anemone cylindrica**.

Anemonella Spach. (Rue Anemone)
RANUNCULACEAE (Buttercup Family)

DESCRIPTION: A genus with a single perennial species, native in deciduous woods in eastern North America; plants with tuberous, fascicled **roots** and basal, compound **leaves**; **flowers** white to pale pink in few-flowered umbels; sepals petallike; stamens numerous.

Anemonella thalictroides (L.) Spach. (Rue Anemone). Hardy in all zones; perennial to 15 cm. tall.
DESCRIPTION: Low, glabrous perennial, native in sheltered woodlands with high, open shade from Minnesota to Maine, south to Oklahoma and Florida; **leaves** basal, delicate, 2- to 3- ternate, resembling meadow rue; leaf segments ovate to oblong, to 2.5 cm. long, 3-toothed at apex; **flowers** white to pale pink, in few-flowered umbels, subtended by 2 to 3 sessile, compound involucral leaves, in May and June; sepals 1.25 cm. long; petals lacking.
USE AND CULTURE: Planted in rock gardens and in woodland wild flower gardens. The double-flowered forms are more compact and bloom for a longer time than the species. 'Shoaf's Double Pink' is a popular, good cultivar. These plants prefer a neutral to slightly acid soil high in organic matter. High, filtered shade and shelter from the wind is important. Propagation is by division of the tuberous roots. They should be planted in the fall so the neck of the root will be about 2.5 cm. deep. Seed planted as soon as ripe will produce flowering plants the second year.

Antennaria Gaertn. (Everlasting, Ladies'-tobacco, Pussy-toes)
COMPOSITAE (Sunflower Family)
Inula Tribe

DESCRIPTION: Nearly 75 species of small, dioecious, white- or gray-woolly perennials native on poor soils in North and South America, Europe, and Asia; **stems** simple, erect; **leaves** simple, in basal rosettes and alternate on the stems; **flower** heads small, discoid, in racemes or in dense corymbs; involucral bracts imbricate with white or colored scarious apices; flowers white, tubular on pistillate plants, funnelform on staminate plants; in some species staminate plants do not exist and seeds are produced parthenocarpically; **fruit** an achene.

Antennaria aprica - see **Antennaria parvifolia**.

Antennaria neglecta Greene. (Field Pussy-toes). Hardy in all zones; perennial to 30 cm. tall.
DESCRIPTION: Low, stoloniferous perennial, native in poor soils in pastures and open woods from southern Canada to California and Virginia; **stolons** slender, leafy at the tip; basal rosette **leaves** oblanceolate, tapering to base, tomentose when young but soon becoming glabrous and green above, to 6 cm. long; stem leaves linear; **flower** heads small, several, from May to July; involucral bracts green or purple with white apices.
USE AND CULTURE: Plant in rock gardens or as a ground cover on slopes where the soil is poor. They prefer full sun and a well-drained soil of low fertility. Propagation is by division of the stolons either in early spring or fall. Once established, the plants will self sow.

Antennaria plantaginifolia (L.) Hook. (Ladies'-tobacco, Pussy-toes). Hardy in all zones; perennial to 15 cm. tall.
DESCRIPTION: Stoloniferous perennial, native in dry, open woods, fields, and pastures from Minnesota to Quebec, south to Texas and Florida; **stolons** forming dense mats; basal **leaves** elliptic to obovate, to 7.5 cm. long; 3- to 5- veined, tomentose when young but becoming glabrous above, petioled; stem leaves lanceolate to linear; **flower** heads several, woolly, clustered at the top of stems, in May and June; involucral bracts green or purple, with white apices.
USE AND CULTURE: Same as for **Antennaria neglecta**.

Antennaria rosea Greene. (Rose Pussy-toes). Hardy in all zones; perennial to 40 cm. tall.
DESCRIPTION: Stoloniferous, mat-forming perennial, native in dry, open meadows and woods from Alaska to Ontario, south to California and Michigan; basal **leaves** oblanceolate or spatulate, gray tomentose; **flower** heads several in a subcapitate or rather loose cyme; pistillate involucres 4 to 7 mm. long, with scarious apices that are deep pink to white.
USE AND CULTURE: Same as for **Antennaria neglecta**.

Apocynum L. (Dogbane)
APOCYNACEAE (Dogbane Family)

Apocynum androsaemifolium (Dogbane).

Aquilegia canadensis (Wild Columbine).

Photographs: Mr. Arvid Lund.

DESCRIPTION: 7 species of perennial herbs with milky juice, native in temperate North America; **bark** tough and fibrous; **leaves** alternate or opposite, entire; **flowers** small, white or pink, in cymes; corolla campanulate to cylindrical, glabrous, with 5 scalelike appendages in the base of the tube; stamens 5, borne at base of corolla tube, alternating with the appendages; **fruit** a pair of slender, spreading follicles; **seed** with a tuft of hairs.

Apocynum androsaemifolium L. (Common Dogbane, Spreading Dogbane). Hardy in all zones; perennial to 60 cm. tall.
DESCRIPTION: Branched perennial, native in upland woods and pastures from British Columbia to Newfoundland, south to Arizona and Georgia; **stems** forked; **leaves** opposite, ovate to oblong-lanceolate, to 10 cm. long, drooping or spreading, petioled; **flowers** pink, campanulate, to 1 cm. long, in terminal or axillary cymes, from June to August; **follicles** to 15 cm. long, mostly erect.
USE AND CULTURE: Used in wild flower gardens. Easy to grow in partial shade in soils that are high in organic matter. Propagation is by seeds or by division in early spring.

Aquilegia L. (Columbine)
RANUNCULACEAE (Buttercup Family)
DESCRIPTION: About 70 species of erect, branched perennials, native in the North Temperate Zone; **leaves** 2- to 3- ternate; **flowers** white, yellow, blue, red, or lavender, showy, pendent or erect, terminating branches; sepals 5, petallike, regular; petals 5, with a short, broad lip and usually with a long, hollow backward projecting spur; stamens many, the inner ones replaced by staminodes; pistils usually 5; **fruit** a many-seeded follicle.

Aquilegia canadensis L. (Wild Columbine, Honeysuckle, Meeting-houses, Rock-bells). Hardy in all zones; perennial to 60 cm. tall.
DESCRIPTION: A branched perennial, native in rocky terrain at the edges of woods and along roadsides from Manitoba to Nova Scotia, south to Texas and Florida; basal **leaves** 2-ternate; **flowers** nodding, glandular-pubescent, red, in May and June; sepals red, divergent, ovate, about 1.25 cm. long; limb of petals yellow, to 8 mm. long; spurs red, straight, to 2.5 cm. long.
USE AND CULTURE: This is one of our choice native wild flowers. They are planted in wild flower gardens in any well-drained soil that is neutral to slightly acid. They will grow in full sun or part shade. Start with young plants grown from seed planted as soon as ripe. Once established, volunteer seedlings will usually be sufficient to maintain a stand. Individual plants are short-lived.

Aralia L. (Aralia)
ARALIACEAE (Ginseng Family)
DESCRIPTION: Over 30 species of perennial herbs, shrubs, and trees, often with spiny stems, native in rich soils, mostly in shady woods in North America, Asia, and the Malay Peninsula; **leaves** alternate, pinnate to 3-pinnate; **flowers** small, white or green in umbels often arranged in panicles; petals 5, more or less imbricate; stamens 5; ovary 2- to 5-celled with 2 to 5 separate styles; **fruit** a small drupe.

Aquilegia canadensis (Wild Columbine).

Photograph: Merv Eisel.

Aralia hispida (Bristly Sarsaparilla).

Aralia hispida Venten. (Bristly Sarsaparilla). Hardy in all zones; perennial to 90 cm. tall.

DESCRIPTION: Bristly perennial, native in dry, sandy woods from Minnesota to Newfoundland, south to North Carolina; **leaves** few, 2-pinnate; leaflets mostly 10 cm. long, oblong to lanceolate; **flowers** white about 2 mm. across, in loose umbels, in June and July; **fruit** purple-black, to 8 mm. across.

USE AND CULTURE: Used in shady wild flower gardens in well-drained soils. Propagation is by seeds which have dormant embryos and impermeable seed coats. Mechanical or chemical scarification may be required.

Aralia nudicaulis L. (Wild Sarsaparilla). Hardy in all zones; perennial to 50 cm. tall.

DESCRIPTION: Rhizomatous perennial, native in dry deciduous woods from Washington to Newfoundland, south to Colorado and Georgia; **stems** usually solitary, emerging from underground rhizomes, with 3 leaves; **leaves** 2- to 3-pinnate; leaflets 3 to 5 on each branch, elliptic to lanceolate, to 15 cm. long, finely serrate; **flowers** yellow, in 2 to 7 umbels terminal on scape, in May and June; **drupe** black, showy.

USE AND CULTURE: Used as a ground cover in wild flower gardens under shade conditions. Roots are used for medicinal purposes. Plants prefer a slightly acid soil. Propagation is by division of the rhizomes in spring or fall, in addition to seeds.

Aralia racemosa L. (American Spikenard, Life-of-man, Petty Morel, Spikenard). Hardy in all zones; perennial to 1 m. tall.

DESCRIPTION: Thornless perennial, native in woods and thickets rich in organic matter from Utah to New Brunswick, south to Arizona and North Carolina; **leaves** few, 2- to 3-pinnate, to 75 cm. long; leaflets ovate, to 20 cm. long, sharply serrate; **flowers** greenish-white, in small umbels clustered in dense axillary or terminal racemes or panicles; with 10 to 25 flowers in each umbel, in June and July; **drupes** red, brown, or purple in September.

USE AND CULTURE: Plant in wild flower gardens for the showy leaves and fruit. They need a neutral to slightly acid soil that is rich in organic matter which remains moist. Propagation is by division in early spring. Root segments as short as 10 to 12 cm. long will grow.

Arisaema Mart. (Jack-in-the-pulpit)
ARACEAE (Arum Family)

DESCRIPTION: About 190 species of stemless, tuberous perennials, native in moist, shady woods in Europe, Asia, and North America; **leaves** 1 to 3, 3-lobed, 3-parted, or deeply dissected with 5 to 19 segments; petioles long; **flowers** small, monoecious or dioecious, without a perianth, borne on an elongated spadix and enclosed by a spathe; spathe convolute below, expanded above into a narrow to very broad blade, often colored or striped with purple; **fruit** a berry.

Arisaema dracontium (L.) Schott. (Dragonroot, Green-dragon). Hardy in all zones; perennial to 1 m. tall.

DESCRIPTION: Perennial, native in moist woods from Minnesota to Quebec, south to Texas and Florida; **tubers** oblong; **leaves** solitary, pedate, with 7 to 19 segments, each oblong to elliptic, to 25 cm. long, on petioles to 1 m. long; **flowers** small, on an elongated spadix ending in a slender, erect appendage to 15 cm. long; spathe to 7.5 cm. long, green, with an erect hood; **berries** orange-red.

USE AND CULTURE: It is often used in moist, shaded wild flower gardens in slightly acid soils with a pH of at least 6.5. Propagation is by division of the tubers or by seeds planted as soon as ripe. Tubers should be planted about 12 cm. deep. It usually takes 3 years for seedlings to reach blooming size.

Arisaema triphyllum (L.) Torr. (Indian Turnip, Jack-in-the-pulpit). Hardy in all zones; perennial to 60 cm. tall.

DESCRIPTION: Perennial, native in moist woods and swamps from Manitoba to New Brunswick, south to Kansas and Florida; **tubers** subglobose; **leaves** mostly 2- to 3-lobed, each lobe elliptic, to 22 cm. long, on petioles to 60 cm. long; **flowers** small,

Arisaema triphyllum (Jack-in-the-pulpit). In flower in May 1961.

on a cylindrical spadix that ends in an appendage that is slightly exserted beyond the tube of the enclosing spathe; spathe to 18 cm. long, green to purple, variously striped with purple and green or white, with a hood that arches over the spadix.

USE AND CULTURE: Plant in a woodland wild flower garden. It is often planted for its curious bloom and handsome foliage. Native Americans used the tubers for food. The tubers must be cooked to remove the acrid, puckering taste. A pH of 5.5 is considered ideal but it can be grown on nearly neutral soil. Propagation is the same as for **Arisaema dracontium**.

Arnica L. (Arnica)
COMPOSITAE (Sunflower Family)
Senecio Tribe

DESCRIPTION: About 30 species of perennial herbs, native in Europe, Asia, and North America; **leaves** opposite; **flower** heads usually solitary on long peduncles, yellow, radiate or discoid; involucral bracts herbaceous, in 2 rows; **fruit** a slender, cylindrical achene; pappus of minutely barbed or plumose bristles.

Arnica cordifolia Hook. (Heartleaf Arnica). Hardy in all zones; perennial to 45 cm. tall.

DESCRIPTION: Rhizomatous perennial, native in dry woods from the Yukon to Michigan, south to California and New Mexico; **leaves** broad-lanceolate to ovate, cordate, mostly coarsely dentate to 7 cm. long, long-petioled; **flower** heads yellow, mostly solitary, radiate, to 7 cm. across, from April to August; ray flowers pistillate, yellow; anthers yellow; **achenes** pubescent; pappus white.

USE AND CULTURE: Planted in wild flower gardens in any fertile soil. Propagation is by division in early spring or by seeds.

Artemisia L. (Wormwood, Mugwort, Sagebrush)
COMPOSITAE (Sunflower Family)
Anthemis Tribe

DESCRIPTION: About 200 species of aromatic herbs and shrubs, native in dry soils mostly in the northern hemisphere; **leaves** alternate, entire to lobed and dissected; **flower** heads small, in spikes, racemes, or panicles, radiate or discoid; involucre cylindrical to globose; involucral bracts imbricate in several rows, dry, at least the inner ones with scarious margins; receptacle flat or hemispherical, naked or with long hairs; disc **flowers** white, yellow, brown, or purple; ray flowers pistillate when present; **fruit** an achene that is ellipsoid, ovoid, or prismatic, 2- to 5-angled or ribbed; pappus absent or a short crown.

Artemisia ludoviciana Nutt. (Western Mugwort, White Sage, Cudweed). Hardy in all zones; perennial to 1 m. tall.

DESCRIPTION: Rhizomatous, aromatic perennial herb, native in dry soils from Washington to Michigan, south to Texas and Arkansas; **leaves** lanceolate to elliptic-lanceolate, to 10 cm. long, entire or lobed, white-tomentose beneath, becoming glabrous above; **flower** heads small, to 3 mm. across, in dense panicles, in August and September.

USE AND CULTURE: Used in flower borders for the silvery foliage and also planted in prairie plantings. 'Silver King' and 'Silver Queen' are cultivars that have been selected for their silvery foliage. They are easy to grow in any well-drained soil. Propagation is by division or seeds planted as soon as ripe. A winter mulch will improve seed germination.

Aruncus Adans. (Goatsbeard)
ROSACEAE (Rose Family)

DESCRIPTION: A small genus of tall, dioecious, perennial herbs, native in shady woods in the northern hemisphere; **leaves** 2- to 3-pinnate, long-petioled; **flowers** small, white, dioecious, in spikes forming large panicles; sepals and petals 5; stamens many; pistils mostly 3; **fruit** a follicle.

Aruncus dioicus (Walt.) Fern. (Goatsbeard). Hardy in zone 4; perennial to 2 m. tall.

Aruncus dioicus (Goatsbeard). In flower at

the Minnesota Landscape Arboretum.

Photograph: Dr. Anne M. Hanchek.

DESCRIPTION: A mostly glabrous perennial, native in woods from Iowa to Pennsylvania, south to Oklahoma and Georgia; **leaves** large, much divided; leaflets ovate to oblong-lanceolate; **flowers** small, in panicles to 40 cm., from May to July.

USE AND CULTURE: Plant in wild flower gardens for bold effects. Plant in shade in a soil that is high in organic matter. Propagation is by seed sown as soon as ripe or in the spring.

Asarum L. (Asarabacca, Wild Ginger)
ARISTOLOCHIACEAE (Birthwort Family)

DESCRIPTION: About 75 species of rhizomatous, perennial herbs, native in moist woods in the North Temperate Zone; **leaves** simple, mostly cordate, long-petioled; **flowers** purple or brown, borne singly near the ground and covered by the leaves; calyx corollalike, campanulate, 3-parted; corolla vestigial or none; stamens 10; **fruit** a fleshy, globose capsule.

Asarum canadense L. (Snakeroot, Wild Ginger). Hardy in all zones; perennial to 15 cm. tall.

DESCRIPTION: A low spreading perennial, native in dense, moist woods from Manitoba to New Brunswick, south to Kansas and North Carolina; **leaves** 2, light green and cordate, to 18 cm. across, pubescent, long-petioled; **flowers** brownish-purple, to 2.5 cm. across, hidden by the leaves.

USE AND CULTURE: Plant as a ground cover in shady wild flower gardens or in a shaded rock garden. Rhizomes have an aromatic odor; when cooked with sugar, they make a fair substitute for true ginger. They grow best in soils that are neutral to slightly acid and in those that are high in organic matter. Propagation is usually by division in early spring or fall. Plant the rhizomes about 2 cm. deep. Cuttings, taken in July, root easily. Plants can also be grown from seeds sown as soon as ripe.

Asclepias L. (Butterfly Flower, Milkweed, Silkweed)
ASCLEPIADACEAE (Milkweed Family)

DESCRIPTION: About 200 species of perennial herbs with milky sap, native mostly in North America and Africa; **leaves** opposite or whorled, rarely alternate; **flowers** white, yellow, red, or purple, in terminal or axillary umbellate cymes; corolla rotate, with 5 reflexed lobes; corona present with 5 hoodlike lobes, each with or without a horn; **fruit** a pair of erect follicles; **seed** with a tuft of silky hairs.

Asclepias incarnata L. (Swamp Milkweed). Hardy in all zones; perennial to 1 m. tall.

DESCRIPTION: Upright perennial, native in wet meadows, along streams and lake shores, and in marshes, from Wyoming to Nova Scotia, south to Oklahoma and Florida; **leaves** opposite, linear to ovate-elliptic, to 15 cm. long; **flowers** pink to wine-colored, rarely white, in paired, axillary cymes, in July and August; corolla with short lobes and stalked hoods, each with a curved horn; **follicles** erect, fusiform, to 8 cm. long.

USE AND CULTURE: An excellent plant for the flower border or near a pool. The plants also attract butterflies and the flowers last well in flower arrangements. Although this plant grows in wet soils, it does surprisingly well in ordinary garden soils if kept moist. It prefers a slightly acid soil. Propagation is by division of old crowns in spring or by seeds sown as soon as ripe.

Asarum canadense (Wild Ginger).

Photograph: Merv Eisel.

Asclepias tuberosa L. (Butterfly Flower, Butterfly Weed, Chigger Flower, Indian Paintbrush, Pleurisy Root, Tuberroot). Hardy in all zones; perennial to 60 cm. tall.
DESCRIPTION: Bushy perennial, native on sandy, well-drained soils in full sun from North Dakota to New England, south to Arizona and Florida; **roots** woody and tuberous; **leaves** spiral and crowded, narrowly lanceolate to oblanceolate, to 12 cm. long; **flowers** orange, red, or yellow, in axillary cymes, in July and August; corolla lobes to 8 mm. long; hoods cucullate, stalked; **follicles** narrowly fusiform, to 15 cm. long.
USE AND CULTURE: Plant in flower borders or in prairie plantings. They require a sandy, well-drained soil that is neutral to slightly acid, and consequently they are short-lived on heavy or poorly-drained soils. They grow best in full sun but will withstand partial shade. Propagation is by root cuttings taken in May and planted vertically in sand. Old plants can be divided in the fall with the roots planted so the buds are 5 cm. deep. Seeds can be planted in May. Mulch the seedlings the first winter. The flowers attract butterflies, and the dried roots also have medicinal value. The dried pods are prized by flower arrangers.

Aster L. (Aster, Frost Flower, Michaelmas Daisy, Starwort).
COMPOSITAE (Sunflower Family)
Aster Tribe
DESCRIPTION: A large genus of mostly perennial herbs, native in North and South America, Europe, Asia, and Africa; plants rhizomatous or fibrous-rooted; **leaves** alternate, simple, entire or dentate; **flower** heads radiate, usually in racemes, corymbs, or panicles; involucres campanulate, hemispherical, or turbinate; involucral bracts in many rows, herbaceous or scarious; receptacles flat, pitted, naked; ray flowers in 1 row, purple, blue, violet, pink, or white; disc flowers, perfect, yellow; **fruit** a compressed, non-ribbed achene; pappus of persistent capillary bristles.

Aster novae-angliae L. (New England Aster). Hardy in all zones; perennial to 1.2 m. tall.
DESCRIPTION: Perennials with a woody root crown or thick rhizomes, native in open meadows and along roadsides from Wyoming to Vermont, south to New Mexico and Alabama; **stems** clustered, much branched glandular and hairy; **leaves** lanceolate, auricled or clasping at base, to 12 cm. long, entire, scabrous; **flower** heads to 5 cm. across, in corymbose clusters, from August to October; ray flowers usually a deep violet-purple to rosy-lilac.
USE AND CULTURE: Plant in flower borders or in prairie plantings. They grow best in full sun in moist, neutral to slightly acid soils. They also like cool roots, so mulch the plants if grown in sunny flower borders. Propagation is mostly by division, either in the fall or early in the spring. Plant only those divisions that have fine, fibrous roots. Divide the plants every 3 years. Seeds are slow to germinate but the plants self sow under prairie conditions.

Aster novi-belgii L. (New York Aster). Hardy in all zones; perennial to 1.3 m. tall.
DESCRIPTION: Rhizomatous perennial, native in rich, moist woods from Newfoundland south to Georgia; **stems** clustered, glabrous or with lines of hairs; **leaves** sessile or auriculate and clasping, linear-lanceolate to lanceolate or elliptic, entire to serrate, to 16 cm. long; **flower** heads to 2.5 cm. across, in paniculate clusters; ray flowers blue or violet.
USE AND CULTURE: Same as for **Aster novae-angliae**. This species is one of the parents of most of our garden hybrids.

Astragalus L. (Milk Vetch)
LEGUMINOSAE (Pea Family)
DESCRIPTION: About 1000 species of perennial herbs, native in temperate regions of the northern hemisphere; **leaves** alternate, odd-pinnate; leaflets entire; stipules

prominent; **flowers** pealike, purple, white, or yellow, 5-merous; stamens 10, 9 united, 1 separate; **fruit** a 1- to 2-celled, leathery, fleshy, or papery legume.

Astragalus alpinus L. (Alpine Milk Vetch). Hardy in all zones; perennial to 35 cm. tall.
DESCRIPTION: Decumbent perennial, native at high elevations in Europe, Asia, and North America, from Canada south to Wisconsin; **leaflets** in 6 to 11 pairs, to 1.25 cm. long; **flowers** blue to violet, in short racemes, in May; **legumes** 1-celled, black, pubescent.
USE AND CULTURE: Plant in rock gardens. Propagation is by seeds sown in early spring in well-drained soil.

Astragalus crassicarpus Nutt. (Ground Plum). Hardy in all zones; perennial to 30 cm. long.
DESCRIPTION: Decumbent perennial, native in open prairies from the Rocky Mountains east to Minnesota; **leaflets** to 1.25 cm.; **flowers** pealike, violet-purple, in short racemes, in April and May; **legumes**, globose inflated, to 2 cm. across.
USE AND CULTURE: Plant in rock gardens or in prairie plantings. Plant seeds where plants are to grow in early spring. Mature plants are difficult to transplant.

Baptisia Venten. (False Indigo, Wild Indigo)
LEGUMINOSAE (Pea Family)
DESCRIPTION: About 30 species of perennial herbs, native in dry soils in North America; **leaves** alternate, mostly with 3 leaflets; **flowers** pealike, in racemes; stamens 10, separate; **fruit** a short, inflated legume.

Baptisia australis (L.) R. Br. (Blue False Indigo, Plains False Indigo, Wild Blue Indigo). Hardy in all zones; perennial to 1 m. tall.
DESCRIPTION: Many-stemmed perennial, native in gravelly soils in open woods and in prairies from Pennsylvania south to Tennessee to South Carolina; **leaflets** oblanceolate to ovate, to 6 cm. long; **flowers** indigo blue to 2.5 cm. long, in terminal racemes, in May and June; **legumes** inflated, black.
USE AND CULTURE: Plant in flower borders, in open areas in the wild flower garden, or in prairie plantings. They have attractive, clean foliage and when established are trouble free and long-lived. They do best in sandy loam soils or on heavier soils if well-drained. Propagation is by division of established clumps in early spring or by seeds sown as soon as ripe. It takes 3 years from seed to develop blooming-sized plants. Space plants 60 cm. apart.

Callirhoe Nutt. (Poppy Mallow)
MALVACEAE (Mallow Family)
DESCRIPTION: About 8 species of perennial herbs, native in the United States and Mexico; **roots** a woody tap root; **stems** branched; basal **leaves** few, orbicular; stem leaves smaller and deeply lobed; **flowers** showy, solitary or few in upper leaf axils; involucral bracts 3 or lacking; petals white to deep red-purple, apically truncate, mostly erose; stamens united in a tubular column; style branches filiform; **fruit** a schizocarp with 10 to 25 mericarps in a single whorl.

Baptisia australis.

Callirhoe involucrata (Torr. & A. Gray) A. Gray. (Wine Cups, Poppy Mallow, Buffalo Rose). Hardy in all zones; perennial to 60 cm. tall.
DESCRIPTION: A procumbent or trailing perennial with a tap root, native in dry, sandy soils in prairies from Wyoming to North Dakota, south to New Mexico and Arkansas; **leaves** orbicular, deeply 5- to 7-palmately parted, the divisions oblanceolate to obovate, lobed or incised; stipules to 2.5 cm. long; **flowers** solitary, erect on elongated pedicels, deep red or paler, to 6 cm. across, from June to August; involucral bracts 3, mostly linear-lanceolate; borne at the base of the calyx; **mericarps** round and flat.
USE AND CULTURE: Plant in rock gardens or flower borders. Plants grow best in slightly acid, sandy loam soil in full sun. To prolong the bloom, remove the faded flowers. Propagation is by seed sown as soon as ripe or in early spring. A winter mulch is needed to protect the plants over winter.

Callirhoe triangulata (Leavenw.) A. Gray. (Clustered Poppy Mallow). Hardy in all zones; perennial to 60 cm. tall.
DESCRIPTION: Stellate-pubescent perennial with a tap root, native in sandy prairies and dry woods from Wisconsin to Indiana, south to Texas and Georgia; **stems** erect, branched; basal **leaves** triangular, acute, truncate or sagittate at base, crenate; stem leaves narrower, sometimes cleft; **flowers** crowded at the ends of axillary peduncles, deep purple, about 5 cm. across, from June to August; involucral bracts spatulate or obovate, just below the calyx.
USE AND CULTURE: Same as for **Callirhoe involucrata**.

Baptisia australis.

Calochortus Pursh. (Butterfly Tulip, Globe Tulip
Mariposa, Mariposa Lily, Sego Lily, Star Tulip)
LILIACEAE (Lily Family)
DESCRIPTION: About 60 species of bulbous, perennial herbs, native in well-drained soils in western North America from South Dakota westward; **bulbs** tunicate with membranous coat, sometimes fibrous-reticulate; **stems** leafy or scapose; **flowers** white, yellow, orange, red, lavender, or purple, erect or nodding, solitary or in clusters; sepals 3; petals 3, often bearded, with a basal, flattened gland; stamens 6 with basifixed anthers; **fruit** a 3-winged or a 3-angled capsule.

Calochortus gunnisonii S. Wats. (Rocky Mountain Mariposa). Hardy in all zones; perennial to 45 cm. tall.
DESCRIPTION: Perennial, native in prairies from Montana to South Dakota, south to Arizona and New Mexico; **stems** erect, unbranched; **leaves** linear; **flowers** campanulate, erect, to 4 cm. long, white to purple, bearded with glandular, branched hairs, often purple-banded, in June and July; **capsules** linear-oblong, 3-angled, erect.
USE AND CULTURE: Plant in rock gardens or prairie plantings. Plant bulbs 10 cm. deep on a bed of gravel 5 cm. deep in the fall. Good drainage is essential to longevity. Mulch over winter. Propagation is by seeds or by division of bulbs.

Calochortus nuttallii Torr. (Mariposa Tulip, Sego Lily). Hardy in all zones; perennial to 45 cm. tall.
DESCRIPTION: Erect perennials, native in prairies from Montana to North Dakota, south to Arizona and New Mexico; **stems** unbranched; **leaves** linear, reduced in size on the stems; **flowers** campanulate, erect; petals to 4 cm. long, white, tinged with lilac, yellow at base, marked with a reddish-brown or purple spot above the glands; **capsule** lanceolate-linear, 3-angled, to 5 cm. long.
USE AND CULTURE: Same as for **Callachortus gunnisonii**.

Camassia Lindl. (Camas, Camass, Quamash)
LILIACEAE (Lily Family)
DESCRIPTION: 5 species of perennial, scapose, bulbous herbs, native on loamy soils in North America; **bulbs** tunicate with brown or black coats; **leaves** basal, linear; **flowers** white, blue, or blue-violet, in terminal racemes; perianth segments 6, separate; stamens 6, with versatile anthers; **fruit** a 3-valved capsule.

Camassia esculenta - see **Camassia quamash**.

Camassia quamash (Pursh) Greene. (Camosh, Common Camass, Quamash, Wild Hyacinth). Hardy in all zones; perennial to 75 cm. tall.
DESCRIPTION: Bulbous, perennial herbs, native in open meadows from British Columbia to Alberta, south to Oregon and Montana; **leaves** linear, to 45 cm. long, glaucous above; **flowers** irregular, white, pale blue, or blue-violet, in June; perianth segments not twisted together after pollination; **fruit** a 3-valved capsule.
USE AND CULTURE: This western species is sometimes planted in flower borders and rock gardens. Plant bulbs in the fall about 10 cm. deep and 15 cm. apart in a fertile, loamy, well-drained soil in full sun. Propagation is by seeds sown as soon as ripe and by division of the bulbs. Native Americans used the bulbs as a staple food.

Camassia scilloides (Raf.) V.L. Cory. (Eastern Camass, Indigo Squill, Meadow Hyacinth, Wild Hyacinth). Hardy in all zones; perennial to 45 cm. tall.
DESCRIPTION: Bulbous perennial, native in damp meadows, prairies, and open woodlands from Minnesota to Pennsylvania, south to Texas and Georgia; **leaves** linear, to 60 cm.; **flowers** regular, white, blue, or blue-violet, to 1.6 cm. long, in May; perianth segments not twisted together after pollination; anthers bright yellow; **capsules** sub-globose.
USE AND CULTURE: Plant in wild flower gardens in light shade or in the flower border. Plant in a fertile, loamy soil that is neutral to slightly acid. Plant bulbs in the fall 10 cm. deep and 15 cm. apart. Seed can be sown as soon as ripe. It takes several years for bulbs to reach a flowering size.

Campanula L. (Bellflower)
CAMPANULACEAE (Bellflower Family)
DESCRIPTION: About 300 species of annual, biennial, or perennial herbs, native throughout the northern hemisphere but chiefly in Europe and North Africa; **leaves** alternate; basal leaves with longer petioles; **flowers** campanulate or rotate, white, pink, or violet-blue, in racemes, spikes, or panicles, rarely solitary; calyx tube regular, fused to the ovary, with 5 needle-shaped or triangular lobes; corolla campanulate to rotate, 5-lobed; stamens 5, with flattened filaments attached to the corolla tube; ovary 3- to 5-celled, with many ovules; style elongate with a 3- to 5-lobed stigma; **fruit** a capsule dehiscing by basal or lateral pores or slits.

Campanula americana L. (Tall Bellflower). Hardy in all zones; annual to 2 m. tall.
DESCRIPTION: An erect annual, native in woods and thickets in moist, shady places from Ontario to New York, south to Missouri and Florida; stem **leaves** lanceolate to ovate-elliptic, to 15 cm. long, narrowed at both ends, serrate; **flowers** blue or white, produced in leaf axils to form a long, terminal spike from June to September; calyx lobes linear, to 1 cm. long; corolla rotate, to 2.5 cm. across; style 3-lobed.
USE AND CULTURE: Plant in shaded flower borders as a background plant. Propagation is by seeds started indoors and transplanted to the flower border in late May. The soil should be kept moist.

Campanula rotundifolia (Bluebell).

Campanula americana (Tall Bellflower).

Campanula petiolata - see **Campanula rotundifolia**.

Campanula rotundifolia L. (Bluebell, Common Harebell, Harebell). Hardy in all zones; perennial to 50 cm. tall.
DESCRIPTION: A much-branched perennial with a basal rosette of leaves, native on rocky ledges, meadows, and woods, often in sandy or rocky soils, circumboreal, from Canada south to Nebraska and Indiana in North America; basal **leaves** with long petioles, ovate to orbicular, to 2.5 cm. across; entire or toothed; stem leaves sessile, linear to lanceolate-ovate; **flowers** campanulate, deep lavender-blue, rarely white, in erect terminal racemes or solitary, nodding to ascending, from July to September; calyx with short lobes and no appendages; corolla campanulate, about 2.5 cm. long.
USE AND CULTURE: Plant in rock gardens. Plants prefer a well-drained, sandy soil. Mulching to control weeds and to keep the soil moist improves growth. Propagation is by division in early spring. Plant so basal leaves are at soil level. Plants can also be grown from seeds planted as soon as ripe.

Cassia L. (Senna)
LEGUMINOSAE (Pea Family)

DESCRIPTION: Over 500 species of trees, shrubs, and annual and perennial herbs, native mostly in tropical and subtropical regions; **leaves** opposite, even-pinnate; **flowers** showy, mostly yellow, nearly regular, 5-merous, in racemes, corymbs, or panicles, rarely solitary; stamens mostly 10, with 7 fertile and 3 abortive anthers; **fruit** a cylindrical legume, sometimes winged.

Cassia fasciculata Michx. (Bee Flower, Golden Cassia, Partridge Pea, Prairie Senna). Annual to 60 cm. tall.
DESCRIPTION: Annual, native in sandy, open areas from South Dakota to Maine, south to Mexico and Florida; **leaflets** in 12 to 44 pairs, sensitive to touch, linear-oblong, to 1.5 cm. long; **flowers** yellow, clustered in leaf axils, to 2 cm. long, from July to September; stamens with fertile anthers 10; **fruit** flat, linear, to 4 cm. long.
USE AND CULTURE: Plant in flower borders or in prairie plantings. Start seeds indoors in March. Transplant to the garden in late May. Plants must have a well-drained soil, preferably a sandy loam. A member of the pea family, it does have nitrogen-fixing properties that help build soils.

Cassia marilandica L. (Wild Senna). Hardy in all zones; perennial to 120 cm. tall.
DESCRIPTION: Coarse, glabrous perennial, native in low ground and in moist, open woods from Kansas to Pennsylvania, south to Texas and Florida; **leaflets** numerous, oblong-lanceolate; **flowers** golden-yellow in loose racemes, in July and August; anthers dark brown; **legumes** flat, thick, to 8 cm. long.
USE AND CULTURE: A coarse perennial best used in a wild flower garden or at the edges of woods. The plants prefer a moist, sandy loam soil that is slightly acid. Propagation is by division in early spring or by seeds sown as soon as ripe. It takes 3 years for seedlings to reach blooming size.

Castilleja Mutis ex L.f. (Paintbrush, Painted-cup)
SCROPHULARIACEAE (Figwort Family)

DESCRIPTION: About 200 species of perennial herbs that are partially parasitic on the roots of other plants in North and South America; **leaves** alternate; **flowers** mostly green, in yellow-, purple-, or red-bracted spikelike racemes; calyx 4-lobed; corolla 2-lipped, upper lip helmet-shaped; stamens 4; **fruit** a capsule.

Castilleja coccinea (Indian Paintbrush).

Photograph: Mr. Arvid Lund.

Castilleja coccinea (Indian Paintbrush).

Caulophyllum thalictroides (Blue Cohosh). Flower.

Photograph: Dr. Anne M. Hanchek.

Caulophyllum thalictroides (Blue Cohosh). Fruit.

Photograph: Mr. Arvid Lund.

Castilleja coccinea (L.) K. Spreng. (Indian Paintbrush, Scarlet Paintbrush). Hardy in all zones; annual to 60 cm. tall.
DESCRIPTION: Hairy annual or biennial, native in moist soil, in moist roadside ditches, along banks where grasses are sparse, and along woodland trails where shade is high and sparse from Manitoba to New Hampshire, south to Oklahoma and Florida; basal **leaves** obovate or oblong, to 7.5 cm. long, mostly entire; stem leaves 3- to 5-lobed; **flowers** pale yellow, about 2.5 cm. long, in June and July; floral bracts scarlet.
USE AND CULTURE: Seldom planted due to parasitic relationship with other plants. This is a rare wild flower and should not be picked. Enjoy it in its natural habitat. Plants can be grown from seed planted as soon as ripe. Success has been reported where oats are planted in the spring and cut back to 15 cm. Plant seeds in the stubble.

Castilleja septentrionalis Lindl. (Northern Painted-cup). Hardy in all zones; perennial to 45 cm. tall.
DESCRIPTION: Perennial herb, native in damp, rocky soil from British Columbia to Newfoundland, south to New Mexico and Maine; **leaves** linear to lanceolate, entire; **floral** bracts pale yellow, rarely white or purple; corolla to 2.5 cm. long.
USE AND CULTURE: Same as for **Castilleja coccinea**.

Castilleja sulphurea - see **Castilleja septentrionalis**.

Caulophyllum Michx. (Blue Cohosh)
BERBERIDACEAE (Barberry Family)
DESCRIPTION: Two species of erect, rhizomatous perennial herbs, native in moist woods in North America and eastern Asia; **leaves** ternately compound; **flowers** small, in clusters, appearing with the unfolding leaves; sepals 6; petals 6; stamens 6; ovary ruptures early, exposing two drupelike seeds.

Caulophyllum thalictroides (L.) Michx. (Blue Cohosh, Papooseroot). Hardy in all zones; perennial to 1 m. tall.
DESCRIPTION: Branched perennial, native in rich, rocky woods and well-drained river bottoms from southern Canada south to Missouri and South Carolina; **leaves** blue-green; **flowers** yellowish-green often with a reddish tinge, about 1 cm. across, in May; **seeds** with a blue, fleshy seed coat, in August.
USE AND CULTURE: Plant in woodland wild flower gardens. Grown for its blue seeds and handsome foliage. Plants prefer a neutral to slightly acid soil and shade. This is a good companion plant for Virginia bluebells since the foliage fills in as the bluebell foliage turns yellow and dies. Propagation is by division in the fall and by seeds sown as soon as ripe. It takes 3 years for seedlings to reach flowering size.

Chelone L. (Snakehead, Turtlehead)
SCROPHULARIACEAE (Figwort Family)
DESCRIPTION: About 5 species of perennial herbs, native in moist soil and partial shade, in North America; **leaves** opposite, serrate; **flowers** white or purple, in spikelike racemes; sepals 5, overlapping; corolla 2-lipped, lower lip bearded inside; fertile stamens 4, woolly; staminode 1, shorter; **fruit** a many-seeded winged capsule.

Chelone glabra L. (White Turtlehead, Snakehead, Balmony). Hardy in all zones; perennial to 60 cm. tall.

DESCRIPTION: Perennial, native in moist soil, along streams, and in moist woods from Minnesota to Newfoundland, south to Missouri and Georgia; **leaves** lanceolate to ovate, to 15 cm. long, subsessile or with a short, winged petiole; **flowers** white or pink, to 2.5 cm. long, from July to September; lower lip of corolla white-bearded; staminode white or green, resembling a turtle's head with an open mouth.

USE AND CULTURE: Plant in wild flower gardens. Plants grow best in moist, slightly acid soil. They tolerate light shade but bloom best in full sun. A good companion plant for **Lobelia cardinalis**. Plants pinched back in June will be bushier and bloom later. Propagation is by division in spring or fall. Plant with rhizomes spread horizontally and barely covered. Stem cuttings taken in July root easily.

Chelone obliqua L. (Red Turtlehead). Hardy in all zones; perennial to 120 cm. tall.

DESCRIPTION: Perennial, native in moist places from Minnesota to Maryland, south to Mississippi and Florida; **leaves** lanceolate to lanceolate-elliptic, short-petioled; **flowers** rose-purple, to 2.5 cm. long, from August to October; lower lip pale, yellow-bearded; staminode white.

USE AND CULTURE: Same as for **Chelone glabra**.

Chimaphila Pursh. (Wintergreen, Pipsissewa, Prince's Pine, Waxflower)
PYROLACEAE (Wintergreen Family)

DESCRIPTION: About 8 species of creeping, glabrous, evergreen, woodland herbs or subshrubs, native in moist, acid, coniferous woods in temperate regions of the northern hemisphere; **leaves** simple, in irregular whorls, dentate; **flowers** white to rose-pink, in few-flowered terminal corymbs, 5-merous; stamens 10, expanded at base, hairy in the middle; **fruit** a 5-celled capsule.

Chimaphila maculata (L.) Pursh. (Spotted Wintergreen, Spotted Pipsissewa). Hardy in all zones; perennial to 20 cm. tall.

DESCRIPTION: Creeping, evergreen perennial, native in moist, acid woods from Minnesota to Massachusetts, south to Alabama to Georgia; **leaves** lanceolate to lanceolate-ovate, to 5 cm. long, variegated white above along veins; **flowers** white, fragrant, to 2 cm. across.

USE AND CULTURE: Plant in woodland wild flower gardens in acid, well-drained soil. Mulching with pine needles helps to maintain moisture and acidity. Propagation is by division. Plant with the rhizomes just barely covered. Cuttings taken in July can be rooted in a sand and acid peat mixture. Plants should be rooted and ready to plant by the following spring.

Chimaphila umbellata var. **cisatlantica** S.F. Blake. (Pipsissewa, Prince's Pine). Hardy in all zones; perennial to 30 cm. tall.

DESCRIPTION: Creeping, evergreen perennial, native in acid, coniferous woods from British Columbia to Michigan, south to California and Colorado; **leaves** oblong-obovate, to 5 cm. long, broadest above the center, sharp-toothed, not variegated, prominently veined on under surface; **flowers** pinkish-white in umbels; calyx lobes broader than long.

USE AND CULTURE: Same as for **Chimaphila maculata**.

Chiogenes hispidula - see **Gaultheria hispidula**.

Chrysopsis (Nutt.) Elliott. (Golden Aster)
COMPOSITAE (Sunflower Family)
Aster Tribe

DESCRIPTION: About 30 species of annual, biennial, or perennial herbs, native in North America; stems leafy, erect to decumbent; **leaves** alternate, simple, usually entire, reduced upward; **flower** heads yellow, radiate, in corymbs; involucre campanulate to

Chelone glabra (White Turtlehead).

Photograph: Mr. Arvid Lund.

Chelone obliqua (Red Turtlehead). In flower in April 197 at the Eloise Butler Wildflower Garden in Minneapolis.

Cimicifuga americana (American Bugbane).

Chimaphila umbellata var. cisatlantica.

hemispherical; involucral bracts imbricate in several rows; receptacle naked; disc and ray flowers yellow; **achenes** obovoid, compressed; pappus double.

Chrysopsis villosa (Pursh.) Nutt. (Golden Aster). Hardy in all zones; perennial to 85 cm. tall.
DESCRIPTION: A variable tap-rooted perennial, native in sandy soils from British Columbia to Wisconsin, south to California and Indiana; **stems** erect to decumbent, often woody at base; **leaves** oblong-elliptic to linear-oblanceolate, obtuse or acute at apex, seldom dentate; **flower** heads yellow, to 4 cm. across.
USE AND CULTURE: Plant in sunny flower borders or in a prairie planting. Plants will grow and bloom in soils of low fertility. Propagation is by division in early spring or by seeds planted in July.

Cimicifuga L. (Bugbane, Rattletop)
RANUNCULACEAE (Buttercup Family)

DESCRIPTION: About 15 species of tall, upright, perennial herbs, native in rich woods in the North Temperate Zone; **leaves** large, ternately compound; **flowers** small, white, in long racemes or rarely in panicles; sepals 2 to 5, petallike, falling early; petals 1 to 8 or none, small, clawed, mostly 2-lobed; stamens many; pistils 1 to 8; **fruit** a follicle.

Cimicifuga americana Michx. (Summer Cohosh, American Bugbane, Mountain Bugbane). Hardy in all zones; perennial to 60 cm. tall.
DESCRIPTION: Upright perennial with slender stems, native in moist, rocky woods, from Pennsylvania south to Tennessee and Georgia; **leaves** 2- to 3-ternate, then pinnate with 3 to 5 leaflets; leaflets ovate, oblong, incised, acuminate, to 7 cm. long; **flowers** white, in loose and feathery, elongate inflorescences, in July and August; petals 2-horned, with a basal concave nectary; **follicles** 3 to 8, shorter than the slender stipe.
USE AND CULTURE: Plant in woodland wild flower gardens or toward the back of flower borders. Plants grow best in a neutral to slightly acid soil that is high in organic matter. They should be kept constantly moist. Propagation is by spring or fall division or by seeds sown as soon as ripe. Mulch seedlings the first winter.

Cimicifuga racemosa (L.) Nutt. (Black Cohosh, Black Snakeroot, Bugbane, Fairy Candles, Rattletop). Hardy in all zones; perennial to 1.5 m. tall.
DESCRIPTION: Tall perennial, native in moist woods or at the edges of woods from Ontario to Massachusetts, south to Missouri and Georgia; **leaves** 2- to 3-ternate, then often pinnate; leaflets cuneate to cordate at base, to 10 cm. long; **flowers** white, in erect, wandlike racemes to 90 cm. long, in July and August; petals, 1- to 2-horned; stamens many, some petallike; **follicle** 1, sessile, rattles when dry.
USE AND CULTURE: Same as for **Cimicifuga americana**. Flowering racemes often harvested in the seed stage for winter bouquets.

Claytonia L. (Spring-beauty)
PORTULACACEAE (Purslane Family)

DESCRIPTION: Between 15 and 20 species of small, succulent, glabrous perennial herbs, native in North and South America and Eurasia; basal **leaves** 1 or more; stem leaves opposite, usually a single pair; **flowers** white or rose, in terminal racemes; **fruit** a capsule.

Claytonia caroliniana Michx. (Carolina Spring-beauty). Hardy in all zones: perennial to 25 cm. tall.
DESCRIPTION: A corm-producing perennial, native in moist woods from Saskatchewan to Newfoundland, south to Tennessee and North Carolina; **stems** weak, to 30 cm. long; **leaves** broadest in the middle, to 2 cm. wide, obtuse; **flowers** pink to white, striped with pink, in 2- to 15-flowered racemes, in April and May.
CUTURE AND USE: Same as for **Claytonia virginica**.

Claytonia lanceolata Pursh. (Lanceleaf, Spring-beauty). Hardy in all zones; perennial to 15 cm. tall.
DESCRIPTION: Corm-producing perennial, native in moist woods, along streams, and on alpine slopes from Washington to New England, south to Colorado and Florida;

basal **leaves** lacking; stem leaves lanceolate or ovate, sessile; **flowers** pink or white, striped with pink, in 1- to 15-flowered racemes, in April and May; petal tips emarginate to retuse.

USE AND CULTURE: Same as for **Claytonia virginica**.

Claytonia virginica L. (Common Spring-beauty). Hardy in all zones; perennial to 30 cm. tall.

DESCRIPTION: Succulent perennial, native in moist woods in eastern North America as far west as South Dakota; **corms** globe-shaped; **stems** one to many, often reclining; basal **leaves** none to many, linear to linear-lanceolate, to 12 cm. long; **flowers** white, striped with pink in racemes, in April and May.

USE AND CULTURE: Plant in rock gardens or in masses in the wild flower garden. Plants grow best in a neutral to slightly acid soil rich in organic matter in open shade. If the soil is kept moist, plants can also be grown in full sun. Propagation is by division of the corms as soon as the plants die down after flowering or by seeds sown as soon as ripe. This is a good companion plant for oak ferns since the ferns cover the soil after the plants die down.

Clintonia Raf. (Wood Lily)
LILIACEAE (Lily Family)

DESCRIPTION: About 6 species of rhizomatous, scapose, perennial herbs, native in acid soil in moist, shady places in North America and eastern Asia; **stems** erect; **leaves** mostly basal; **flowers** white to greenish-yellow or rose-purple, mostly in terminal umbels, rarely solitary or in racemes; perianth segments 6, separate; stamens 6 with basifixed anthers; **fruit** a blue or black berry.

Clintonia borealis (Ait.) Raf. (Bluebead Lily, Corn Lily). Hardy in all zones; perennial to 45 cm. tall.

DESCRIPTION: Plants with erect flowering stems, native in eastern North America; **leaves** 2 to 5, oblong to elliptic or obovate, to 30 cm. long, glossy green, ciliolate; **flowers** greenish-yellow, nodding, to 2 cm. long, in 3- to 8-flowered umbels, on erect, leafless peduncles, in May and June; **berries** blue, rarely white, in August.

USE AND CULTURE: Plant in woodland wild flower gardens. Plants require an acid soil rich in organic matter with constantly moist conditions. Nursery grown plants can be transplanted at any time. Rhizome divisions should be planted in the fall with the rhizomes about 3 cm. deep. Plants can be grown from seed planted as soon as ripe but it takes up to 10 years for the seedlings to bloom.

Collinsonia L. (Horse Balm, Horseweed)
LABIATAE (Mint Family)

DESCRIPTION: Five species of aromatic perennial herbs, native in eastern North America; **stems** square; **leaves** opposite, ovate, large; **flowers** yellow, in verticillasters arranged in a panicle; calyx ovoid, 2-lipped; corolla elongated with inflated throat, tube with bearded ring inside, limb 2-lipped; stamens 2, exserted; **fruit** of 4 nutlets.

Collinsonia canadensis L. (Citronella, Richweed, Stoneroot). Hardy in all zones; perennial to 1.2 m. tall.

DESCRIPTION: Smooth perennial, native in rich, moist woodlands where spring foliage is protected from spring frosts, native from Ontario to Vermont, south to Arkansas and Florida; **leaves** ovate, to 2.5 cm. long, coarsely serrate, lemon-scented when crushed, long-petioled; **flowers** yellow, small, lemon-scented, in panicles to 3.5 cm. long.

USE AND CULTURE: Plant toward the back of the flower border for the fragrance of the leaves and flowers. Plants require a fertile soil kept constantly moist in either light shade or full sun. Propagation is by division of the woody rhizomes in spring. An axe or chisel may be needed to cut the rhizome. The buds on the rhizome should be set 5 cm. deep. A winter mulch is advisable. Do not remove the mulch too early in the spring as the new growth is very susceptible to spring frosts.

Coptis Salisb. (Goldthread)
RANUNCULACEAE (Buttercup Family)

Claytonia virginica (Spring-beauty).

Clintonia borealis (Bluebead Lily).

Photograph: Mr. Arvid Lund.

DESCRIPTION: About 10 species of small, perennial herbs with slender rhizomes, native in moist woods in peaty soils in the North Temperate Zone; **leaves** basal, evergreen, often ternately divided; **flowers** small, white or yellow, on scapes; sepals 5 to 7, petallike, deciduous; petals 5 to 7, fleshy, tubular at apex; stamens 15 to 25; pistils 3 to 9, on slender stalks; **fruit** a follicle.

Coptis groenlandica (Oed.) Fern. (Goldthread, Cankerroot). Hardy in all zones; trailing perennial to 15 cm. tall.
DESCRIPTION: Trailing evergreen perennial herb with erect flowering scapes, native in moist, mossy woods and acid peat bogs from Canada south to Iowa and North Carolina; **rhizomes** yellow, threadlike; **leaves** with 3 leaflets; leaflets cuneate-obovate, shining, coarsely dentate; **flowers** white, usually solitary on peduncles, 1.25 cm. across, from May to July; sepals not clawed; petals broader than long.
USE AND CULTURE: Plant under evergreens where the soil is acid and high in organic matter. A winter mulch with pine needles is advisable to prevent winter burn. Propagation is by division in spring or fall or by root cuttings taken in the spring and planted in acid peat. Seedlings can also be grown from seed planted as soon as ripe in an acid peat-sand mixture. Seedlings should bloom the second year.

Coreopsis L. (Coreopsis, Tickseed)
COMPOSITAE (Sunflower Family)
Helianthus Tribe

DESCRIPTION: Over 100 species of annual or perennial herbs, native in North and South America and Africa; **leaves** opposite or alternate, entire or variously lobed or cut; **flower** heads yellow, purple, rose, or often bicolored, mostly solitary, rarely in corymbose panicles; involucral bracts in 2 rows; **fruit** a compressed achene, usually winged; pappus of smooth or barbed awns, or short scales.

Coreopsis lanceolata L. (Lance-leaved Coreopsis). Hardy in all zones; perennial to 60 cm. tall.
DESCRIPTION: Erect perennial, native in dry, often sandy soils from Ontario south to New Mexico and Florida; **leaves** opposite, mostly simple, sometimes pinnately lobed with lobes linear to oblanceolate, petioled; **flower** heads with yellow ray flowers, to 6 cm. across, on long peduncles, from May to July.
USE AND CULTURE: Plant in sunny flower borders or naturalize in prairie plantings or along roadsides. They are short-lived but reseed readily. Plants grow best in a well-drained sandy or gravelly soil. Too rich of a soil inhibits flowering. Propagation is by division or by seeds sown as soon as ripe. Seeds need light to germinate, so sow seeds on the surface of the soil and keep moist.

Coreopsis palmata Nutt. (Tickseed). Hardy in all zones; perennial to 90 cm. tall.
DESCRIPTION: Rhizomatous perennial, native in prairies and open woods from Manitoba to Michigan, south to Texas and Arkansas; **leaves** narrow, nearly sessile, 3-lobed to near middle with linear-oblong lobes; **flower** heads in short peduncles with yellow ray flowers, to 3 cm. long; involucral bracts linear-clavate; **achenes** cuneate-oblong, black, narrowly winged.
USE AND CULTURE: Same as for **Coreopsis lanceolata**.

Coreopsis tinctoria Nutt. (Calliopsis). Annual to 120 cm. tall.
DESCRIPTION: A much-branched annual, rarely biennial, native in prairies from Saskatchewan to Minnesota, south to California and Louisiana; **leaves** opposite, 1- to 2-pinnate; leaflets linear or linear-lanceolate; **flowers** in radiate heads to 3 cm. across, arranged in corymbs, from June to September; involucral bracts of variable length with the outer bracts only one-fourth as long as the inner; disc flowers dark red or purple; ray flowers sterile, bicolored, yellow with a brown base; **achenes** slender, wingless, black, without a pappus.
USE AND CULTURE: Plant in sunny flower borders. Plants thrive in any well-drained soil in full sun. Plants are started from seed either indoors or seeded directly where plants are to bloom about May 1.

Coreopsis tinctoria (Calliopsis). In the Oslo Botanic Garden in August 1983.

Cornus canadensis (Bunchberry). In fruit in

Palmer, Minnesota in August 1968.

Cornus canadensis (Bunchberry). In flower in June 1978.

Cornus L. (Dogwood, Cornel)
CORNACEAE (Dogwood Family)
DESCRIPTION: About 45 species of mostly deciduous shrubs or small trees, native in North America, Europe, Asia, and in Africa; **leaves** usually opposite, simple, entire; **flowers** white, greenish-white, or yellow, in terminal cymes, panicles, umbels, or heads, small, 4-merous, sometimes surrounded by an involucre of showy bracts; **fruit** a 2-seeded drupe.

Cornus canadensis L. (Bunchberry, Crackerberry, Dwarf Cornel, Puddingberry). Hardy in all zones; perennial to 15 cm. tall.
DESCRIPTION: Perennial herb with woody rhizomes, native in moist, acid woods or bogs from Alberta to Greenland, south to New Mexico and West Virginia, also in Asia; **leaves** in whorls, ovate to elliptic or obovate, to 8 cm. long; **flowers** small, in dense heads, subtended by 4 large, white, petallike bracts; **drupes** clustered in heads, red.
USE AND CULTURE: Plant as a ground cover under evergreens. A good companion plant for stemless lady's slipper or bluebead lily. Plants require an acid soil high in organic matter and light shade. Dormant plants should be planted in early spring about 15 cm. apart. Potted plants can be planted at any time. Propagation is by seeds sown as soon as ripe in an acid peat-sand mixture. It takes 3 years from seed to get bloom.

Corydalis Venten. (Corydalis)
FUMARIACEAE (Fumitory Family)
DESCRIPTION: About 300 species of annual and perennial herbs, native in the North Temperate Zone and in South Africa; perennial species with rhizomes or tuber; **leaves** pinnately decompound; **flowers** irregular, in racemes; sepals 2 or lacking; petals 4, one of the outer pair with a basal spur; stamens 6, in 2 bundles; **fruit** a slender, dehiscent capsule.

Corydalis aurea (Muhlenb. ex Willd.) Willd. (Golden Corydalis). Hardy in all zones; mostly annuals to 50 cm. tall.
DESCRIPTION: Annual or biennial, prostrate-ascending herbs, native in sandy or gravelly soil in prairies or in bottom lands, widely distributed in North America; plants many-stemmed, glaucous; **leaves** 3-pinnate; **flowers** yellow, to 2 cm. long, in terminal racemes, from April to September; spur of corolla one half as long as the rest of the petal; floral bracts toothed; **capsules** spreading or pendulous, to 2.5 cm. long.
USE AND CULTURE: Plant in rock gardens or prairie plantings. Plants are easy to grow in soils of low fertility. Propagation is by seeds sown as soon as ripe. Plants frequently self sow.

Corydalis glauca - see **Corydalis sempervirens**.

Corydalis sempervirens (L.) Pers. (Pale Corydalis). Hardy in all zones; annual to 60 cm. tall.
DESCRIPTION: A much-branched, very glaucous annual or biennial herb, native in rocky woods and clearings from Alaska to Newfoundland, south to Minnesota and

Coryphantha vivipara (Nipple Cactus).

Cypripedium acaule (Moccasin Flower). Photographed

in flower in northern Wisconsin.

Photograph: Bonnie E. Harper Lore.

Georgia; **leaves** typical of the genus; **flowers** pale pink to purple with yellow tips, to 2 cm. long, in loose panicles, from May to September; spur of corolla very short, blunt; **capsules** erect, narrowly linear, to 5 cm. long.

USE AND CULTURE: Same as for **Corydalis aurea**.

Coryphantha (Engelm.) Lem. (Nipple Cactus)
CACTACEAE (Cactus Family)

DESCRIPTION: About 60 species of low, tubercled, barrel-shaped cacti, native in dry, sandy soils in Mexico and the United States; **stems** simple or cespitose, globose to oblong, with a watery sap; **tubercles** succulent, cylindrical or angled, grooved on the upper surface; **flowers** formed in grooves of young tubercles, large and showy for the size of the plant; ovary naked or rarely scaly; **fruit** globose or ovoid to oblong.

Coryphantha vivipara (Nutt.) Britt. ex Rose. (Nipple Cactus). Hardy in zone 3; perennial to 15 cm.

DESCRIPTION: Barrel-shaped cactus, native in rocky soils from Oregon to Minnesota, south to New Mexico to Texas; **stems** solitary or cespitose, depressed-globose to cylindrical; **tubercles** to 1.25 cm. long; radial spines 12 to 40, needle-shaped, to 1.5 cm. long; **flowers** pink to purple, rarely yellowish-green, to 5 cm. across.

USE AND CULTURE: Plant in a sunny rock garden in well-drained soil. Propagation is by division of offsets or by seeds.

Crotalaria L. (Rattlebox)
LEGUMINOSAE (Pea Family)

DESCRIPTION: Over 500 species of herbs and shrubs, native mostly in warm climates; **leaves** alternate, simple or compound, with 3 to 7 leaflets; **flowers** pealike, in racemes, with an orbicular or 2-auricled standard and with keel petals curved and beaked; stamens 10, with long filaments and globose anthers alternating with short stamens with narrow anthers; **fruit** an elongated, inflated, dehiscent legume.

Crotalaria sagittalis L. (Arrow Rattlebox). Hardy in all zones; annual to 40 cm. tall.

DESCRIPTION: Annual with spreading hairs, native in dry open places from Minnesota to Vermont, south to Texas and Florida; **stems** simple or branched above, **leaves** simple, lanceolate to linear, sessile or nearly so, to 8 cm. long; stipules on upper leaves; **flowers** yellow, to 8 mm. long, in 2- to 4-flowered racemes, from June to September; calyx villous; **legumes** to 3 cm. long, much inflated.

USE AND CULTURE: Plant in flower borders or in prairie plantings. Plants are easy to grow in any well-drained soil. Propagation is by seeds sown in early spring. Soak seeds in warm water before planting.

Cypripedium L. (Lady-slipper,
Lady's-slipper, Moccasin Flower)
ORCHIDACEAE (Orchid Family)

DESCRIPTION: About 50 species of terrestrial perennial herbs, native in Eurasia and North America; **leaves** broad, plicate; **flowers** solitary or in few-flowered terminal racemes, showy; lip inflated, saclike; column with 2 fertile anthers flanking a glandlike staminode; **fruit** a capsule.

Cypripedium acaule Ait. (Moccasin Flower, Nerveroot, Pink Lady's-slipper, Stemless Lady's-slipper, Two-leaved Lady's-slipper). Hardy in all zones; perennial to 20 cm. tall.

DESCRIPTION: Stemless perennial, native in acid, sandy coniferous woods or acid bogs from Alberta to Newfoundland, south to Alabama and Georgia; **leaves** 2, basal, to 20 cm. long and 7 cm. wide; **flowers** solitary, rose, rarely white, on a scape, in May and June; sepals and petals greenish-brown; lip rose-colored, veined with darker crimson; **capsules** elongated, erect.

USE AND CULTURE: Plant under pines or in acid bogs. This orchid is on the protected list and should not be moved from native stands. Plants are sold by licensed nurserymen. This orchid is difficult to grow unless you have ideal conditions. It is best to enjoy this orchid in its natural stands. If you do attempt to grow it, transplant in the fall and set the dormant rhizomes about 2 cm. deep.

Cypripedium calceolus L. (Yellow Lady's-slipper). Hardy in all zones; perennial to 50 cm. tall.

DESCRIPTION: Leafy-stemmed perennial, native on hummocks in bogs, swamps, and in deciduous woods from British Columbia to Newfoundland, south to Texas and Georgia; **leaves** alternate, ovate to elliptic-lanceolate, to 20 cm. long; **flowers** yellow, fragrant, 1 or 2 per stem, in May and June; sepals and petals long, greenish-yellow to purplish-brown; lip light to deep yellow, usually veined or spotted with purple.

USE AND CULTURE: Plant in woodland wild flower gardens among ferns. This orchid is also on the protected list. It is one of the easiest of the lady's-slippers to grow requiring partial shade and a soil high in organic matter. It helps to bring in some woods soil from where this orchid was cultivated in the nursery to supply a needed mycorrhizal fungus. Two varieties, based on flower and plant size are recognized. These are:

Cypripedium calceolus var. **parviflorum** (Salisb.) Fern. (Small Yellow Lady's-slipper, Small Yellow Moccasin Flower, Small Golden-slipper).

Cypripedium calceolus var. **pubescens** (Willd.) Correll. (Large Yellow Lady's-slipper, Large Yellow Moccasin Flower, Golden-slipper, Whippoorwill-shoe, American Valerian, Umbiroot, Nerveroot, Yellow Indian-shoe, Venus'-shoe, Noah's-ark).

Cypripedium candidum Muhlenb. ex Willd. (Small White Lady's-slipper). Hardy in all zones. Perennial to 30 cm. tall.

DESCRIPTION: Leafy perennial with many stems, native in wet pastures and meadows, usually near outcrops from North Dakota to New York, south to Missouri and Kentucky; **leaves** 3 or 4, to 13 cm. long; **flowers** solitary on leafy stems, in May and June; sepals and petals green, veined with purple-brown, lip white with purple spots inside.

USE AND CULTURE: The same as for **Cypripedium calceolus**. Plant in moist soil either in full sun or partial shade in a neutral or slightly alkaline soil.

Cypripedium reginae Walt. (Showy Lady's-slipper). Hardy in all zones; perennial to 60 cm. tall.

DESCRIPTION: A leafy, densely hairy perennial, native in mossy, evergreen swamps, bogs, and moist woodlands in slightly acid soil from Manitoba to Newfoundland, south to Missouri and Georgia; **leaves** to 20 cm. long and 10 cm. wide; **flowers** white, striped with rose or purple, solitary or in 2's or 3's, to 7.5 cm. across, in June and July; sepals and petals white; lip white, striped with rose and purple, rarely entirely white.

USE AND CULTURE: Plant only nursery-grown specimens in woodland wild flower gardens. Plant in fall with buds on rhizomes about 3 cm. deep. The soil should be high in organic matter and on the acid side. It is advisable to bring in some soil from the nursery where this lady's-slipper is growing to provide the needed mycorrhizal fungi. Do not dig plants from the wild as this orchid is on the protected list. This is the Minnesota State Flower.

Cypripedium calceolus (Yellow Lady's-slipper).

Cypripedium reginae (Showy Lady's-slipper).

Minnesota's State Flower.

Delphinium virescens (Plains Larkspur).

Flowering along a roadside near Bay City, Wisconsin.

Photograph: Bonnie E. Harper Lore.

Delphinium L. (Larkspur)
RANUNCULACEAE (Buttercup Family)

DESCRIPTION: About 300 species of annual or perennial herbs, native throughout the North Temperate Zone; **leaves** palmate, variously cut and divided; **flowers** mostly blue, in racemes; calyx showy, with 5 sepals, one of which is spurred; petals 2 or 4, much smaller, crowded in the throat of the calyx and called the "bee", the upper pair with spurs that project into the calyx spur; stamens many; pistils 2 to 5; **fruit** a follicle.

Delphinium tricorne Michx. (Dwarf Larkspur, Three-horned Larkspur). Hardy in all zones; perennial to 60 cm. tall.
DESCRIPTION: Perennial with tuberous roots, native in open woods and rocky slopes from Minnesota to Pennsylvania, south to Oklahoma and Georgia; **stems** simple, succulent; **leaves** mostly basal, pedately 5-parted, then cleft into narrow lobes; **flowers** blue or purple, often variegated with white, to 4 cm. long, in open racemes, from April to June; spur straight, ascending, to 2 cm. long.
USE AND CULTURE: Sometimes planted in wild flower gardens. Plants grow well in most soils, either in full sun or in partial shade. Propagation is by seeds sown as soon as ripe or indoors in early spring. Seeds should be stored in a refrigerator for spring sowing.

Delphinium virescens Nutt. (Plains Larkspur). Hardy in all zones; perennial to 1.5 m. tall.
DESCRIPTION: Pubescent perennial, native in prairies and open woods; from Manitoba to Wisconsin, south to Texas and Louisiana; **leaves** chiefly basal or below the center of the stem, deeply dissected into linear segments; **flowers** white with a greenish tint, rarely pale blue; spur twice as long as the limb of the calyx.
USE AND CULTURE: Same as for **Delphinium tricorne**.

Dentaria L. (Pepperroot, Toothwort)
CRUCIFERAE (Mustard Family)

DESCRIPTION: About 10 species of perennial herbs with long fleshy rhizomes, native in moist woods throughout the northern hemisphere; **leaves** often emerging directly from the rhizomes, compound or deeply cleft, with petioles; **flowers** white to rose-purple or bluish-purple in terminal corymbs or racemes; **fruit** a linear, flat, erect silique.

Dentaria diphylla Michx. (Crinkleroot, Two-leaved Toothwort). Hardy in all zones; perennial to 25 cm. tall.
DESCRIPTION: Erect perennials, native in moist woods and along streams from Minnesota to Nova Scotia, south to Alabama and Georgia; **rhizomes** slender, white, brittle and crinkled; **leaves** usually 2, opposite, with 3 ovate, toothed or shallowly lobed divisions or leaflets; **flowers** white, turning pink with age, in glabrous clusters, in April and May; sepals and petals 4.
USE AND CULTURE: Plant as a ground cover in wild flower gardens or in rock gardens. Plants prefer a moist soil high in organic matter and high filtered shade. The soil should be neutral to slightly acid. Propagation is by division in early spring or in

the fall. Plant rhizomes 2.5 cm. deep and 25 cm. apart. Plants can also be grown from seeds sown as soon as ripe. Plants often self sow.

Dentaria laciniata Muhlenb. (Cut-leaved Toothwort, Pepperroot). Hardy in all zones; perennial to 30 cm. tall.
DESCRIPTION: Perennial with jointed rhizomes, native in moist woods and along streams that overflow in the spring from Minnesota to Quebec, south to Kansas and Florida; **roots** spindle-shaped; stem **leaves** commonly 3, more or less whorled with narrow divisions, similar to leaves emerging directly from the rhizomes; **flowers** white or purple in a pubescent cluster, in April and May.
USE AND CULTURE: Same as for **Dentaria diphylla**.

Desmodium Desv. (Beggar's-ticks, Sticktight,
Tick Clover, Tick Trefoil)
LEGUMINOSAE (Pea Family)
DESCRIPTION: More than 300 species of perennial herbs, native in open woods worldwide; **leaves** with 3 leaflets; **flowers** small, pealike, mostly pink or purple, in racemes or panicles; stamens 10, united into a tube or 1 separate at base only; **fruit** a flat, jointed legume with hooked hairs and separating readily into 1-seeded segments.

Desmodium canadense (L.) DC. (Tick Trefoil). Hardy in all zones; perennial to 2 m. tall.
DESCRIPTION: Perennial, native in dry woods and fields from Alberta to Nova Scotia, south to Oklahoma and North Carolina; **leaflets** oblong to oblong-lanceolate, to 10 cm. long; **flowers** purple to 2 cm. long; **legumes** 3- to 5-jointed.
USE AND CULTURE: Plant in flower borders or in wild flower gardens. Plants are easy to grow in most soils. Propagation is by seeds sown as soon as ripe. The ripe legume segments can cling to clothing, so it is best to cut the flowering stems as soon as the flowers fade.

Dicentra Bernh. (Bleeding-heart, Dicentra)
FUMARIACEAE (Fumitory Family)
DESCRIPTION: About 20 species of perennial herbs, often with rhizomes or tubers, native in moist woods in North America and Asia; **leaves** alternate or basal, mostly ternately compound or dissected; **flowers** showy, in racemes, usually nodding, irregular; corolla laterally flattened, cordate or 2-spurred at base, closed at the apex, composed of an outer and an inner pair of petals; stamens 6, united in 2 bundles; pistil with 2- to 4-crested or horned stigma; **fruit** an oblong or linear capsule.

Dicentra canadensis (J. Goldie) Walp. (Squirrel Corn). Hardy in all zones; perennial to 30 cm. tall.
DESCRIPTION: Perennial with filiform rhizomes and many small yellow tubers, native in moist woods from Minnesota to Nova Scotia, south to Missouri and North Carolina; **leaves** all basal, finely cut, blue-green, dying down after flowering and fruiting; **flowers** greenish-white, tinged with purple, fragrant, in May; corolla cordate, with inner petals crested.
USE AND CULTURE: Grows well in combination with **Adiantum pedatum** in wild flower gardens. Plants require a neutral soil high in organic matter. Tubers are planted

Dentaria laciniata. In flower May 1978.

Dicentra canadensis (Squirrel Corn). In flower at the Arboretum in May 1983.

Dicentra cucullaria (Dutchman's-breeches).

In flower in May 1961.

in the fall about 5 cm. deep. Squirrels and chipmunks often dig up the tubers so cover newly planted area with hardware cloth. Plants often self sow.

Dicentra cucullaria (L.) Bernh. (Dutchman's-breeches). Hardy in all zones; perennial to 25 cm. tall.
DESCRIPTION: Perennial with small yellow tubers, native in moist woods from North Dakota to Quebec, south to Kansas and Georgia; **leaves** all basal with ultimate segments linear, dark green and fernlike; **flowers** nodding, in simple racemes, white, tipped with creamy-yellow, in May; corolla with prolonged, divergent spurs.
USE AND CULTURE: Same as for **Dicentra canadensis**.

Dicentra eximia (Ker-Gawl.) Torr. (Fern-leaved Bleeding-heart, Staggerweed, Turkey Corn, Wild Bleeding-heart). Hardy in all zones; perennial to 40 cm. tall.
DESCRIPTION: Perennial with short, fleshy rhizomes, native in dry or moist woods from New York south to Tennessee and Georgia; **leaves** all basal, much divided; **flowers** pink to purple, nodding, in panicles, from May to frost.
USE AND CULTURE: Plant in rock gardens and in wild flower gardens. This eastern species is widely planted and easy to grow in most soils. Propagation is by division or by seeds sown as soon as ripe. Once established, volunteer seedlings will keep appearing year after year. The everblooming habit and the fernlike foliage make this a valuable addition to any wild flower garden.

Dicentra eximia (Fern-leaved Bleeding-heart).

In flower in May 1978.

Disporum Salisb. ex D. Don. (Fairy-bells, Mandarin)
LILIACEAE (Lily Family)
DESCRIPTION: About 15 species of rhizomatous, perennial herbs, native in woods in North America and Asia; **stems** branched, leafy; **leaves** alternate, sessile or clasping; **flowers** white or greenish-yellow, usually nodding, solitary or in few-flowered umbels; perianth segments 6; stamens 6; **fruit** a berry.

Disporum lanuginosum (Michx.) Nichols. (Yellow Mandarin). Hardy in all zones; perennial to 75 cm. tall.
DESCRIPTION: Branched perennial, native in moist woods from Ontario to New York, south to Alabama and Georgia, chiefly in the mountains; **stems** forked above; **leaves** ovate to lanceolate-ovate, to 12 cm. long, hairy beneath; **flowers** yellowish-green, 6 mm. long, in May and June; stigma 3-lobed; **berries** red, glabrous.
USE AND CULTURE: Plant in woodland wild flower gardens. Plants grow well in any soil that is high in organic matter and shaded. Propagation is by spring division and by seeds sown as soon as ripe. The seeds may be slow to germinate.

Disporum maculatum (Buckl.) Britt. (Nodding Mandarin). Hardy in all zones; perennial to 60 cm. tall.
DESCRIPTION: Branched perennial, native in moist woods from Michigan to Ohio, south to Alabama and Georgia; **stems** forked; **leaves** oblong or oblong-ovate, to 10 cm. long, with stiff spreading hairs beneath; **flowers** white, cream-colored, or yellow, with purple spots, to 2 cm. long, nodding, in May and June; stigma 3-lobed; **berries** yellow, hairy.
USE AND CULTURE: Same as for **Disporum lanuginosum**.

Dodecatheon L. (American Cowslip, Shooting-star)
PRIMULACEAE (Primrose Family)
DESCRIPTION: About 14 species of scapose perennial herbs, native in well-drained soils in partial shade in North America and Siberia; small ricelike **bulblets** often formed on roots; **leaves** simple, in a basal rosette; **flowers** white, magenta, lavender, or purple, nodding, in umbels; calyx and corolla 4- to 5-parted; corolla tube usually maroon with a yellow band at the throat, with reflexed lobes; stamens 4 or 5, free or united into a tube; **fruit** a capsule that opens by valves or a cap.

Dodecatheon meadia L. (American Cowslip, Common Shooting-star). Hardy in all zones; perennial to 40 cm. tall.
DESCRIPTION: Glabrous perennial, native in open woods, fertile prairies, and meadows from North Dakota to Pennsylvania, south to Texas and Alabama; **leaves** in

a basal rosette, ovate to spatulate, to 30 cm. long; **flowers** magenta or lavender to white, 5-merous, in 4- to 125-flowered umbels on scapes to 40 cm. tall, in May and June; pollen sacs yellow.

USE AND CULTURE: Plant in rock gardens, prairie gardens, and wild flower gardens. The plants grow best in a neutral or slightly acid, well-drained soil that is high in organic matter. Moisture is needed during the blooming period. Plants die down in summer after the seeds ripen. Propagation is by fall division. Plant with the bud about 2 cm. deep. Seeds are slow to germinate and the seedlings are fragile.

Echinacea Moench. (Purple Coneflower)
COMPOSITAE (Sunflower Family)
Helianthus Tribe

DESCRIPTION: Five species of coarse perennial herbs, native in North America; **leaves** alternate, simple coarse; **flower** heads radiate, solitary or few, on long peduncles; receptacle conical with stiff spiny scales; ray flowers purple, rarely white; disc flowers purple-brown; **fruit** a 4-angled achene; pappus a short crown.

Echinacea angustifolia D.C. (Pink Coneflower). Hardy in all zones; perennial to 60 cm. tall.
DESCRIPTION: Coarse perennial, native in open woods and open fields, usually in sandy or gravelly soil from Saskatchewan to Minnesota, south to Texas and Tennessee; **leaves** oblong-lanceolate to linear-lanceolate, entire, with 3 to 5 parallel veins; lower leaves long-petioled, upper sessile; ray **flowers** rose-purple, rarely white, to 4 cm. long, from May to August.
USE AND CULTURE: Plant in sunny flower borders or in prairie gardens. It is easy to grow in any well-drained soil. Propagation is by spring division or by seeds started indoors or in a cold frame. When seedlings are large enough, transplant to their permanent location.

Disporum maculatum (Nodding Mandarin). In flower at the Arboretum in May 1981.

Elymus species (Wild Rye).

Photograph: Bonnie E. Harper Lore.

Echinacea pallida (Nutt.) Nutt. (Pale Purple Coneflower). Hardy in all zones; perennial to 90 cm. tall.
DESCRIPTION: Coarse perennial, native in prairies and barrens from Montana to Illinois, south to Texas and Georgia; **leaves** linear-lanceolate to lanceolate-elliptic, gradually tapering at base; **flower** heads solitary, on long peduncles, in June and July; ray flowers purple, rarely paler, to 8 cm. long, reflexed.
USE AND CULTURE: Same as for **Echinacea angustifolia**.

Echinacea purpurea (L.) Moench. (Purple Coneflower). Hardy in all zones; perennial to 1 m. tall.
DESCRIPTION: Coarse perennial, native in dry, open woods or in prairies from Montana to Michigan, south to Colorado and Georgia; basal **leaves** ovate to broadly lanceolate, coarsely dentate, long-petioled; upper stem leaves narrower, nearly entire, sessile; **flower** heads to 15 cm. across, in July and August; ray flowers rose-purple.
USE AND CULTURE: Same as for **Echinacea angustifolia**.

Elymus L. (Lyme Grass, Wild Rye)
GRAMINEAE (Grass Family)
DESCRIPTION: About 50 species of erect, annual or perennial grasses, native in the North Temperate Zone; **leaves** linear, flat, rarely convolute; **flowers** crowded in slender, sometimes bristly spikes; spikelets usually rigid, 2- to 6-flowered; glumes equal, acute or aristate; **fruit** a caryopsis.

Elymus glaucus Buckl. (Blue Wild Rye). Hardy in all zones; perennial to 1.2 m. tall.
DESCRIPTION: Erect, tufted perennial, native in open woods and thickets from Alaska to Ontario, south to California and Arkansas; **leaves** flat, usually lax, to 1.6 cm. wide, bluish-green, usually scabrous on both surfaces; **flowers** in slender, dense spikes to 20 cm. long; spikelets 3- to 6-flowers, appressed; glumes lanceolate, to 1.6 cm. long, acuminate, awn-pointed.
USE AND CULTURE: Plant in flower borders for a bold accent. The plants grow well in any well-drained soil. Propagation is by seeds sown in the spring. Seedlings can be transplanted.

Epilobium angustifolium (Fireweed). In flower in Norway in August 1983.

In fruit in September 1967.

Epigaea L. (Ground Laurel)
ERICACEAE (Heath Family)

DESCRIPTION: Two species of creeping, evergreen shrubs, native in acid, sandy soil in partial shade in Japan and North America; **leaves** simple, alternate, leathery; **flowers** white to rose, fragrant, clustered toward the tips of the branches; sepals 5; corolla urceolate or salverform, hairy inside; stamens 10; ovary superior; **fruit** a many-seeded capsule.

Epigaea repens L. (Mayflower, Trailing Arbutus). Hardy in all zones; creeping shrub to 10 cm. tall.
DESCRIPTION: Hairy-stemmed, creeping shrub native in acid, sandy soils, usually under jack pines from Saskatchewan to Labrador, south to Minnesota and North Carolina; **leaves** oblong-ovate, ovate, or suborbicular, to 7.5 cm. long, cordate at base, rounded at apex, bright green, hairy; **flowers** white to pink, very fragrant, in April and May; corolla salverform with spreading lobe.
USE AND CULTURE: Plant as a ground cover in woodland wild flower gardens. Effective on the north side of stumps. Mature plants are difficult to transplant. It is best to start plants from seeds or from cuttings. Seeds are difficult to collect as the mature capsule forcibly discharges its seed as soon as ripe. Seeds should be sown as soon as ripe in an acid sand-peat mixture. Cuttings should be taken just after bloom and rooted in an acid sand-peat mixture. Cuttings should be rooted by fall. It takes 3 years for seedlings to bloom. The practice of moving mature plants should be discouraged as this plant is becoming rare and such transplants seldom grow.

Epilobium L. (Fireweed, Willow Herb)
ONAGRACEAE (Evening Primrose Family)

DESCRIPTION: About 200 species of annual or perennial herbs, native on burned over land and in swamps in temperate regions; **leaves** alternate, opposite, or sometimes whorled, simple, entire or dentate; **flowers** 4-merous, usually in terminal racemes or panicles; sepals separate; petals entire or deeply emarginate; stamens 8; ovary inferior; **fruit** a capsule; **seeds** many, each with a tuft of silky hairs.

Epilobium angustifolium L. (Fireweed, Great Willow Herb, Wickup). Hardy in all zones; perennial to 2 m. tall.
DESCRIPTION: Rhizomatous perennial, native in disturbed soils, especially abundant after a fire in North America and Eurasia; **leaves** alternate, willowlike, to 15 cm. long, acute, scarcely dentate; **flowers** showy, rose to purple, rarely white, to 2 cm. across, in terminal spikelike racemes, from July to September; styles pubescent at base.
USE AND CULTURE: Plant toward the back of the flower border or in the wild flower garden. They thrive in neutral to slightly acid soils of low fertility. Propagation is by seeds and by crown division in the spring. Seed sown as soon as ripe will produce seedlings that bloom the following year. Plants self sow and can become a weed.

Erigeron L. (Fleabane)
COMPOSITAE (Sunflower Family)
Aster Tribe

DESCRIPTION: About 200 species of annual, biennial, or perennial herbs, native worldwide but most abundant in North America; **leaves** alternate, rarely all basal, frequently sessile; **flower** heads mostly radiate, solitary or few, or sometimes numerous in corymbs or panicles; involucre campanulate to hemispherical; involucral bracts in 2 or 3 rows, narrow; receptacle flat, naked; ray flowers in usually 2 rows, narrow, white, pink, blue, or purple; disc flowers yellow; **fruit** a compressed achene; pappus of few to many soft capillary hairs.

Erigeron asper - see **Erigeron glabellus**.

Erigeron glabellus Nutt. (Daisy Fleabane). Hardy in all zones; biennial or perennial to 50 cm. tall.
DESCRIPTION: Hairy biennial or perennial, native in dry barrens, prairies, and rolling hills from Alaska to Ontario, south to Colorado and Wisconsin; **roots** fibrous; basal and lower stem **leaves** oblanceolate, persistent, to 15 cm. long; upper stem leaves linear to lanceolate, much reduced; **flower** heads in clusters of 1 to 15, to 5 cm. across, from late May to July; ray flowers blue, pink, or white.
USE AND CULTURE: Plant in rock gardens or in prairie plantings. They are similar to asters and are of easy culture in any well-drained soil. Propagation is by division or by seeds.

Erigeron pulchellus Michx. (Poor Robin's Plantain, Robin's Plantain). Hardy in all zones; biennial or perennial to 60 cm. tall.
DESCRIPTION: Fibrous-rooted biennial or short-lived perennial with slender, stoloniferous rhizomes, native in meadows and open woodlands from Minnesota to Maine, south to Texas and Georgia; basal **leaves** lanceolate-oblong or ovate, to 7 cm. long; **flower** heads 1 to 6 in a corymb, to 4 cm. across, from April to July; ray flowers blue, pink, or white.
USE AND CULTURE: Same as for **Erigeron glabellus**.

Eryngium L. (Eryngo)
UMBELLIFERAE (Carrot Family)

DESCRIPTION: About 200 species of perennial herbs, native in sunny places in rich soil, worldwide; **leaves** simple, spiny-toothed, variously lobed or divided; **flowers** small, white or blue, sessile, in dense, bracted heads; calyx prominent, persistent; **fruits** ovoid.

Eryngium yuccifolium Michx. (Button Snake-root, Rattlesnake-master). Hardy in all zones; perennial to 90 cm. tall.
DESCRIPTION: Spiny-leaved perennial, native in moist or dry sandy soil in open woods and prairies from Minnesota to Connecticut, south to Texas and Florida; **leaves** rigid, broadly linear, bristle-tipped, parallel-veined; **flowers** small, white, in heads to 2.5 cm. long.
USE AND CULTURE: Plant in flower borders and prairie gardens. Plants are easy to grow on any well-drained soil. Propagation is by division in early spring or by seeds sown as soon as ripe.

Erythronium L. (Adder's-tongue, Dog-tooth Violet,
Fawn Lily, Trout Lily)
LILIACEAE (Lily Family)

DESCRIPTION: About 25 species of spring-flowering perennial herbs with membranous-coated corms, native in moist woods in North America, Europe, and Asia; **leaves** 2, basal or nearly so, nearly opposite, often mottled; **flowers** white, yellow, pink, rose, or purple, solitary or several in racemes, nodding; perianth segments 6, separate, usually recurved; stamens 6 with basifixed anthers; **fruit** a 3-valved capsule.

Erythronium albidum (White Dog-tooth Violet).

Photograph: Dr. Anne M. Hanchek.

Erythronium albidum (White Dog-tooth Violet).

Near Faribault, Minnesota.

Erythronium albidum Nutt. (Blonde Lilian, White Dog-tooth Violet, White Trout Lily). Hardy in all zones; perennial to 30 cm. tall.
DESCRIPTION: Corm producing perennial, native in moist woods from Minnesota to New York, south to Texas and Kentucky; **leaves** elliptic, to 15 cm. long, green, rarely mottled; **flowers** solitary, to 5 cm. long, nodding, bluish- to pinkish-white, yellow at base inside, in April and May; anthers creamy-white; stigmas deeply lobed, spreading.
USE AND CULTURE: Plant in wild flower gardens among ferns. They grow best in a soil that is high in organic matter. Mulching heavily is recommended. Propagation is by division of corms in the fall or by seeds sown as soon as ripe. It takes 3 or more years for seedlings to bloom. Plant corms about 5 cm. deep and 15 cm. apart. Leaves die down after flowering.

Erythronium americanum Ker-Gawl. (Amberbell, Trout Lily, Yellow Adder's-tongue, Yellow Dog-tooth Violet). Hardy in all zones; perennial to 30 cm. tall.
DESCRIPTION: Corm producing perennial, native in moist, deciduous woods from Minnesota to Nova Scotia, south to Alabama and Florida; **leaves** elliptic, to 15 cm. long, mottled with brown spots; **flowers** solitary, bell-shaped, to 5 cm. long, yellow, often spotted at base inside; anthers brown or yellow; stigmas with short lobes.
USE AND CULTURE: Same as for **Erythronium albidum**. It takes up to 8 years for seedlings to bloom, so division of corms is the principal method of propagation.

Eupatorium L. (Boneset, Joe-pye Weed, Thoroughwort)
COMPOSITAE (Sunflower Family)
Eupatorium Tribe

DESCRIPTION: Nearly 500 species of mostly perennial herbs, native worldwide but mainly in tropical America; **leaves** simple, mostly opposite, sometimes alternate or whorled, usually petioled, entire to dissected; **flower** heads discoid, usually in corymbs, rarely solitary or in panicles; involucral bracts in 2 to 3 rows; receptacle flat to convex, naked; disc flowers all tubular, purple, rose, or white; **fruit** a 5-angled achene; pappus of capillary bristles in a single row.

Eupatorium maculatum L. (Joe-pye Weed, Smokeweed). Hardy in all zones; perennial to 2 m. tall.
DESCRIPTION: Coarse perennial, native in wet, calcareous soils and roadside ditches from British Columbia to Newfoundland, south to New Mexico and Maryland; **stems** speckled or blotched with purple; **leaves** in whorls of 3 to 6, lanceolate, elliptic-lanceolate or ovate-lanceolate, to 20 cm. long, sharply serrate; **flower** heads to 6 mm. across with 8 to 10 flowers, in flat-topped corymbs, from July to September; involucral bracts often purple; disc flowers purple.
USE AND CULTURE: These perennials can be striking when planted toward the back of the flower border or in prairie plantings. Plants require a moist soil. Propagation is by spring division or by seeds. Seeds should be sown in the fall as soon as ripe. Mulching with evergreen boughs will assure winter survival.

Eupatorium perfoliatum L. (Common Boneset, Thoroughwort). Hardy in all zones; perennial to 1.2 m. tall.
DESCRIPTION: Rhizomatous, pubescent perennial, native in moist or wet soils in open woods, roadside ditches, and river bottoms from southern Canada south to Oklahoma and Louisiana; **leaves** opposite, lanceolate, to 20 cm. long, acuminate, mostly connate-perfoliate, crenate-serrate, rugose; **flower** heads about 6 mm. across, with 10 to 40 flowers, in flat-topped corymbs, from July to October; disc flowers white.
USE AND CULTURE: Plant in wild flower gardens. They require a moist soil. Propagation is mainly by seeds sown as soon as ripe. Plants are difficult to divide. Young plants can be moved successfully in early spring.

Eupatorium purpureum L. (Green-stemmed Joe-pye Weed, Sweet Joe-pye Weed). Hardy in all zones; perennial to 3 m. tall.
DESCRIPTION: Coarse perennial, native in moist thickets and open woods from Wisconsin to New Hampshire, south to Oklahoma and Georgia; **stems** green or green with purple nodes; **leaves** usually in whorls of 3 to 5, elliptic or lanceolate to ovate, to 30 cm. long, sharply serrate, vanilla-scented; **flower** heads to 9 mm. across, with 5 to

Erythronium americanum (Trout Lily).

In flower in May 1978.

7 flowers, in rounded corymbose panicles, from July to September; disc flowers pink to purple, rarely white.

USE AND CULTURE: Same as for **Eupatorium maculatum**. According to legend, Joe Pye was a Native American who used this plant to cure typhus fever.

Eupatorium rugosum Houtt. (White Snakeroot, Snow Thoroughwort, White Sanicle). Hardy in all zones; perennial to 1 m. tall.

DESCRIPTION: Perennial, native in moist open woods, along streams, and in moist meadows from Saskatchewan to Nova Scotia, south to Texas and Georgia; **leaves** opposite, thin, ovate, to 18 cm. long, acuminate, sharply and coarsely serrate, glabrous or hairy; **flower** heads about 6 mm. across, with 12 to 24 flowers, in corymbs, in August and September; disc flowers white.

USE AND CULTURE: Plant in flower borders, wild flower gardens, or in prairie plantings. Plants thrive in moist soil either in full sun or partial shade. Propagation is by spring division or by seeds sown as soon as ripe. Plants often self sow. This species is poisonous to livestock if eaten.

Euphorbia L. (Spurge)
EUPHORBIACEAE (Spurge Family)

DESCRIPTION: Over 1600 species of monoecious or dioecious herbs, shrubs, or trees with milky juice, native worldwide; **stems** often spiny and cactuslike; **leaves** alternate, opposite, or whorled, simple, entire, or dentate, sometimes rudimentary or lacking; **flowers** in cyathia; cyathia solitary and terminal, clustered in leaf axils, or arranged in a simple umbel, panicle, or cyme; involucre of cyathium cup-shaped, with 5 inner lobes alternating with glands; ovary 3-celled; **fruit** a 3-valved capsule.

Euphorbia corollata L. (Flowering Spurge, Tramp's Spurge, Wild Hippo). Hardy in all zones; perennial to 90 cm. tall.

DESCRIPTION: Slender herbaceous perennial, native in open fields, roadsides, woods, and prairies, mostly in sandy soils from Minnesota to Massachusetts, south to Texas and Florida; **leaves** elliptic, ovate, oblong, or linear, alternate on stems, whorled below primary branches, to 5 cm. long; **cyathia** in umbellike cymes; glands 5, with showy white, petallike appendages, from June to October.

USE AND CULTURE: Plant in flower borders or woodland wild flower gardens. They require a sandy, well-drained soil. Propagation is by spring division, root cuttings, and seeds. The plant makes an excellent substitute for baby's-breath for use in flower arrangements.

Euphorbia cyathophora J. Murr. (Fiddler's Spurge, Fire-on-the-mountain, Mexican Fire Plant, Painted Leaf, Wild Poinsettia). Hardy in all zones; annual to 90 cm. tall.

DESCRIPTION: Upright annual, native in disturbed soils from South Dakota to Virginia, south to Texas and Florida; **leaves** ovate to linear, or sometimes fiddle-shaped, entire or dentate, glossy green; upper leaves and floral bracts red or red at base; **cyathea** in terminal clusters; glands 1 or 2, broad, more or less 2-lipped, in August and September.

USE AND CULTURE: Plant in flower borders. Plants grow well in any well-drained soil in either full sun or partial shade. Propagation is by seeds sown in early spring. Thin the seedlings to 30 cm. apart.

Euphorbia heterophylla - see **Euphorbia cyathophora.**

Euphorbia marginata Pursh. (Ghostweed, Snow-on-the-mountain). Hardy in all zones; annual to 60 cm. tall.

DESCRIPTION: Erect annual, native in fields and prairies from Montana to Minnesota, south to New Mexico and Missouri; **leaves** ovate to oblong, to 7.5 cm. long, alternate on stems, whorled below inflorescences; upper leaves with white margins; **cyathia** in 3-rayed umbels; glands 4, with broad, white, petallike appendages, from June to October.

USE AND CULTURE: Plant in flower borders or in prairie plantings. They are most effective when planted in mass. The culture is the same as for **Euphorbia cyathophora**. In flower borders they should be pinched back early in the spring to induce side

Euphorbia corollata (Flowering Spurge).

Eustoma grandiflorum (Prairie Gentian).

branching, but don't get its sap on your hands. The milky juice from crushed leaves can cause skin irritations.

Eustoma Salisb. (Tulip Gentian)
GENTIANACEAE (Gentian Family)

DESCRIPTION: Three species of glaucous annual or perennial herbs, native in the southwestern and plains states; **stems** leafy; **leaves** opposite; **flowers** white or blue, solitary or in panicles; calyx keeled; corolla 5- to 6-lobed; **fruit** an ellipsoid, many-seeded capsule.

Eustoma grandiflorum (Raf.) Shinn. (Prairie Gentian). Hardy in all zones; annual to 90 cm. tall.
DESCRIPTION: Weak-stemmed annual or biennial, native in grasslands and moist meadows near springs from Colorado to Nebraska, south to Mexico and Texas; **stems** erect to ascending; **leaves** ovate to oblong, to 7.5 cm. long, glaucous; **flowers** showy, pale purple to white, cup-shaped to 5 cm. across, from June to September; petals joined at base.
USE AND CULTURE: Plant in rock gardens or flower borders. Seeds, which can be difficult to start, should be planted indoors in March. Transplant seedlings in late May, spacing the plants about 30 cm. apart. Keep the soil moist. The flowers are showy in the garden and are excellent for cutting.

Filipendula Mill. (Meadowsweet)
ROSACEAE (Rose Family)

DESCRIPTION: A small genus of perennial herbs, native in the North Temperate Zone; **leaves** alternate, usually pinnate; **flowers** numerous, small, in terminal corymbose panicles on leafy stems; sepals and petals usually 5; stamens 20 to 40; **fruit** an achene.

Filipendula rubra (J. Hill.) B.L. Robinson. (Queen-of-the-prairie). Hardy in all zones; perennial to 2 m. tall.
DESCRIPTION: Glabrous perennial, native in moist meadows and prairies in full sun from Minnesota to Pennsylvania, south to Kentucky and Georgia; **leaves** interruptedly pinnate, green, paler beneath, with a large terminal leaflet, to 10 cm. across; **flowers** deep, peach-blossom pink, from June to August.

Fragaria vesca (Woodland Strawberry).

In flower in May 1978.

USE AND CULTURE: Plant toward the back of the flower border or in a prairie garden. They grow best in a moist, neutral to slightly acid soil. Propagation is largely by spring division. Space plants about 30 cm. apart.

Fragaria L. (Strawberry)
ROSACEAE (Rose Family)

DESCRIPTION: About 12 species of low, stoloniferous perennial herbs that root at the nodes, native in the North Temperate Zone; **leaves** palmate compound; leaflets 3, coarsely serrate, obovate-cuneate; **flowers** mostly white, in cymes or racemes on scapes; sepals 5 with bractlets in each sinus; petals 5, rounded; stamens few to many; **fruit** a fleshy edible receptacle in which achenes are embedded.

Fragaria vesca L. (Sow-teat Strawberry, Woodland Strawberry). Hardy in all zones; perennial to 20 cm. tall.
DESCRIPTION: Stoloniferous perennial, native on cut-over lands and roadside ditches in North America and Europe; **runners** long, arching, rooting at nodes; **leaflets** to 6 cm. long; **flowers** white, in racemelike clusters, to 2 cm. across, in May and June; **fruits** red, to 2 cm. across.
USE AND CULTURE: Plant as a ground cover and for the edible fruit. Plants do well in most soils either in full sun or light shade. Plants tolerate very acid soil conditions. Propagation is by division in eary spring. Set plants with the crown at ground level, spaced about 30 cm. apart.

Gaillardia Foug. (Blanket Flower, Gaillardia)
COMPOSITAE (Sunflower Family)
Helenium Tribe

DESCRIPTION: About 14 species of annual, biennial, and perennial herbs, native in full sun and well-drained soils in North and South America; basal **leaves** entire, dentate or pinnatifid, pubescent; **flower** heads radiate or discoid, solitary, large, showy; receptacle hemispherical; ray flowers yellow or red, with 3-lobed ligules; disc flowers hairy, reddish-purple or yellow; **fruit** a hairy, obconical achene; pappus of awned scales.

Gaillardia aristata Pursh. (Blanket Flower). Hardy in all zones; perennial to 45 cm. tall.
DESCRIPTION: Upright perennial, native in dry meadows and other open areas from British Columbia to North Dakota, south to Colorado and Kansas; **leaves** obovate to linear-lanceolate; lower leaves often pinnately lobed, to 25 cm. long, petioled; upper leaves entire, sessile; **flower** heads to 10 cm. across, from May to September; ray flowers yellow, often purple at base; disc flowers yellow or purple.
USE AND CULTURE: Plant in flower borders, rock gardens, or prairie plantings. They require a well-drained soil and full sun. Do not provide too rich of a soil. Propagation is by spring division or by direct seeding as soon as seeds are ripe. Plants may be short-lived on heavy soils.

Fragaria vesca (Woodland Strawberry).

In fruit in June 1979.

Galium boreale (Northern Bedstraw).

Gaillardia pulchella Foug. (Annual Gaillardia). Hardy in all zones; annual to 60 cm. tall.

DESCRIPTION: Annual, native in dry, sandy prairies from Minnesota to Virginia, south to Mexico and Florida; lower **leaves** oblanceolate to spatulate, to 10 cm. long; dentate or pinnately lobed, sessile or short-petioled; stem leaves oblong or oblanceolate, usually entire, sessile; **flower** heads solitary on long-peduncles, to 5 cm. across, from July to October; involucral bracts green, with papery bases; ray flowers red, tipped with yellow, or entirely red or yellow; disc flowers yellow or yellow with red tips.

USE AND CULTURE: Plant in flower borders. They are free bloomers. The culture is the same as for **Gaillardia aristata** except propagation is only by seeds started indoors each year. It takes 3 months from seeding to bloom.

Galium L. (Bedstraw, Cleavers)
RUBIACEAE (Madder Family)
DESCRIPTION: About 300 species of slender, weak-stemmed herbs with square stems, native in temperate regions; **leaves** whorled, slender, sessile; **flowers** small, in axillary or terminal panicles, usually 4-merous; corolla rotate, deeply 4-parted; **fruit** 2-lobed, 2-seeded, dry, indehiscent, sometimes bristly or hairy.

Galium boreale L. (Northern Bedstraw). Hardy in all zones; perennial to 90 cm. tall.
DESCRIPTION: Stoloniferous perennial, native in open woods throughout North America; **leaves** in whorls of 4, lanceolate, to 4 cm. long; **flowers** white, quite showy, in June and July.

USE AND CULTURE: Plant in wild flower gardens. Plants are easy to grow in partial shade in soils high in organic matter. Propagation is by spring division or by seeds sown as soon as ripe.

Galium septentrionale - see **Galium boreale**.

Gaultheria L. (Wintergreen)
ERICACEAE (Heath Family)
DESCRIPTION: About 100 species of evergreen shrubs, rarely small trees, native in moist, sandy or peaty soils in woods, widespread in North and South America, Asia, and Australia; **leaves** alternate, rarely opposite, simple; **flowers** pink or white, solitary, or in racemes or panicles; calyx 5-parted; corolla urceolate or campanulate, rarely tubular; stamens 8 to 10 with awned anthers; ovary superior; **fruit** a capsule enclosed by a fleshy, bright-colored calyx.

Gaultheria hispidula (L.) Muhlenb. ex Bigel. (Maidenhair Berry, Moxie Plum, Creeping Snowberry). Hardy in all zones; trailing shrub to 12 cm. tall.
DESCRIPTION: Trailing, mat-forming, semi-herbaceous, evergreen shrub, native in acid bogs or wet woods, often on logs, from British Columbia to Newfoundland, south to Minnesota and North Carolina; **leaves** ovate, to 1 cm. long, revolute, bristly beneath; **flowers** white, bell-shaped, less than 5 mm. long, in May and June; **fruits** white, berrylike.

USE AND CULTURE: Plant as a ground cover in acid soil in shade. This is a difficult plant to grow. It does best in a specially prepared soil consisting of a mixture of coarse sand, rotted pine logs, and sphagnum peat. Keep plants constantly moist. Propagation is by spring division or by cuttings taken in May and rooted in a sand-peat mixture.

Gaultheria procumbens L. (Checkerberry, Ivry-leaves, Mountain Tea, Teaberry, Wintergreen). Hardy in all zones; evergreen shrub to 15 cm. tall.
DESCRIPTION: Creeping plants, native in acid, sandy soils in dry or moist woods, occasionally on hummocks in peat bogs from Manitoba to Newfoundland, south to Alabama and Georgia; **leaves** elliptic to narrowing obovate, to 5 cm. long, bristly serrate, shiny above; young leaves with a minty flavor; **flowers** solitary, nodding, white, to 7 mm. long, in July and August; **fruits** scarlet, with a minty flavor, remaining on plants over winter.

USE AND CULTURE: Plant as a ground cover in wild flower gardens or in rock gardens. Young leaves are used to make a mint-flavored tea. Berries are also tasty with a minty flavor. Plant in an acid, sandy soil or in a soil that has been specially prepared

Gentiana andrewsii (Bottle Gentian).
In August 1978 at the Schaefer Prairie in Glencoe, Minnesota.

by adding sand, acid peat, and rotted pine or oak sawdust. Propagation is by spring division, cuttings taken in July and rooted in a sand-peat mixture, or by seeds planted as soon as ripe. Germination is often poor.

Gentiana L. (Gentian)
GENTIANACEAE (Gentian Family)

DESCRIPTION: About 300 species of mostly perennial herbs, native in moist areas, mostly in temperate and arctic regions or in the mountains in the tropics; **leaves** opposite, sometimes clasping; **flowers** white, yellow, blue, purple, or red, often spotted, solitary to many in elongated or capitate clusters, usually 4- to 5-merous; calyx tubular to campanulate, variously cleft or lobed; corolla funnelform, campanulate, or salverform, sometimes tubular or club-shaped, variously lobed, with pleats, teeth, or appendages between the lobes; stamens united with corolla tube; **fruit** a capsule.

Gentiana affinis Griseb. ex Hook. (Northern Gentian). Hardy in all zones; perennial to 40 cm. tall.
DESCRIPTION: Perennial with clustered stems, native in meadows and valleys from British Columbia to Ontario, south to California and Arizona; **leaves** oblong to linear, to 2.5 cm. long; **flowers** blue, in many-flowered terminal or axillary clusters, from July to September; calyx lobes unequal; corolla narrowly funnelform, to 2.5 cm. long; the pleats or appendages lacerate into narrow segments.
USE AND CULTURE: Plant in rock gardens or near pools. Plants are easy to grow in moist soil. Propagation is by spring division or by seeds. Sow seeds as soon as ripe in a cold frame. Transplant seedlings to their permanent location the following spring.

Gentiana amarella - see **Gentianella amarella**.

Gentiana andrewsii Grieseb. (Blind Gentian, Bottle Gentian, Closed Gentian). Hardy in all zones; perennial to 60 cm. tall.
DESCRIPTION: Perennial, native in wet, sunny meadows, and along streams and lake shores from Saskatchewan to Quebec, south to Missouri and North Carolina; **leaves** ovate to lanceolate; **flowers** blue, becoming purple, in terminal, sessile clusters or in upper leaf axils; corolla completely closed, to 4 cm. long.
USE AND CULTURE: Plant along streams or at the edges of pools. Plants are easy to grow in any moist soil that is neutral to slightly acid. Propagation is mainly by division. Fall planting is preferable to spring. Set crowns about 2 cm. deep. Seeds can also be planted as soon as ripe. Mulch with evergreen boughs the first winter.

Gentiana crinita - see **Gentianopsis crinita**.

Gentiana puberula - see **Gentiana puberulenta**.

Gentiana puberulenta Pringle. (Downy Gentian). Hardy in all zones; perennial to 50 cm. tall.
DESCRIPTION: Perennial with downy stems, native in sandy or rocky soils on prairies and grasslands from Manitoba to Ontario, south to Kansas and Arkansas; **leaves** oblong-lanceolate or nearly linear, 1-veined; **flowers** blue above, colorless below, in 1- to 6-flowered clusters, vase-shaped when fully open, to 4 cm. long, in July and August.
USE AND CULTURE: Same as for **Gentiana andrewsii**.

Gentiana saponaria L. (Soapwort Gentian). Hardy in all zones; perennial to 75 cm. tall.
DESCRIPTION: Perennial, native in sandy soils, in roadside ditches, wet lake shores, marshes, and damp meadows from Minnesota to Pennsylvania, south to Louisiana and Alabama; **leaves** lanceolate or oblong; **flowers** blue, in terminal and axillary clusters, in July and August; calyx tubular, with linear-lanceolate lobes to 1 cm. long; corolla club-shaped to 4 cm. long.
USE AND CULTURE: Same as for **Gentiana andrewsii**.

Gentiana puberulenta (Downy Gentian).

Gentianella Moench. (Gentian)
GENTIANACEAE (Gentian Family)
DESCRIPTION: About 200 species of annual or perennial herbs, native in Europe, Asia, North and South America, and New Zealand; **stems** often square; **leaves** opposite; **flowers** blue, lavender, or white, clustered in 3- to 10-flowered cymes, on short, bracted pedicels, 5-merous; calyx tubular, sometimes spathelike, lobes with green margins; corolla tubular, funnelform, or campanulate to rotate, without appendages, lobes entire; ovary sessile; **fruit** a capsule.

Gentianella amarella (L.) Borner. (Felwort). Hardy in all zones; annual to 30 cm. tall.
DESCRIPTION: Annual, native in moist, gravelly soil, circumboreal, south to California and Maine in North America; basal **leaves** spatulate, to 3 cm. long; stem leaves lanceolate, smaller; **flowers** pale lilac, in leaf axils, to 1.25 cm. long, in July and August.
USE AND CULTURE: Plant in flower borders or in prairie plantings. Plants require a moist, well-drained soil in full sun. Propagation is by seeds started indoors.

Gentianopsis Ma. (Fringed Gentian)
GENTIANACEAE (Gentian Family)
DESCRIPTION: About 15 species of annual or biennial herbs, native in the northern hemisphere; **leaves** opposite; **flowers** showy, blue or purple, rarely white, solitary, on slender, bractless pedicels, 4-merous; calyx tubular, 4-angled, lobes in 2 unequal pairs; corolla funnelform to campanulate, lobes fringed; stamens attached to upper 1/3 of corolla tube; ovary stalked; **fruit** a capsule.

Gentianopsis crinita (Froel.) Ma. (Fringed Gentian). Hardy in all zones; annual or biennial to 90 cm. tall.
DESCRIPTION: Annual or biennial, native in low woods, wet meadows, stream banks, and lake shores from Manitoba to Maine, south to Iowa and Georgia; **leaves** ovate to lanceolate; **flowers** bright blue, few to many, to 5 cm. across, with lobes fringed all around, from August to October.
USE AND CULTURE: Plant in wild flower gardens. This beautiful wild flower is difficult to grow. The soil must be alkaline, high in humus, preferably sandy, and moist. Sow seeds as soon as ripe either directly where plants are to grow or in flats. Cover with evergreen boughs or winter in a cold frame. If conditions are right the plants will self sow. Seeds can also be stored in a cool, moist place over winter and planted early in the spring. This rare wild flower should not be picked. Allow the plants to mature their seeds.

Geranium L. (Cranesbill, Geranium)
GERANIACEAE (Geranium Family)
DESCRIPTION: Over 300 species of annual or perennial herbs, native in temperate regions and in the mountains in the tropics; **leaves** alternate, palmately cleft, divided, or lobed; **flowers** white, pink, or purple, solitary and axillary, or clustered and terminal; sepals and petals 5; stamens 10; ovary 5-celled; **fruit** a capsule with axis prolonged into a beak.

Geranium maculatum L. (Alumroot, Spotted Cranesbill, Wild Cranesbill, Wild Geranium). Hardy in all zones; perennial to 60 cm. tall.
DESCRIPTION: Rhizomatous perennial, native in moist woods from Manitoba to Maine, south to Arkansas and Georgia; **rhizomes** thick; **stems** appressed-pubescent; **leaves** deeply 3- to 5-parted; **flowers** rose-purple, to 2.5 cm. across, in terminal clusters, in May and June; petals entire, barbate-ciliate at base; stamen filaments short-ciliate.
USE AND CULTURE: Plant in wild flower gardens or in flower borders. Plants require a neutral to slightly acid soil that is high in organic matter. Propagation is by spring division or by seeds sown as soon as ripe. It takes two to three years for seedlings to bloom. Seeds are forcibly discharged from their capsule as soon as ripe so it is necessary to harvest them at just the right time.

Geum L. (Avens)
ROSACEAE (Rose Family)
DESCRIPTION: Over 50 species of perennial herbs, native in temperate regions; **leaves** mostly basal, pinnate or lyrate, usually with large terminal lobes; stem leaves alternate,

Geranium maculatum (Wild Geranium). In flower in Cumberland, Wisconsin in May 1985.

much smaller; **flowers** solitary or in corymbs, white, yellow, or red; calyx tube bell-shaped or flat; sepals 5, usually with 5 bractlets between the lobes; petals 5, usually broad and showy; stamens many; **fruit** an achene, often with a plumose style.

Geum rivale L. (Chocolate Root, Indian Chocolate, Purple Avens, Water Avens). Hardy in all zones; perennial to 60 cm. tall.
DESCRIPTION: Pubescent perennial, native in wet meadows and bogs from British Columbia to Labrador, south to California and West Virginia, also native in Europe and Asia; **leaves** with 3 to 6 pairs of unequal lateral leaflets and a large terminal leaflet to 5 cm. across; **flowers** few, nodding, from May to July; calyx purple; corolla dull orange-pink; **achenes** in stalked heads.
USE AND CULTURE: Plant in flower borders or near pools. Plants require a moist soil and full sun. Propagation is by spring division or seeds sown as soon as ripe.

Geum triflorum Pursh. (Old Man's Whiskers, Prairie-smoke, Torch Flower). Hardy in all zones; perennial to 45 cm. tall.
DESCRIPTION: Soft, hairy perennial, native in open woods and open prairies in sandy or rocky soil from British Columbia to Ontario, south to California and Illinois; **leaves** with many cuneate, shallowly cut leaflets; **flowers** rose-pink, nodding, usually in 3's, in June and July; sepals purple, shorter than the bractlets; petals crimson to rose-pink; styles not jointed, feathery in fruit, to 5 cm. long; **achenes** elongated, mauve-pink.
USE AND CULTURE: Plant in rock gardens or in prairie gardens. They grow best in a well-drained, neutral to slightly acid soil in full sun. Prairie-smoke can withstand dryer, poorer soils. The fruiting stage of this plant is much more conspicuous than its flowering. Propagation is by spring division or by seeds sown as soon as ripe. Seed germination is often poor.

Gilia - see **Ipomopsis**

Gillenia Moench. (Gillenia)
ROSACEAE (Rose Family)
DESCRIPTION: Two species of erect, branching, perennial herbs, native in North America; **leaves** alternate, compound, with 3 leaflets; **flowers** white or pink, in terminal panicles; calyx 5-lobed; petals 5; stamens 10 to 20; **fruit** a follicle.

Gillenia trifoliata (L.) Moench. (Bowman's-root, Indian-physic). Hardy in all zones; perennial to 1 m. tall.
DESCRIPTION: Branched perennial, native in rich, open woods under high, filtered shade from Ontario to New York, south to Alabama and Georgia; **leaflets** oblong-ovate, serrate; **stipules** small, subulate, entire or slightly incised; **flowers** white to pale pink, to 2.5 cm. long, in June and July.
USE AND CULTURE: Plant in wild flower gardens in masses interspersed with ferns. These plants prefer a moist, moderately acid soil in sun or high, filtered shade. Propagation is by spring division or by seeds sown as soon as ripe. Plant with crowns at soil level and space 45 cm. apart.

Gillenia trifoliata. In flower at the Arboretum.

Goodyera pubescens (Downy Rattlesnake Orchid).

Goodyera R.Br. (Latticeleaf, Rattlesnake Plantain)
ORCHIDACEAE (Orchid Family)
DESCRIPTION: About 40 species of rhizomatous perennial herbs, native worldwide; **stems** leafy; **leaves** variegated with white; **flowers** in many-flowered terminal racemes or spikes; sepals and petals meeting at the tips and forming a helmet; lip saccate; column short; **fruit** a capsule.

Goodyera pubescens (Willd.) R.Br. (Downy Rattlesnake Orchid, Downy Rattlesnake Plantain, Scrofula Weed). Hardy in all zones; perennial to 40 cm. tall.
DESCRIPTION: Perennial, native in acid soil in coniferous and deciduous woods from Minnesota to Newfoundland, south to Arkansas and Georgia; **leaves** 3 to 8, in a basal rosette, to 7.5 cm. long, dark green with white reticulations; **flowers** small, white, pubescent, in many-flowered racemes, to 12 cm. long, from May to October.
USE AND CULTURE: Plant in rock gardens or in wild flowers gardens. These plants must have an acid soil and continuous moisture. Propagation is mainly by division of the rhizomes in fall or early spring. This orchid should not be dug in the wild. Purchase plants from a licensed dealer.

Grindelia Willd. (Gum Plant, Gumweed,
Rosinweed, Sticky-heads, Tarweed)
COMPOSITAE (Sunflower Family)
Aster Tribe
DESCRIPTION: About 50 species of coarse annual, biennial, or perennial herbs, mostly tap-rooted, native along roadsides and in poor, gravelly soils in western North America and in South America; **stems** simple or much-branched; **leaves** alternate, usually sessile, often clasping, glandular-dotted; **flower** heads radiate or discoid, usually gummy, solitary; involucre hemispherical; involucral bracts imbricate in several rows, often spreading or revolute; receptacle flat to slightly convex, pitted, naked; ray flowers pistillate or lacking; disc flowers perfect; **fruit** a glabrous, compressed to 4-angled achene; pappus of 2 to 10 stiff, deciduous awns.

Grindelia squarrosa (Pursh) Dunal. (Curly-cup Gumweed). Hardy in all zones; annual, biennial, or short-lived perennial to 1 m. tall.
DESCRIPTION: Erect annual, biennial, or short-lived perennial, native in prairies, and along streams and pond margins from Montana to Minnesota, south to Texas; **leaves** oblong or ovate, glandular-dotted, wavy-margined, or entire to dentate; basal leaves clasping stem at base; **flower** heads yellow, usually radiate, to 3 cm. across, from July to September; ray flowers lemon-yellow or bright yellow, rarely absent.
USE AND CULTURE: Plant in flower borders or prairie plantings. Native Americans used the plants for medicinal purposes. Plants are easy to grow on most soils. Propagation is by seeds sown as soon as ripe, or indoors in March for transplanting to the garden.

Habenaria Willd. (Fringed Orchid, Fringed Orchis,
Rein Orchid, Rein Orchis)
ORCHIDACEAE (Orchid Family)

DESCRIPTION: About 100 species of terrestrial perennial herbs, native in bogs, moist woods, and wet meadows in temperate and tropical areas; **stems** erect, simple, leafy; **leaves** linear to oblanceolate; stem leaves smaller than the basal ones; **flowers** in 1- to many-flowered terminal racemes; petals usually smaller than the sepals; lip entire, lobed, or often fringed, spurred at base; anthers firmly fused to column; **fruit** a capsule.

Habenaria ciliaris (L.) R. Br. (Orange-fringe, Orange-plume, Yellow Fringed Orchid). Hardy in all zones; perennial to 1 m. tall.
DESCRIPTION: Leafy perennial, native in bogs, swamps, meadows, and pine barrens from Ontario to Massachusetts, south to Texas and Florida; **stems** leafy; **leaves** to 30 cm. long; **flowers** bright yellow to deep orange, in racemes to 20 cm. long, from July to September; lip to 1.25 cm. long, copiously ciliate-fringed, with a slender spur.
USE AND CULTURE: Plant in wild flower or bog gardens. This fringed orchid requires an acid soil and partial shade. The soil should be kept moist. Propagation is by division. Seed propagation has not been successful. This is one of the easiest of the fringed orchids to grow.

Habenaria fimbriata - see **Habenaria psycodes** var. **grandiflora**.

Habenaria psycodes (L.) K. Spreng. (Butterfly Orchid, Fairy-fringe, Lesser Purple Fringed Orchid, Small Purple Fringed Orchid, Soldier's-plume). Hardy in all zones; perennial to 1 m. tall.
DESCRIPTION: Perennial, native in mossy woods, swamps, and roadside ditches from Alaska to Greenland, south to Wyoming and New York; **stems** leafy; **leaves** several, up to 22 cm. long; **flowers** showy, purple, lilac, or rarely white, in many-flowered racemes, fragrant, from June to August; upper sepal and petals forming a hood; lip 3-lobed, with fringed margins; spur to 2 cm. long.
USE AND CULTURE: The same as for **Habenaria ciliaris**.
VARIETIES: var. **grandiflora** (Bigel.) A. Gray. (Greater Purple Fringed Orchid, Large Butterfly Orchid, Large Purple Fringed Orchid, Plume-royal).
DESCRIPTION: Plants more robust than the species with flowers twice as large. It has the same range as the species.

Hedyotis L. (Bluets, Hedyotis)
RUBIACEAE (Madder Family)
DESCRIPTION: About 400 species of shrubs or perennial herbs, native in tropical, subtropical, and sometimes temperate regions; **leaves** opposite with interpetiolar stipules; **flowers** solitary or in axillary or terminal cymes, 4-merous; corolla funnelform or salverform; **fruit** a capsule.

Hedyotis angustifolia - see **Hedyotis nigricans**

Hedyotis caerulea (L.) Hook. (Bluets, Creeping Bluets, Eyebright, Innocence, Quaker-ladies). Hardy in all zones; perennial to 18 cm. tall.
DESCRIPTION: Tufted perennial, native in moist meadows from Wisconsin to Nova Scotia, south to Arkansas and Georgia; **leaves** opposite, oblanceolate, to 1.25 cm. long; **flowers** solitary, violet, blue, or white with yellow eye, in May and June; corolla salverform, to 1.25 cm. long; **capsules** short, 3 mm. across.
USE AND CULTURE: Plant in rock gardens or prairie plantings. Plants are easy to grow in any well-drained soil that is kept moist in the spring. They die down after flowering but new plants form from the tips of the rhizomes around the parent plant. Propagation is by division and by seeds sown as soon as ripe.

Hedyotis nigricans (Lam.) Fosb. (Bluets). Hardy in zone 4; perennial to 60 cm. tall.
DESCRIPTION: Branched perennial, native in dry soils and barrens from Iowa to Indiana, south to Texas and Florida; **leaves** clustered, sessile, linear to threadlike, to 3 cm. long; **flowers** white to purple in terminal cymes grouped to form a panicle, in June and July; corolla salverform, to 6 mm. long; **fruit** oblong to cylindrical.
USE AND CULTURE: The same as for **Hedyotis caerulea**.

Hedyotis caerulea (Bluets). In flower at the Arboretum in May 1983.

Hedyotis purpurea (L.) Torr. & A. Gray. (Purple Bluets). Hardy in all zones; perennial to 45 cm. tall.

DESCRIPTION: Branched perennial, native in dry woods, pine barrens, and in prairies from Michigan to New England, south to Texas and Alabama; **leaves** ovate to ovate-lanceolate, to 5 cm. long; **flowers** purple or lilac, in terminal cymes; corolla funnelform, to 1 cm. long; **capsules** globose to 3 mm. long.

USE AND CULTURE: The same as for **Hedyotis caerulea**.

VARIETIES: var. **longifolia** (Gaertn.) Fosb.

DESCRIPTION: Leaves are narrower than the species. Native from Saskatchewan to Ontario, south to Arkansas and South Carolina.

Helenium L. (Sneezeweed)
COMPOSITAE (Sunflower Family)
Helenium Tribe

DESCRIPTION: About 40 species of annual or perennial herbs, native in rich soil and full sun in North and South America; **leaves** alternate, glandular-dotted, frequently decurrent; **flower** heads radiate or discoid, solitary or in cymes; involucral bracts in 2 rows, deflexed or spreading; receptacle convex to ovoid or globose, naked; ray flowers mostly yellow, present or absent, pistillate or sterile; disc flowers yellow, perfect; **fruit** an achene; achenes turbinate or obpyramidal, 4- to 5-angled, red-brown or red-purple; pappus of 5 to 10 scarious, awn-tipped scales.

Helenium autumnale L. (Common Sneezeweed). Hardy in all zones; perennial to 1.5 m. tall.

DESCRIPTION: Fibrous-rooted perennial, native along streams, in meadows, and other wet areas from British Columbia, south to Arizona and Florida; **stems** branched, winged due to decurrent leaf bases; **leaves** linear-lanceolate to elliptic or ovate-lanceolate, to 15 cm. long, serrate, nearly glabrous; **flower** heads to 5 cm. across, from July to September; receptacle nearly globose to hemispherical; ray flowers yellow; disc flowers yellow.

USE AND CULTURE: Plant toward the back of the flower border or in prairie plantings. Sneezeweed grows best in rich, well-drained soils that are kept moist. Propagation is by division, cuttings taken in July, or by seeds sown as soon as ripe or in the spring.

Helianthemum Mill. (Frostweed, Rock Rose, Sun Rose)
CISTACEAE (Rock Rose Family)

DESCRIPTION: About 110 species of herbs or subshrubs, native in full sun and in limestone soils in Europe, Asia, and North and South America; **leaves** opposite or alternate, usually small and narrow, pubescent with stellate hairs; **flowers** 5-merous; stamens numerous; stigma capitate; **fruit** an ovoid, 3-valved capsule.

Helianthemum canadense (L.) Michx. (Frostweed). Hardy in all zones; perennial to 50 cm. tall.

DESCRIPTION: Erect perennial with stellate pubescence, native in dry soils in full sun from Minnesota to Nova Scotia, south to Missouri and North Carolina; **leaves** elliptic-lanceolate, to 2.5 cm. long, densely pubescent on under surface; **flowers** of two kinds, cleistogamous that never open and the normal with open flowers to 2.5 cm. across, yellow, from May to July.

USE AND CULTURE: Plant in rock gardens in full sun. Frostweed requires a well-drained soil of low fertility. Propagation is by seeds sown as soon as ripe. Late in the season the bark splits open and frost forms as strings of ice crystals, thus giving the plant its common name.

Helianthus L. (Sunflower)
COMPOSITAE (Sunflower Family)
Helianthus Tribe

DESCRIPTION: About 150 species of annual or perennial herbs, native in sunny areas in North America; **roots** fibrous or tuberous; **leaves** often opposite below and alternate above, simple; **flower** heads radiate, rarely discoid, usually solitary on long peduncles or several in corymbs; involucre mostly saucer-shaped to hemispherical; involucral bracts in from 2 to 4 rows; receptacle flat to convex, scaly; ray flowers yellow, in 1 row, pistillate or sterile; disc flowers numerous, perfect; **fruit** an achene; achene with deciduous pappus consisting of two awns with scalelike bases.

Helianthus annuus L. (Common Sunflower, Mirasol). Hardy in all zones; annual to 3 m. tall.
DESCRIPTION: Coarse, rough-hairy annual, native in prairies and dry areas throughout North America; **leaves** mostly alternate, ovate, to 30 cm. long, truncate to cordate at base, dentate; **flower** heads radiate, to 30 cm. across, from July to September; ray flowers orange-yellow; disc flowers red or purple.
USE AND CULTURE: Cultivars are sometimes planted toward the back of the sunny flower border. The species is planted in prairie plantings and for bird food. Annual sunflowers are easy to grow in any fertile soil in full sun. Seeds are planted in early spring.

Helianthus laetiflorus Pers. (Showy Sunflower). Hardy in all zones; perennial to 2 m. tall.
DESCRIPTION: Perennial, nearly glabrous to rough-hairy, native in dry prairies and plains from Montana to Minnesota, south to New Mexico and Indiana; **leaves** mostly opposite, lanceolate to narrowly ovate, frequently rhombic-lanceolate, to 27 cm. long, acute, firm, serrate, and scabrous; **flower** heads to 10 cm. across, from August to October; ray flowers yellow; disc flowers usually yellow, rarely brown or purple.
USE AND CULTURE: Plant toward the back of flower borders or in prairie plantings. The showy sunflower is easy to grow on most soils. Propagation is by seeds sown as soon as ripe or in early spring. Division of established plants in early spring is also successful.

Helianthus maximiliani Schrad. (Maximilian Sunflower). Hardy in all zones; perennial to 3 m. tall.
DESCRIPTION: Stout perennial with woody crowns, native in prairies from Canada south to Texas and North Carolina; **leaves** mostly alternate, lanceolate, to 30 cm. long, acuminate at both ends, entire to serrate, sessile, gray-green; **flower** heads to 7.5 cm. across, in racemes or panicles, from June to October; ray flowers yellow; disc flowers yellow.
USE AND CULTURE: The same as for **Helianthus laetiflorus**.

Helianthus tuberosus L. (Girasole, Jerusalem Artichoke). Hardy in all zones; perennial to 2.4 m. tall.
DESCRIPTION: Stout, branched perennial, producing edible tubers, native in waste lands and damp areas from Manitoba to Nova Scotia, south to Texas and Florida; **leaves** mostly alternate, ovate-lanceolate or oblong-lanceolate to ovate, to 20 cm. long, acuminate, serrate-dentate, scabrous above; petioles winged; **flower** heads to 8 cm. across, from August to October; ray flowers yellow; disc flowers yellow.
USE AND CULTURE: It is sometimes planted toward the back of the flower border, in prairie plantings, or in the vegetable garden for the edible tubers. The Jerusalem artichoke is easy to grow. Propagation is by division of the fleshy tubers in the fall. Portions of the tubers that break off will often produce new plants. The tubers contain inulin and are an important food for diabetics.

Heliopsis Pers. (Oxeye)
COMPOSITAE (Sunflower Family)
Helianthus Tribe

DESCRIPTION: 12 species of annual or perennial herbs, native in North America; **leaves** opposite, simple; **flower** heads radiate, solitary; involucral bracts in 1 or 2 rows, nearly equal; receptacle convex to conical, scaly, often hollow; ray flowers pistillate, orange-yellow or yellow, rarely purple; disc flowers perfect, yellow to brownish-yellow, purple, or red; **fruit** an achene; achenes 4-sided, or triangular with outer surface convex; pappus of a few teeth, an irregular crown, or lacking.

Heliopsis helianthoides (L.) Sweet. (Oxeye). Hardy in all zones; perennial to 1.5 m. tall.

DESCRIPTION: Short-lived, nearly glabrous perennial, native on dry slopes, open sunny woods, roadsides, railroad banks, and other disturbed sites from North Dakota to New York, south to Colorado and Georgia; **leaves** lanceolate-ovate to oblong-ovate, to 12 cm. long, serrate; petioles to 4 cm. long; **flower** heads to 6 cm. across, from late July until frost; ray flowers yellow; disc flowers brownish-yellow.

USE AND CULTURE: Plant in flower borders or in prairie gardens. The oxeye thrives in neutral to slightly acid soils in full sun or light shade. Propagation is by division or seeds. Strong clumps can be divided in early spring. Trim the roots back to about 10 cm. when transplanting. Seeds should be planted as soon as ripe or they can be started indoors in early April for late summer bloom. A number of named cultivars are sold.

Hepatica Mill. (Liverleaf)
RANUNCULACEAE (Buttercup Family)

DESCRIPTION: About 10 species of small, mostly hairy perennial herbs, native in rich, well-drained woodlands in the northern hemisphere; **leaves** long-petioled, cordate, 3- to 5-lobed, evergreen; **flowers** white to purple or blue, solitary, terminal on a scape; involucre calyxlike, of 3 small bracts; sepals petallike; petals lacking; stamens numerous; **fruit** a conical to fusiform achene.

Hepatica acutiloba DC. (Sharplobe Liverleaf). Hardy in all zones; perennial to 10 cm. tall.
DESCRIPTION: Low, cespitose perennial, native in dry or moist upland woods on calcareous soils, often found under sugar maples from Minnesota to Quebec, south to Maine and Georgia; **leaves** 3-, rarely 5- or 7-lobed, deeply cordate at base, broad, acute; **flowers** blue to white or pink, to 2.5 cm. across, in April and May; involucral bracts acute, about as long as the sepals.
USE AND CULTURE: Plant in rock gardens or wild flower gardens. Hepaticas need a neutral soil that is high in organic matter. Grow in the shade. Propagation is by division of established clumps soon after flowering or by seeds sown as soon as ripe. Seeds are forcibly ejected so it is necessary to catch the seeds in a paper bag placed over the seed pod. Plant the seeds immediately.

Hepatica americana (DC.) Ker-Gawl. (Roundlobe Liverleaf). Hardy in all zones; perennial to 10 cm. tall.
DESCRIPTION: Cespitose perennial, native in moist, acid woods, often found under oaks from Manitoba to Nova Scotia, south to Missouri and Florida; **leaves** oblate-reniform with rounded lobes, wine-colored on under surface; **flowers** lavender-blue to white or rose, to 2.5 cm. across, in April and May; sepals 5 to 7, elliptic to oblong; involucral bracts broadly elliptic, obtuse.
USE AND CULTURE: The same as for **Hepatica acutiloba** except that an acid soil is required for best results.

Heracleum L. (Cow Parsnip)
UMBELLIFERAE (Carrot Family)

Hepatica acutiloba. In flower at the Arboretum in April 1982.

Hepatica acutiloba. Close-up.

DESCRIPTION: About 60 species of coarse, biennial or perennial herbs, native in Eurasia and North America; **leaves** large, pinnately or ternately compound; **flowers** small, white, pink, green, or yellow, in compound umbels; **fruit** a flattened mericarp.

Heracleum lanatum - see **Heracleum sphondylium** subsp. **montanum**.

Heracleum sphondylium subsp. **montanum** (Schleich. ex Gaudin) Briq. (American Cow Parsnip, Masterwort). Hardy in all zones; biennial to 3 m. tall.
DESCRIPTION: Coarse biennial, native in moist, usually shaded soils from Alaska to Newfoundland, south to California and Georgia; **leaves** ternately compound; leaflets broadly ovate, lobed and dentate, hairy beneath; **flowers** small, white, in large 15- to 30-rayed umbels, to 20 cm. across, in July; **mericarps** pubescent.
USE AND CULTURE: The cow parsnip is a good plant to grow in moist soils. Propagation is by seeds sown as soon as ripe. Plants self sow.

Heuchera L. (Alumroot)
SAXIFRAGACEAE (Saxifrage Family)
DESCRIPTION: About 40 species of perennial herbs, native on cliffs, hills, and mountains, mostly in western North America; **leaves** mostly basal, rounded-cordate or broadly 5- to 9-lobed, dentate, long-petioled; **flowers** small, green, white, red, or purple, in panicles or racemes, on upright scapes; calyx tube cup-shaped, urn-shaped, or saucer-shaped, united to the ovary, 5-lobed; petals and stamens 5; ovary partly inferior with 2 apical beaks; **fruit** a capsule dehiscing on inner surface of beaks.

Heuchera americana L. (Crevice Alumroot, Rock Geranium). Hardy in all zones; perennial to 1 m. tall.
DESCRIPTION: Perennial, native in dry upland woods and in rocky crevices from Ontario, south to Illinois and Georgia; **leaves** mottled when young, becoming green; **flowers** greenish-white, about as long as the calyx tube, in June; stamens exserted.
USE AND CULTURE: Plant in rock gardens or wild flower gardens. They grow best in a neutral to slightly acid soil in open shade. Propagation is by spring division or by seeds sown as soon as ripe.

Heuchera richardsonii R.Br. (Alumroot). Hardy in all zones; perennial to 90 cm. tall.
DESCRIPTION: Tufted perennial, native in prairies and in dry woods from Saskatchewan to Manitoba, south to Colorado and Indiana; **leaves** mostly basal, rounded-cordate, dentate, long-petioled; **flowers** small, greenish, in narrow panicles; petals spatulate, about as long as the calyx lobes.
USE AND CULTURE: The same as for **Heuchera americana**.

Hibiscus L. (Giant Mallow, Mallow, Rose Mallow)
MALVACEAE (Mallow Family)
DESCRIPTION: About 250 species of herbs, shrubs, and trees, native mostly in warm, temperate, and tropical regions; **leaves** alternate, usually simple and palmately veined, lobed, or parted; **flowers** large, showy, mostly solitary in leaf axils; involucral bracts 4 to 20, sometimes basally united; calyx mostly bell-shaped, 5-lobed; petals 5, longer than the sepals, white to yellow, red, or purple, generally with a basal maroon spot; stamens united into a tube; style 5-branched; **fruit** a 5-celled capsule.

Hibiscus militaris Cav. (Halberd-leaved Rose Mallow, Soldier Rose Mallow). Hardy in zone 3; perennial to 2 m. tall.
DESCRIPTION: Glabrous perennial, native in wet soils from Minnesota to Pennsylvania, south to Texas and Florida; lower **leaves** to 15 cm. long, mostly cordate-ovate; upper leaves triangular and hastately 3- to 5-lobed; **flowers** solitary in upper leaf axils, pale pink to nearly white, crimson or purple at base, from July to October; involucral bracts 10 to 14, filiform to linear-lanceolate, to 2.5 cm. long; calyx tubular-campanulate; petals to 7.5 cm. long.
USE AND CULTURE: Plant in moist soil in wild flower gardens or flower borders. Propagation is by division in early spring or by seeds sown as soon as ripe. Plants are slow to start growing in the spring.

Hibiscus moscheutos ssp. palustris (Marsh Mallow).

Photograph of cultivar 'Southern Belle'.

Photograph: Dr. Anne M. Hanchek.

Hibiscus moscheutos subsp. **palustris** (L.) R.T. Clausen. (Marsh Mallow, Sea Hollyhock). Hardy in zone 4; perennial to 2 m. tall.
DESCRIPTION: Perennial, native in swamps and wet meadows in eastern United States; **leaves** ovate to rounded, commonly 3-lobed, green above, white-pubescent beneath, **flowers** solitary, axillary on long pedicels, white, pink, or rose, usually with a crimson base from July to September; involucral bracts mostly 10 to 14, lanceolate-linear, to 2.5 cm. long; calyx to 4 cm. long, slightly enlarged in fruit; petals to 10 cm. long; **capsule** ovoid, short-beaked, glabrous.
USE AND CULTURE: Same as for **Hibiscus militaris**. Garden hybrids have been produced by crossing **Hibiscus militaris** with **Hibiscus moscheutos**.

Hibiscus palustris - see **Hibiscus moscheutos** ssp. **palustris**.

Houstonia - see **Hedyotis**.

Hydrastis Ellis (Orangeroot, Yellow Puccoon)
RANUNCULACEAE (Buttercup Family)

DESCRIPTION: Two species of low, perennial herbs, native in rich, moist woods in Japan and North America; **leaves** palmately lobed; **flowers** small, solitary; sepals 3, petallike; petals lacking; stamens many, clavate; **fruit** a berry.

Hydrastis canadensis L. (Goldenseal, Orangeroot, Turmeric). Hardy in all zones; perennial to 30 cm. tall.
DESCRIPTION: Rhizomatous perennial, native in moist maple woods, usually found with ginseng, becoming very rare from Minnesota to Vermont, south to Arkansas and Georgia; **rhizomes** thick, yellow; basal **leaves** cordate at base, 5- to 9-lobed, to 20 cm. across, with lobes doubly serrate; stem leaves 2, the upper one under the flower sessile; **flowers** greenish-white, to 1.25 cm. across, in April and May; stamens many, yellow; **berries** dark red, 1- to 2-seeded, forming a head.
USE AND CULTURE: Sometimes planted in wild flower gardens mainly because of its romantic history. The goldenseal requires a rich, moist soil and deep shade. Propagation is by rhizome division either in the fall or early spring. Seeds should be sown as soon as ripe. Because of its rarity, nursery grown plants should be planted. The rhizomes contain berberine, once used in medicines. Like ginseng, this plant was dug in the wild and sold to pharmaceutical companies.

Hypoxis L. (Star Grass)
HYPOXIDACEAE (Star Grass Family)

DESCRIPTION: About 110 species of stemless perennial herbs, native in well-drained soils mostly in the southern hemisphere; rhizomes short, cormlike; **leaves** linear, grasslike; **flowers** white or yellow, 1 to several on a scape; perianth of 6 separate segments; stamens 6, in 1 series with slender filaments and erect or versatile anthers; **fruit** a capsule or an indehiscent pod.

Impatiens pallida. In flower in August 1977.

Hypoxis hirsuta (L.) Cov. (Star Grass, Yellow Star Grass). Hardy in all zones; perennial to 20 cm. tall.
DESCRIPTION: Rhizomatous perennial, native in prairies and in open woods from Manitoba to Maine, south to Texas and Florida; **rhizomes** short, cormlike; **leaves** linear, grasslike, to 30 cm. long, hairy; **flowers** bright yellow, starlike, 1 to 7 on a scape, from May to July, occasionally all summer; perianth segments 1.25 cm. long; anthers versatile; ovary pilose; **fruit** an indehiscent pod.
USE AND CULTURE: Plant in rock gardens or prairie gardens. It is attractive when grown with blue-eyed grass. Plants grow best in a slightly acid soil in full sun or open shade. Propagation is by division of the cormlike rhizomes. Plant about 4 cm. deep in the fall or early spring. Seeds should be planted as soon as ripe and barely covered.

Impatiens L. (Balsam, Jewelweed, Snapweed, Touch-me-not)
BALSAMINACEAE (Balsam Family)

DESCRIPTION: About 500 species of annual or perennial herbs or subshrubs, native in moist soils, widespread, especially in the tropics and subtropics of Asia and Africa; **stems** nearly transparent showing vascular bundles; **leaves** simple, generally without stipules; **flowers** solitary or variously clustered; sepals usually 3, the upper 2 small and green, the lower 1 petaloid, asymmetrically funnelform, usually with a long necateriferous spur; petals 5. the upper (standard) flat or helmet-shaped, the lower 4 united in lateral pairs (wings); stamens 5, united in a short tube; ovary superior, 5-celled; **fruit** a 5-valved capsule, explosively dehiscent.

Impatiens capensis Meerb. (Jewelweed, Lady's-earrings, Spotted Touch-me-not). Annual to 1.2 m. tall.
DESCRIPTION: Glabrous annual, native in moist, shaded areas from Saskatchewan to Newfoundland, south to Oklahoma and Alabama; **stems** transparent; **leaves** ovate to elliptic, to 8 cm. long, coarsely toothed; **flowers** orange-yellow, spotted with reddish-brown, in few-flowered, axillary racemes, from July to frost; spurs to 2.5 cm. long, strongly incurved.
USE AND CULTURE: Plant in wild flower gardens. The jewelweed requires a moist soil with some shade. Propagation is by seeds sown as soon as ripe. Plants will self sow once the plants are established. Volunteer seedlings will keep the planting going if conditions are right. This is a fun plant to grow. Mature seed capsules will explode to discharge their seeds when touched, hence one of its common names, touch-me-not.

Impatiens pallida Nutt. (Jewelweed, Pale Touch-me-not). Annual to 1.2 m. tall.
DESCRIPTION: Succulent annual, native in moist soils from Saskatchewan to New-foundland, south to Kansas and Georgia; **stems** glaucous; **leaves** ovate to elliptic, to 8 cm. long; **flowers** canary yellow, usually unspotted, from June to September; spur short, bent at right angles.
USE AND CULTURE: The same as for **Impatiens capensis**.

Ipomoea L. (Morning-glory)
CONVOLVULACEAE (Morning-glory Family)

DESCRIPTION: About 500 species of prostrate, twining, or erect annuals or perennial herbs, native mostly in tropical and warm-temperate regions; **leaves** alternate, entire, lobed, or divided; **flowers** axillary, solitary, or in few- to many-flowered clusters; corolla funnelform or campanulate, 5-lobed with 5 stripes; stamens and styles included; style solitary; stigmas entire or 2- to 3-lobed; **fruit** a 4- to 6-valved capsule.

Ipomoea leptophylla Torr. (Bush Moonflower, Bush Morning-glory, Man-of-the-earth, Manroot). Hardy in zone 4; perennial to 1.3 m. tall.
DESCRIPTION: Perennial with large, tuberous roots, native in dry plains from Wyoming to Nebraska, south to New Mexico; **stems** erect or ascending; **leaves** linear, to 12 cm. long, entire; **flowers** purple or pink, to 7.5 cm. across, in May and June.
USE AND CULTURE: Plant in flower borders or in prairie gardens. Plants require a well-drained soil. Propagation is by seeds sown in the spring. Because of the hard seed coats which are impervious to water, it is advisable to file through the seed coat before

Impatiens capensis (Jewelweed).

planting. This is a beautiful wild flower when in bloom. It should be kept in mind that plants produce a large, tuberous root.

Ipomopsis Michx (Gilia)
POLEMONIACEAE (Phlox Family)

DESCRIPTION: About 24 species of annual, biennial, or perennial herbs, native mostly in North America, one species native in Argentina; **stems** leafy; **leaves** alternate, entire to pinnately dissected, with sharp-tipped segments, variously hairy; **flowers** of various colors, in cymes or panicles, each subtended by a bract; calyx 5-lobed; corolla salverform or tubular; stamens 5, often unequal in length; **fruit** a capsule.

Ipomopsis rubra (L.) Wherry. (Scarlet Gilia, Spanish Larkspur, Standing Cypress). Hardy in zone 4; biennial to 2 m. tall.
DESCRIPTION: Unbranched biennial or short-lived perennial, native from Oklahoma to South Carolina, south to Texas and Florida; **leaves** pinnately parted into filiform segments, about 2.5 cm. long; **flowers** scarlet outside, yellow and dotted red inside, in a narrow panicle, in July and August.
USE AND CULTURE: Plant in flower borders. This southern native wild flower is occasionally planted in our area. The blooms are very showy and make it worth the effort to grow. Being primarily a biennial, it is best to sow the seed in a cold frame where the seedlings can be wintered. Transplant to the flower border in the spring. Seedlings, started early indoors, will sometimes bloom the first year. This plant attracts hummingbirds.

Ipomopsis rubra (Scarlet Gilia).

Iris cristata (Crested Iris). In flower in

Dr. Snyder's garden in May 1982.

Iris L. (Flag, Fleur-de-lis, Iris)
IRIDACEAE (Iris Family)

DESCRIPTION: About 200 species of rhizomatous or bulbous, perennial herbs, native in the North Temperate Zone; **leaves** mostly basal, 2-ranked, linear to sword-shaped; **flowers** showy, in many colors, 1 or more in unbranched or branched inflorescences; perianth segments 6, the outer 3 (falls) narrowed basally, sometimes bearded, the inner 3 (standards) narrowed into a claw, usually erect and arching; stamens 3, born at the base of the falls; style branches 3, bifid or crested, petallike; **fruit** a 3- or 6-angled, leathery capsule.

Iris cristata Ait. (Crested Dwarf Iris, Crested Iris, Dwarf Crested Iris). Hardy in all zones; perennial to 20 cm. tall.
DESCRIPTION: Low, rhizomatous perennial, native from Wisconsin to Maryland, south to Missouri and Georgia; **leaves** about 6, sword-shaped, to 22 cm. long; **flowers** in 1- to 2-flowered spathes, in April and May; perianth tube longer than the spathe; falls obovate, to 4 cm. long; crest white and yellow, dotted lilac-purple; standards oblanceolate.
USE AND CULTURE: This is a popular rock garden plant that can also be used as a ground cover in sun or open shade. Plants grow best on a well-drained, slightly acid soil in full sun or half shade. Propagation is by division, preferably about 6 weeks after bloom although, with proper care, plants can be moved at any time.

Iris lacustris Nutt. (Lake Iris). Hardy in all zones; perennial to 7.5 cm. tall.
DESCRIPTION: Rhizomatous perennial, native in gravelly soils around the Great Lakes; **leaves** broadly linear, to 18 cm. long; **flowers** about 5 cm. across, from May to July; perianth tube scarcely longer than the spathe valves, dull yellow; segments blue; falls obovate; standards emarginate.
USE AND CULTURE: Plant in rock gardens or as a ground cover. This iris must have a well-drained, preferably sandy, soil. Propagation is mainly by division about 6 weeks after bloom. Seeds can also be sown as soon as ripe. Seedlings will bloom the third year.

Iris versicolor L. (Blue Flag, Poison Flag, Wild Iris). Hardy in all zones; perennial to 90 cm. tall.
DESCRIPTION: A tufted, often branched perennial, native in marshes, wet meadows, along lake shores and streams, and in wet roadside ditches from Manitoba to Labrador, south to Arkansas and West Virginia; **stems** often branched; **leaves** firm, linear to

sword-shaped, to 90 cm. long, somewhat glaucous; **flowers** in 2- to 3-flowered spathes, in June and July; perianth tube funnelform, to 1.25 cm. long; falls ovate to reniform-ovate, to 7.5 cm. long, lavender, violet, or blue-violet, rarely red-violet or white; standards erect.

USE AND CULTURE: Plant at the edges of pools or in flower borders. This iris can be grown in any fertile garden soil that is kept moist. Bloom is best when grown in full sun. Propagation is by division in late summer or by seeds sown as soon as ripe. Seedlings should bloom the third year.

Isopyrum biternatum (False Rue Anemone).

In flower in May 1978.

Jeffersonia diphylla (American Twinleaf).

Photograph: Dr. Anne M. Hanchek.

Isopyrum L. (Isopyrum)
RANUNCULACEAE (Buttercup Family)

DESCRIPTION: About 30 species of small, delicate, perennial herbs, native in the northern hemisphere; **leaves** decompound, columbinelike; **flowers** white, solitary or in panicles or umbellate cymes; sepals 5 to 6, petallike, deciduous; petals abortive or lacking; stamens many; filaments club-shaped; **fruit** a follicle.

Isopyrum biternatum (Raf.) Torr. & A. Gray. (False Rue Anemone). Hardy in all zones; perennial to 30 cm. tall.
DESCRIPTION: Delicate perennial with scattered tuberous roots, native in woods from Minnesota to Ontario, south to Texas and Florida; **leaves** 2-ternate; leaflets glabrous beneath; **flowers** solitary, terminal or axillary, in April and May; sepals white; petals lacking; filaments white; follicles 4, widespreading.
USE AND CULTURE: Plant in woodland wild flower gardens. These plants grow well in most soils that are high in organic matter. They need shade. Propagation is by division of the tubers in fall or early spring. Seeds can be planted as soon as ripe.

Jeffersonia B. Barton. (Twinleaf)
BERBERIDACEAE (Barberry Family)

DESCRIPTION: Two species of small perennial herbs, native in woods in eastern North America and northeastern Asia; **leaves** basal, palmately veined or lobed; **flowers** white or blue, solitary, terminal on long scapes; perianth of about 12 segments, the inner ones petaloid; stamens 6; ovary ovoid; **fruit** a leathery capsule.

Jeffersonia diphylla (L.) Pers. (American Twinleaf). Hardy in all zones; perennial to 25 cm. tall.
DESCRIPTION: Perennial, native in open, deciduous woods rich in leafmold from Wisconsin to Ontario, south to Alabama and Maryland; **leaves** to 15 cm. long, divided into 2 kidney-shaped, entire or lobed divisions, glaucous beneath; petioles as long as the flower scapes; **flowers** white, solitary on long scapes, to 2.5 cm. across, in May and June; **capsules** yellow-green, dehiscent by a lid.
USE AND CULTURE: Plant in woodland wild flower gardens. The twinleaf needs soils that are neutral to moderately acid that are high in organic matter. Plant in open shade. Propagation is by fall division or by seeds sown as soon as ripe. Space plants about 20 cm. apart.

Lathyrus L. (Vetchling, Wild Pea)
LEGUMINOSAE (Pea Family)
DESCRIPTION: Over 100 species of mostly climbing annual and perennial herbs, native in north temperate regions and in Africa and South America; **stems** winged or angled; **leaves** alternate, even-pinnate with branched tendrils on climbing species; **flowers** showy, axillary, pealike, solitary or in racemes; style flattened, bearded on inner surface; **fruit** a dehiscent, flattened legume.

Lathyrus japonicus Willd. (Beach Pea, Heath Pea, Seaside Pea). Hardy in all zones; perennial to 60 cm. tall.
DESCRIPTION: Decumbent perennial, native on shores of lakes and streams around the Great Lakes and in Europe and Asia; **stems** creeping, wingless; **leaflets** in 3 to 6 pairs, oblong or ovate, to 5 cm. long; **stipules** broadly ovate; **flowers** purple, in 6- to 10-flowered racemes, from June to August.
USE AND CULTURE: Plant in flower borders. These plants require a well-drained soil. Propagation is by seeds sown in the spring where the plants are to grow. Plants can also be increased by cuttings.

Lathyrus maritimus - see **Lathyrus japonicus**

Lathyrus venosus Muhlenb. ex Willd. (Vetchling ,Wild Pea). Hardy in all zones; perennial to 1 m. tall.
DESCRIPTION: Stout, upright perennial, native in woods from Alberta to New Brunswick, south to Texas and Georgia; **stems** stout, 4-angled, pubescent; **leaflets** in 4 to 6 pairs, oblong-ovate, to 5 cm. long; **stipules** narrow, semi-sagittate; **flowers** purple, to 2 cm. long, in crowded clusters, in June and July; **legumes** smooth.
USE AND CULTURE: Plant in flower borders in sun or shade. The culture is the same as for **Lathyrus japonicus**.

Leucocrinum Nutt. (Mountain Lily, Sand Lily, Star Lily)
LILIACEAE (Lily Family)
DESCRIPTION: A single species of stemless, perennial herbs, native in sandy prairie soils in western North America; **rhizomes** deep-seated with fleshy roots; **leaves** narrowly linear; **flowers** white, emerging in a cluster from the rhizomes; perianth segments salverform; 6-lobed; stamens 6, attached near the tip of the perianth tube; **fruit** a capsule.

Leucocrinum montanum Nutt. (Sand Lily). Hardy in all zones; perennial to 12 cm. tall.
DESCRIPTION: Native in sandy soils from Oregon to South Dakota, south to California and Nebraska; **leaves** several, linear, to 12 cm. long; **flowers** pure white, fragrant, to 12 cm. long, in May; stamens with yellow anthers.
USE AND CULTURE: Plant in rock gardens or prairie gardens. The plants require full sun, and a sandy, well-drained soil. Propagation is by division in the fall or by seeds sown as soon as ripe. Capsules and seeds are produced underground.

Liatris Gaertn. ex. Schreb. (Blazing-star,
Button Snakeroot, Gay-feather)
COMPOSITAE (Sunflower Family)
Eupatorium Tribe
DESCRIPTION: About 40 species of perennial herbs with corms or rhizomes, native in sunny roadside ditches and open prairies in the Great Plains of North America; **leaves** alternate, simple, mostly linear to linear-lanceolate, entire, usually resin-dotted; **flower** heads discoid, in spikes, racemes, or panicles, the uppermost heads flowering first; involucral bracts imbricate in several rows, lanceolate to orbicular, with scarious, ciliate to deeply erose margins; receptacle flat, naked; disc flowers tubular, perfect, purple or rose-purple, rarely white; **fruit** a cylindrical 10-ribbed achene; pappus of 15 to 40 plumose bristles.

Liatris aspera Michx. (Gay-feather). Hardy in all zones; perennial to 2 m. tall.

DESCRIPTION: A stout, erect perennial, native in dry, often sandy soils from North Dakota to Ontario, south to Texas and South Carolina; lower **leaves** rhombic lanceolate, to 40 cm. long, petioled; upper leaves linear to linear-lanceolate, reduced upward; **flower** heads to 2.5 cm. across, in spikes of 20 to 150 heads, in August and September; involucre campanulate to nearly globose; involucral bracts wrinkled, glabrous, purple, with lacerate margins.

USE AND CULTURE: Plant in flower borders or prairie gardens. Plants are easy to grow on well-drained soil in full sun. Propagation is by division and by seeds sown in May.

Liatris ligulistylis (A. Nelson) K. Schum. (Rocky Mountain Gay-feather). Hardy in all zones; perennial to 1 m. tall.

DESCRIPTION: Perennial, native in moist, low areas, often along roadsides, from Alberta to Wisconsin, south to New Mexico; **leaves** glabrous to densely pubescent, ciliate; basal leaves lanceolate-oblong to oblanceolate, to 15 cm. long, usually petioled; upper leaves lanceolate, reduced upward; **flower** heads to 3 cm. across with 40 to 70 disc flowers, in racemes of 2 to 30 heads, in August and September; involucre broadly campanulate or hemispherical; involucral bracts often purple with scarious, lacerate margins.

USE AND CULTURE: The same as for **Liatris aspera**.

Liatris punctata Hook. (Dotted Gay-feather). Hardy in all zones; perennial to 30 cm. tall.

DESCRIPTION: Glabrous perennial with numerous stems from a crown, native in dry prairies from Alberta to Minnesota, south to New Mexico and Iowa; **leaves** rigid, conspicuously punctate, basal leaves linear, to 10 cm. long, ciliate; upper leaves gradually reduced; **flower** heads 4- to 8-flowered, 2 cm. long, in dense spikes; involucre cylindrical; involucral bracts white-ciliate.

USE AND CULTURE: The sames as for **Liatris aspera**.

Liatris pycnostachya Michx. (Cattail Gay-feather, Kansas Gay-feather). Hardy in all zones; perennial to 1.5 m. tall.

DESCRIPTION: Coarse, upright perennial, native in moist prairies and roadside ditches from South Dakota to Indiana, south to Texas and Florida; **stems** with fleshy, underground corms; **leaves** punctate, glabrous to hairy; lower leaves to 40 cm. long, reduced upward; **flower** heads to 1 cm. across, 5- to 10-flowered, in dense cylindrical spikes to 45 cm. long, in August and September; involucre cylindrical to narrowly turbinate; involucral bracts with spreading tips.

USE AND CULTURE: Plant in flower borders for accent and also in prairie gardens. This is the most widely planted species of Liatris. For propagation, the corms are cut vertically very much as you would cut potatoes, being sure that each piece has a bud. Let the cut surfaces dry for at least an hour before replanting. Seeds are slow to germinate and seelings take 3 years to bloom.

Liatris spicata (L.) Willd. (Spike Gay-feather). Hardy in all zones; perennial to 1.5 m. tall.

DESCRIPTION: Stiff, erect perennial, native in moist soils from Michigan to New York, south to Louisiana and Florida; lower **leaves** linear-lanceolate, to 10 cm. long, reduced upwards; **flower** heads about 1 cm. across, many in spikelike inflorescences to 75 cm. long, in August and September; involucre turbinate-campanulate; involucral bracts often purple with scarious margins.

USE AND CULTURE: The same as for **Liatris aspera**. This species requires soils that are more moist than other **Liatris** species.

Liatris squarrosa (L.) Michx. (Gay-feather). Hardy in all zones; perennial to 1 m. tall.

DESCRIPTION: Stout perennial, native in prairies and roadside ditches from South Dakota to Delaware, south to Texas and Alabama; **stems** several to many, pubescent; **leaves** rigid, punctate, lowest ones to 25 cm. long, shorter above; **flower** heads to 3 cm. across, 20- to 45-flowered, solitary to many in a raceme or panicle, in August and September; involucre cylindrical; involucral bracts with long, tapered, spreading tips.

USE AND CULTURE: The same as for **Liatris aspera**.

Lilium michiganense (Michigan Lily). Along Interstate 35 in Northeastern Minnesota.

Photograph: Bonnie L. Harper Lore.

Lilium canadense (Canada Lily).

Photograph: Mr. Arvid Lund

Lilium superbum (Turk's-cap Lily).

Photograph: Dr. Anne M. Hanchek.

Lilium L. (Lily)
LILIACEAE (Lily Family)

DESCRIPTION: Nearly 100 species of perennial herbs with scaly bulbs, native in the North Temperate Zone; **stems** leafy, unbranched; **leaves** alternate or whorled, usually many; **flowers** solitary and terminal or in terminal racemes, panicles, or umbels, white, orange, red, purple, or maroon; perianth funnelform, cup-shaped, or campanulate with 6 segments (tepals); stamens 6, with versatile anthers; **fruit** a 3-valved capsule.

Lilium canadense L. (Canada Lily, Field Lily, Meadow Lily, Wild Yellow Lily, Yellow-bell Lily, Yellow Lily). Hardy in all zones; perennial to 1.5 m. tall.
DESCRIPTION: Tall perennial, native in moist, open ground and meadows from Minnesota to Nova Scotia, south to Kentucky and Virginia; **bulbs** renewed annually at the tips of rhizomes; **leaves** whorled, lanceolate to oblanceolate, to 15 cm. long, margins often scabrous, **flowers** 1 to 20, in 1- to 4-flowered umbels from upper leaf axils, campanulate, nodding, to 7.5 cm. long and wide, orange-yellow to red, spotted with purple-brown spots, in June and July; tepals recurved outward.
USE AND CULTURE: Plant in flower borders or prairie gardens. Plants require a moist soil. They also need protection from winds. Bulbs should be planted in the fall about 15 cm. deep and 30 cm. apart. Plants will tolerate some shade but bloom best in full sun.

Lilium michiganense Farw. (Michigan Lily). Hardy in all zones; perennial to 1.5 m. tall.
DESCRIPTION: Stoloniferous perennial, native in moist meadows from Manitoba to Ontario, south to Kansas and Tennessee; new **bulbs** form at the tips of horizontal rhizomes; **leaves** whorled, lanceolate, to 10 cm. long; **flowers** 1 to 8 in an umbel, nodding to 7 cm. long, orange-red, spotted with reddish-maroon spots and with a green basal spot on inside, in July; tepals strongly recurved; stigmas purple.
USE AND CULTURE: The same as for **Lilium canadense**. This species is similar to **Lilium canadense** and considered by some to be a western form of the Canada lily.

Lilium philadelphicum L. (Orange-cup Lily, Wood Lily). Hardy in all zones; perennial to 1 m. tall.
DESCRIPTION: Perennial, native in open woods and clearings, also in prairies from British Columbia to Quebec, south to New Mexico and Kentucky; **leaves** in whorls of 4 to 8, linear-lanceolate, to 10 cm. long; **flowers** 1 to 5, open-campanulate, facing upward, to 10 cm. across, orange to vivid orange-red, spotted with purple, from June to August; tepals with long claws.
USE AND CULTURE: Plant in prairie planting or in the flower border. Plants will tolerate some shade but bloom best where they receive morning sun. Plant bulbs in the fall. This lily is on the protected list and should not be dug in the wild. Bulbs can be grown from scales in a sand-humus mixture. Seedlings take 5 years to bloom from seed.
VARIETIES: var. **andinum** (Nutt.) Ker-Gawl. (Western Orange-cup Lily). Plants smaller; **leaves** mostly alternate.
Lilium superbum L. (American Turk's-cap Lily, Lily-royal, Swamp Lily, Turk's-cap, Turk's-cap Lily). Hardy in all zones; perennial to 2 m. tall.

DESCRIPTION: Stoloniferous perennial, native in wet meadows and marshy lowlands from Minnesota to New Brunswick, south to Missouri and Florida; **bulbs** white; **leaves** whorled below, alternate above, lanceolate, to 15 cm. long; **flowers** few to many in a terminal raceme, nodding, to 10 cm. across, orange-scarlet, spotted with purple-brown, from June to September; tepals strongly reflexed; anthers orange-red; filaments curved outward.
USE AND CULTURE: The same as for **Lilium canadense**.

Lilium umbellatum - see **Lilium philadelphicum** var. **andinum**.

Linnaea L. (Twinflower)
CAPRIFOLIACEAE (Honeysuckle Family)

DESCRIPTION: A single species of trailing evergreen subshrub, native in acid woods, bogs, and peaty soils, circumpolar; **leaves** opposite, simple, rounded; **flowers** in pairs, campanulate, nodding, on slender terminal peduncles; calyx and corolla 5-lobed; stamens 4; ovary inferior, 3-celled but only one cell fertile; **fruit** a 1-seeded achene.

Linnaea borealis L. (Twinflower). Hardy in all zones; subshrub to 10 cm. tall.
DESCRIPTION: Creeping evergreen subshrub, native along logging trails in cut-over evergreen woods covering logs and stumps, circumpolar south to California and West Virginia in the United States; **leaves** crenate, to 2.5 cm. long; **flowers** rose or white, to 8 mm. long, fragrant, borne in pairs and nodding, from June to August; **fruits** yellow, to 3 mm. long.
USE AND CULTURE: Plant in wild flower gardens or rock gardens. The twinflower requires a rich, acid soil with a pH of about 4.5. Adding acid peat moss to the soil helps. Propagation is by seeds planted as soon as ripe or by cuttings taken in the spring before growth starts. Stem cuttings should be rooted in a cold frame in a sand-peat mixture. The soil must be kept moist.

Linum L. (Flax)
LINACEAE (Flax Family)

DESCRIPTION: About 200 species of annual or perennial herbs, native in temperate or subtropical regions of the world; **leaves** simple, usually alternate, narrow, entire; **flowers** red, yellow, blue, or white, in terminal or axillary racemes, corymbs, cymes, or panicles, 5-merous; petals drop early; stamens united at base; pistil 1, with 5 styles; **fruit** a 5- to 10-celled capsule.

Linum lewisii - see **Linum perenne** subsp. **lewisii**.

Linum perenne subsp. **lewisii** (Pursh) Hult. (Prairie Flax). Hardy in all zones; perennial to 60 cm. tall.
DESCRIPTION: Glabrous perennial, native in dry soils in western North America from Alaska to Wisconsin, south to California and West Virginia; **leaves** linear to lanceolate, to 3 cm. long; **flowers** blue, to 2.5 cm. across in much-branched panicles, from May to September.

Lilium philadelphicum (Wood Lily). In flower in August 1983 in Fort Wing, Wisconsin.

Linum perenne ssp. lewisii (Prairie Flax).

Photograph: Dr. Anne M. Hanchek.

USE AND CULTURE: Plant in flower borders or in rock gardens. Plants require a well-drained soil and full sun. Propagation is by spring division, cuttings, and by seeds. Seeds can be planted directly where plants are to be grown.

Linum rigidum Pursh. (Flax). Hardy in all zones; perennial to 50 cm. tall.
DESCRIPTION: Glabrous perennial, native in rocky soils from Alberta to Manitoba, south to Utah and Oklahoma; **stems** rigid, fastigiate, angled; **leaves** few, erect, linear, with stipular glands; **flowers** yellow with reddish centers, to 3 cm. across.
USE AND CULTURE: Plant in rock gardens. The culture is the same as for **Linum perenne** ssp. **lewisii**.

Linum sulcatum Ridd. (Flax). Annual to 75 cm. tall.
DESCRIPTION: Erect annual, native in prairies from Montana to Ontario, south to Texas and Georgia; **stems** angled; **leaves** linear, to 1.25 cm. long, with minute glands on either side of leaf base; **flowers** yellow, to 1.25 cm. across, from June to October; sepals lanceolate, glandular-serrate, longer than the capsule.
USE AND CULTURE: Plant in flower borders. Plants will grow in most any well-drained soil in full sun. Propagation is by seeds started indoors in early April. Space plants about 20 cm. apart.

Lisianthus russellianus - see **Eustoma grandiflorum**.

Lithospermum L. (Gromwell, Puccoon)
BORAGINACEAE (Borage Family)
DESCRIPTION: About 45 species of hairy, perennial herbs, native in sunny fields and roadsides, usually in sandy soils on all continents except Australia; **roots** often with a red or purple dye; **leaves** alternate, simple, sessile, entire; **flowers** orange, yellow, or white, in simple or branched scorpioid cymes; calyx and corolla 5-lobed with glands in the throat of the corolla; stamens 5, never exserted; **fruit** of 4 nutlets, usually polished, white.

Lithospermum canescens (Michx.) Lehm. (Indian-paint, Hoary Puccoon). Hardy in all zones; perennial to 45 cm. tall.
DESCRIPTION: Perennial with hoary pubescence, native in sandy soils from North Dakota to Ontario, south to Texas and Georgia; **roots** contain a red dye; **leaves** oblong to linear; **flowers** orange-yellow, 1.4 cm. long, in May and June; corolla lobes entire, with tube glabrous inside; **nutlets** yellow, smooth, and shining.
USE AND CULTURE: Plant in rock gardens or prairie gardens. Plants require full sun and a sandy soil of low fertility. Propagation is by seeds sown as soon as ripe, or by root cuttings. Root cuttings should be about the size of a lead pencil and 5 cm. long. Plant in early spring spacing the plants about 30 cm. apart.

Lithospermum caroliniense (Walt.) MacMill. (Puccoon). Hardy in all zones; perennial to 60 cm. tall.

Lobelia siphilitica (Great Blue Lobelia).

DESCRIPTION: Perennial, native in upland woods, lake shores, and prairies, usually in sandy soils, from Wyoming to Ontario, south to Texas and Florida; **stems** erect, from a woody root, villous or hirsute; **leaves** linear to lanceolate, to 6 cm. long, rough-hirsute; **flowers** bright yellow or orange, in leafy-bracted cymes; corolla tube to 1.4 cm. long; **nutlets** ivory-white.

USE AND CULTURE: The same as for **Lithospermum canescens**.

Lobelia L. (Lobelia)
LOBELIACEAE (Lobelia Family)

DESCRIPTION: About 375 species of herbs, shrubs, or trees, native in moist soils, mostly in tropical and warm-temperate regions; **leaves** alternate, simple; **flowers** blue, violet, red, yellow, or white, in bracted racemes; calyx 5-toothed; corolla irregular, mostly 2-lipped, the upper lip 2-lobed, the lower lip 3-cleft, tube slit nearly to base; stamens 5, attached at base of corolla; anthers united into a tube around style; ovary 2-celled; stigma lobes rounded, spreading; **fruit** a capsule.

Lobelia cardinalis L. (Cardinal Flower, Indian Pink). Hardy in all zones; perennial to 1 m. tall.

DESCRIPTION: Perennial, native in wet soils along streams from Minnesota to New Brunswick, south to Texas; **stems** glabrous, often a purple-red; **leaves** lanceolate to oblong, to 10 cm. long, acute; **flowers** scarlet, rarely pink or white, in bracted racemes, from July to September; corolla to 4 cm. long; anthers exserted, lower 2 tufted; **capsules** subglobose, to 1 cm. across.

USE AND CULTURE: Plant in flower borders or in wild flower gardens. Plants require a moist soil and either full sun or partial shade. The soil should be neutral to slightly acid. Propagation is by seeds sown as soon as ripe or started indoors in mid-March. Established plants can be divided in early spring. This plant should not be dug in the wild. Once established, this plant will self sow. Although a perennial, individual plants are short-lived. A winter mulch is advised. Cutting back the plants after flowering, to prevent seed development, prolongs the life of the plants.

Lobelia siphilitica L. (Blue Cardinal Flower, Great Blue Lobelia). Hardy in all zones; perennial to 1 m. tall.

DESCRIPTION: Unbranched perennial, native in moist soils in meadows and along streams from South Dakota to Maine, south to Kansas and North Carolina; **leaves** ovate to broadly lanceolate, to 10 cm. long, acute, irregularly serrate; **flowers** blue, rarely white, in dense racemes, in August and September; calyx lobes auricled at base; corolla to 2.5 cm. long; lower 2 anthers tufted.

USE AND CULTURE: The same as for **Lobelia cardinalis**.

Lobelia spicata Lam. (Pale-spike Lobelia). Hardy in all zones; biennial to 60 cm. tall.

DESCRIPTION: Biennial, rarely perennial, native in roadside ditches and other disturbed soils from Minnesota to New Brunswick, south to Arkansas and Georgia; **stems** sparsely branched; **leaves** mostly basal, obovate to lanceolate, sessile, serrate; **flowers** bluish-violet, rarely white, in terminal spikes, in June; calyx tube scarcely inflated, about 6 mm. long.

USE AND CULTURE: Plant in flower borders or prairie gardens. Effective in masses. Plants grow well in most soils. Propagation is by seeds sown as soon as ripe. Once established, this species self sows.

Lupinus L. (Lupine)
LEGUMINOSAE (Pea Family)

DESCRIPTION: About 200 species of annual or perennial herbs or subshrubs, native in sandy or well-drained soils, worldwide but mainly in North America; **leaves** palmately compound, rarely reduced to a single leaflet; stipules united to the petioles; **flowers** showy, pealike, in terminal spikes or racemes; standards erect with reflexed margins; stamens 10, united; **fruit** a legume, often constricted between the seeds.

Lupinus perennis L. (Sundial Lupine, Wild Lupine). Hardy in all zones; perennial to 60 cm. tall.

Lobelia cardinalis (Cardinal Flower). In flower in July 1977.

Lupinus perennis (Wild Lupine). In flower at

the Arboretum in June 1982.

DESCRIPTION: Pubescent perennial, native in sandy soils along roadsides, waste lands, and pastures from Ontario south to Minnesota and Florida; **leaflets** 7 to 11, blue-green, to 5 cm. long; **flowers** blue, varying to pink or white, in racemes, in May and June; **legumes** pubescent to 4 cm. long.

USE AND CULTURE: Plant in flower borders or prairie gardens. Plants require a well-drained soil that is slightly acid. They need full sun. Plants go dormant in August after the seeds mature. Propagation is by spring division or by seeds. Seeds can be started indoors or seeded directly. Due to the hard seed coat, germination is improved by soaking for 15 minutes in warm water. Seedlings will bloom the second year. Plants self sow once established. The foliage is reported to be poisonous to livestock.

Lysimachia L. (Loosestrife)
PRIMULACEAE (Primrose Family)

DESCRIPTION: About 165 species of annual or perennial herbs, rarely shrubs, native in moist soils, widely distributed in temperate and subtropical regions; **stems** leafy; **leaves** simple, alternate, opposite, or whorled, often glandular-dotted; **flowers** yellow or white, rarely pink, blue, or purple; calyx 5- to 6-parted; corolla rotate to campanulate, 5- to 7-parted; stamens 5 to 7, inserted on the corolla tube; **fruit** a 5-valved capsule.

Lysimachia ciliata L. (Fringed Loosestrife). Hardy in all zones; perennial to 1 m. tall.
DESCRIPTION: Perennial, native in wet meadows and thickets from British Columbia to Nova Scotia, south to New Mexico and Florida; **stems** lightly branched; **leaves** opposite, ovate to ovate-lanceolate, to 15 cm. long; petioles conspicuously ciliate; **flowers** yellow, to 2.5 cm. across, solitary in the upper leaf axils, from June to August.
USE AND CULTURE: Plant in flower borders or wild flower gardens. Plants are easy to grow in any moist soil. Propagation is by division. Plants have a tendency to spread and should be divided every few years.

Lysimachia lanceolata Walt. Hardy in all zones; perennial to 75 cm. tall.
DESCRIPTION: Perennial, native in swamps and damp meadows from Wisconsin to Pennsylvania, south to Iowa and Florida; **stems** 4-angled; **leaves** opposite, lower ones elliptic to ovate, upper ones linear to lanceolate; **flowers** yellow, solitary in upper leaf axils or panicled, from June to August.
USE AND CULTURE: The same as for **Lysimachia ciliata**.

Lysimachia quadrifolia L. (Whorled Loosestrife). Hardy in all zones; perennial to 90 cm. tall.
DESCRIPTION: Erect perennial, native in moist or dry upland soils, chiefly in open woods from Wisconsin to Maine, south to Alabama and South Carolina; **stems** rarely branched, glabrous or sparsely hairy; **leaves** in whorls of 3 to 6, mostly in 4's, narrowly or broadly lanceolate, to 10 cm. long, hairy beneath; **flowers** yellow, usually solitary in leaf axils, in June and July.
USE AND CULTURE: The same as for **Lysimachia ciliata**.

Lysimachia terrestris (L.) BSP. (Swamp Candles). Hardy in all zones; perennial to 40 cm. tall.

DESCRIPTION: Erect, glabrous perennial, native in swamps and wet roadside ditches from Minnesota to Newfoundland, south to Tennessee and South Carolina; **stems** often branched; **rhizomes** creeping; **bulbils** often form in leaf axils; **leaves** opposite, narrowly lanceolate, to 10 cm. long; **flowers** yellow, starlike, in many-flowered terminal racemes, from June to August.

USE AND CULTURE: Plant in wild flower gardens. Plants prefer light shade and a moist soil. Propagation is by division of the rhizomes or by bulbils. Plant rhizomes about 2.5 cm. deep either in the fall or early spring. Bulbils planted as soon as mature will bloom the second year.

Lysimachia thyrsiflora L. (Tufted Loosestrife). Hardy in all zones; perennial to 75 cm. tall.

DESCRIPTION: Perennial with creeping rhizomes, native circumboreal, south to Missouri and Ohio in North America; **leaves** opposite, lanceolate to elliptic, to 15 cm. long, sessile; **flowers** pale yellow, in short, axillary, spikelike racemes, from May to July.

USE AND CULTURE: The same as for **Lysimachia ciliata**.

Lythrum L. (Loosestrife)
LYTHRACEAE (Loosestrife Family)

DESCRIPTION: About 30 species of annual or perennial herbs, native in moist soils in North America and Eurasia; **stems** 4-angled or winged; **leaves** mostly opposite or alternate toward the top of the stems, entire; **flowers** purple to white, regular, solitary, paired in leaf axils, or in clusters in axils of a terminal, leafy inflorescence; calyx tube with lobes alternating with appendages; petals 4 to 8; stamens 2 to 8; **fruit** a 2-valved capsule.

Lythrum alatum Pursh. (Winged Loosestrife). Hardy in all zones; perennial to 1 m. tall.

DESCRIPTION: Perennial, native in swamps and meadows from British Columbia to Ontario, south to Texas and Georgia; **stems** erect; 4-angled; **leaves** mostly alternate, oblong-ovate to linear-lanceolate; **flowers** purple, solitary in leaf axils, from June to September; calyx appendages longer than the lobes; ovary with a fleshy, thickened basal ring.

USE AND CULTURE: Plant in wild flower gardens. Plants thrive in moist soils in full sun or light shade. Propagation is by division, stem cuttings, or seeds. Stem cuttings should be taken in July and rooted under mist. Plants self sow once established. The European species, **Lythrum salicaria**, has escaped from cultivation and is spreading rapidly in swamps and roadside ditches. It crowds out native plants which are more valuable for wildlife. The planting of this European species and its hybrids is discouraged and in some areas prohibited.

Machaeranthera Nees (Tahoka Daisy)
COMPOSITAE (Sunflower Family)
Aster Tribe

DESCRIPTION: About 30 species of tap-rooted annual, biennial, or perennial herbs, native in western North America; **leaves** alternate, spinulose-dentate to pinnately parted or pinnatifid, rarely entire; **flower** heads usually radiate, solitary or in corymbs or panicles; involucre hemispherical to turbinate; involucral bracts in several rows; receptacle flat to slightly convex, rough; disc flowers many, perfect; ray flowers pistillate, blue, purple, or white; **fruit** a turbinate to linear achene; pappus of barbed bristles.

Machaeranthera tanacetifolia (HBK) Nees. (Tahoka Daisy). Annual to 60 cm. tall.
DESCRIPTION: Annual, native in prairies from Alberta to South Dakota, south to New Mexico; **stems** densely leafy, nearly glabrous; **leaves** 2-pinnately parted, to 7.5 cm. long; **flower** heads solitary, to 6 cm. across, from June to October; ray flowers violet, blue, or white.

USE AND CULTURE: Plant in flower borders. Plants are easy to grow in any good garden soil. Propagation is by seeds sown indoors in early April. Space plants 30 cm. apart in the garden.

Maianthemum canadense (Canada Mayflower).

Maianthemum Wiggers. (False Lily-of-the-valley)
LILIACEAE (Lily Family)
DESCRIPTION: Three species of low, perennial herbs with slender roots and creeping rhizomes, native in Europe, Asia, and North America; **leaves** 2 to 3, simple; **flowers** white, in terminal racemes; perianth segments 4, separate, spreading; stamens 4; ovary 2-celled; fruit a 1- to 2-seeded berry.

Maianthemum canadense Desf. (Canada Mayflower, Two-leaved Solomon's-seal, Wild Lily-of-the-valley). Hardy in all zones; perennial to 15 cm. tall.
DESCRIPTION: Rhizomatous perennial, native in moist woods from British Columbia to Newfoundland, south to Iowa and Georgia; **leaves** 1 to 3, ovate to ovate-oblong, to 10 cm. long, glabrous, subcordate, with a narrow, v-shaped sinus, almost sessile; **flowers** white, fragrant, in racemes to 5 cm. long, in May and June; **fruit** pale red.
USE AND CULTURE: Plant as a ground cover in the wild flower garden. Plants prefer a slightly acid soil high in organic matter. Plant in shade. They are propagated by seeds and by division of the rhizomes in the fall. Plant rhizomes horizontally, 2.5 cm. deep, and 20 cm. apart. Seeds should be sown as soon as ripe. It takes several years for seedlings to bloom. A light winter mulch should be used after fall planting.

Mammillaria vivipara - see **Coryphantha vivipara**.

Medeola L. (Indian Cucumber Root)
LILIACEAE (Lily Family)
DESCRIPTION: A single species of perennial herb with thickened, tuberlike rhizomes, native in eastern North America; **leaves** in whorls; **flowers** greenish-yellow, in sessile, few-flowered, terminal umbels; perianth segments (tepals) 6, separate, recurved; stamens 6 with versatile anthers; **fruit** a globose berry.

Medeola virginica L. (Indian Cucumber Root). Hardy in all zones; perennial to 60 cm. tall.
DESCRIPTION: Perennials, native in moist woods and mossy slopes from Minnesota to Nova Scotia, south to Louisiana and Florida; tuberous **rhizomes** white, with a cucumberlike flavor; **leaves** whorled to 12 cm. long in lower whorls, to 5 cm. long in upper whorls; **flowers** 2 to 9, greenish-yellow, drooping, to 1.25 cm. long, in a terminal umbel, in May and June; **berries** dark purple to black in the fall.
USE AND CULTURE: Plant in wild flower gardens among ferns. They thrive in slightly acid soils high in organic matter. Grow in shade. Propagation is by division and by seeds sown as soon as ripe. Plants should be divided either in the early spring or in the fall. Plant rhizomes 5 cm. deep and 20 cm. apart. Native Americans used the tuberous rhizomes for food.

Mentzelia L. (Mentzelia)
LOASACEAE (Loasa Family)

DESCRIPTION: About 60 species of herbs or shrubs with barbed hairs, native in the prairies of North America; **leaves** mostly alternate; **flowers** white, yellow, or orange, often very showy; petals separate; **fruit** a capsule.

Mentzelia decapetala (Pursh) Urb. & Gilg. (Sand Lily, Tenpetal Mentzelia). Hardy in all zones; biennial to 1.2 m. tall.
DESCRIPTION: Biennial or short-lived perennial native in prairies from Alberta to Iowa, south to Mexico and Texas; **leaves** lanceolate to oblong-lanceolate, pinnately lobed; **flowers** white or yellow, to 7.5 cm. across, opening in the evening, fragrant, from July to September; petals 10, stamens many.
USE AND CULTURE: Plant in flower borders or prairie gardens. They require full sun and a well-drained soil. Propagation is by seeds sown as soon as ripe where the plants are to bloom. Seedlings should be thinned to 30 cm. apart.

Mertensia Roth. (Bluebells, Lungwort)
BORAGINACEAE (Borage Family)
DESCRIPTION: About 40 species of perennial herbs, native in woods and thickets in Europe, Asia, and North America; **leaves** simple, alternate, entire, often with pellucid dots; basal leaves petioled; stem leaves nearly sessile; **flowers** blue, purple, or white, in loose or crowded, bractless, scorpioid racemes or panicled cymes; calyx 5-lobed; corolla tubular, 5-lobed, usually with crests in the throat; stamens 5; ovary 2-lobed; **fruit** of 4 erect, usually rough nutlets.

Mertensia paniculata (Ait.) G. Don. (Panicled Bluebells). Hardy in all zones; perennial to 1 m. tall.
DESCRIPTION: Perennial, native along stream banks, in meadows, and damp thickets from Alaska to Quebec, south to Washington and Michigan; **leaves** ovate to lanceolate, rough-hairy on both surfaces; **flowers** blue, pink when young, rarely white, crested, to 1.25 cm. long, from May to August.
USE AND CULTURE: Plant in wild flower gardens. They like a soil high in organic matter in partial shade. Propagation is by spring division and by seeds sown as soon as ripe. Space plants about 30 cm. apart.

Mertensia virginica (Virginia Bluebells).

Photograph: Dr. Anne M. Hanchek.

Mertensia paniculata. In flower in

Duluth, Minnesota in June 1969.

Mertensia virginica (L.) Pers. (Cowslip, Roanoke-bells, Virginia Bluebells). Hardy in all zones; perennial to 60 cm. tall.
DESCRIPTION: Erect, glabrous perennial, native in woods and moist bottom lands along streams from Kansas to New York, south to Alabama; **rhizomes** tuberlike; **leaves** elliptic to ovate, glabrous, dying down after flowering and fruiting; **flowers** blue-purple, rarely white or pink, in nodding clusters, in May and June; corolla to 2.5 cm. long, with conspicuous crests.
USE AND CULTURE: Plant in wild flower gardens with other wild flowers that will cover the ground when the bluebells' tops die down. Merrybells make a good companion planting. Bluebells prefer a rich soil that is neutral to slightly acid in shade. The soil should be moist in the spring but can become dry in summer. Propagation is mainly by division of the tuberous rhizomes in the fall. Seeds should be planted as soon as they are ripe. Plant self sows once established.

Mimulus L. (Monkey Flower)
SCROPHULARIACEAE (Figwort Family)
DESCRIPTION: About 150 species of annual or perennial herbs, rarely shrubs, native in South Africa, Asia, Australia, and North and South America; **stems** decumbent to erect, often viscid or glandular-pubescent; **leaves** opposite, simple, entire or toothed; **flowers** yellow, orange, red, blue, violet, or purple, solitary and axillary or in terminal spikelike racemes; calyx 5-angled, 5-toothed; corolla 2-lipped to nearly regular, upper lip 2-lobed, lower lip 3-lobed, with open throat or closed by a palate; stamens 4; **fruit** a capsule.

Mimulus moschatus Dougl. ex Lindl. (Musk Flower, Musk Plant). Hardy in all zones; perennial to 30 cm. tall.
DESCRIPTION: Rhizomatous perennial, native in cool wet soils, especially along streams and around springs from British Columbia to Newfoundland, south to Califor-

nia and West Virginia; **stems** covered with sticky hairs; **leaves** ovate or oblong-ovate, to 5 cm. long, with a musklike odor; **flowers** pale yellow, lightly dotted with brown, in July and August; corolla to 2.5 cm. long.

USE AND CULTURE: Plant in flower borders or around pools, as these plants require a moist soil. Propagation is by seeds sown as soon as ripe or by division of established plants in early spring. Seeds can also be started indoors in late March.

Mimulus ringens L. (Allegheny Monkey Flower). Hardy in all zones; perennial to 75 cm. tall.

DESCRIPTION: Glabrous perennial, native in wet woods and swamps from Saskatchewan to Nova Scotia, south to Texas and Georgia; **stems** 4-angled; **leaves** oblong, elliptic, or oblanceolate, to 10 cm. long; **flowers** blue to blue-violet, rarely pink or white, from June to September; corolla to 4 cm. long, 2-lipped with a narrow throat.

USE AND CULTURE: The same as for **Mimulus moschatus**.

Mitchella L. (Partridgeberry)
RUBIACEAE (Madder Family)

DESCRIPTION: Two species of trailing evergreen perennial herbs, native in acid woods in North America and Asia; **stems** trailing, rooting at the nodes; **leaves** opposite; **flowers** white, 4-merous, in axillary or terminal pairs; corolla funnelform with short lobes; **fruit** a red, rarely white, twin berry.

Mitchella repens L. (Partridgeberry, Running Box, Squawberry, Squaw Vine, Twinberry, Two-eyed Berry). Hardy in all zones; perennial to 25 cm. long.

DESCRIPTION: Trailing evergreen vine, native in acid woods, often creeping over fallen aspen and birch logs and stumps from Minnesota to Nova Scotia, south to Texas and Florida; **leaves** orbicular-ovate, to 2 cm. long, dark green and glossy above with white lines; **flowers** white, fragrant, to 1.25 cm. long, bearded inside, in June and July; 2 **berries** unite to form a 2-calyxed red berry.

USE AND CULTURE: Plant in wild flower gardens to cover fallen logs or stumps. Partridgeberry must have an acid soil rich in organic matter. Propagation is by cuttings taken in June and rooted in a sand-peat mixture. Division is possible but such plants are difficult to establish. Plants are often used in terrariums for the red berries.

Mitella L. (Bishop's-cap, Miterwort)
SAXIFRAGACEAE (Saxifrage Family)

DESCRIPTION: About 12 species of delicate, rhizomatous, perennial herbs, native in moist woods in North America and northeastern Asia; **leaves** mostly basal, cordate, long-petioled; **flowers** small, in simple racemes; calyx tube saucer-shaped with 5 lobes; petals 5, pinnately cut; stamens 5 or 10; ovary partly or nearly inferior with 2 short styles; **fruit** a capsule, dehiscing apically.

Mitella diphylla L. (Common Bishop's-cap, Coolwort, Miterwort). Hardy in all zones; perennial to 25 cm. tall.

Mimulus moschatus (Musk Flower).

DESCRIPTION: Rhizomatous perennial, native in moist, humus rich woods or on hummocks in bogs from Ontario to Quebec, south to Missouri and Virginia; **stems** forming clumps; **leaves** mostly basal, with one pair of opposite leaves on the flowering stems; **flowers** white, to 6 mm. across, in racemes, in May and June; petals deeply fimbriate-pinnatifid; **capsules** dehisce to expose black seeds.

USE AND CULTURE: Plant in rock gardens or use as a ground cover in wild flower gardens. The plants prefer a humus-rich, slightly acid soil with some shade. Propagation is by seeds sown as soon as ripe or by fall division. Seedlings take 3 years to bloom.

Mitella nuda L. (Bishop's-cap). Hardy in all zones; perennial to 20 cm. tall.
DESCRIPTION: Perennial, native in damp woods and acid bogs from Canada south to Washington and Pennsylvania; **leaves** mostly basal, cordate; **flowers** yellowish-green, to 1 cm. across, in few-flowered racemes, in May and June; petals fimbriate-pinnatifid into 8 opposite segments; stamens 10.

USE AND CULTURE: The same as for **Mitella diphylla**.

Monarda L. (Horsemint, Monarda, Wild Bergamot)
LABIATAE (Mint Family)

DESCRIPTION: About 12 species of annual or perennial aromatic herbs, native in North America; **stems** square; **leaves** opposite, entire or toothed; **flowers** showy, in densely-flowered verticillasters, subtended by leafy bracts; calyx tubular, 15-veined; corolla tube longer than the calyx, with 2-lipped limb; upper lip erect, often emarginate; lower lip spreading, 3-lobed; fertile stamens 2, usually exserted; **fruit** a glabrous nutlet, produced in 4's.

Monarda didyma L. (Bee Balm, Oswego Bee Balm, Oswego Tea). Hardy in all zones; perennial to 1.2 m. tall.
DESCRIPTION: Glabrescent perennial, native in rich woods and along streams from New England south to Tennessee and Georgia; **leaves** ovate-acuminate, to 10 cm. long, serrate-dentate, sparsely pubescent; **flowers** scarlet-red, in a single terminal verticillaster, in July and August; bracts tinged red, leaflike; calyx with bristly teeth, to 1.25 cm. long; corolla to 3 cm. long.

USE AND CULTURE: Plant in flower borders or wild flower gardens. These plants prefer a moist soil that is neutral to slightly acid either in full sun or partial shade. Propagation is by seeds sown as soon as ripe, by divisions, or cuttings. Since plants become crowded, it is best to divide and replant every spring. Cuttings should be taken in July, rooted in sand, and wintered in a cold frame. Powdery mildew can be a serious problem with bee balm. Several named cultivars are on the market.

Monarda fistulosa L. (Wild Bergamot). Hardy in all zones; perennial to 90 cm. tall.
DESCRIPTION: Pubescent perennial, native in upland woods, thickets, prairies, and roadside ditches, mostly in sandy soils from British Columbia to Quebec, south to Arizona and Georgia; **stems** square; **leaves** ovate-lanceolate to broadly ovate, to 10 cm.

Monarda didyma (Bee Balm).

Monarda fistulosa (Wild Bergamot). In bloom in July 1981 in Hayward, Wisconsin.

long, acute or acuminate, sparsely serrate or nearly entire, generally pubescent; **flowers** bright lavender, rarely white, usually in single headlike verticillasters, from July to September; calyx to 2 cm. long, with bristle teeth; corolla to 3 cm. long, pubescent outside.

USE AND CULTURE: The same as for **Monarda didyma**. Leaves steeped in water make a good tea.

Monarda punctata L. (Dotted Mint, Dotted Monarda, Horsemint). Hardy in all zones; perennial to 90 cm. tall.

DESCRIPTION: Annual, biennial, or perennial, native in sandy soils from Minnesota to Vermont, south to Texas and Florida; **leaves** lanceolate to oblong, to 8 cm. long, serrate to nearly entire; **flowers** yellow, spotted purple, in several superposed, headlike verticillasters, from July to October; calyx to 1 cm. long with narrow, triangular teeth; corolla to 2 cm. long.

USE AND CULTURE: Plant in flower borders or prairie gardens. They prefer a sandy soil in full sun. Propagation is the same as for **Monarda didyma**.

Moneses Salisb. (Moneses)
PYROLACEAE (Wintergreen Family)

DESCRIPTION: A single species of glabrous, rhizomatous perennial, native in cool, moist, acid woods in Eurasia and North America; **leaves** simple, in basal clusters; **flowers** white or pink, nodding, solitary, on scapes, 5-merous; stamens 10 with filaments swollen at base; **fruit** a 5-valved capsule.

Moneses uniflora (L.) A. Gray. (One-flowered Pyrola, One-flowered Shinleaf, One-flowered Wintergreen). Hardy in all zones; perennial to 12 cm. tall.

DESCRIPTION: Low perennial, native mostly in moist, coniferous acid woods, circumboreal, south to California and Florida in North America; **leaves** orbicular or ovate, to 2.5 cm. long, wavy-toothed, evergreen; **flowers** white to pink, fragrant, to 2 cm. across, from June to August; **capsule** to 6 mm. across.

USE AND CULTURE: Plant in wet areas of wild flower gardens. They require a moist, acid soil high in humus. Propagation is by seeds sown as soon as ripe or by spring division of established plants.

Oenothera L. (Evening Primrose, Sundrops)
ONAGRACEAE (Evening Primrose Family)

DESCRIPTION: About 80 species of annual, biennial, and perennial herbs, native in sunny areas in North and South America; **stems** erect or lacking; **leaves** basal or alternate, simple, entire to pinnatifid; **flowers** solitary and axillary or in racemes or panicles, 4-merous; calyx tube usually well developed; stamens 8 with versatile anthers; ovary inferior, 4-celled, cylindrical or clavate; **fruit** a capsule.

Oenothera caespitosa Nutt. (Gumbo Lily, Tufted Evening Primrose). Hardy in all zones; perennial to 30 cm. tall.

DESCRIPTION: Short-lived, cespitose perennial, native in dry soil that is often a heavy clay in the Rocky Mountain states and adjoining plains as far east as the badlands of South Dakota; **leaves** basal, to 10 cm. long, entire to sinuate-toothed, glabrous; **flowers** white, to 10 cm. across, fragrant, opening in the evening, from April to September; calyx tube to 7 cm. long; **capsules** lanceolate-ovoid, to 2 cm. long.

USE AND CULTURE: Plant in rock gardens. Plants prefer a heavy, clay soil in full sun. Propagation is by seeds sown as soon as ripe or in the spring. Plants do not bloom until the second year.

Oenothera fruticosa L. (Sundrops). Hardy in all zones; perennial to 60 cm. tall.

DESCRIPTION: Rhizomatous perennial, native in open woods and fields in eastern United States as far west as Oklahoma; **stems** numerous, slender, strigose; basal **leaves** oblanceolate, to 20 cm. long; stem leaves lanceolate, shorter; **flowers** yellow, day-flowering, to 5 cm. across, from May to August; **capsules** clavate, to 1 cm. long.

Oenothera fruticosa (Sundrops).

USE AND CULTURE: Plant in rock gardens or use as a ground cover. They require a sunny location and a moist soil. Propagation is mainly by spring division. Space plants 20 cm. apart. Plants wilt if the soil becomes dry.

Oenothera missouriensis Sims (Flutter-mills, Glade Lily, Missouri Evening Primrose). Hardy in all zones; perennial to 40 cm. tall.
DESCRIPTION: Low perennial, native in prairies and rocky hillsides from Nebraska to Missouri, south to Texas; **stems** decumbent to erect, strigose; **leaves** lanceolate, petioled to 10 cm. long, entire; **flowers** yellow, becoming red with age, to 10 cm. across, very showy, opening in the evening; **capsules** woody, 4-winged, to 7.5 cm. long.
USE AND CULTURE: Plant in rock gardens and prairie gardens. The culture is the same as for **Oenothera caespitosa**.

Oenothera perennis L. (Sundrops). Hardy in all zones; perennial to 50 cm. tall.
DESCRIPTION: Rhizomatous perennial, native in fields, meadows, and open woods from Manitoba to Quebec, south to Missouri and North Carolina; lower **leaves** oblanceolate to spatulate, to 5 cm. long; **flowers** yellow, to 2 cm. across, day-flowering, from June to August; **capsules** ellipsoid.
USE AND CULTURE: The same as for **Oenothera fruticosa**.

Oenothera tetragona Roth. (Sundrops). Hardy in all zones; perennial to 50 cm. tall.
DESCRIPTION: Perennial, native in fields and open woods from Michigan to Nova Scotia, south to Louisiana and South Carolina; **stems** branched above, hairy; **leaves** ovate to nearly linear, to 10 cm. long, smaller above; **flowers** yellow, in clusters, up-facing, from May to August; **capsules** oblong-ellipsoid, with gland-tipped hairs.
USE AND CULTURE: The same as for **Oenothera fruticosa**.

Opuntia Mill. (Cholla, Cholla Cactus, Prickly Pear, Tuna)
CACTACEAE (Cactus Family)
DESCRIPTION: About 300 species of prostrate or erect, jointed cacti, native in dry prairies and deserts in sandy or gravelly soils in western North America; **stems** divided into either flat or rounded joints; **leaves** cylindrical to conical, soon deciduous; spines naked or sheathed; smaller spines clustered at the tips of areoles; **flowers** usually yellow, showy, sessile, sometimes clustered; stamens shorter than petals; **fruit** a dry or fleshy berry.

Opuntia fragilis (Nutt.) Haw. (Brittle Prickly Pear). Hardy in all zones; perennial to 10 cm. tall.
DESCRIPTION: Plants prostrate, with tuberous roots, native in dry soils from British Columbia to Manitoba, south to Arizona and Texas; **stem** joints ovoid or flattened, to 5 cm. long, easily detached; areoles white-woolly; spines 5 to 9, slender, to 3 cm. long; **flowers** yellow, green, or purple, to 5 cm. across, in June and July; **fruits** dry, spiny.
USE AND CULTURE: Plant in rock gardens. They require a dry, well-drained soil in full sun. Propagation is largely by separation of the joints. A joint, pushed into the soil, will root and produce a new plant. Seeds can also be planted as soon as ripe.

Opuntia humifusa (Raf.) Raf. (Common Prickly Pear). Hardy in all zones; perennial to 15 cm. tall.

Opuntia humifusa (Prickly Pear). In bloom at the Arboretum in July 1979.

Opuntia polyacantha (Plains Prickly Pear).

DESCRIPTION: Plants prostrate and spreading, with fibrous roots, native in prairies from Montana to Massachusetts, south to Texas and Florida; **stem** joints orbicular to obovate, flattened, to 15 cm. long; areoles few, spineless or nearly so; spines 1 or 2, to 2 cm. long; **flowers** yellow, very showy, to 10 cm. across, in June and July; **fruits** ovoid, green to purple, to 5 cm. long.
USE AND CULTURE: The same as for **Opuntia fragilis**.

Opuntia polyacantha Haw. (Plains Prickly Pear). Hardy in all zones; perennial to 15 cm. tall.
DESCRIPTION: Plants low and spreading, native in prairies in dry sandy soil from Alberta to North Dakota, south to Arizona and Texas; **stem** joints orbicular, to 10 cm. wide; areoles close together; spines 7 to 10, cylindrical, mostly deflexed, to 2 cm. long; **flowers** mostly yellow, to 5 cm. across, in June and July; **fruits** obovoid, dry, spiny, to 2.5 cm. long.
USE AND CULTURE: The same as for **Opuntia fragilis**.

Orchis L. (Orchid)
ORCHIDACEAE (Orchid Family)
DESCRIPTION: About 50 species of terrestrial herbs with tuberous roots or rhizomes, native in moist woods in North America and Eurasia; **stems** leafy; **leaves** 1 or more; **flowers** showy, few to many in a raceme; sepals separate, spreading; petals similar but smaller, meeting with the upper sepal to form a hood over the column; lip simple or more or less 3-lobed, united with the lower part of the column; **fruit** a capsule.

Orchis rotundifolia Banks ex Pursh. (Small Round-leaved Orchid, Spotted Kirtle Pink). Hardy in all zones; perennial to 30 cm. tall.
DESCRIPTION: Plants stoloniferous, native in mossy woods and swamps from Alaska to Greenland, south to Wyoming and Michigan; **leaves** solitary, elliptic, to 10 cm. long; **flowers** showy, in 1- to 16-flowered racemes, in June and July; sepals white to mauve-pink, to 1 cm. long; petals pale white to mauve, ovate-oblong; lip white, spotted with magenta or purple, 3-lobed, ovate, to 1 cm. long.
USE AND CULTURE: Plant in rock gardens or wild flower gardens. These plants require a moist, humus-rich soil that is neutral or slightly acid. Plant in the shade. Propagation is by division in the fall after the plants go dormant. Purchase plants from a licensed nursery that sells wild flowers. This is a protected species.

Orchis spectabilis L. (Kirtle Pink, Purple-hooded Orchid, Showy Orchid, Woodland Orchid). Hardy in all zones; perennial to 25 cm. tall.
DESCRIPTION: Perennial, native in moist woods and on moist slopes from Minnesota to Quebec, south to Arkansas and Georgia; **stems** naked, 4- to 5-angled; **leaves** usually 2, basal, oblong-ovate, to 15 cm. long; **flowers** showy, in 2- to 15-flowered racemes, in May and June; sepals and petals pink to mauve, rarely white; lip white, entire, orbicular-ovate, to 10 cm. long, crenate on margin, with a conspicuous spur.
USE AND CULTURE: Plant in rock gardens or wild flower gardens. They require a humus-rich, slightly acid soil in light shade. Each plant sends out two offshoots in the fall. The mother plant then dies. These offshoots can be divided in the fall to increase the number of plants. This is a protected species, so plants must be purchased from a licensed nursery.

Oxalis L. (Lady's Sorrel, Wood Sorrel)
OXALIDACEAE (Oxalis Family)
DESCRIPTION: About 850 species of annual or perennial herbs, native on all continents, especially numerous in Africa and South America; underground **stems** bulbous, tuberous, or rhizomatous; **leaves** alternate, cauline or basal, cloverlike, palmate, 3- to many-foliate, pinnately 3-foliate, or sometimes reduced to 1 or 2 leaflets, often closing at night; **flowers** in most colors except blue, in 1- to several-flowered scapes, umbellate cymes; sepals and petals 5, cohering basally; stamens 10, in 2 series, the outer shorter than the inner, all fertile; **fruit** a capsule.

Oxalis violacea L. (Violet Wood Sorrel). Hardy in all zones; perennial to 25 cm. tall.

Orchis spectabilis (Showy Orchid). In bloom at the Arboretum in May 1981.

DESCRIPTION: Scapose perennial, with brown, scaly bulbs, native in fields and prairies from North Dakota to Maine, south to Colorado and Florida; **leaflets**, 3 obreniform, to 2.5 cm. wide; **flowers** violet to rose-purple, rarely white, in 3- to 10-flowered umbels on peduncles to 25 cm. long.

USE AND CULTURE: Plant in rock gardens or prairie gardens. Plants grow well in any well-drained soil that is slightly acid. Propagation is by seeds or by division of the bulbs. Bulbs should be planted in the fall about 5 cm. deep and 15 cm. apart. Plants self sow. There are several introduced species with yellow flowers that can become troublesome weeds.

Oxytropis DC. (Crazyweed, Locoweed)
LEGUMINOSAE (Pea Family)

DESCRIPTION: About 300 species of low perennial herbs, native in the North Temperate Zone; **leaves** odd-pinnate; leaflets obtuse at base; flowers pealike, in racemes or spikes; keel beaked; stamens 10, 9 united, 1 separate; **fruit** a legume.

Oxytropis campestris (L.) DC. (Locoweed). Hardy in all zones; perennial to 20 cm. tall.

DESCRIPTION: A variable perennial, native near rocks, cliffs, and gravelly lake shores, circumboreal, from British Columbia to Manitoba, south to Colorado and Wisconsin; **leaves** to 15 cm. long, with linear-oblong to oblong-lanceolate leaflets; **flowers** white to yellow, rarely purple, in many-flowered racemes, from May to July; **legumes** thin-walled, to 2 cm. long.

USE AND CULTURE: Plant in flower borders or in prairie gardens. They will grow in any well-drained soil. Propagation is by direct seeding. Plants have a tap root and do not transplant well. Plants are poisonous to livestock when eaten.

Panax L. (Ginseng)
ARALIACEAE (Ginseng Family)

DESCRIPTION: About 6 species of glabrous perennial herbs with thick roots and simple stems, native in moist woods in North America and Asia; **leaves** palmately compound, in whorls; leaflets dentate or lobed; **flowers** small, in single, terminal umbels; petals 5, overlapping, sometimes united; stamens 5; ovary 2- to 3-celled, with 2 to 3 styles; **fruit** a drupe.

Panax quinquefolius L. (American Ginseng, Ginseng). Hardy in all zones; perennial to 50 cm. tall.

DESCRIPTION: Perennial with tuberous, fusiform roots, native in cool, moist woods rich in leaf mold from North Dakota to Quebec, south to Oklahoma and Georgia; **leaflets** 3 to 5, long-petioled, somewhat obovate, to 15 cm. long, abruptly acuminate, coarsely dentate; **flowers** mostly perfect, greenish-white, in July; styles 2; **drupes** bright red, about 1 cm. across.

USE AND CULTURE: Plant in wild flower gardens. They are sometimes grown under artificial shade for the fleshy roots that are exported to China for medicinal purposes. These plants require a soil rich in humus, deep shade, and constantly moist conditions. Propagation is by seeds collected when ripe and stratified until the following August. It is best to purchase nursery grown plants. Plants can also be increased by division in the fall. Since plants have been dug for the fleshy roots, this species is now very rare.

Panax trifolius L. (Dwarf Ginseng, Groundnut). Hardy in all zones; perennial to 12 cm. tall.

DESCRIPTION: Perennial with glabrous roots, native in rich, moist woods from North Dakota to Nova Scotia, south to Oklahoma and Georgia; **leaflets** 3 to 5, to 4 cm. long, sessile or nearly so, acute, finely toothed; **flowers** often imperfect, white, tinged with pink, from April to June; styles 3; **drupes** yellow.

USE AND CULTURE: The same as for **Panax quinquefolius**. The soil should be acid. These roots are not used in medicine.

Pedicularis L. (Lousewort, Wood Betony)
SCROPHULARIACEAE (Figwort Family)

Panax trifolius (Dwarf Ginseng). In bloom in June 1978.

DESCRIPTION: Over 350 species of annual, biennial, or perennial herbs, native mostly in the northern hemisphere; **leaves** alternate, opposite, or rarely whorled, dentate, lobed, or pinnatifid; **flowers** purple, red, rose, white, or yellow, axillary or in showy terminal bracted racemes or spikes; calyx tubular, 2- to 5-toothed; corolla tubular, 2-lipped, with upper lip helmet-shaped, often beaked and lower lip 3-lobed; stamens 4; **fruit** a capsule.

Pedicularis canadensis L. (Common Lousewort, Wood Betony). Hardy in all zones; perennial to 45 cm. tall.
DESCRIPTION: Pubescent perennial, native in upland woods and prairies from Manitoba to Quebec, south to New Mexico and Florida; **stems** unbranched, clustered; **leaves** mostly basal, pinnately parted, to 12 cm. long, alternate; **flowers** yellow or red, rarely white, to 2 cm. long, from April to June; **capsule** 3 times as long as the calyx.
USE AND CULTURE: Plant in rock gardens or in wild flower gardens. They grow well in any well-drained soil. Propagation is mainly by spring division or by seeds. Sometimes the plants die down soon after transplanting and do not come up again until the following spring. Seeds should be sown as soon as ripe.

Pedicularis lanceolata Michx. (Lousewort). Hardy in all zones; perennial to 90 cm. tall.
DESCRIPTION: Glabrous perennial, native in swamps and wet soils from Minnesota to Massachusetts, south to Missouri and North Carolina; **leaves** opposite to subopposite, oblong-lanceolate, to 12 cm. long, pinnately lobed, sessile; **flowers** yellow, to 2 cm. long, in August and September; **capsule** about as long as the calyx.
USE AND CULTURE: The same as for **Pedicularis canadensis**.

Penstemon Mitch. (Beard-tongue)
SCROPHULARIACEAE (Figwort Family)
DESCRIPTION: About 250 species of perennial herbs or rarely shrubs, native mostly in moist rocky soils in full sun chiefly in western North America; **leaves** opposite, rarely in whorls of 3, or upper alternate; **flowers** scarlet, purple, blue, white, or yellow, solitary or in terminal racemes or panicles; calyx 5-parted; corolla tubular, more or less 2-lipped; fertile stamens 4; staminode 1, naked or bearded; **fruit** a capsule.

Penstemon albidus Nutt. (White Beard-tongue). Hardy in all zones; perennial to 40 cm. tall.
DESCRIPTION: Perennial, native in dry prairies from Alberta to Minnesota, south to New Mexico and Iowa; **leaves** lanceolate-oblong, to 8 cm. long, entire or with a few shallow teeth, rounded or truncate at base; **flowers** white, occasionally tinged violet, in May and June; corolla tube to 2 cm. long, gradually dilated upward.
USE AND CULTURE: Plant in rock gardens, flower borders, or prairie gardens. They require a well-drained soil and full sun. Propagation is by division, seeds, or cuttings. Seeds should be sown in the fall or stored in an airtight container at 32 to 40 degrees Fahrenheit for spring planting. Seeds should be covered with screened peat that is kept moist.

Penstemon digitalis Nutt. (Foxglove Penstemon). Hardy in all zones; perennial to 1 m. tall.
DESCRIPTION: Glabrous perennial, native in moist open woods or prairies from South Dakota to Maine, south to Texas; basal **leaves** oblanceolate to elliptic, entire or dentate; stem leaves lanceolate, oblanceolate, or oblong-ovate, to 17 cm. long; **flowers** white or pink, in June and July; corolla to 2.5 cm. long; anthers bearded; staminodes bearded.
USE AND CULTURE: The same as for **Penstemon albidus**.

Penstemon gracilis Nutt. (Slender Beard-tongue). Hardy in all zones; perennial to 60 cm. tall.
DESCRIPTION: Slender perennials, native in sandy or gravelly soils, in prairies, and in open woods from British Columbia to Ontario, south to New Mexico and Wisconsin; basal **leaves** oblanceolate to elliptic, finely dentate to entire, thin, glabrous; stem leaves linear-lanceolate; **flowers** lilac to white, in June and July; corolla to 2 cm. long, strongly 2-lipped; staminode densely yellow-bearded.
USE AND CULTURE: The same as for **Penstemon albidus**.

Panax quinquefolius (American Ginseng). In fruit at the Arboretum in October 1961.

Penstemon grandiflorus Nutt. (Shell-leaf Beard-tongue). Hardy in all zones; biennial to 1 m. tall.

DESCRIPTION: Glabrous, glaucous biennial or short-lived perennial, native in dry fields and in prairies from North Dakota to Illinois, south to Wyoming and Texas; **leaves** entire, thick, fleshy; basal leaves ovate; stem leaves elliptic to round-ovate or orbicular, clasping; **flowers** lilac or blue-lavender, in May and June; corolla to 5 cm. long; staminode hooked, minutely bearded at apex.

USE AND CULTURE: Plant in flower borders or in prairie gardens. The culture is the same as for **Penstemon albidus**.

Phlox L. (Phlox)
POLEMONIACEAE (Phlox Family)

DESCRIPTION: About 60 species of erect, diffuse, or cespitose annual or perennial herbs, native mostly in North America, one species in Siberia; **leaves** mostly opposite, simple; **flowers** blue, purple, crimson, pink, or white, solitary or in terminal cymes or panicles; calyx 5-cleft; corolla salverform, 5-lobed; stamens 5; **fruit** a 3-valved capsule, rupturing the calyx at maturity.

Phlox divaricata L. (Blue Phlox, Wild Sweet William). Hardy in all zones; perennial to 30 cm. tall.

DESCRIPTION: Spreading perennial with decumbent branches rooting at nodes, native in rich, moist woods and shady roadsides from Minnesota to Quebec, south to Oklahoma and Georgia; **leaves** elliptic, ovate, or oblong, to 5 cm. long; **flowers** pale violet-blue to lavender, rarely white, in terminal clusters, in May and June; corolla lobes notched or erose.

USE AND CULTURE: Plant in flower borders, wild flower gardens, or rock gardens. They prefer a rich, woodsy soil that is neutral to slightly acid. Plant either in light shade or full sun. Propagation is by spring division, cuttings, or seeds sown as soon as ripe. Plants from seeds will flower the second year. Space plants about 30 cm. apart. Plants cut back after flowering will often bloom again.

Phlox paniculata L. (Autumn Phlox, Fall Phlox, Perennial Phlox, Summer Perennial Phlox). Hardy in all zones; perennial to 2 m. tall.

DESCRIPTION: Clump-forming perennial, native in rich, moist woods from Iowa to New York, south to Arkansas and Georgia; **leaves** elliptic-lanceolate or ovate, to 15 cm. long, thin, veiny; **flowers** pink-purple or magenta (various colors in named cultivars), to 2.5 cm. across, in large panicles, from July to September.

USE AND CULTURE: Sometimes planted in wild flower gardens. The named cultivars are some of the most popular summer blooming perennials, and are often planted in the flower border. Plants are easy to grow in most garden soils. Propagation is mainly by division or root cuttings in named cultivars. Seedlings frequently volunteer. Powdery mildew and other leaf diseases can be a problem where summers are hot and humid. The named cultivars are planted more often than the species.

Phlox pilosa L. (Prairie Phlox). Hardy in all zones; perennial to 30 cm. tall.

DESCRIPTION: Hairy perennial, native in open upland woods, in dry prairies, and common in roadside ditches from Manitoba to Connecticut, south to Texas and Florida; **leaves** linear to lanceolate, to 7.5 cm. long; **flowers** purple to pink, rarely white, to 2 cm. across, in small clusters, in June.

USE AND CULTURE: Plant in rock gardens and prairie gardens. Plants prefer a slightly acid, sandy loam soil in full sun. Propagation is mainly by seeds since the plants are difficult to divide. Although this phlox usually blooms in late spring, seedlings often bloom the first year in August. Foliage dies down soon after bloom, but under cultivation, this plant can rebloom later in the season.

Physostegia Benth. (False Dragonhead, Lion's-heart,
Obedience, Obedient Plant)
LABIATAE (Mint Family)

Phlox divaricata (Blue Phlox). In bloom in May 1978.

Phytolacca americana (Poke). In fruit at Egeskov Castle in Denmark in August 1983.

DESCRIPTION: About 15 species of glabrous or puberulous perennial herbs, native in North America; **stems** mostly square in cross section; **leaves** opposite, often toothed; **flowers** showy, white, purple, red, or pink, solitary in leaf axils or in panicled, leafless spikes; calyx tubular or campanulate, 10-veined, slightly inflated in fruit; corolla tube longer than the calyx; limb 2-lipped; **fruit** of 4 smooth nutlets.

Physostegia virginiana (L.) Benth. (False Dragonhead, Obedience). Hardy in all zones; perennial to 90 cm. tall.
DESCRIPTION: Stoloniferous, glabrous perennial, native in swampy thickets and wet woods, sometimes in prairies from Minnesota to New Brunswick, south to Oklahoma and South Carolina; **leaves** lanceolate, to 12 cm. long, acute, sharply-serrate; **flowers** showy, rose-purple, in closely flowered spikes clustered in a panicle, from June to September; calyx tubular-campanulate, viscid-glandular, with sharp triangular teeth; corolla to 3 cm. long, inflated at mouth.
USE AND CULTURE: Plant in flower borders, wild flower gardens, or prairie gardens. They thrive in any good garden soil. Plants spread rapidly, especially in moist soils. Propagation is mainly by division either in the spring or fall. Plant with the buds near the surface and space the plants 30 cm. apart. Divide plants every third year. Plants grown from seeds sown as soon as ripe will bloom the second year.

Phytolacca L. (Pokeberry, Pokeweed)
PHYTOLACCACEAE (Pokeweed Family)
DESCRIPTION: About 25 species of coarse, sometimes dioecious herbs, shrubs, or treelike plants, native mostly in tropical and warm climates; **leaves** often large, alternate, simple; **flowers** small, in racemes or panicles, sometimes imperfect; sepals 5; petals 0; stamens 6 to 33; carpels 5 to 16, separate or sometimes united; **fruit** a depressed, globose berry with each carpel 1-seeded.

Phytolacca americana L. (Garget, Pigeon Berry, Pocan, Poke, Scoke, Virginia Poke). Hardy in all zones; perennial to 2 m. tall.
DESCRIPTION: Poisonous perennial with an unpleasant odor and large fleshy roots, native in moist woods, roadside ditches, and in open fields from Minnesota to Maine, south to Texas and Florida; **leaves** oblong to ovate-lanceolate, to 15 cm. long; **flowers** perfect, white or purple, in racemes to 15 cm. long, from July to October; stamens and styles 10; **fruit** a black-purple berry with red juice.
USE AND CULTURE: Use as a background plant in flower borders or plant in wild flower gardens. Children often use the red juice in the berries for a war paint. Plants also used as a remedy for the garget disease in cattle. Young shoots are sometimes used as a potherb. Discard the cooking water as it may contain a poisonous substance since all parts of the plant should be considered poisonous. The potherbs are safe to eat as the poisonous ingredient is water soluble and will leach into the cooking water. Plants are easy to grow. The usual method of propagation is by seeds sown as soon as ripe.

Podophyllum L. (Mayapple)
BERBERIDACEAE (Barberry Family)
DESCRIPTION: Two species of rhizomatous perennial herbs, native in moist woods in North America and Asia; basal **leaves** large, peltate, solitary, lobed; stem leaves

Podophyllum peltatum (Mayapple).

Photograph: Dr. Anne M. Hanchek.

smaller, in pairs, palmately lobed; **flowers** showy, born in the fork between the paired leaves, nodding; sepals 6, petals 6 or 9; stamens as many or twice as many as the petals; **fruit** an ellipsoid, fleshy berry.

Podophyllum peltatum L. (Mandrake, Mayapple, Raccoon Berry, Wild Jalap, Wild Lemon). Hardy in all zones; perennial to 45 cm. tall.
DESCRIPTION: Rhizomatous perennial, native in moist, open woods, on hillsides, and in meadows from Minnesota to Quebec, south to Texas and Florida; **leaves** large, to 30 cm. across, 5- to 9-lobed, forming an umbrella over the flowers, **flowers** solitary, white, showy but covered by leaves, in May and June; stamens 12 to 18; **fruits** yellow, rarely red, to 5 cm. long, edible but somewhat insipid.
USE AND CULTURE: Plant as a ground cover in wild flower gardens. If space is limited, plant in a bottomless gallon can to prevent spreading. Plants prefer a slightly acid soil high in organic matter in light shade. This is a good companion plant to grow with Virginia bluebells to cover the ground after the bluebells die down. Propagation is by seed sown as soon as ripe or by fall division after the plants go dormant. Plant the rhizomes about 4 cm. deep and 30 cm. apart.

Polemonium L. (Greek Valerian, Jacob's-ladder)
POLEMONIACEAE (Phlox Family)
DESCRIPTION: About 25 species of decumbent, annual or rhizomatous perennial herbs, native in Europe, Asia, and in North and South America; **leaves** alternate, pinnate; **flowers** blue, purple, yellow, or white, solitary or in axillary cymes; calyx 5-lobed, enlarging in fruit; corolla campanulate to funnelform; stamens equal, regularly inserted; **fruit** a 3-celled capsule.

Polemonium reptans L. (Greek Valerian, Jacob's-ladder). Hardy in all zones; perennial to 30 cm. tall.
DESCRIPTION: Tufted perennial, native in rich, moist woods from North Dakota to New Hampshire, south to Oklahoma and Georgia; **leaflets** 7 to 19, ovate to lanceolate, to 5 cm. long; **flowers** blue, to 2 cm. across, in small cluster at the tips of arching stems, in May and June; **capsules** stipitate.
USE AND CULTURE: Plant in flower borders, wild flower gardens, and rock gardens. Plants grow well in any soil that is neutral to slightly acid either in sun or shade. Propagation is by spring division or by seeds sown as soon as ripe or early in the spring. Plants self sow.

Polygala L. (Milkwort)
POLYGALACEAE (Milkwort Family)
DESCRIPTION: Nearly 600 species of herbs, shrubs, and trees, widely distributed throughout the world; **leaves** simple, entire; **flowers** showy, irregular, in terminal or axillary racemes; sepals 5, the inner 2 petallike; petals 3 to 5, often united, the lower one (keel) often crested; stamens usually 8, the filaments united to a sheath that is split on the upperside; **fruit** a capsule.

Polygala paucifolia Willd. (Bird-on-the-wing, Flowering Wintergreen, Fringed Milkwort, Gay Wings). Hardy in all zones; perennial to 12 cm. tall.

Polygala paucifolia (Gay Wings).

Polygonatum commutatum (Great Solomon's-seal).

Photograph taken at Hidcote Manor in England in May 1979.

DESCRIPTION: Rhizomatous perennial, native in acid woods rich in organic matter from Saskatchewan to New Brunswick, south to Minnesota and Georgia; lower **leaves** few, scalelike; upper leaves clustered, ovate to oblong, to 3 cm. long; **flowers** dainty, orchidlike, rose-purple or rarely white, in small clusters of 1 to 4, in May and June; wings obovate; keel fringed; stamens 6; **capsules** orbicular.

USE AND CULTURE: Plant in wild flower gardens. Plants require an acid soil with a pH of between 5 and 6. The soil must be well-drained and high in organic matter. Propagation is by fall division or by root or stem cuttings taken in July. Dip the cuttings in a rooting hormone and root in a sand-peat mixture. Potted plants are easiest to transplant. This is a delightful wild flower worth trying.

Polygonatum Mill. (Solomon's-seal).
LILIACEAE (Lily Family)

DESCRIPTION: About 30 species of rhizomatous perennial herbs, native in rich, shady woods in temperate regions in Europe, Asia, and North America; **rhizomes** horizontal, much-jointed, with many leafscars; **stems** erect or arching; **leaves** alternate, opposite, or whorled; **flowers** green to yellow, axillary, solitary or in clusters; perianth cylindrical, 6-lobed; stamens 6, borne on perianth tube; **fruit** a blue-black or red berry.

Polygonatum biflorum (Walt.) Elliott. (Small Solomon's-seal). Hardy in all zones; perennial to 1 m. tall.

DESCRIPTION: Perennial with erect or arching stems, native in moist woods from Ontario to Connecticut, south to Texas and Florida; **leaves** alternate, sessile, elliptic-lanceolate, to 10 cm. long, glabrous or glaucous beneath; **flowers** pale yellow or greenish white, on 1- to 3-flowered peduncle from May to July; **fruit** a blue berry in the fall.

USE AND CULTURE: Plant among ferns in wild flower gardens. Plants prefer a slightly acid soil rich in humus. Propagation is by seeds sown as soon as ripe, or more commonly, by division of the rhizomes either in the fall or early in the spring before growth starts. Plant rhizomes about 4 cm. deep and 30 cm. apart.

Polygonatum commutatum (Schult.f.) A. Dietr. (Great Solomon's-seal). Hardy in all zones; perennial to 2 m. tall.

DESCRIPTION: Rhizomatous perennial, native in moist woods from Manitoba to New Hampshire, south to Mexico and Georgia; **stems** stout, arching, naked below; **leaves** alternate, ovate-lanceolate to ovate, to 18 cm. long, glabrous; **flowers** yellowish-green to greenish-white, to 2 cm. long, on mostly 2- to 10-flowered peduncles; **fruit** a blue berry.

USE AND CULTURE: The same as for **Polygonatum biflorum**. Some authors consider this species to be a tetraploid form of **Polygonatum biflorum**.

Potentilla L. (Cinquefoil, Five-finger)
ROSACEAE (Rose Family)

DESCRIPTION: About 500 species of mostly annual or perennial herbs, rarely shrubs, native in temperate regions; **leaves** alternate, pinnately or palmately compound; **flowers** yellow, white, or red, perfect, solitary or in cymes; sepals 5, alternating with bractlets; petals 5, showy; stamens many; pistils many; **fruit** an achene.

Potentilla tridentata Ait. (Three-toothed Cinquefoil, Wineleaf Cinquefoil). Hardy in all zones; perennial to 25 cm. tall.
DESCRIPTION: Rhizomatous perennial, native along rocky or gravelly lake shores from Minnesota to Greenland, south to Iowa and Georgia; **leaflets** 3, palmate, leathery, more or less evergreen, cuneate-oblong, 3- to 5-toothed at apex, nearly glabrous, turning wine-colored in the fall; **flowers** white, in stiff cymes, from June to August.
USE AND CULTURE: Plant as a ground cover or in rock gardens. Plants grow well in any well-drained soil. Propagation is chiefly by division in early spring. Seeds can be planted as soon as ripe.

Primula L. (Primrose)
PRIMULACEAE (Primrose Family)
DESCRIPTION: About 400 species of scapose perennial herbs, native in moist soils, mostly in north temperate zones; **leaves** simple, mostly basal; **flowers** showy, in many colors; borne in heads, umbels, or in superimposed whorls; calyx 5-toothed; corolla funnelform or salverform, the tube longer than the calyx, the lobes entire or 2-lobed; stamens 5; **fruit** a 5- to 10-valved capsule.

Primula mistassinica Michx. (Bird's-eye Primrose). Hardy in all zones; perennial to 20 cm. tall.
DESCRIPTION: Plants cespitose herbaceous, native in North America; **leaves** oblanceolate to cuneate-obovate, to 7 cm. long, dentate; **flowers** pink to pale blue, with a yellow eye, to 1.25 cm. wide, in 2- to 8-flowered umbels, in May and June.
USE AND CULTURE: Plant in rock gardens or near pools. Plants require a moist soil. Propagation is by seeds started indoors in March or outdoors as soon as ripe. Space the plants about 20 cm. apart.

Psoralea L. (Scurfy Pea)
LEGUMINOSAE (Pea Family)
DESCRIPTION: About 130 species of scented herbs or shrubs, native in North America and South Africa; **leaves** alternate, odd-pinnate, rarely with 1 leaflet, with translucent dots, with a scurfy surface due to scalelike glands; **flowers** pealike, solitary or in heads, racemes, or spikes; stamens 10, united or separate; **fruit** a short, 1-seeded, indehiscent legume.

Psoralea esculenta Pursh. (Indian Breadroot, Indian Turnip, Pomme Blanche, Prairie Potato). Hardy in all zones; perennial to 40 cm. tall.
DESCRIPTION: Hairy perennial with edible tuberous roots, native in prairies and in dry open woods from Saskatchewan to Wisconsin, south to Texas; **leaflets** 5, oblong to oblanceolate, to 6 cm. long, smooth above, hairy beneath; **flowers** yellow to blue, in dense spikes, to 10 cm. long, from May to July.
USE AND CULTURE: Plant in flower borders or prairie gardens. Roots are edible. Plants require a well-drained soil. Propagation is by seeds. Space plants 45 cm. apart.

Pyrola L. (Pyrola, Shinleaf, Wintergreen)
PYROLACEAE (Wintergreen Family)
DESCRIPTION: About 12 species of evergreen perennial herbs with scaly rhizomes, native in moist, acid woods in north temperate regions; **leaves** simple, mostly basal; **flowers** white, green, pink, or purple, in terminal, scapose racemes; calyx 5-parted; petals 5; stamens 10; **fruit** a 5-valved capsule.

Pyrola asarifolia Michx. (Pink Pyrola, Pink Wintergreen). Hardy in all zones; perennial to 30 cm. tall.
DESCRIPTION: Rhizomatous perennial, native in moist, acid woods from British Columbia to New Brunswick, south to New Mexico and Indiana; **leaves** basal, reniform, petioled, leathery, shiny, to 5 cm. long; **flowers** crimson to pale pink, in spiral racemes, from June to September.
USE AND CULTURE: Plant in rock gardens or in wild flower gardens. Plants require a moist, acid soil rich in organic matter. Propagation is mainly by division. Plant when

Potentilla tridentata (Wineleaf Cinquefoil).

dormant, either in the fall or spring. Seed germination is usually poor. Space plants 20 cm. apart.

Pyrola elliptica Nutt. (Shinleaf, Wild Lily-of-the-valley). Hardy in all zones; perennial to 30 cm. tall.
DESCRIPTION: Perennial, native in acid woods from British Columbia to Quebec, south to Iowa and West Virginia; **leaves** elliptic, oblong, or obovate, to 8 cm. long, thin, dull; **flowers** white or cream-colored, in spiral racemes, from June to September; calyx lobes triangular-ovate.
USE AND CULTURE: The same as for **Pyrola asarifolia**.

Ratibida Raf. (Prairie Coneflower)
COMPOSITAE (Sunflower Family)
Helianthus Tribe

DESCRIPTION: Five species of biennial or perennial rough-hairy herbs, native in prairies of North America; **leaves** alternate, pinnatifid; **flower** heads radiate, solitary; involucral bracts green in one row; receptacle globose to conical, scaly; ray flowers yellow or rarely purple, drooping; disc flowers brown; **fruit** a compressed achene, partially enclosed by a scale; pappus lacking or of 2 awns.

Ratibida columnifera (Nutt.) Woot. & Standl. (Upright Prairie Coneflower). Hardy in all zones; perennial to 1 m. tall.
DESCRIPTION: Short-lived perennial, native in prairies from British Columbia to Minnesota, south to Mexico and Texas; **stems** branching from the base; **leaf** segments linear to narrowly lanceolate, entire; **flower** heads several to many, from June to September; receptacle columnar, to 5 cm. long; ray flowers yellow or purple, to 2 cm. long, drooping; disc flowers brown.
USE AND CULTURE: Plant in flower borders or in prairie gardens. Plants require full sun and a well-drained soil. Propagation is by seeds sown as soon as ripe.

Ratibida pinnata (Venten.) Barnh. (Prairie Coneflower). Hardy in all zones; perennial to 1 m. tall.
DESCRIPTION: Coarse perennial with hairy stems, native in dry, often sandy soils from Minnesota to Ontario, south to Oklahoma and Georgia; **stems** branched above; **leaf** segments narrowly to broadly lanceolate, serrate; **flower** heads solitary or several, from June to August; receptacle ellipsoid to oblong, to 2 cm. long; ray flowers pale yellow, 5 to 10, to 5 cm. long, spreading or reflexed; **achenes** smooth; pappus lacking.
USE AND CULTURE: The same as for **Ratibida columnifera**.

Rudbeckia L. (Coneflower)
COMPOSITAE (Sunflower Family)
Helianthus Tribe

DESCRIPTION: About 25 species of annual, biennial, or perennial herbs throughout North America; **leaves** alternate, simple, pinnatifid or pinnate; **flower** heads radiate, showy, terminal; receptacle hemispherical to columnar, scaly, the scales shorter than or equalling the disc flowers; ray flowers sterile, yellow to reddish-brown; disc flowers perfect; **fruit** a 4-angled achene; pappus a short crown or lacking.

Rudbeckia hirta L. (Black-eyed Susan). Hardy in all zones; annual, biennial, or perennial to 90 cm. tall.
DESCRIPTION: Hairy annual, biennial, or perennial herb, native in open disturbed soils throughout North America; **leaves** mostly basal, simple, lanceolate, petioled; stem leaves sessile above; **flower** heads showy to 8 cm. across, from June to September; receptacle conical; ray flowers mostly orange-yellow; disc flowers purple-brown; pappus lacking.
USE AND CULTURE: Plant in flower borders or in prairie gardens. Plants grow well in most any well-drained soil in full sun. Propagation is by seeds sown as soon as ripe or started indoors in early April. Plants will bloom the first year if seeds are planted early. By cutting back the flower stalks after bloom, the plants will persist for several years. Plants can self sow. Tetraploid strains of this species are sold as gloriosa daisies.

Pyrola elliptica (Shinleaf). In flower in Deer River, Minnesota in July 1971.

Rudbeckia laciniata L. (Cutleaf Coneflower). Hardy in all zones; perennial to 3 m. tall.

DESCRIPTION: Tall perennial, native in wet fields, ditches, and ravines from Montana to Quebec, south to Arizona and Florida; **leaves** pinnate, nearly glabrous; leaflets deeply lobed; **flower** heads to 8 cm. across, from July to September; receptacle hemispherical, becoming conic-oblong in age; ray flowers yellow, drooping; disc flowers greenish-yellow.

USE AND CULTURE: The same as for **Rudbeckia hirta**. The cultivar 'Hortensia', called Goldenglow, is a double form of this species.

Ruellia L. (Ruellia)
ACANTHACEAE (Acanthus Family)

DESCRIPTION: About 250 species of mostly tropical perennial herbs or shrubs, native in tropical America, Africa, and Asia, one in northern United States; **leaves** opposite, simple, mostly entire; **flowers** large, showy, solitary, or in axillary cymes or terminal panicles; calyx deeply 5-parted or 5-cleft; corolla with funnelform throat, 5-lobed, spreading; stamens 4 in 2 pairs with each pair united at base; **fruit** a cylindrical or clavate capsule.

Ruellia humilis Nutt. (Wild Petunia). Hardy in zone 4; perennial to 45 cm. tall.

DESCRIPTION: Pubescent, branched perennial, native in dry, sandy soil in open fields and wood edges from Nebraska to Pennsylvania, south to Texas and Florida; **leaves** ovate to lanceolate, to 7.5 cm. long, sessile or nearly so; **flowers** lavender-blue, in cymose clusters in upper leaf axils, from June to September; corolla to 5 cm. long with tube about equaling the throat.

USE AND CULTURE: Plant in flower borders or in rock gardens. Plants grow well in a well-drained fertile soil that is slightly acid, either in full sun or in partial shade. Propagation is by seeds, division, or by cuttings. Seeds should be sown as soon as ripe. Spring division is recommended. Cuttings taken in June or July are easy to root. Rooted cuttings should be wintered in a cold frame.

Salvia L. (Ramona, Sage, Salvia)
LABIATAE (Mint Family)

DESCRIPTION: Over 750 species of herbs, subshrubs, and shrubs, native in dry or rocky soils worldwide; **stems** square in cross section; **leaves** opposite, simple to pinnatifid, upper ones reduced to scales; **flowers** in axillary verticillasters; calyx 2-lipped with unequal teeth; corolla 2-lipped; stamens 2; **fruit** of 4 ovoid, 3-angled nutlets.

Salvia azurea Lam. (Azure Salvia, Blue Sage). Hardy in all zones; perennial to 60 cm. tall.

DESCRIPTION: Erect perennial, native in dry prairies from Minnesota to Kentucky, south to Texas; basal **leaves** lanceolate or oblong, to 7.5 cm. long, serrate, tapering at base; upper leaves narrow, often linear; **flowers** deep blue, rarely white, in spikes, in June and July; calyx with upper lip entire; corolla to 2 cm. long.

Sanguinaria canadensis (Bloodroot). In flower on May 7, 1961.

USE AND CULTURE: Plant in flower borders or prairie gardens. Plants prefer a sunny location and a fertile garden loam. Propagation is by seeds or division. Plant seeds as soon as ripe or in early spring. Seedlings bloom the second year. Plants can be divided either in the spring or fall. Space plants about 20 cm. apart and slightly deeper than they were growing.

VARIETIES: var. **grandiflora** Benth. Flowers larger than in the species. This variety has the same range as the species.

Salvia pitcheri - see **Salvia azurea** var. **grandiflora**

Sanguinaria L. (Bloodroot)
PAPAVERACEAE (Poppy Family)

DESCRIPTION: A single species of perennial herb with red sap and prominent rhizomes, native in eastern North America; **rhizomes** with a red sap; **leaves** lobed, emerging from the rhizomes; **flowers** white, showy; sepals 2, early deciduous; petals 8 to 16; stamens many with linear anthers; ovary narrowed above to a short style and a 2-lobed stigma; **fruit** a fusiform capsule.

Sanguinaria canadensis L. (Bloodroot, Red Puccoon). Hardy in all zones; perennial to 20 cm. tall.

DESCRIPTION: Rhizomatous perennial, native in woods, often on dry, rocky slopes or along streams from Manitoba to Quebec, south to Oklahoma and Florida; **leaves** solitary, basal, petioled, palmately lobed, to 30 cm. across; **flowers** solitary on a scape, white, sometimes tinged pink, to 4 cm. across, in April and May; **capsule** ellipsoid, to 2.5 cm. long.

USE AND CULTURE: Plant in rock gardens or wild flower gardens. Plants grow well in a soil high in organic matter, either in shade or full sun. Propagation is by seeds or division. Seeds should be sown as soon as ripe. Seedlings bloom the third year. Division of rhizomes should be done in the fall.

Saxifraga L. (Rockfoil, Saxifrage)
SAXIFRAGACEAE (Saxifrage Family)

DESCRIPTION: About 300 species of mostly perennial herbs, native in moist, rocky soils in subarctic, alpine, and temperate regions of Europe, Asia, North and South America, and North Africa; **leaves** mostly basal and clustered in a rosette; stem leaves alternate and smaller; **flowers** white, pink, purple, or yellow, in racemose, paniculate, or cymose clusters, 5-merous; calyx 5-cleft, free or adhering to the base of the ovary; petals entire, often deciduous; carpels 2, fused except at the top; ovary inferior to superior; **fruit** a bilobed capsule or of two follicles.

Saxifraga aizoides L. (Yellow Mountain Saxifrage). Hardy in all zones; perennial to 15 cm. tall.

DESCRIPTION: Cespitose perennial, native circumboreal south to British Columbia and New York; **leaves** linear-oblong, thick, to 25 cm. long; **flowers** yellow to orange, often with red spots, to 1 cm. long, in terminal, somewhat leafy cymes, from June to August.

USE AND CULTURE: Plant in rock gardens or wild flower gardens. Plants require a cool, moist soil in sun or shade. Propagation is by spring division or by seeds sown as soon as ripe. Cuttings taken after flowering can also be rooted.

Saxifraga aizoon - see **Saxifraga paniculata**.

Saxifraga paniculata Mill. (Saxifrage). Hardy in all zones; perennial to 30 cm. tall.

DESCRIPTION: Cespitose perennial, native circumboreal, south to Minnesota and Vermont in North America; **leaves** narrow-spatulate, in dense basal rosettes, to 3 cm. long; **flowers** creamy-white marked with purple, to 1.25 cm. across, in upright panicles, in July.

USE AND CULTURE: The same as for **Saxifraga aizoides**. Numerous named cultivars of this species are on the market.

Saxifraga virginiensis Michx. (Early Saxifrage). Hardy in all zones; perennial to 30 cm. tall.

DESCRIPTION: Cespitose perennial, native in moist or dry, open woods and on rock ledges from Manitoba to New Brunswick, south to Oklahoma and Georgia; **leaves** ovate to oblong, to 7 cm. long, dentate, in basal rosettes; **flowers** white, to 8 mm. across, in open clusters on a scape, in May and June.

USE AND CULTURE: The same as for **Saxifraga aizoides**.

Scutellaria L. (Skullcap)
LABIATAE (Mint Family)

DESCRIPTION: About 300 species of rhizomatous perennial herbs, native in open woods around the world; **stems** mostly square in cross section; **leaves** opposite, simple; **flowers** blue or violet, rarely pink or white, in pairs or in dense paniculate racemes; calyx campanulate, 2-lipped with crestlike projections on back of upper lip; corolla tube long, curved upwards, glabrous inside, with 2-lipped limb; stamens 4 with hairy anthers; **fruit** of 4 nutlets.

Scutellaria lateriflora L. (Mad-dog Skullcap). Hardy in all zones; perennial to 70 cm. tall.

DESCRIPTION: Rhizomatous perennial, native in moist woods from British Columbia to Newfoundland, south to California and Georgia; **stems** solitary from slender rhizomes; **leaves** thin, pinnately veined, ovate or lanceolate-ovate, with broadly rounded or subcordate bases, dentate, to 5 cm. long; **flowers** blue, rarely white or pink, in axillary racemes, from July to September.

USE AND CULTURE: Plant in flower borders or in wild flower gardens. Plants require a neutral to slightly acid soil kept constantly moist. Propagation is by division in early spring and by seeds sown as soon as ripe. Seedlings bloom the second year.

Scutellaria ovata Hill. (Early Blue Skullcap). Hardy in all zones; perennial to 70 cm. tall.

DESCRIPTION: Rhizomatous perennial, native in moist open woods in full sun along streams and in meadows from Minnesota to Maryland, south to Mexico and South Carolina; **leaves** ovate to round-ovate, crenate, cordate at base, long-petioled; **flowers** blue, to 2.5 cm. long, in racemes to 10 cm. long.

USE AND CULTURE: The same as for **Scutellaria lateriflora**.

Senecio L. (Groundsel)
COMPOSITAE (Sunflower Family)
Senecio Tribe

DESCRIPTION: About 3000 species of annual or perennial herbs, shrubs, or trees, native in all parts of the world; **leaves** alternate, sometimes all basal; **flower** heads usually radiate, rarely discoid, solitary or clustered; involucral bracts in one row; ray flowers commonly yellow; **fruit** a cylindrical ribbed achene; pappus of soft white bristles.

Senecio aureus L. (Golden Groundsel, Golden Ragwort). Hardy in all zones; perennial to 75 cm. tall.

DESCRIPTION: Perennial, native in moist woods and swamps from Minnesota to Newfoundland, south to Texas and Florida; **stems** lightly tomentose when young, becoming glabrous; basal **leaves** cordate-ovate, to 15 cm. long, dentate; stem leaves pinnately cut; **flower** heads to 2 cm. across, in corymbs, in June; ray flowers 8 to 12, yellow.

USE AND CULTURE: Plant in flower borders or in wild flower gardens. Plants require a moist soil of ordinary fertility. Propagation is by division in early spring or by seeds sown as soon as ripe. Space plants 30 cm. apart.

Sieversia triflorum - see **Geum triflorum**.

Silene L. (Campion, Catchfly)
CARYOPHYLLACEAE (Pink Family)

DESCRIPTION: About 500 species of annual, biennial, or perennial herbs, native in the northern hemisphere; **leaves** opposite or whorled, without stipules; **flowers** white, pink, or red, solitary, in cymes or panicles; calyx tubular, 5-lobed; petals 5, 2-lobed or notched at apex; stamens 10; ovary 1- to 5-celled; styles 3 to 5; **fruit** a capsule.

Silene stellata (L.) Ait.f. (Starry Campion, Widow's-frill). Hardy in all zones; perennial to 1 m. tall.
DESCRIPTION: Perennial, native in woods from South Dakota to Massachusetts, south to Texas and Georgia; **stems** puberulent to glabrous; **leaves** in whorls of 4, linear-lanceolate, to 10 cm. long, pubescent; **flowers** white, in panicles, from June to September; calyx pubescent, 1.25 cm. long; petals laciniate, lanate at base.
USE AND CULTURE: Plant in flower borders or wild flower gardens. Plants grow in any good garden soil either in partial shade or in full sun. Propagation is by division or by seeds sown as soon as ripe.

Silene virginica L. (Fire Pink). Hardy in all zones; perennial to 40 cm. tall.
DESCRIPTION: Perennial, native in open woods from Minnesota to New Jersey, south to Oklahoma and Georgia; **stems** puberulent, glandular, or glabrous; **leaves** opposite, oblanceolate, to 10 cm. long, with ciliate petioles below, sessile above; **flowers** scarlet, to 2.5 cm. long, in 7- to 10-flowered clusters, from April to June; calyx 2 cm. long, pubescent; petals 2-lobed.
USE AND CULTURE: The same as for **Silene stellata**.

Silphium L. (Rosinweed)
COMPOSITAE (Sunflower Family)
Helianthus Tribe
DESCRIPTION: About 25 species of coarse perennial herbs, native in open areas in eastern North America; **stems** sparingly branched, scabrous-hispid; **leaves** opposite below, alternate above, usually scabrous; **flower** heads radiate, in racemes or corymbose panicles; involucre shallowly campanulate; involucral bracts nearly equal, in 2 to several rows; receptacle flat to convex, scaly; ray flowers in 2 to 3 rows, pistillate, yellow or rarely white; disc flowers yellow, sterile; **fruit** a compressed achene with winged edges.

Silphium laciniatum L. (Compass Plant). Hardy in all zones; perennial to 2 m. tall.
DESCRIPTION: Coarse perennial, native in prairies from Minnesota to Ohio, south to Texas and Alabama; **stems** stout, very hispid; **leaves** alternate, deeply pinnatifid, to 50 cm. long; **flower** heads to 12 cm. across, in racemes, from July to September.
USE AND CULTURE: Plant toward the back of flower borders or in prairie gardens. Plants are easy to grow in any well-drained garden soil in full sun. Propagation is by division in early spring or by seeds sown as soon as ripe. Space plants about 30 cm. apart.

Silphium perfoliatum L. (Carpenter Weed, Compass Plant, Cup Plant). Hardy in all zones; perennial to 2.5 m. tall.
DESCRIPTION: Nearly glabrous perennial, native in open fields and open woods from South Dakota to Ontario, south to Oklahoma and Georgia; **stems** 4-angled; **leaves** connate-perfoliate with triangular to ovate blades, to 35 cm. long, coarsely dentate; **flower** heads to 7.5 cm. across, in corymbs, from July to September; ray flowers yellow.
USE AND CULTURE: The same as for **Silphium laciniatum**.

Sisyrinchium L. (Blue-eyed Grass)
IRIDACEAE (Iris Family)
DESCRIPTION: About 75 species of clump-forming herbs, native in sunny locations in the western hemisphere; **rhizomes** very short or none; **leaves** grasslike, linear or cylindrical; **flowers** blue, yellow, or white, in terminal, solitary or fascicled clusters, each cluster subtended by a spathe; perianth rotate or campanulate with 6 segments; stamens 3 with filaments united at the base; style branches 3; **fruit** a 3-valved capsule.

Sisyrinchium albidum Raf. (White Blue-eyed Grass). Hardy in all zones; perennial to 45 cm. tall.
DESCRIPTION: Perennial, native in dry, sandy soils from North Dakota to New York, south to Oklahoma and Georgia; **stems** flattened, slightly winged; **leaves** flat, persisting or withering; **flowers** white or pale violet, to 1.25 cm. across, in May and June; spathe sessile, subtended by an erect leaflike bract.
USE AND CULTURE: Plant in rock gardens, flower borders, and prairie gardens. Plants grow best in a sunny location and in a well-drained sandy loam soil. Propagation is by division or by seeds sown as soon as ripe. Space plants about 20 cm. apart.

Sisyrinchium angustifolium Mill. (Blue-eyed Grass). Hardy in all zones; perennial to 30 cm. tall.
DESCRIPTION: Perennial, native in sunny meadows from North Dakota to Newfoundland, south to Texas and Florida; **stems** forked, usually winged; **leaves** mostly basal, grasslike, deep green; **flowers** pale blue or violet, to 1.25 cm. across, from May to July; spathes on stout, flattened, or winged peduncles.
USE AND CULTURE: The same as for **Sisyrinchium albidum**

Sisyrinchium campestre Bickn. Hardy in all zones; perennial to 50 cm. tall.
DESCRIPTION: Perennial, native in dry prairies, meadows, and open woods from Manitoba to Wisconsin, south to Texas and Louisiana; **stems** tufted, slender, flat, winged, glaucous; **leaves** grasslike, to 30 cm. long; **flowers** light blue to white, about 1.25 cm. across, from April to June; spathes sessile, solitary, half as long as the subtending bract.
USE AND CULTURE: The same as for **Sisyrinchium albidum**.

Sisyrinchium montanum Greene. Hardy in all zones; perennial to 60 cm. tall.
DESCRIPTION: Perennial, native in meadows and along lake shores from British Columbia to Quebec, south to Colorado and North Carolina; **stems** simple, flattened, pale green; **leaves** grasslike, shorter than the stem; **flowers** blue-violet on erect pedicels, from May to July; spathes sessile.
USE AND CULTURE: The same as for **Sisyrinchium albidum**.

Smilacina Desf. (False Solomon's-seal,
False Spikenard, Solomon's-feather,
Solomon's-plumes)
LILIACEAE (Lily Family)

DESCRIPTION: About 25 species of rhizomatous, perennial herbs, native in moist, shady areas in North America and Asia; **stems** unbranched, leafy; **leaves** alternate; **flowers** white, pink, or purple, in terminal racemes or panicles; perianth segments 6, persistent; stamens 6; **fruit** a many-seeded berry.

Smilacina stellata (Starflower).

Photograph: Mr. Arvid Lund.

Smilacina racemosa. In flower at

Royal Botanic Gardens, Kew, England on May 24, 1979.

Smilacina racemosa (L.) Desf. (False Spikenard, Solomon's plumes, Solomon's-zig-zag, Treacleberry). Hardy in all zones; perennial to 1 m. tall.
DESCRIPTION: Rhizomatous perennial, native in open woods in humus-rich soils from British Columbia to Quebec, south to Missouri and Virginia; **stems** arching to ascending, finely pubescent; **leaves** elliptic to lanceolate-ovate, short-petioled, to 15 cm. long, acuminate, pubescent beneath; **flowers** white, many, in terminal panicles to 15 cm. long, from May to July; **berries** red, sometimes spotted with purple, in August.
USE AND CULTURE: Plant in flower borders and in wild flower gardens. Plants are easy to grow in any humus-rich soil in partial shade. Propagation is mostly by division either in the fall or early in the spring. Seeds, sown as soon as ripe, take two years to germinate. Seedlings take 5 more years to bloom. Space plants 30 cm. apart. Plant rhizomes 2.5 cm. deep and horizontal. Fruits furnish valuable food for grouse.

Smilacina stellata (L.) Desf. (Starflower, Star-flowered Lily-of-the-valley). Hardy in all zones; perennial to 50 cm. tall.
DESCRIPTION: Rhizomatous perennial, native in gravelly or sandy soils in thickets from British Columbia to Newfoundland, south to California and West Virginia; **stems** arching, zig-zag; **leaves** lanceolate to oblong-lanceolate, to 15 cm. long, usually folded lengthwise, finely pubescent beneath; **flowers** white, in sessile racemes to 5 cm. long, in May and June; **berries** dark red to almost black, in August.
USE AND CULTURE: The same as for **Smilacina racemosa**.

Solidago L. (Goldenrod)
COMPOSITAE (Sunflower Family)
Aster Tribe

DESCRIPTION: About 150 species of perennial herbs, native mostly in North America, a few in Europe, Asia, and South America; **stems** emerging from rhizomes or a crown; **leaves** alternate, simple, entire or dentate; **flower** heads yellow, radiate, small, often clustered in racemes, corymbs, and panicles; involucral bracts in few rows; involucre nearly cylindrical to campanulate; receptacle flat or convex, naked, pitted; ray flowers pistillate; disc flowers perfect; **fruit** an angled or nearly cylindrical achene; pappus of many capillary bristles.

Solidago canadensis L. (Canada Goldenrod). Hardy in all zones; perennial to 1.5 m. tall.
DESCRIPTION: Rhizomatous perennial, native in moist soil in open woods and meadows from Manitoba to Newfoundland, south to Colorado and Virginia; **leaves** numerous, lanceolate-linear to elliptic-lanceolate, to 15 cm. long attenuate, 3-veined, glabrous or scabrous above, pubescent beneath, sharply serrate, losing lower leaves early; **flower** heads in panicles, from July to October.
USE AND CULTURE: Plant in flower borders or prairie gardens. Plants are easy to grow in most soils in full sun. Propagation is by division. Replant only the outer divisions that have young rhizomes. Space plants about 30 cm. apart. Plants often self sow and can spread in fertile soils. This species is but one of many that can be planted. The goldenrods are falsely accused of causing hayfever. Actually, the pollen is sticky and spread by insects. The fluffy panicles possibly can catch ragweed pollen and, when used in flower arrangements, could cause hayfever sufferers to sneeze. In Europe goldenrods are popular garden flowers.

Specularia perfoliata - see **Triodanis perfoliata**.

Sphaeralcea St.-Hil. (False Mallow, Globe Mallow)
MALVACEAE (Mallow Family)

DESCRIPTION: About 50 species of annual or perennial herbs or small shrubs, native in dry soils in North and South America; **leaves** linear-lanceolate to orbicular, scarcely 3-lobed to deeply palmately parted or divided, the lobes serrate; **flowers** yellow, orange, lavender, or white, in racemes or panicles; involucral bracts 3, usually early deciduous; corolla cuplike; stamens united in a tubular column; style branches 10 to 20; **fruit** a schizocarp with 10 to 20 mericarps in a single whorl.

Sphaeralcea coccinea (Pursh.) Rydb. (Prairie Mallow, Red False Mallow). Hardy in all zones; perennial to 60 cm. tall.
DESCRIPTION: A decumbent perennial with gray-white pubescence, native in dry prairies from Manitoba, south to Arizona and Texas; root a tap root; **leaves** pedately parted or divided, usually broader than long; **flowers** orange to red, in short racemes, in April and May; involucral bracts absent; **mericarps** 10 or 11, suborbicular.
USE AND CULTURE: Plant in flower borders or prairie gardens. Plants require a well-drained soil and full sun. Due to the tap root, plants are difficult to transplant. Sow seeds as soon as ripe where plants are to grow. Thin plants to about 20 cm. apart.

Stachys L. (Betony, Glistening Mint, Hedge Nettle, Woundwort)
LABIATAE (Mint Family)
DESCRIPTION: About 300 species of herbs or subshrubs, native in temperate and subtropical regions; **stems** mostly square; **leaves** opposite, entire or dentate; **flowers** small, purple, red, pink, yellow, or white, in 2- to many-flowered verticillasters arranged in terminal spikelike inflorescences; calyx tubular-campanulate, 5- to 10-veined, 5-toothed with bristly teeth; corolla tube cylindrical, often hairy inside, upper lip concave, often 2-lobed, lower lip 3-lobed; stamens 4; **fruit** of 4 ovoid nutlets.

Stachys palustris L. (Woundwort). Hardy in all zones; perennial to 1 m. tall.
DESCRIPTION: Rhizomatous perennial, native in moist or wet soils from Alaska to Quebec, south to Arizona and New York, also native in Europe and Asia; **stems** hairy and often glandular; **leaves** lance-triangular to lance-ovate, sessile or short-petioled; **flowers** purple, spotted white, in 6-flowered verticillasters, from June to August.
USE AND CULTURE: Plant in flower borders or in wild flower gardens. Plants require a moist soil. Propagation is by seeds sown as soon as ripe or by division in early spring. Space plants 30 cm. apart. Plants may self sow.

Stachys tenuifolia Willd. (Hedge Nettle). Hardy in all zones; perennial to 1 m. tall.
DESCRIPTION: Creeping perennial with erect, mostly glabrous stems, native in meadows, bottom lands, and moist woods from Minnesota to New York, south to Texas and Alabama; **leaves** narrowly lanceolate to ovate, to 8 cm. long, short-petioled, acute, dentate; **flowers** small, purple, in few-flowered verticillasters.
USE AND CULTURE: The same as for **Stachys palustris**.

Steironema - see **Lysimachia**.

Streptopus Michx. (Mandarin, Twisted-stalk)
LILIACEAE (Lily Family)
DESCRIPTION: About 7 species of rhizomatous perennial herbs, native in moist woods in North America, Europe, and Asia; **stems** simple or branched, leafy; **leaves** alternate, sessile or clasping; **flowers** white, pink, rose, or purple, nodding, solitary or in pairs, axillary on twisted pedicels; perianth segments 6, separate; stamens 6, with dilated filaments; **fruit** a berry.

Streptopus amplexifolius var. **americanus** Schult. (Liverberry, Scootberry). Hardy in all zones; perennial to 1 m. tall.
DESCRIPTION: Rhizomatous perennial, native in moist woods, circumboreal, south to Arizona and North Carolina in North America; **stems** glabrous; **leaves** lanceolate-ovate to ovate or oblong-ovate, to 12 cm. long, glaucous beneath, clasping; **flowers** greenish-white, to 1.25 cm. long, in pairs, in June and July; **berries** red, ellipsoid, to 2 cm. long, in August.
USE AND CULTURE: Plant in wild flower gardens. Plants prefer a humus-rich, moist soil in shade. Propagation is by seeds sown as soon as ripe or by division either in the fall or early in the spring. Rabbits are fond of the foliage. Birds eat the fruits.

Streptopus roseus Michx. (Rose Mandarin). Hardy in all zones; perennial to 60 cm. tall.
DESCRIPTION: Rhizomatous perennial, native in moist, humus-rich woods from Minnesota to Labrador, south to Tennessee and Georgia; **stems** finely pubescent; **leaves**

lanceolate to ovate-lanceolate, tapering to a point, to 8 cm. long, sessile, not clasping, ciliate; **flowers** solitary, on glabrous pedicels, rose or purple, bell-shaped, axillary, drooping, to 1.25 cm. long, from May to July; perianth segments recurved; **berries** red, to 1 cm. in diameter, in July and August.

USE AND CULTURE: The same as for **Streptopus amplexifolius**.

Stylophorum Nutt. (Celandine Poppy)
PAPAVERACEAE (Poppy Family)

DESCRIPTION: About 6 species of perennial herbs with yellow sap, native in moist woods in North America and eastern Asia; **leaves** mostly basal, pinnately lobed; **flowers** yellow, few in terminal umbels; sepals 3; petals 4; stamens many; **fruit** a bristly, 2- to 4-valved capsule.

Stylophorum diphyllum (Michx.) Nutt. (Celandine Poppy, Wood Poppy). Hardy in all zones; perennial to 35 cm. tall.

DESCRIPTION: Rhizomatous perennial, native in humus-rich, moist woods from Wisconsin to Pennsylvania, south to Missouri and Virginia; basal **leaves** usually 2, 5- to 7-lobed, gray-green; **flowers** yellow, to 5 cm. across, in May and June.

USE AND CULTURE: Plant in wild flower gardens. Plants prefer a moist, humus-rich soil either in full sun or shade. Propagation is by seeds sown as soon as ripe or by fall division. Plant rhizomes 2.5 cm. deep and 30 cm. apart.

Talinum Adans. (Fameflower, Sunbright)
PORTULACACEAE (Purslane Family)

DESCRIPTION: About 50 species of annual or perennial succulent herbs, native in rocky or sandy soils mostly in North America with a few species in South America, Africa, and Asia; **leaves** basal, linear; **flowers** showy, ephemeral, in erect, terminal cymes or panicles; sepals 2, deciduous; petals 5 or more; stamens few to many; **fruit** a 3-valved capsule.

Talinum parviflorum Nutt. (Fameflower, Sunbright). Hardy in all zones; perennial to 20 cm. tall.

DESCRIPTION: Fleshy-rooted perennial, native in thin, acid soils overlying rocks from South Dakota to Minnesota, south to Arizona and Texas; **leaves** linear, cylindrical, to 5 cm. long; **flowers** pink, about 1.5 cm. across, in few-flowered clusters on upright stems, from May to September; stamens 4 to 8.

USE AND CULTURE: Plant in rock gardens. Plants must have an acid, well-drained soil. Propagation is by seeds sown as soon as ripe in a sand-peat mixture.

Thalictrum L. (Meadow Rue)
RANUNCULACEAE (Buttercup Family)

DESCRIPTION: About 100 species of perennial herbs, native in north temperate regions; **leaves** ternately compound; **flowers** small, in open panicles, racemes, or corymbs; sepals 4 or 5, deciduous; petals lacking; stamens numerous, sometimes brightly colored; pistils few; **fruit** a ribbed, angled, or winged achene.

Thalictrum dasycarpum Fisch. & Ave-Lall. (Purple Meadow Rue). Hardy in all zones; perennial to 2 m. tall.

DESCRIPTION: Mostly dioecious perennials with short, thick crowns and erect stems, native in meadows and swamps from Alberta to Ontario, south to Arizona and Ohio; **stems** often purple; **leaflets** firm with prominent veins and pubescent beneath; **flowers** small, in corymbs or panicles, from May to July; sepals acuminate; filaments filiform, soon drooping; anthers subulate at apex.

USE AND CULTURE: Plant in wild flower gardens. Plants require a moist soil in either full sun or partial shade. Propagation is by spring division or by seeds sown as soon as ripe.

Thalictrum dioicum L. (Early Meadow Rue, Quicksilver Weed). Hardy in all zones; perennial to 60 cm. tall.

DESCRIPTION: Dioecious perennial with leaves emerging from a thick crown, native in woods from Manitoba to Quebec, south to Mississippi and Georgia; **leaves** 1 to 3,

ternately compound; leaflets reniform to obovate with blunt lobes; **flowers** small, greenish-yellow, in large terminal or axillary panicles, in May and June; sepals green or purple; filaments filiform; anthers mucronate-acuminate, yellow.
USE AND CULTURE: Plant in wild flower gardens. Plants prefer a humus-rich soil that is slightly acid in light shade. Propagation is by division in fall or early spring, or by seeds sown as soon as ripe. Plants self sow once established.

Thalictrum polygamum Muhlenb. (King-of-the-meadow, Muskrat Weed, Tall Meadow Rue). Hardy in all zones; perennial to 2.5 m. tall.
DESCRIPTION: Polygamous perennial, native along brooks, in wet meadows, and roadside ditches from Ontario to Newfoundland, south to Tennessee and Georgia; stem **leaves** sessile; leaflets firm; **flowers** small, white, in plumelike panicles, from June to September; stamens with clavate filaments and blunt anthers; achenes nearly sessile.
USE AND CULTURE: The same as for **Thalictrum dasycarpum**.

Thermopsis R. Br. (False Lupine, Golden Banner, Golden Pea)
LEGUMINOSAE (Pea Family)
DESCRIPTION: About 20 species of perennial herbs, native in well-drained soils in North America and northeastern Asia; **leaves** palmately compound with 3 leaflets; stipules leaflike; **flowers** pealike, in racemes; stamens 10, separate; **fruit** a narrow flat legume.

Thermopsis caroliniana M.A. Curtis (Aaron's Rod, Carolina Lupine). Hardy in all zones; perennial to 1 m. tall.
DESCRIPTION: Sparsely branched perennial, native in open woods from Virginia to Georgia; **leaflets** ovate to obovate, to 7.5 cm. long, pubescent and glaucous on under surface; **flowers** yellow, in terminal spikes, in June and July; **legumes** erect, densely hairy, to 5 cm. long.
USE AND CULTURE: Plant in flower borders or in prairie gardens. Plants require a well-drained soil of low fertility. Propagation is by division of dormant plants or by seeds sown as soon as ripe. Seedlings should be transplanted in early spring. Space plants 45 cm. apart. This southern species is hardy and widely planted in our area.

Tiarella L. (False Miterwort)
SAXIFRAGACEAE (Saxifrage Family)
DESCRIPTION: Six species of rhizomatous perennial herbs, native in shady woods in acid soils in North America and Asia; **leaves** mostly basal, cordate and palmately lobed, or with 3 leaflets; **flowers** small, white or red, in simple or branched racemes; calyx tube campanulate, united to base of ovary; calyx lobes triangular; petals 5; stamens 10; ovary superior with 2 beaklike projections; **fruit** a capsule of 2 unequal parts.

Tiarella cordifolia L. (Foamflower). Hardy in all zones; perennial to 20 cm. tall.
DESCRIPTION: Rhizomatous perennial, native in moist, acid woods from Ontario to Nova Scotia, south to Alabama and Georgia; **leaves** ovate-cordate, to 10 cm. long, dentate, with petioles to 10 cm. long; **flowers** white or red, from April to July.

Trientalis borealis (Starflower). In flower in June 1971.

USE AND CULTURE: Plant in rock gardens or use as a ground cover in wild flower gardens. Plants require an acid soil that is kept moist in the shade. Propagation is by seeds or division. Rhizomes can be planted either in the fall or early in the spring.

Townsendia Hook. (Easter Daisy)
COMPOSITAE (Sunflower Family)
Aster Tribe.

DESCRIPTION: About 20 species of annual, biennial, or perennial herbs, native mostly in western North America; **leaves** alternate, spatulate to linear, entire; **flower** heads radiate, solitary, sessile or peduncled, many-flowered; ray flowers white, pink, or purple; disc flowers yellow; **fruit** a glabrate or pubescent achene with forked hairs; pappus of bristles.

Townsendia exscapa (Richardson) T.C. Porter. (Stemless Easter Daisy). Hardy in all zones; perennial to 7.5 cm. tall.
DESCRIPTION: Cespitose perennial, native in plains and hills from Manitoba south to Utah and Oklahoma; **leaves** narrowly oblanceolate, to 5 cm. long, strigose-pubescent; **flower** heads sessile or on short peduncles, to 5 cm. across; ray flowers white or pink.
USE AND CULTURE: Plant in rock gardens or in prairie gardens. Plants require a well-drained soil. Propagation is by seeds sown as soon as ripe or in the spring. Space seedlings about 20 cm. apart.

Tradescantia L. (Spiderwort)
COMMELINACEAE (Spiderwort Family)

DESCRIPTION: About 20 species of perennial herbs, native along roadsides and in open woods in North and South America; **stems** erect or trailing; **leaves** linear, folded lengthwise; **flowers** blue, rose, purple, or white, in terminal or axillary clusters, subtended by spathelike bracts; sepals and petals 3, separate; stamens 6, with hairy filaments; **fruit** a capsule.

Tradescantia virginiana L. (Common Spiderwort, Virginia Spiderwort, Widow's Tears). Hardy in all zones; perennial to 90 cm. tall.
DESCRIPTION: Perennial, native in woods, meadows, and on roadsides from Minnesota to Maine, south to Missouri and Georgia; **leaves** linear-lanceolate, to 30 cm. long; **flowers** violet-purple, rarely rose or white, from May to July; sepals bright green, somewhat inflated, pubescent.
USE AND CULTURE: Plant in flower borders or wild flower gardens. Plants grow best in a moist soil either in partial shade or in full sun. Propagation is by seeds or division in early spring. Plants tend to be floppy due to weak stems. Flowers open in the morning and last but a single day. Several other native species occur and can be planted.

Trientalis L. (Chickweed Wintergreen, Starflower)
PRIMULACEAE (Primrose Family)

DESCRIPTION: Four species of perennial herbs, native in Europe, Asia, and North America; **leaves** mostly clustered at the top of the stem, frequently with a few smaller or scalelike leaves below; **flowers** white or pink, solitary, axillary, on slender pedicels; calyx 5-parted; corolla rotate; stamens 5; **fruit** a capsule.

Trientalis borealis Raf. (Starflower). Hardy in all zones; perennial to 20 cm. tall.
DESCRIPTION: Single-stemmed perennial, native from Labrador south to Illinois and Virginia; **leaves** in a whorl of 5 to 10, lanceolate, to 10 cm. long, acuminate; **flowers** white, starlike, to 1.25 cm. across; on slender pedicels to 5 cm. long, in May and June.
USE AND CULTURE: Plant as a ground cover or in wild flower gardens. Plants must have an acid soil, constant moisture, and rich leafmold mixed into the soil. Propagation is by seeds or division. Fall planting is best. In moving plants from the woods, take some adjacent soil for inoculation. Seeds should be sown as soon as ripe in a soil containing leafmold. This delicate plant is difficult to establish but worth the effort.

Trillium L. (Birthroot, Trillium, Wake-robin)
LILIACEAE (Lily Family)

Trillium grandiflorum (Large White Trillium).

In flower in Wayzata, Minnesota on May 17, 1981.

DESCRIPTION: About 30 species of perennial herbs, native in fertile, moist woods in North America, eastern Asia, and the Himalayas; **stems** simple with thick, underground rootstocks; **leaves** in terminal whorls of 3, subtending a single sessile or peduncled flower; **flowers** white, yellow-green, pink, or purple; sepals 3, green; petals 3, separate; stamens 6 with basifixed anthers; **fruit** a 3-celled berry.

Trillium cernuum L. (Nodding Trillium). Hardy in all zones; perennial to 45 cm. tall.
DESCRIPTION: Perennial, native in damp woods rich in organic matter and at the edges of evergreen swamps from Manitoba to Newfoundland, south to Iowa and Georgia; **leaves** broadly rhombic-ovate, to 10 cm. long, narrowed to an obscure petiole; **flowers** white, sweet-scented, nodding, on peduncles to 3 cm. long, in May and June; petals wavy; anthers deep rose to maroon; **berries** triangular, turning red in July.
USE AND CULTURE: Plant in wild flower gardens. Plants are easy to grow in a humus rich soil in shade. Propagation is by seeds or division of the tuberous rootstocks. Plant tubers about 15 cm. deep. Seeds should be sown as soon as ripe. It takes about 10 years for seedlings to bloom. Slugs often feed on the foliage.

Trillium grandiflorum (Michx.) Salisb. (Large White Trillium, Showy Trillium, White Wake-robin). Hardy in all zones; perennial to 45 cm. tall.
DESCRIPTION: Perennial, native in moist woods and thickets from Minnesota to Quebec, south to Arkansas and Georgia; **leaves** broadly ovate to rhombic or subcircular, to 12 cm. long, acuminate, cuneate at base, usually sessile; **flowers** white, changing to rosy-pink, to 7.5 cm. across, in May and June; petals spreading, wavy-margined; filaments as long as the anthers; **berries** 6-angled, greenish-white.
USE AND CULTURE: The same as for **Trillium cernuum**. This is the showiest of our native trilliums.

Trillium nivale Ridd. (Dwarf White Trillium, Snow Trillium). Hardy in all zones; perennial to 15 cm. tall.

Trillium nivale (Dwarf White Trillium).

Photograph: Dr. Anne M. Hanchek.

DESCRIPTION: Perennial, native in rich woods from Minnesota to Pennsylvania, south to Missouri and Kentucky; **leaves** elliptic to ovate, to 5 cm. long, obtuse, petioled; **flowers** erect, white, marked with purple, to 4 cm. across on 2.5 cm. peduncles recurved in fruit, in April and May.

USE AND CULTURE: Plant in rock gardens or wild flower gardens. The culture is the same as for **Trillium cernuum**.

Trillium undulatum Willd. (Painted Trillium). Hardy in all zones; perennial to 30 cm. tall.

DESCRIPTION: Perennial, native in moist, acid woods and swamps from Manitoba to Quebec, south to Tennessee and Georgia; **leaves** ovate, to 18 cm. long, acuminate, petioled; **flowers** white, veined with purple blotches at base, to 4 cm. across, erect to somewhat nodding, on 6 cm. peduncles, in May and June; petals wavy; **berries** bright red.

USE AND CULTURE: The culture is the same as for **Trillium cernuum** except it requires an acid soil.

Triodanis Raf. (Venus's-looking-glass)
CAMPANULACEAE (Bellflower Family)

DESCRIPTION: Eight species of annual herbs, native mostly in North America; **stems** unbranched; **leaves** simple, sessile, clasping at base, alternate, dentate; **flowers** also sessile, formed in leaf axils; some flowers open with 5 petals joined only at the base; other flowers do not open (cleistogamous), being self-pollinating; stamens separate with ciliate filaments; **fruit** a linear to obovate capsule opening by pores.

Triodanis perfoliata (L.) Nieuwl. (Venus's-looking-glass). Annual to 1 m. tall.

DESCRIPTION: Annual with unbranched stems, native from British Columbia to New England, south to tropical America; **leaves** and bracts sessile, clasping, rounded-cordate, to 3 cm. long; **flowers** deep purple to lavender, about 1.25 cm. long, in June and July; **capsules** oblong to obovate, to 1.25 cm. long with a pore opening from the middle.

USE AND CULTURE: Plant in flower borders. Plants are easy to grow in any good garden soil. Propagation is by seeds started indoors or by direct seeding in early May.

Triosteum L. (Feverwort, Horse Gentian, Tinker's Weed)
CAPRIFOLIACEAE (Honeysuckle Family)

DESCRIPTION: Six species of perennial herbs, native in eastern Asia and eastern North America; **leaves** opposite, simple, entire, sessile, fiddle-shaped or obovate; **flowers** yellow or purple, axillary, solitary or clustered; calyx lobes leafy; corolla tubular, 5-lobed; ovary 3-celled, inferior; **fruit** a leathery drupe with 3 nutlets.

Triosteum perfoliatum L. (Feverroot, Tinker's Weed, Wild Coffee). Hardy in zone 4; perennial to 1.2 m. tall.

DESCRIPTION: Coarse perennial, native in rocky, open woods from Minnesota to Massachusetts, south to Kansas and South Carolina; **leaves** ovate or elliptic, to 20 cm. long, often united at base; **flowers** purple, to 2 cm. long, from May to July; **fruits** orange-yellow.

USE AND CULTURE: Plant in wild flower gardens in open shade. Plants require a moist, slightly acid soil high in organic matter. Plants are usually started from seeds sown in the fall. Due to the hard seed coats, filing through the seed coat will improve germination. Divisions are difficult to establish.

Uvularia L. (Bellwort, Merrybells)
LILIACEAE (Lily Family)

DESCRIPTION: Five species of rhizomatous perennial herbs, native in eastern North America; **stems** simple or branched, leafy; **leaves** alternate, sessile or perfoliate; **flowers** yellow, campanulate, pendulous, usually solitary; perianth segments 6, separate; stamens 6; style 3-parted; **fruit** a 3-lobed or 3-winged capsule.

Uvularia grandiflora Sm. (Bellwort, Merrybells). Hardy in all zones; perennial to 40 cm. tall.

DESCRIPTION: Rhizomatous perennial, native in rich woods, often in limestone regions from Minnesota to Quebec, south to Oklahoma and Tennessee; **stems** forked; **leaves** perfoliate, oblong to lanceolate-ovate, to 12 cm. long, pubescent beneath; **flowers** lemon yellow, to 5 cm. long, from April to June; **capsules** green, 3-cornered.
USE AND CULTURE: Plant in wild flower gardens. Plants are easy to grow in a humus-rich soil in shade. Propagation is by seeds or division. Plants can be divided either in the fall or spring. Seeds should be sown as soon as ripe. Space plants 30 cm. apart. Plants often self sow.

Uvularia perfoliata L. (Strawbell, Wood Merrybells). Hardy in all zones; perennial to 40 cm. tall.
DESCRIPTION: Rhizomatous perennial, native in open, often acid woods from Ontario to Quebec, south to Louisiana and Florida; **leaves** perfoliate, oblong to lanceolate-ovate, to 8 cm. long, glabrous; **flowers** pale yellow, drooping, bell-shaped, to 3 cm. long; perianth segments glandular-papillose on inside; **capsules** green, 3-cornered.
USE AND CULTURE: The same as for **Uvularia grandiflora**. Plants prefer an acid soil.

Uvularia sessilifolia L. (Little Merrybells, Wild Oats). Hardy in all zones; perennial to 30 cm. tall.
DESCRIPTION: Perennial with creeping rhizomes, native in woods and thickets from North Dakota to New Brunswick, south to Oklahoma and Alabama; **leaves** sessile, oblong-lanceolate, to 7.5 cm. long; **flowers** greenish-yellow, to 3 cm. long; styles parted only for one third its length; **capsules** stalked, 3-cornered.
USE AND CULTURE: The same as for **Uvularia grandiflora**.

Vernonia Schreb. (Ironweed)
COMPOSITAE (Sunflower Family)
Vernonia Tribe

DESCRIPTION: About 1000 species of perennial herbs, subshrubs, shrubs, or rarely trees or woody climbers, native in moist, rich soils in warmer parts of North and South America, Asia, Africa, and Australia; **leaves** alternate, rarely opposite; **flower** heads solitary or in corymbs or panicled cymes; involucre cylindrical, globose, urceolate, campanulate, or turbinate; receptacle flat or convex, naked, pitted; flowers all tubular, perfect; **fruit** a columnar or turbinate, ribbed achene; pappus consisting of 2 rows of bristles.

Vernonia altissima Nutt. (Tall Ironweed). Hardy in all zones; perennial to 2 m. tall.
DESCRIPTION: Perennial, native in lowlands and banks of lakes and streams from Nebraska to New York, south to Louisiana and Georgia; **stems** glabrous, leafy; **leaves** lanceolate to lanceolate-oblong or lanceolate-ovate, to 25 cm. long, long acuminate, glabrous above, thinly hairy below, entire to irregularly serrate; **flower** heads to 1 cm. across in loose cymes; flowers, purple from August to October.

Uvularia grandiflora (Merrybells). In bloom on April 28, 1981 at the Arboretum.

Uvularia grandiflora (Merrybells).

Photograph: Mr. Arvid Lund.

USE AND CULTURE: Plant toward the back of flower borders or plant in prairie gardens. Plants can be grown in most garden soils if kept moist. Propagation is mainly by division in fall or spring. Seedlings take 4 years to bloom.

Vernonia fasciculata Michx. (Western Ironweed). Hardy in all zones; perennial to 2 m. tall.
DESCRIPTION: Perennial, native in low, wet places and in prairies from North Dakota to Ohio, south to Texas and Missouri; **leaves** linear to oblong-lanceolate, acuminate, spinulose-dentate; **flower** heads campanulate in dense cymes; flowers purple, from July to September; **achenes** glabrous, to 3 mm. long.
USE AND CULTURE: The same as for **Vernonia altissima**.

Veronica L. (Brooklime, Speedwell)
SCROPHULARIACEAE (Figwort Family)
DESCRIPTION: About 250 species of annual or perennial herbs, native in the north temperate regions of the world, but mostly in Europe; **stems** erect or prostrate; **leaves** mostly opposite, rarely alternate or whorled near the top of the stem, simple, entire or dentate; **flowers** small, white, rose, purple, or blue, in axillary or terminal spikes, racemes, or corymbs; calyx 4- to 5-parted; corolla rotate; stamens 2; **fruit** a flattened, notched capsule.

Veronica americana (Raf.) Schweinitz ex Benth. (American Brooklime). Hardy in all zones; perennial to 1 m. tall.
DESCRIPTION: Creeping perennial, native in swamps and marshes, often in shallow water, from Alaska to Newfoundland, south to California and North Carolina, also in Asia; **stems** fleshy, prostrate or ascending; **leaves** elliptic, oblong to suborbicular, serrate to crenate, glabrous; **flowers** violet to blue in loose racemes, from May to August.
USE AND CULTURE: Plant in moist soil near water. Plants must have a continuously moist soil. Propagation is by division or by seeds sown as soon as ripe. Space plants 30 cm. apart.

Veronica virginica - see **Veronicastrum virginicum**.

Veronicastrum Fabr. (Culver's-physic, Culver's-root)
SCROPHULARIACEAE (Figwort Family)
DESCRIPTION: Two species of tall, perennial herbs, native in eastern North America and eastern Asia; **leaves** whorled, simple; **flowers** tubular, nearly regular, in spikes; calyx deeply 4- to 5-parted, the 2 lobes of the lower lip longer than the 2 or 3 lobes of the upper lip; corolla tubular with the lobes shorter than the tube; stamens 2, inserted below the middle of the corolla tube; anther sacs parallel, exserted beyond the corolla tube; **fruit** a capsule opening by 4 short terminal slits.

Veronicastrum virginicum (L.) Farw. (Blackroot, Bowman's-root, Culver's-physic, Culver's-root). Hardy in all zones; perennial to 2 m. tall.
DESCRIPTION: Tall perennial, native in open woods and in prairies from Manitoba to Massachusetts, south to Texas and Florida; **leaves** in whorls of 5, lanceolate to oblong-lanceolate, to 15 cm. long, dentate; **flowers** small, pale blue or white, in tapering terminal racemes to 20 cm. long, from June to September.
USE AND CULTURE: Plant towards the back of flower borders, in prairie gardens, or at the edges of woods. Plants thrive in any good garden soil either in full sun or in partial shade. Propagation is by division or by seeds. Plants can be divided either in the fall or early in the spring. Seeds should be sown as soon as ripe. Space plants 45 cm. apart.

Vicia L. (Tare, Vetch)
LEGUMINOSAE (Pea Family)
DESCRIPTION: About 150 species of mostly trailing or climbing perennial herbs, native in temperate regions; **leaves** alternate, even-pinnate, terminating in tendrils except in erect species; **flowers** pealike; stamens 10, 9 united, 1 separate; style with tuft of hairs toward the tip; **fruit** a flat, dehiscent legume.

Viola canadensis (Canada Violet).

Photograph: Dr. Anne M. Hanchek.

Vicia americana Muhl. (American Vetch). Hardy in all zones; perennial to 1 m. tall.
DESCRIPTION: Trailing or climbing perennial, native in moist woods from Ontario to New York, south to Missouri and Virginia; **leaflets** 8 to 14, each 3 cm. long; **flowers** blue-purple, to 2.5 cm. long, in loose racemes, from April to July.
USE AND CULTURE: Plant as a bank cover. Also planted as a forage plant. Plants grow well in moist soil either in full sun or in partial shade. Propagation is by seeds planted in the spring directly where the plants are to grow.

Viola L. (Violet)
VIOLACEAE (Violet Family)

DESCRIPTION: About 500 species of mostly perennial herbs, rarely subshrubs, native mostly in rich, moist soil in temperate regions; **stems** leafy or lacking; **leaves** usually heart-shaped, petioled; stipules present and often leaflike; **flowers** often of two types, those in early spring showy and sterile, those in summer cleistogamous, fertile, and without petals; showy spring flowers nodding, the lower petal spurred, the other 4 in 2 unequal pairs; **fruit** a capsule dehiscing by 3 boat-shaped keeled valves.

Viola blanda Willd. (Sweet White Violet). Hardy in all zones; perennial to 10 cm. tall.

DESCRIPTION: Stemless, stoloniferous perennial, native in cool, damp swamps, moist meadows, and open woods from Minnesota to Quebec, south to Louisiana and Georgia; **leaves** ovate, acute, somewhat hairy on upper surface; spring **flowers** fragrant, white with purple veins, with narrow, reflexed petals, in May and June.
USE AND CULTURE: Plant in wild flower gardens or use as a ground cover under shrubs. Plants prefer a moist, humus-rich soil in partial shade. Propagation is by spring division or by seeds sown as soon as ripe. Plants often self sow.

Viola canadensis L. (Canada Violet, Tall White Violet). Hardy in all zones; perennial to 25 cm. tall.
DESCRIPTION: Perennial, native in cool, moist woods, often in rocky soils, from Canada south to Arizona and Alabama; **stems** leafy growing from thick rhizomes; **leaves** broad-ovate, cordate, acute, dentate, nearly glabrous; **flowers** fragrant, white with a yellow spot at base, often tinged violet outside, with a short spur, in May and June.
USE AND CULTURE: The same as for **Viola blanda**.

Viola papilionacea - see **Viola sororia**

Viola pedata L. (Bird-foot Violet, Crowfoot Violet, Pansy Violet). Hardy in all zones; perennial to 12 cm. tall.
DESCRIPTION: Stemless, glabrous perennial with short, thick, vertical rhizomes, native in acid, sandy soils in full sun from Minnesota to Maine, south to Texas and Florida; **leaves** 3- to 5-divided with segments 2- to 4-cleft or toothed near apex; **flowers** flattened, pansylike, to 2.5 cm. across, in May and June; 2 upper petals dark violet, 3 lower petals light violet.

Viola pedata (Bird-foot Violet). Blooming at

McKnight Prairie, Carleton College, Northfield, Minnesota.

Photograph: Bonnie E. Harper Lore.

USE AND CULTURE: Plant in rock gardens or in prairie gardens. Plants require an acid, sandy soil in full sun. Propagation is by fall division in late August or by seeds sown as soon as ripe. Space plants 30 cm. apart with rhizomes 2 cm. deep.

Viola pubescens Ait. (Downy Yellow Violet). Hardy in all zones; perennial to 30 cm. tall.
DESCRIPTION: Rhizomatous perennial, native in rich, deciduous woods from North Dakota to Nova Scotia, south to Oklahoma and Georgia; **stems** leafy, pubescent; **leaves** ovate-cordate, usually wider than long, crenate-dentate, white-downy underneath; stipules broadly ovate; **flowers** yellow with purple-brown markings near base, in May and June.
USE AND CULTURE: The same as for **Viola blanda**.

Viola sororia Willd. (Woolly Blue Violet). Hardy in all zones; perennial to 15 cm. tall.
DESCRIPTION: Stemless, rhizomatous perennial, native in open meadows and along roadsides from Minnesota to Quebec, south to Oklahoma and North Carolina; **leaves** ovate-cordate, wider than long, usually pubescent on both surfaces; **flowers** blue or purple, rarely red or white, in May and June.
USE AND CULTURE: The same as for **Viola blanda**.

Waldsteinia Willd. (Barren Strawberry)
ROSACEAE (Rose Family)
DESCRIPTION: A few species of strawberrylike, perennial herbs with shallow, creeping rhizomes, native in north temperate regions; **leaves** mostly basal, 3- to 5-lobed or divided; **flowers** small, yellow, on bracted scapes; sepals 5, alternating with 5 bracteoles; petals 5; stamens many; **fruit** a cluster of 2 to 6 achenes with slender, deciduous styles.

Viola pubescens (Downy Yellow Violet).

Blooming in Michigan in June 1983.

Waldsteinia fragarioides (Barren Strawberry).

Blooming at Grandview Lodge (Minnesota) in May 1986.

Waldsteinia fragarioides (Michx.) Tratt. (Barren Strawberry). Hardy in all zones; perennial to 15 cm. tall.

DESCRIPTION: Stoloniferous perennial, native in dry or moist woods and in cut- over lands, especially under oaks and aspens from Minnesota to New Brunswick, south to Missouri and Georgia; **leaflets** 3, to 5 cm. long, broadly cuneate, dentate at apex; **flowers** yellow, to 2 cm. across, on several-flowered scapes to 15 cm. tall, in May and June.

USE AND CULTURE: Plant in rock or wall gardens or use as a ground cover in sun or shade. Plants are easy to grow. The soil should be slightly acid and rich in humus. Propagation is by division in early spring or by seeds sown as soon as ripe. Plant with the crown even with soil surface much as you would plant strawberries. Space plants 30 cm. apart.

Yucca L. (Yucca)
AGAVACEAE (Agave Family)

DESCRIPTION: About 40 species of stemless or erect, woody plants, native in well-drained soils in full sun mostly in warmer parts of North America; **leaves** stiff, sword-shaped or rarely stilettolike; **flowers** white or violet, in racemes or panicles; perianth cup- or saucer-shaped with 6 segments that are separate or partly united; stamens 6; ovary superior, 3-celled; **fruit** a fleshy, indehiscent capsule or sometimes a dry, dehiscent capsule.

Yucca glauca Nutt. ex J. Fraser. (Soapweed, Soapwell). Hardy in all zones; shrub to 1 m. tall.

DESCRIPTION: Shrubs with short, prostrate stems, native in sandy, prairie soils from Montana to South Dakota, south to Arizona and Missouri; **leaves** linear, to 70 cm. long, pale green with white or greenish-white, thread-bearing margins; **flowers** greenish-cream, fragrant, in racemes to 1 m. long, from May to July; perianth segments 6, separate or briefly united at base, to 6 cm. long; style dark green, swollen; **capsules** dry and dehiscent, to 5 cm. long.

USE AND CULTURE: Plant in rock gardens or in prairie gardens. Plants grow best in a well-drained, sandy soil in full sun. Propagation is by seeds or root cuttings. It takes many years for seedlings to bloom.

PRAIRIE PLANTS

Heliopsis helianthoides and other prairie plants.

Allium L. (Onion)
AMARYLLIDACEAE (Amaryllis Family)
DESCRIPTION: About 400 species of strongly odorous, rhizomatous or bulbous, perennial herbs, native in the northern hemisphere; **leaves** narrow, sheathing, solid or hollow, flat to cylindrical; **flowers** small, borne in few- to many-flowered umbels terminal on a scape and subtended by a spathe; perianth segments 6; stamens 6; ovary superior; **fruit** a capsule.

Allium cernuum Roth. (Wild Onion, Nodding Onion, Lady's Leek). Hardy in all zones; perennial to 50 cm. tall.
DESCRIPTION: Bulbous perennial, native in sandy or gravelly soil in open woods and prairies from British Columbia to New York, south to California and Georgia; **bulb** coat membranous; **leaves** linear, flat; **flowers** white or rose lavender with a pinkish cast in many-flowered, nodding umbels, in July and August; stamens and styles exserted; ovary 6-crested.
USE AND CULTURE: Used in rock gardens and prairies. Grows best on a well-drained soil that is neutral or slightly acid. Plant in colonies in full sun for best landscape effect. Propagation is by seeds or by division of the bulbs in fall.

Allium stellatum Ker. (Prairie Onion). Hardy in all zones; perennial to 45 cm. tall.
DESCRIPTION: A bulbous perennial, native in prairies and on open, rocky slopes; **bulbs** elongated with membranous coats; **leaves** linear and flat; **flowers** lavender-pink, in many-flowered umbels that face upward, from July to September; stamens and styles exserted.
USE AND CULTURE: Same as for **Allium cernuum**.

Amorpha L. (Lead Plant, False Indigo)
LEGUMINOSAE (Pea Family)
DESCRIPTION: About 20 species of shrubs, native in North America; **leaves** alternate, odd-pinnate, deciduous, with many leaflets; **flowers** small, blue or white, in dense terminal, often panicled spikes; sepals 5; petals 1, the standard enclosing 10 exserted stamens; **fruit** a short, mostly glabrous, indehiscent legume.

Amorpha canescens Pursh. (Lead Plant). Hardy in all zones; shrub to 1 m. tall.
DESCRIPTION: Small, densely white-hairy shrub native in prairies and dry woodlands from Manitoba south to New Mexico and Louisiana; **leaves** spreading, to 12 cm. long, with up to 45 leaflets; leaflets elliptic to oblong-lanceolate, to 2 cm. long, acute or obtuse, rounded at base, hairy and gray on both surfaces; **flowers** blue, in dense, clustered spikelike racemes to 15 cm. long, from May to August; **fruits** densely villous-gray-pubescent.
USE AND CULTURE: Is often used for prairie plantings. It is of easy culture in any well-drained soil in full sun. Propagation is by cuttings, division, or by seeds planted as soon as they are ripe or in the spring following stratification.

Amorpha nana Nutt. (Fragrant False Indigo). Hardy in all zones; shrub to 50 cm. tall.
DESCRIPTION: Small shrubs, native in dry prairies from Saskatchewan south to Colorado and Iowa; **leaves** green with up to 41 leaflets; leaflets small, to 1.25 cm. long; **flowers** purple, in usually solitary racemes to 5 cm. long; **fruits** short, smooth, and glandular.
USE AND CULTURE: Same as for **Amorpha canescens**.

Andropogon L. (Beard Grass, Bluestem)
GRAMINEAE (Grass Family)
DESCRIPTION: About 20 species of perennial grasses, native in prairies in warm, temperate and tropical regions; **stems** solid, often coarse; **leaves** linear; **flowers** in racemes or spikelets on a common peduncle and usually enclosed by a spathelike sheath; spikelets in pairs at each node of a jointed rachis, one sessile and perfect, the other pedicelled and either staminate or reduced to a pedicel; **fruit** a caryopsis.

Allium stellatum (Prairie Onion).

Amorpha canescens (Lead Plant).

Andropogon gerardii (Big Bluestem). Flowering in

McKnight Prairie, Carleton College, Northfield, Minnesota.

Photograph: Bonnie E. Harper Lore.

Andropogon gerardii Vitm. (Big Bluestem, Turkeyfoot). Hardy in all zones; perennial to 3 m. tall.
DESCRIPTION: A glaucous, branched, perennial grass, native in prairies from Saskatchewan to Quebec, south to Arizona and Florida; **leaves** elongate, flat, villous, to 1 cm. wide; **flowers** inflorescences of 3 to 6, usually purplish racemes to 10 cm. long on a long, exserted terminal peduncle; **awns** geniculate and tightly twisted below, usually scabrous.
USE AND CULTURE: Grown for forage and planted in prairie plantings. It is easy to grow in fertile, well-drained soil in full sun. Propagation is by seeds planted as soon as mature or in the spring.

Andropogon scoparius - see **Schizachyrium scoparium**

Anemone L. (Anemone, Lily-of-the-field, Windflower)
RANUNCULACEAE (Buttercup Family).
DESCRIPTION: About 120 species of perennial herbs, native in the North Temperate Zone, often in high mountains; **leaves** more or less divided or dissected, or even compound; stem leaves forming an involucre below the flowers; **flowers** mostly showy, solitary; sepals yellow, white, rose, red, purple, or violet; petals 0; stamens many; pistils many; **fruit** an achene with a long plumose style.

Anemone canadensis L. (Canada Anemone, Meadow Anemone). Hardy in all zones; perennial to 60 cm. tall.
DESCRIPTION: Perennial with slender rhizomes, forming large patches in moist meadows, along stream banks, and in roadside ditches from British Columbia to Quebec, south to New Mexico and Maryland; **stems** branched; basal **leaves** long-petioled, deeply 3-parted, sharply dentate; involucral leaves similar but sessile; **flowers** 1 to 3 on long peduncles; white, to 5 cm. across, from May to July; stamens golden yellow.
USE AND CULTURE: Used in prairie plantings although it can be weedy. It thrives in any moist soil in full sun. Propagation is by seeds sown as soon as ripe or by division in spring or fall. Seedlings bloom the second year from seed.

Anemone caroliniana Walt. (Carolina Anemone). Hardy in zone 4; perennial to 30 cm. tall.
DESCRIPTION: Perennial with tuberous rhizomes, native in dry prairies and barrens from South Dakota to Indiana, south to Texas and Georgia; **leaves** ternate or 3-parted, with lobed segments, petioled; involucral leaves sessile; **flowers** solitary, erect, purple, red, or white, to 4 cm. across, in April and May; sepals 10 to 20, hairy underneath.
USE AND CULTURE: Used in rock gardens or prairie plantings. Requires full sun and a well-drained soil. Propagation is by seeds sown as soon as ripe and by fall division of rhizomes.

Anemone canadensis (Canada Anemone). In flower at

Superior, Wisconsin in June 1984.

Anemone cylindrica A. Gray. (Long-headed Anemone, Sheep's Wool, Thimbleweed). Hardy in all zones; perennial to 90 cm. tall.
DESCRIPTION: Erect perennial, native in sandy soil in open woods and thickets from British Columbia to Maine, south to Arizona and New Jersey; basal **leaves** few, long-petioled, deeply 5-parted with rhombic segments; involucral leaves similar; **flowers** 2 to 6 on erect peduncles to 25 cm. long, greenish-white, to 2 cm. across, from May to July; **fruit** achenes woolly, in cylindrical, thimblelike heads.
USE AND CULTURE: Used in prairie plantings or wild flower gardens. It is of easy culture in any well-drained soil in full sun or partial shade. Propagation is by seed sown as soon as ripe or by division in spring.

Artemisia L. (Wormwood, Mugwort, Sagebrush)
COMPOSITAE (Sunflower Family)
Anthemis Tribe
DESCRIPTION: About 200 species of aromatic herbs and shrubs, native in dry soils mostly in the northern hemisphere; **leaves** alternate, entire to lobed and dissected; **flower** heads small, in spikes, racemes, or panicles, radiate or discoid; involucre cylindrical to globose; involucral bracts imbricate in several rows, dry, at least the inner ones with scarious margins; receptacle flat or hemispherical, naked or with long hairs; disc **flowers** white, yellow, brown, or purple; ray flowers pistillate when present; **fruit** an achene that is ellipsoid, ovoid, or prismatic, 2- to 5-angled or ribbed; pappus absent or a short crown.

Artemisia ludoviciana Nutt. (Western Mugwort, White Sage, Cudweed). Hardy in all zones; perennial to 1 m. tall.
DESCRIPTION: Rhizomatous, aromatic perennial herb, native in dry soils from Washington to Michigan, south to Texas and Arkansas; **leaves** lanceolate to elliptic-lanceolate, to 10 cm. long, entire or lobed, white-tomentose beneath, becoming glabrous above; **flower** heads small, to 3 mm. across, in dense panicles, in August and September.
USE AND CULTURE: Used in flower borders for the silvery foliage and also planted in prairie plantings. 'Silver King' and 'Silver Queen' are cultivars that have been selected for their silvery foliage. They are easy to grow in any well-drained soil. Propagation is by division or seeds planted as soon as ripe. A winter mulch will improve seed germination.

Asclepias L. (Butterfly Flower, Milkweed, Silkweed)
ASCLEPIADACEAE (Milkweed Family)
DESCRIPTION: About 200 species of perennial herbs with milky sap, native mostly in North America and Africa; **leaves** opposite or whorled, rarely alternate; **flowers** white, yellow, red, or purple, in terminal or axillary umbellate cymes; corolla rotate, with 5 reflexed lobes; corona present with 5 hoodlike lobes, each with or without a horn; **fruit** a pair of erect follicles; **seed** with a tuft of silky hairs.

Anemone cylindrica (Thimbleweed).

Photograph: Bonnie E. Harper Lore.

Asclepias tuberosa (Butterfly Flower). In flower

at Wassau Lakes, Wisconsin in July 1984.

Asclepias tuberosa L. (Butterfly Flower, Butterfly Weed, Chigger Flower, Indian Paintbrush, Pleurisy Root, Tuberroot). Hardy in all zones; perennial to 60 cm. tall.

DESCRIPTION: Bushy perennial, native in sandy, well-drained soils in full sun from North Dakota to New England, south to Arizona and Florida; **roots** woody and tuberous; **leaves** spiral and crowded, narrowly lanceolate to oblanceolate, to 12 cm. long; **flowers** orange, red, or yellow, in axillary cymes, in July and August; corolla lobes to 8 mm. long; hoods cucullate, stalked; **follicles** narrowly fusiform, to 15 cm. long.

USE AND CULTURE: Plant in flower borders or in prairie plantings. The flowers attract butterflies. The dried roots also have medicinal value. They require a sandy, well-drained soil that is neutral to slightly acid, and consequently they are short-lived on heavy or poorly-drained soils. Propagation is by root cuttings taken in May and planted vertically in sand. Old plants can be divided in the fall with the roots planted so the buds are 5 cm. deep. Seeds can be planted in May. Mulch the seedlings the first winter.

Aster L. (Aster, Frost Flower, Michaelmas Daisy, Starwort).
COMPOSITAE (Sunflower Family)
Aster Tribe
DESCRIPTION: A large genus of mostly perennial herbs, native in North and South America, Europe, Asia, and Africa; plants rhizomatous or fibrous-rooted; **leaves** alternate, simple, entire, or dentate; **flower** heads radiate, usually in racemes, corymbs, or panicles; involucres campanulate, hemispherical, or turbinate; involucral bracts in many rows, herbaceous or scarious; receptacles flat, pitted, naked; ray flowers in 1 row, purple, blue, violet, pink, or white; disc flowers, perfect, yellow; **fruit** a compressed, non-ribbed achene; pappus of persistent capillary bristles.

Aster novae-angliae L. (New England Aster). Hardy in all zones; perennial to 1.2 m. tall.

DESCRIPTION: Perennials with a woody root crown or thick rhizomes, native in open meadows and along roadsides from Wyoming to Vermont, south to New Mexico and Alabama; **stems** clustered, much branched glandular and hairy; **leaves** lanceolate, auricled or clasping at base, to 12 cm. long, entire, scabrous; **flower** heads to 5 cm. across, in corymbose clusters, from August to October; ray flowers usually a deep violet-purple to rosy-lilac.

USE AND CULTURE: Plant in flower borders or in prairie plantings. They grow best in full sun in moist, neutral to slightly acid soils. Propagation is mostly by division, either in the fall or early in the spring. Plant only those divisions that have fine, fibrous roots. Divide the plants every 3 years. Seeds are slow to germinate but the plants self sow under prairie conditions.

Aster novae-angliae (New England Aster)

In bloom at the Arboretum in October 1965.

Aster novi-belgii L. (New York Aster). Hardy in all zones; perennial to 1.3 m. tall.
DESCRIPTION: Rhizomatous perennial, native in rich, moist woods from Newfoundland south to Georgia; **stems** clustered, glabrous or with lines of hairs; **leaves** sessile or auriculate and clasping, linear-lanceolate to lanceolate or elliptic, entire to serrate, to 16 cm. long; **flower** heads to 2.5 cm. across, in paniculate clusters; ray flowers blue or violet.
USE AND CULTURE: Same as for **Aster novae-angliae**. This species is one of the parents of most of our garden hybrids.

Astragalus L. (Milk Vetch)
LEGUMINOSAE (Pea Family)
DESCRIPTION: About 1000 species of perennial herbs, native in temperate regions of the northern hemisphere; **leaves** alternate, odd-pinnate; leaflets entire; stipules prominent; **flowers** pealike, purple, white, or yellow, 5-merous; stamens 10, 9 united, 1 separate; **fruit** a 1- to 2-celled, leathery, fleshy, or papery legume.

Astragalus crassicarpus Nutt. (Ground Plum). Hardy in all zones; perennial to 30 cm. long.
DESCRIPTION: Decumbent perennial, native in open prairies from the Rocky Mountains east to Minnesota; **leaflets** to 1.25 cm.; **flowers** pealike, violet-purple, in short racemes, in April and May; **legumes**, globose inflated, to 2 cm. across.
USE AND CULTURE: Plant in rock gardens or in prairie plantings. Plant seeds where plants are to grow in early spring. Mature plants are difficult to transplant.

Baptisia Venten. (False Indigo, Wild Indigo)
LEGUMINOSAE (Pea Family)
DESCRIPTION: About 30 species of perennial herbs, native in dry soils in North America; **leaves** alternate, mostly with 3 leaflets; **flowers** pealike, in racemes; stamens 10, separate; **fruit** a short, inflated legume.

Baptisia australis (L.) R. Br. (Blue False Indigo, Plains False Indigo, Wild Blue Indigo). Hardy in all zones; perennial to 1 m. tall.
DESCRIPTION: Many-stemmed perennial, native in gravelly soils in open woods and in prairies from Pennsylvania south to Tennessee to South Carolina; **leaflets** oblanceolate to ovate, to 6 cm. long; **flowers** indigo blue to 2.5 cm. long, in terminal racemes, in May and June; **legumes** inflated, black.
USE AND CULTURE: Plant in flower borders, in open areas in the wild flower garden, or in prairie plantings. They do best in sandy loam soils or in heavier soils if well-drained. Propagation is by division of established clumps in early spring or by seeds sown as soon as ripe. It takes 3 years from seed to develop blooming-sized plants. Space plants 60 cm. apart.

Astragalus crassicarpus (Ground Plum).

Photograph: Mr. Arvid Lund.

Calochortus gunnisonii (Rocky Mountain Mariposa).

In bloom near Custer, South Dakota in August 1976.

Baptisia tinctoria (L.) V̇enten. (Horsefly Weed, Rattleweed, Wild Indigo). Hardy in all zones; perennial to 1.2 m. tall.
DESCRIPTION: Perennial, native in sterile, sandy soils from Minnesota to Massachusetts, south to Florida; **leaflets** to 2.5 cm. long; **flowers** bright yellow, on semi-drooping, branched spikes; **legumes** inflated, with loose seeds that rattle.
USE AND CULTURE: A dye plant used for prairie plantings. Culture is the same as for **Baptisia australis**. Because it was placed in the harnesses of horses to keep away flies, this plant was commonly called horsefly weed.

Calochortus Pursh. (Butterfly Tulip, Globe Tulip
Mariposa, Mariposa Lily, Sego Lily, Star Tulip)
LILIACEAE (Lily Family)
DESCRIPTION: About 60 species of bulbous, perennial herbs, native in well-drained soils in western North America from South Dakota westward; **bulbs** tunicate with membranous coat, sometimes fibrous-reticulate; **stems** leafy or scapose; **flowers** white, yellow, orange, red, lavender, or purple, erect or nodding, solitary or in clusters; sepals 3; petals 3, often bearded, with a basal, flattened gland; stamens 6 with basifixed anthers; **fruit** a 3-winged or a 3-angled capsule.

Calochortus gunnisonii S. Wats. (Rocky Mountain Mariposa). Hardy in all zones; perennial to 45 cm. tall.
DESCRIPTION: Perennial, native in prairies from Montana to South Dakota, south to Arizona and New Mexico; **stems** erect, unbranched; **leaves** linear; **flowers** campanulate, erect, to 4 cm. long, white to purple, bearded with glandular, branched hairs, often purple-banded, in June and July; **capsules** linear-oblong, 3-angled, erect.
USE AND CULTURE: Plant in rock gardens or prairie plantings. Plant bulbs 10 cm. deep on a bed of gravel 5 cm. deep in the fall. Good drainage is essential to longevity. Mulch over winter. Propagation is by seeds or by division of bulbs.

Calochortus nuttallii Torr. (Mariposa Tulip, Sego Lily). Hardy in all zones; perennial to 45 cm. tall.
DESCRIPTION: Erect perennials, native in prairies from Montana to North Dakota, south to Arizona and New Mexico; **stems** unbranched; **leaves** linear, reduced in size on the stems; **flowers** campanulate, erect; petals to 4 cm. long, white, tinged with lilac, yellow at base, marked with a reddish-brown or purple spot above the glands; **capsule** lanceolate-linear, 3-angled, to 5 cm. long.
USE AND CULTURE: Same as for **Calochortus gunnisonii**.

Cassia L. (Senna)
LEGUMINOSAE (Pea Family)
DESCRIPTION: Over 500 species of trees, shrubs, and annual and perennial herbs, native mostly in tropical and subtropical regions; **leaves** opposite, even-pinnate; **flowers** showy, mostly yellow, nearly regular, 5-merous, in racemes, corymbs, or panicles, rarely solitary; stamens mostly 10, with 7 fertile and 3 abortive anthers; **fruit** a cylindrical legume, sometimes winged.

Cassia fasciculata Michx. (Bee Flower, Golden Cassia, Partridge Pea, Prairie Senna). Hardy in all zones; annual to 60 cm. long.
DESCRIPTION: Annual, native in sandy, open areas from South Dakota to Maine, south to Mexico and Florida; **leaflets** in 12 to 44 pairs, sensitive to touch, linear-oblong, to 1.5 cm. long; **flowers** yellow, clustered in leaf axils, to 2 cm. long, from July to September; stamens with fertile anthers 10; **fruit** flat, linear, to 4 cm. long.
USE AND CULTURE: Plant in flower borders or in prairie plantings. Start seeds indoors in March. Transplant to the garden in late May. Plants must have a well-drained soil, preferably a sandy loam.

Cassia marilandica L. (Wild Senna). Hardy in all zones; perennial to 120 cm. tall.
DESCRIPTION: Coarse, glabrous perennial, native in low ground and in moist, open woods from Kansas to Pennsylvania, south to Texas and Florida; **leaflets** numerous,

oblong-lanceolate; **flowers** golden-yellow in loose racemes, in July and August; anthers dark brown; **legumes** flat, thick, to 8 cm. long.

USE AND CULTURE: A coarse perennial best used in a wild flower garden or at the edges of woods. The plants prefer a moist, sandy loam soil that is slightly acid. Propagation is by division in early spring or by seeds sown as soon as ripe. It takes 3 years for seedlings to reach blooming size.

Chrysopsis (Nutt.) Elliott. (Golden Aster)
COMPOSITAE (Sunflower Family)
Aster Tribe
DESCRIPTION: About 30 species of annual, biennial, or perennial herbs, native in North America; stems leafy, erect to decumbent; **leaves** alternate, simple, usually entire, reduced upward; **flower** heads yellow, radiate, in corymbs; involucre campanulate to hemispherical; involucral bracts imbricate in several rows; receptacle naked; disc and ray flowers yellow; **achenes** obovoid, compressed; pappus double.

Chrysopsis villosa (Pursh.) Nutt. (Golden Aster). Hardy in all zones; perennial to 85 cm. tall.
DESCRIPTION: A variable tap-rooted perennial, native in sandy soils from British Columbia to Wisconsin, south to California and Indiana; **stems** erect to decumbent, often woody at base; **leaves** oblong-elliptic to linear-oblanceolate, obtuse or acute at apex, seldom dentate; **flower** heads yellow, to 4 cm. across.
USE AND CULTURE: Plant in sunny flower borders or in a prairie planting. Plants will grow and bloom in soils of low fertility. Propagation is by division in early spring or by seeds planted in July.

Coreopsis L. (Coreopsis, Tickseed)
COMPOSITAE (Sunflower Family)
Helianthus Tribe
DESCRIPTION: Over 100 species of annual or perennial herbs, native in North and South America and Africa; **leaves** opposite or alternate, entire or variously lobed or cut; **flower** heads yellow, purple, rose, or often bicolored, mostly solitary, rarely in corymbose panicles; involucral bracts in 2 rows; **fruit** a compressed achene, usually winged; pappus of smooth or barbed awns, or short scales.

Coreopsis lanceolata L. (Lance-leaved Coreopsis). Hardy in all zones; perennial to 60 cm. tall.
DESCRIPTION: Erect perennial, native in dry, often sandy soils from Ontario south to New Mexico and Florida; **leaves** opposite, mostly simple, sometimes pinnately lobed with lobes linear to oblanceolate, petioled; **flower** heads with yellow ray flowers, to 6 cm. across, on long peduncles, from May to July.
USE AND CULTURE: Plant in sunny flower borders or naturalize in prairie plantings or along roadsides. Plants grow best in a well-drained sandy or gravelly soil. Propagation is by division or by seeds sown as soon as ripe.

Coreopsis palmata Nutt. (Tickseed). Hardy in all zones; perennial to 90 cm. tall.
DESCRIPTION: Rhizomatous perennial, native in prairies and open woods from Manitoba to Michigan, south to Texas and Arkansas; **leaves** narrow, nearly sessile, 3-lobed to near middle with linear-oblong lobes; **flower** heads in short peduncles with yellow ray flowers, to 3 cm. long; involucral bracts linear-clavate; **achenes** cuneate-oblong, black, narrowly winged.
USE AND CULTURE: Same as for **Coreopsis lanceolata**.

Coreopsis tinctoria Nutt. (Calliopsis). Annual to 120 cm. tall.
DESCRIPTION: A much-branched annual, rarely biennial, native in prairies from Saskatchewan to Minnesota, south to California and Louisiana; **leaves** opposite, 1- to 2-pinnate; leaflets linear or linear-lanceolate; **flowers** in radiate heads to 3 cm. across, arranged in corymbs, from June to September; involucral bracts of variable length with the outer bracts only one-fourth as long as the inner; disc flowers dark red or purple; ray flowers sterile, bicolored, yellow with a brown base; **achenes** slender, wingless, black, without a pappus.

Corydalis aurea (Golden Corydalis). In bloom July 1985.

USE AND CULTURE: Plant in sunny flower borders. Plants thrive in any well-drained soil in full sun. Plants are started from seed either indoors or seeded directly where plants are to bloom about May 1.

Corydalis Venten. (Corydalis)
FUMARIACEAE (Fumitory Family)
DESCRIPTION: About 300 species of annual and perennial herbs, native in the North Temperate Zone and in South Africa; perennial species with rhizomes or tubers; **leaves** pinnately decompound; **flowers** irregular, in racemes; sepals 2 or lacking; petals 4, one of the outer pair with a basal spur; stamens 6, in 2 bundles; **fruit** a slender, dehiscent capsule.

Corydalis aurea (Muhlenb. ex Willd.) Willd. (Golden Corydalis). Hardy in all zones; mostly annuals to 50 cm. tall.
DESCRIPTION: Annual or biennial, prostrate-ascending herbs, native in sandy or gravelly soil in prairies or in bottom lands, widely distributed in North America; plants many-stemmed, glaucous; **leaves** 3-pinnate; **flowers** yellow, to 2 cm. long, in terminal racemes, from April to September; spur of corolla one half as long as the rest of the petal; floral bracts toothed; **capsules** spreading or pendulous, to 2.5 cm. long.
USE AND CULTURE: Plant in rock gardens or prairie plantings. Plants are easy to grow in soils of low fertility. Propagation is by seeds sown as soon as ripe. Plants frequently self sow.

Corydalis glauca - see **Corydalis sempervirens**.

Corydalis sempervirens (L.) Pers. (Pale Corydalis). Hardy in all zones; annual to 60 cm. tall.
DESCRIPTION: A much-branched, very glaucous annual or biennial herb, native in rocky woods and clearings from Alaska to Newfoundland, south to Minnesota and Georgia; **leaves** typical of the genus; **flowers** pale pink to purple with yellow tips, to 2 cm. long, in loose panicles, from May to September; spur of corolla very short, blunt; **capsules** erect, narrowly linear, to 5 cm. long.
USE AND CULTURE: Same as for **Corydalis aurea**.

Crotalaria L. (Rattlebox)
LEGUMINOSAE (Pea Family)
DESCRIPTION: Over 500 species of herbs and shrubs, native mostly in warm climates; **leaves** alternate, simple or compound, with 3 to 7 leaflets; **flowers** pealike, in racemes, with an orbicular or 2-auricled standard and with keel petals curved and beaked; stamens 10, with long filaments and globose anthers alternating with short stamens with narrow anthers; **fruit** an elongated, inflated, dehiscent legume.

Crotalaria sagittalis L. (Arrow Rattlebox). Hardy in all zones; annual to 40 cm. tall.
DESCRIPTION: Annual with spreading hairs, native in dry open places from Minnesota to Vermont, south to Texas and Florida; **stems** simple or branched above, **leaves** simple, lanceolate to linear, sessile or nearly so, to 8 cm. long; stipules on upper leaves;

flowers yellow, to 8 mm. long, in 2- to 4-flowered racemes, from June to September; calyx villous; **legumes** to 3 cm. long, much inflated.

USE AND CULTURE: Plant in flower borders or in prairie plantings. Plants are easy to grow in any well-drained soil. Propagation is by seeds sown in early spring. Soak seeds in warm water before planting.

Dodecatheon L. (American Cowslip, Shooting-star)
PRIMULACEAE (Primrose Family)
DESCRIPTION: About 14 species of scapose perennial herbs, native in well-drained soils in partial shade in North America and Siberia; small ricelike **bulblets** often formed on roots; **leaves** simple, in a basal rosette; **flowers** white, magenta, lavender, or purple, nodding, in umbels; calyx and corolla 4- to 5-parted; corolla tube usually maroon with a yellow band at the throat, with reflexed lobes; stamens 4 or 5, free or united into a tube; **fruit** a capsule that opens by valves or a cap.

Dodecatheon meadia L. (American Cowslip, Common Shooting-star). Hardy in all zones; perennial to 40 cm. tall.
DESCRIPTION: Glabrous perennial, native in open woods, fertile prairies, and meadows from North Dakota to Pennsylvania, south to Texas and Alabama; **leaves** in a basal rosette, ovate to spatulate, to 30 cm. long; **flowers** magenta or lavender to white, 5-merous, in 4- to 125-flowered umbels on scapes to 40 cm. tall, in May and June; pollen sacs yellow.
USE AND CULTURE: Plant in rock gardens, prairie gardens, and wild flower gardens. The plants grow best in a neutral or slightly acid, well-drained soil that is high in organic matter. Moisture is needed during the blooming period. Plants die down in summer after the seeds ripen. Propagation is by fall division. Plant with the bud about 2 cm. deep. Seeds are slow to germinate and the seedlings are fragile.

Echinacea Moench. (Purple Coneflower)
COMPOSITAE (Sunflower Family)
Helianthus Tribe
DESCRIPTION: Five species of coarse perennial herbs, native in North America; **leaves** alternate, simple coarse; **flower** heads radiate, solitary or few, on long peduncles; receptacle conical with stiff spiny scales; ray flowers purple, rarely white; disc flowers purple-brown; **fruit** a 4-angled achene; pappus a short crown.

Echinacea angustifolia DC. (Pink Coneflower). Hardy in all zones; perennial to 60 cm. tall.
DESCRIPTION: Coarse perennial, native in open woods and open fields, usually in sandy or gravelly soil from Saskatchewan to Minnesota, south to Texas and Tennessee; **leaves** oblong-lanceolate to linear-lanceolate, entire, with 3 to 5 parallel veins; lower leaves long-petioled, upper sessile; ray **flowers** rose-purple, rarely white, to 4 cm. long, from May to August.

Dodecatheon meadia (Shooting-star).

Echinacea angustifolia (Pink Coneflower). In bloom at the Arboretum in September 1983.

Echinacea purpurea (Purple Coneflower).

Photograph: Dr. Anne M. Hanchek

USE AND CULTURE: Plant in sunny flower borders or in prairie gardens. It is easy to grow in any well-drained soil. Propagation is by spring division, or by seeds started indoors or in a cold frame. When seedlings are large enough, transplant to their permanent location.

Echinacea pallida (Nutt.) Nutt. (Pale Purple Coneflower). Hardy in all zones; perennial to 90 cm. tall.
DESCRIPTION: Coarse perennial, native in prairies and barrens from Montana to Illinois, south to Texas and Georgia; **leaves** linear-lanceolate to lanceolate-elliptic, gradually tapering at base; **flower** heads solitary, on long peduncles, in June and July; ray flowers purple, rarely paler, to 8 cm. long, reflexed.
USE AND CULTURE: Same as for **Echinacea angustifolia**.

Echinacea purpurea (L.) Moench. (Purple Coneflower). Hardy in all zones; perennial to 1 m. tall.
DESCRIPTION: Coarse perennial, native in dry, open woods or in prairies from Montana to Michigan, south to Colorado and Georgia; basal **leaves** ovate to broadly lanceolate, coarsely dentate, long-petioled; upper stem leaves narrower, nearly entire, sessile; **flower** heads to 15 cm. across, in July and August; ray flowers rose-purple.
USE AND CULTURE: Same as for **Echinacea angustifolia**.

Erigeron L. (Fleabane)
COMPOSITAE (Sunflower Family)
Aster Tribe
DESCRIPTION: About 200 species of annual, biennial, or perennial herbs, native worldwide but most abundant in North America; **leaves** alternate, rarely all basal, frequently sessile; **flower** heads mostly radiate, solitary or few, or sometimes numerous in corymbs or panicles; involucre campanulate to hemispherical; involucral bracts in 2 or 3 rows, narrow; receptacle flat, naked; ray flowers in usually 2 rows, narrow, white, pink, blue, or purple; disc flowers yellow; **fruit** a compressed achene; pappus of few to many soft capillary hairs.

Erigeron asper - see **Erigeron glabellus**.

Erigeron glabellus Nutt. (Daisy Fleabane). Hardy in all zones; biennial or perennial to 50 cm. tall.
DESCRIPTION: Hairy biennial or perennial, native in dry barrens, prairies, and rolling hills from Alaska to Ontario, south to Colorado and Wisconsin; **roots** fibrous; basal and lower stem **leaves** oblanceolate, persistent, to 15 cm. long; upper stem leaves linear to lanceolate, much reduced; **flower** heads in clusters of 1 to 15, to 5 cm. across, from late May to July; ray flowers blue, pink, or white.
USE AND CULTURE: Plant in rock gardens or in prairie plantings. They are of easy culture in any well-drained soil. Propagation is by division or by seeds.

Erigeron pulchellus Michx. (Poor Robin's Plantain, Robin's Plantain). Hardy in all zones; biennial or perennial to 60 cm. tall.

DESCRIPTION: Fibrous-rooted biennial or short-lived perennial with slender, stoloniferous rhizomes, native in meadows and open woodlands from Minnesota to Maine, south to Texas and Georgia; basal **leaves** lanceolate-oblong or ovate, to 7 cm. long; **flower** heads 1 to 6 in a corymb, to 4 cm. across, from April to July; ray flowers blue, pink, or white.
USE AND CULTURE: Same as for **Erigeron glabellus**.

Eryngium L. (Eryngo)
UMBELLIFERAE (Carrot Family)
DESCRIPTION: About 200 species of perennial herbs, native in sunny places in rich soil, worldwide; **leaves** simple, spiny-toothed, variously lobed or divided; **flowers** small, white or blue, sessile, in dense, bracted heads; calyx prominent, persistent; **fruits** ovoid.

Eryngium yuccifolium Michx. (Button Snake-root, Rattlesnake-master). Hardy in all zones; perennial to 90 cm. tall.
DESCRIPTION: Spiny-leaved perennial, native in moist or dry sandy soil in open woods and prairies from Minnesota to Connecticut, south to Texas and Florida; **leaves** rigid, broadly linear, bristle-tipped, parallel-veined; **flowers** small, white, in heads to 2.5 cm. long.
USE AND CULTURE: Plant in flower borders and prairie gardens. Plants are easy to grow in any well-drained soil. Propagation is by division in early spring or by seeds sown as soon as ripe.

Eupatorium L. (Boneset, Joe-pye Weed, Thoroughwort)
COMPOSITAE (Sunflower Family)
Eupatorium Tribe
DESCRIPTION: Nearly 500 species of mostly perennial herbs, native worldwide but mainly in tropical America; **leaves** simple, mostly opposite, sometimes alternate or whorled, usually petioled, entire to dissected; **flower** heads discoid, usually in corymbs, rarely solitary or in panicles; involucral bracts in 2 to 3 rows; receptacle flat to convex, naked; disc flowers all tubular, purple, rose, or white; **fruit** a 5-angled achene; pappus of capillary bristles in a single row.

Eupatorium maculatum L. (Joe-pye Weed, Smokeweed). Hardy in all zones; perennial to 2 m. tall.
DESCRIPTION: Coarse perennial, native in wet, calcareous soils and roadside ditches from British Columbia to Newfoundland, south to New Mexico and Maryland; **stems** speckled or blotched with purple; **leaves** in whorls of 3 to 6, lanceolate, elliptic-lanceolate, or ovate-lanceolate, to 20 cm. long, sharply serrate; **flower** heads to 6 mm. across with 8 to 10 flowers, in flat-topped corymbs, from July to September; involucral bracts often purple; disc flowers purple.
USE AND CULTURE: Plant toward the back of the flower border or in prairie plantings. Plants require a moist soil. Propagation is by spring division or by seeds. Seeds should be sown in the fall as soon as ripe. Mulching with evergreen boughs will assure winter survival.

Eryngium yuccifolium. In bloom at the Arboretum.

Eupatorium maculatum (Joe-pye Weed).

Photograph: Mr. Arvid Lund.

Eupatorium purpureum L. (Green-stemmed Joe-pye Weed, Sweet Joe-pye Weed). Hardy in all zones; perennial to 3 m. tall.
DESCRIPTION: Coarse perennial, native in moist thickets and open woods from Wisconsin to New Hampshire, south to Oklahoma and Georgia; **stems** green or green with purple nodes; **leaves** usually in whorls of 3 to 5, elliptic or lanceolate to ovate, to 30 cm. long, sharply serrate, vanilla-scented; **flower** heads to 9 mm. across, with 5 to 7 flowers, in rounded corymbose panicles, from July to September; disc flowers pink to purple, rarely white.
USE AND CULTURE: Same as for **Eupatorium maculatum**. According to legend, Joe Pye was a Native American who used this plant to cure typhus fever.

Eupatorium rugosum Houtt. (White Snakeroot, Snow Thoroughwort, White Sanicle). Hardy in all zones; perennial to 1 m. tall.
DESCRIPTION: Perennial, native in moist open woods, along streams, and in moist meadows from Saskatchewan to Nova Scotia, south to Texas and Georgia; **leaves** opposite, thin, ovate, to 18 cm. long, acuminate, sharply and coarsely serrate, glabrous or hairy; **flower** heads about 6 mm. across, with 12 to 24 flowers, in corymbs, in August and September; disc flowers white.
USE AND CULTURE: Plant in flower borders, wild flower gardens, or in prairie plantings. Plants thrive in moist soil either in full sun or partial shade. Propagation is by spring division or by seeds sown as soon as ripe. Plants often self sow. This species is poisonous to livestock if eaten.

Euphorbia L. (Spurge)
EUPHORBIACEAE (Spurge Family)
DESCRIPTION: Over 1600 species of monoecious or dioecious herbs, shrubs, or trees with milky juice, native worldwide; **stems** often spiny and cactuslike; **leaves** alternate, opposite, or whorled, simple, entire, or dentate, sometimes rudimentary or lacking; **flowers** in cyathia; cyathia solitary and terminal, clustered in leaf axils, or arranged in a simple umbel, panicle, or cyme; involucre of cyathium cup-shaped, with 5 inner lobes alternating with glands; ovary 3-celled; **fruit** a 3-valved capsule.

Euphorbia marginata Pursh. (Ghostweed, Snow-on-the-mountain). Hardy in all zones; annual to 60 cm. tall.
DESCRIPTION: Erect annual, native in fields and prairies from Montana to Minnesota, south to New Mexico and Missouri; **leaves** ovate to oblong, to 7.5 cm. long, alternate on stems, whorled below inflorescences; upper leaves with white margins; **cyathia** in 3-rayed umbels; glands 4, with broad, white, petallike appendages, from June to October.
USE AND CULTURE: Plant in flower borders or in prairie plantings. They grow well in any well-drained soil in full sun. Propagation is by seeds sown in early spring. The milky juice from crushed leaves can cause skin irritations.

Gaillardia aristata (Blanket Flower). In bloom at the Arboretum in June 1981.

Filipendula Mill. (Meadowsweet)
ROSACEAE (Rose Family)
DESCRIPTION: A small genus of perennial herbs, native in the North Temperate Zone; **leaves** alternate, usually pinnate; **flowers** numerous, small, in terminal corymbose panicles on leafy stems; sepals and petals usually 5; stamens 20 to 40; **fruit** an achene.

Filipendula rubra (J. Hill.) B.L. Robinson. (Queen-of-the-prairie). Hardy in all zones; perennial to 2 m. tall.
DESCRIPTION: Glabrous perennial, native in moist meadows and prairies in full sun from Minnesota to Pennsylvania, south to Kentucky and Georgia; **leaves** interruptedly pinnate, green, paler beneath, with a large terminal leaflet, to 10 cm. across; **flowers** deep, peach-blossom pink, from June to August.
USE AND CULTURE: Plant toward the back of the flower border or in a prairie garden. They grow best in a moist, neutral to slightly acid soil. Propagation is largely by spring division. Space plants about 30 cm. apart.

Gaillardia Foug. (Blanket Flower, Gaillardia)
COMPOSITAE (Sunflower Family)
Helenium Tribe
DESCRIPTION: About 14 species of annual, biennial, and perennial herbs, native in full sun and well-drained soils in North and South America; basal **leaves** entire, dentate or pinnatifid, pubescent; **flower** heads radiate or discoid, solitary, large, showy; receptacle hemispherical; ray flowers yellow or red, with 3-lobed ligules; disc flowers hairy, reddish-purple or yellow; **fruit** a hairy, obconical achene; pappus of awned scales.

Gaillardia aristata Pursh. (Blanket Flower). Hardy in all zones; perennial to 45 cm. tall.
DESCRIPTION: Upright perennial, native in dry meadows and other open areas from British Columbia to North Dakota, south to Colorado and Kansas; **leaves** obovate to linear-lanceolate; lower leaves often pinnately lobed, to 25 cm. long, petioled; upper leaves entire, sessile; **flower** heads to 10 cm. across, from May to September; ray flowers yellow, often purple at base; disc flowers yellow or purple.
USE AND CULTURE: Plant in flower borders, rock gardens, or prairie plantings. They require a well-drained soil and full sun. Propagation is by spring division or by direct seeding as soon as seeds are ripe. Plants may be short-lived on heavy soils.

Gaura L. (Gaura)
ONAGRACEAE (Evening Primrose Family)
DESCRIPTION: About 18 species of annual or perennial herbs, native in North and South America; **leaves** alternate, simple; **flowers** white or pink, in spikelike racemes or panicles, mostly 4-merous; ovary inferior; **fruit** a small, woody capsule, nutlike, and indehiscent.

Gaura coccinea Nutt. ex Pursh. (Scarlet Gaura). Hardy in all zones; perennial to 60 cm. tall.
DESCRIPTION: Bush perennial, native along streams and in disturbed soils from Alberta to Manitoba, south to California and Texas; **stems** several; **leaves** oblong-lanceolate, about 2.5 cm. long, mostly pubescent; **flowers** white to pink, aging to red, to 1.25 cm. across, in crowded spikes; **capsules** 4-angled, to 6 mm. long.
USE AND CULTURE: Plant in prairie gardens. The plants are of easy culture in any well-drained soil in full sun. Propagation is mainly by division in early spring. Seeds can also be planted as soon as ripe. Plants spread by rhizomes and can become weedy.

Gentianella Moench. (Gentian)
GENTIANACEAE (Gentian Family)
DESCRIPTION: About 200 species of annual or perennial herbs, native in Europe,

Geum triflorum (Prairie-smoke). In flower.

Photograph: Dr. Anne M. Hanchek.

Geum triflorum (Prairie-smoke). Seed heads at the McKnight Prairie, Carleton College, Northfield, Minnesota.

Photograph: Bonnie E. Harper Lore.

Asia, North and South America, and New Zealand; **stems** often square; **leaves** opposite; **flowers** blue, lavender, or white, clustered in 3- to 10-flowered cymes, on short, bracted pedicels, 5-merous; calyx tubular, sometimes spathelike, lobes with green margins; corolla tubular, funnelform, or campanulate to rotate, without appendages, lobes entire; ovary sessile; **fruit** a capsule.

Gentianella amarella (L.) Borner. (Felwort). Annual to 30 cm. tall.
DESCRIPTION: Annual, native in moist, gravelly soil, circumboreal, south to California and Maine in North America; basal **leaves** spatulate, to 3 cm. long; stem leaves lanceolate, smaller; **flowers** pale lilac, in leaf axils, to 1.25 cm. long, in July and August.
USE AND CULTURE: Plant in flower borders or in prairie plantings. Plants require a moist, well-drained soil in full sun. Propagation is by seeds started indoors.

Geum L. (Avens)
ROSACEAE (Rose Family)
DESCRIPTION: Over 50 species of perennial herbs, native in temperate regions; **leaves** mostly basal, pinnate or lyrate, usually with large terminal lobes; stem leaves alternate, much smaller; **flowers** solitary or in corymbs, white, yellow, or red; calyx tube bell-shaped or flat; sepals 5, usually with 5 bractlets between the lobes; petals 5, usually broad and showy; stamens many; **fruit** an achene, often with a plumose style.

Geum triflorum Pursh. (Old Man's Whiskers, Prairie-smoke, Torch Flower). Hardy in all zones; perennial to 45 cm. tall.
DESCRIPTION: Soft, hairy perennial, native in open woods and open prairies in sandy or rocky soil from British Columbia to Ontario, south to California and Illinois; **leaves** with many cuneate, shallowly cut leaflets; **flowers** rose-pink, nodding, usually in 3's, in June and July; sepals purple, shorter than the bractlets; petals crimson to rose-pink; styles not jointed, feathery in fruit, to 5 cm. long; **achenes** elongated, mauve-pink.
USE AND CULTURE: Plant in rock gardens or in prairie gardens. They grow best in a well-drained, neutral to slightly acid soil in full sun. Propagation is by spring division or by seeds sown as soon as ripe. Seed germination is often poor.

Grindelia Willd. (Gum Plant, Gumweed, Rosinweed, Sticky-heads, Tarweed)
COMPOSITAE (Sunflower Family)
Aster Tribe
DESCRIPTION: About 50 species of coarse annual, biennial, or perennial herbs, mostly tap-rooted, native along roadsides and in poor, gravelly soils in western North America and in South America; **stems** simple or much-branched; **leaves** alternate, usually sessile, often clasping, glandular-dotted; **flower** heads radiate or discoid, usually gummy, solitary; involucre hemispherical; involucral bracts imbricate in several rows, often spreading or revolute; receptacle flat to slightly convex, pitted, naked; ray flowers pistillate or lacking; disc flowers perfect; **fruit** a glabrous, compressed to 4-angled achene; pappus of 2 to 10 stiff, deciduous awns.

Grindelia squarrosa (Pursh) Dunal. (Curly-cup Gumweed). Hardy in all zones; annual, biennial, or short-lived perennial to 1 m. tall.

DESCRIPTION: Erect annual, biennial, or short-lived perennial, native in prairies, and along streams and pond margins from Montana to Minnesota, south to Texas; **leaves** oblong or ovate, glandular-dotted, wavy-margined, or entire to dentate; basal leaves clasping stem at base; **flower** heads yellow, usually radiate, to 3 cm. across, from July to September; ray flowers lemon-yellow or bright yellow, rarely absent.

USE AND CULTURE: Plant in flower borders or prairie plantings. Native Americans used the plants for medicinal purposes. Plants are easy to grow in most soils. Propagation is by seeds sown as soon as ripe, or indoors in March for transplanting to the garden.

Hedyotis L. (Bluets, Hedyotis)
RUBIACEAE (Madder Family)
DESCRIPTION: About 400 species of shrubs or perennial herbs, native in tropical, subtropical, and sometimes temperate regions; **leaves** opposite with interpetiolar stipules; **flowers** solitary or in axillary or terminal cymes, 4-merous; corolla funnelform or salverform; **fruit** a capsule.

Hedyotis angustifolia - see **Hedyotis nigricans**

Hedyotis caerulea (L.) Hook. (Bluets, Creeping Bluets, Eyebright, Innocence, Quaker-ladies). Hardy in all zones; perennial to 18 cm. tall.
DESCRIPTION: Tufted perennial, native in moist meadows from Wisconsin to Nova Scotia, south to Arkansas and Georgia; **leaves** opposite, oblanceolate, to 1.25 cm. long; **flowers** solitary, violet, blue, or white with yellow eye, in May and June; corolla salverform, to 1.25 cm. long; **capsules** short, 3 mm. across.
USE AND CULTURE: Plant in rock gardens or prairie plantings. Plants are easy to grow in any well-drained soil that is kept moist in the spring. They die down after flowering but new plants form from the tips of the rhizomes around the parent plant. Propagation is by division and by seeds sown as soon as ripe.

Hedyotis nigricans (Lam.) Fosb. (Bluets). Hardy in zone 4; perennial to 60 cm. tall.
DESCRIPTION: Branched perennial, native in dry soils and barrens from Iowa to Indiana, south to Texas and Florida; **leaves** clustered, sessile, linear to threadlike, to 3 cm. long; **flowers** white to purple in terminal cymes grouped to form a panicle, in June and July; corolla salverform, to 6 mm. long; **fruit** oblong to cylindrical.
USE AND CULTURE: The same as for **Hedyotis caerulea**.

Hedyotis purpurea (L.) Torr. & A. Gray. (Purple Bluets). Hardy in all zones; perennial to 45 cm. tall.
DESCRIPITON: Branched perennial, native in dry woods, pine barrens, and in prairies from Michigan to New England, south to Texas and Alabama; **leaves** ovate to ovate-lanceolate, to 5 cm. long; **flowers** purple or lilac, in terminal cymes; corolla funnelform, to 1 cm. long; **capsules** globose to 3 mm. long.
USE AND CULTURE: The same as for **Hedyotis caerulea**.
VARIETIES: var. **longifolia** (Gaertn.) Fosb.
DESCRIPTION: Leaves are narrower than the species. Native from Saskatchewan to Ontario, south to Arkansas and South Carolina.

Helenium L. (Sneezeweed)
COMPOSITAE (Sunflower Family)
Helenium Tribe
DESCRIPTION: About 40 species of annual or perennial herbs, native in rich soil and full sun in North and South America; **leaves** alternate, glandular-dotted, frequently decurrent; **flower** heads radiate or discoid, solitary or in **cymes**; involucral bracts in 2 rows, deflexed or spreading; receptacle convex to ovoid or globose, naked; ray flowers mostly yellow, present or absent, pistillate or sterile; disc flowers yellow, perfect; **fruit** an achene; achenes turbinate or obpyramidal, 4- to 5-angled, red-brown or red-purple; pappus of 5 to 10 scarious, awn-tipped scales.

Helenium autumnale L. (Common Sneezeweed). Hardy in all zones; perennial to 1.5 m. tall.

DESCRIPTION: Fibrous-rooted perennial, native along streams, in meadows, and other wet areas from British Columbia, south to Arizona and Florida; **stems** branched, winged due to decurrent leaf bases; **leaves** linear-lanceolate to elliptic or ovate-lanceolate, to 15 cm. long, serrate, nearly glabrous; **flower** heads to 5 cm. across, from July to September; receptacle nearly globose to hemispherical; ray flowers yellow; disc flowers yellow.

USE AND CULTURE: Plant toward the back of the flower border or in prairie plantings. Sneezeweed grows best in rich, well-drained soils that are kept moist. Propagation is by divison, cuttings taken in July, or by seeds sown as soon as ripe, or in the spring.

Helianthus L. (Sunflower)
COMPOSITAE (Sunflower Family)
Helianthus Tribe
DESCRIPTION: About 150 species of annual or perennial herbs, native in sunny areas in North America; **roots** fibrous or tuberous; **leaves** often opposite below and alternate above, simple; **flower** heads radiate, rarely discoid, usually solitary on long peduncles or several in corymbs; involucre mostly saucer-shaped to hemispherical; involucral bracts in from 2 to 4 rows; receptacle flat to convex, scaly; ray flowers yellow, in 1 row, pistillate or sterile; disc flowers numerous, perfect; **fruit** an achene; achene with deciduous pappus consisting of two awns with scalelike bases.

Helianthus annuus L. (Common Sunflower, Mirasol). Hardy in all zones; annual to 3 m. tall.

DESCRIPTION: Coarse, rough-hairy annual, native in prairies and dry areas throughout North America; **leaves** mostly alternate, ovate, to 30 cm. long, truncate to cordate at base, dentate; **flower** heads radiate, to 30 cm. across, from July to September; ray flowers orange-yellow; disc flowers red or purple.

USE AND CULTURE: Cultivars are sometimes planted toward the back of the sunny flower border. The species is planted in prairie plantings and for bird food. Annual sunflowers are easy to grow in any fertile soil in full sun. Seeds are planted in early spring.

Helianthus laetiflorus Pers. (Showy Sunflower). Hardy in all zones; perennial to 2 m. tall.

DESCRIPTION: Perennial, nearly glabrous to rough-hairy, native in dry prairies and plains from Montana to Minnesota, south to New Mexico and Indiana; **leaves** mostly opposite, lanceolate to narrowly ovate, frequently rhombic-lanceolate, to 27 cm. long, acute, firm, serrate, and scabrous; **flower** heads to 10 cm. across, from August to October; ray flowers yellow; disc flowers usually yellow, rarely brown or purple.

USE AND CULTURE: Plant toward the back of flower borders or in prairie plantings. The showy sunflower is easy to grow in most soils. Propagation is by seeds sown as soon as ripe or in early spring. Division of established plants in early spring is also successful.

Helianthus annuus (Sunflower).

Photograph: Mr. Arvid Lund.

Heliopsis helianthoides (Oxeye). In flower at the Arboretum in August 1977.

Helianthus maximiliani Schrad. (Maximilian Sunflower). Hardy in all zones; perennial to 3 m. tall.
DESCRIPTION: Stout perennial with woody crowns, native in prairies from Canada south to Texas and North Carolina; **leaves** mostly alternate, lanceolate, to 30 cm. long, acuminate at both ends, entire to serrate, sessile, gray-green; **flower** heads to 7.5 cm. across, in racemes or panicles, from June to October; ray flowers yellow; disc flowers yellow.
USE AND CULTURE: The same as for **Helianthus laetiflorus**.

Helianthus tuberosus L. (Girasole, Jerusalem Artichoke). Hardy in all zones; perennial to 2.4 m. tall.
DESCRIPTION: Stout, branched perennial, producing edible tubers, native in waste lands and damp areas from Manitoba to Nova Scotia, south to Texas and Florida; **leaves** mostly alternate, ovate-lanceolate or oblong-lanceolate to ovate, to 20 cm. long, acuminate, serrate-dentate, scabrous above; petioles winged; **flower** heads to 8 cm. across, from August to October; ray flowers yellow; disc flowers yellow.
USE AND CULTURE: It is sometimes planted toward the back of the flower border, in prairie plantings, or in the vegetable garden for the edible tubers. The Jerusalem artichoke is easy to grow. Propagation is by division of the fleshy tubers in the fall. Portions of the tubers that break off will often produce new plants. The tubers contain inulin and are an important food for diabetics.

Heliopsis Pers. (Oxeye)
COMPOSITAE (Sunflower Family)
Helianthus Tribe
DESCRIPTION: 12 species of annual or perennial herbs, native in North America; **leaves** opposite, simple; **flower** heads radiate, solitary; involucral bracts in 1 or 2 rows, nearly equal; receptacle convex to conical, scaly, often hollow; ray flowers pistillate, orange-yellow or yellow, rarely purple; disc flowers perfect, yellow to brownish-yellow, purple, or red; **fruit** an achene; achenes 4-sided, or triangular with outer surface convex; pappus of a few teeth, an irregular crown, or lacking.

Heliopsis helianthoides (L.) Sweet. (Oxeye). Hardy in all zones; perennial to 1.5 m. tall.
DESCRIPTION: Short-lived, nearly glabrous perennial, native on dry slopes, open sunny woods, roadsides, railroad banks, and other disturbed sites from North Dakota to New York, south to Colorado and Georgia; **leaves** lanceolate-ovate to oblong-ovate, to 12 cm. long, serrate; petioles to 4 cm. long; **flower** heads to 6 cm. across, from late July until frost; ray flowers yellow; disc flowers brownish-yellow.
USE AND CULTURE: Plant in flower borders or in prairie gardens. The oxeye thrives in neutral to slightly acid soils in full sun or light shade. Propagation is by division or seeds. Strong clumps can be divided in early spring. Trim the roots back to about 10 cm. when transplanting. Seeds should be planted as soon as ripe or they can be started indoors in early April for late summer bloom. A number of named cultivars are sold.

Hypoxis hirsuta (Star Grass).

Photograph: Mr. Arvid Lund.

Hypoxis L. (Star Grass)
HYPOXIDACEAE (Star Grass Family)
DESCRIPTION: About 110 species of stemless perennial herbs, native in well-drained soils mostly in the southern hemisphere; rhizomes short, cormlike; **leaves** linear, grasslike; **flowers** white or yellow, 1 to several on a scape; perianth of 6 separate segments; stamens 6, in 1 series with slender filaments and erect or versatile anthers; **fruit** a capsule or an indehiscent pod.

Hypoxis hirsuta (L.) Cov. (Star Grass, Yellow Star Grass). Hardy in all zones; perennial to 20 cm. tall.
DESCRIPTION: Rhizomatous perennial, native in prairies and in open woods from Manitoba to Maine, south to Texas and Florida; **rhizomes** short, cormlike; **leaves** linear, grasslike, to 30 cm. long, hairy; **flowers** bright yellow, starlike, 1 to 7 on a scape, from May to July, occasionally all summer; perianth segments 1.25 cm. long; anthers versatile; ovary pilose; **fruit** an indehiscent pod.
USE AND CULTURE: Plant in rock gardens or prairie gardens. It is attractive when grown with blue-eyed grass. Plants grow best in a slightly acid soil in full sun or open shade. Propagation is by division of the cormlike rhizomes. Plant about 4 cm. deep in the fall or early spring. Seeds should be planted as soon as ripe and barely covered.

Ipomoea L. (Morning-glory)
CONVOLVULACEAE (Morning-glory Family)
DESCRIPTION: About 500 species of prostrate, twining, or erect annuals, or perennial herbs, native mostly in tropical and warm-temperate regions; **leaves** alternate, entire, lobed, or divided; **flowers** axillary, solitary, or in few- to many-flowered clusters; corolla funnelform or campanulate, 5-lobed with 5 stripes; stamens and styles included; style solitary; stigmas entire or 2- to 3-lobed; **fruit** a 4- to 6-valved capsule.

Ipomoea leptophylla Torr. (Bush Moonflower, Bush Morning-glory, Man-of-the-earth, Manroot). Hardy in zone 4; perennial to 1.3 m. tall.
DESCRIPTION: Perennial with large, tuberous roots, native in dry plains from Wyoming to Nebraska, south to New Mexico; **stems** erect or ascending; **leaves** linear, to 12 cm. long, entire; **flowers** purple or pink, to 7.5 cm. across, in May and June.
USE AND CULTURE: Plant in flower borders or in prairie gardens. Plants require a well-drained soil. Propagation is by seeds sown in the spring. Because of the hard seed coats which are impervious to water, it is advisable to file through the seed coat before planting. This is a beautiful wild flower when in bloom. It should be kept in mind that plants produce a large, tuberous root.

Lespedeza Michx. (Bush Clover)
LEGUMINOSAE (Pea Family)
DESCRIPTION: About 120 species of herbs or low shrubs, native in well-drained soils in temperate regions of North America, eastern Asia, and Australia; **leaves** alternate, with 3 leaflets; **flowers** pealike, in axillary racemes, stamens 10, 9 united and 1 separate; **fruit** a flat, ovate-acuminate, very small legume, 1-seeded, and indehiscent.

Lespedeza capitata Michx. (Dusty Clover). Hardy in all zones; perennial to 1.5 m. tall.
DESCRIPTION: Silvery-pubescent perennial, native in dry soils from Ontario south to Louisiana and Florida; **leaflets** oblong to narrowly elliptic; **flowers** yellowish-white with a purple spot on the standard, in dense headlike racemes, from July to September; calyx longer than the fruit.
USE AND CULTURE: Plant in prairie gardens. Plants will grow in any well-drained soil. Propagation is by spring division or by seeds sown in the spring and inoculated with a cowpea inoculum.

Lespedeza violacea (L.) Pers. (Violet Bush Clover). Hardy in all zones; perennial to 80 cm. tall.
DESCRIPTION: A glabrous to sparsely pubescent perennial, native in dry upland woods from Wisconsin to Vermont, south to Texas and Florida; **stems** erect or

Liatris spicata (Spike Gay-feather). In flower at Egeskov Castle in Denmark in August 1983.

ascending, usually much-branched; **leaflets** elliptic, to 4 cm. long, appressed-hairy beneath, glabrous above; **flowers** purple, to 1 cm. long, in loose, few-flowered racemes, in August and September.
USE AND CULTURE: The same as for **Lespedeza capitata**.

Lespedeza virginica (L.) Britt. (Slender Bush Clover). Hardy in all zones; perennial to 90 cm. tall.
DESCRIPTION: Strigose perennial, native in dry upland woods from Wisconsin to New Hampshire, south to Texas and Georgia; **stems** erect or nearly so, simple or branched above; **leaflets** linear to narrowly oblong, to 2.5 cm. long, short-strigose on both surfaces; **flowers** purple, to 8 mm. long, in short, few-flowered racemes in the upper leaf axils; **legumes** thinly strigose.
USE AND CULTURE: The same as for **Lespedeza capitata**.

Leucocrinum Nutt. (Mountain Lily, Sand Lily, Star Lily)
LILIACEAE (Lily Family)
DESCRIPTION: A single species of stemless, perennial herbs, native in sandy prairie soils in western North America; **rhizomes** deep-seated with fleshy roots; **leaves** narrowly linear; **flowers** white, emerging in a cluster from the rhizomes; perianth segments salverform; 6-lobed; stamens 6, attached near the tip of the perianth tube; **fruit** a capsule.

Leucocrinum montanum Nutt. (Sand Lily). Hardy in all zones; perennial to 12 cm. tall.
DESCRIPTION: Native in sandy soils from Oregon to South Dakota, south to California and Nebraska; **leaves** several, linear, to 12 cm. long; **flowers** pure white, fragrant, to 12 cm. long, in May; stamens with yellow anthers.
USE AND CULTURE: Plant in rock gardens or prairie gardens. The plants require full sun and a sandy, well-drained soil. Propagation is by division in the fall or by seeds sown as soon as ripe. Capsules and seeds are produced underground.

Liatris Gaertn. ex. Schreb. (Blazing-star, Button Snakeroot, Gay-feather)
COMPOSITAE (Sunflower Family)
Eupatorium Tribe
DESCRIPTION: About 40 species of perennial herbs with corms or rhizomes, native in sunny roadside ditches and open prairies in the Great Plains of North America; **leaves** alternate, simple, mostly linear to linear-lanceolate, entire, usually resin-dotted; **flower** heads discoid, in spikes, racemes, or panicles, the uppermost heads flowering first; involucral bracts imbricate in several rows, lanceolate to orbicular, with scarious, ciliate to deeply erose margins; receptacle flat, naked; disc flowers tubular, perfect, purple or rose-purple, rarely white; **fruit** a cylindrical 10-ribbed achene; pappus of 15 to 40 plumose bristles.

Liatris aspera Michx. (Gay-feather). Hardy in all zones; perennial to 2 m. tall.
DESCRIPTION: A stout, erect perennial, native in dry, often sandy soils from North Dakota to Ontario, south to Texas and South Carolina; lower **leaves** rhombic lanceolate,

Liatris aspera (Gay-feather). Blooming in the McKnight Prairie, Carleton College, Northfield, Minnesota.
Photograph: Bonnie E. Harper Lore.

to 40 cm. long, petioled; upper leaves linear to linear-lanceolate, reduced upward; **flower** heads to 2.5 cm. across, in spikes of 20 to 150 heads, in August and September; involucre campanulate to nearly globose; involucral bracts wrinkled, glabrous, purple, with lacerate margins.

USE AND CULTURE: Plant in flower borders or prairie gardens. Plants are easy to grow in well-drained soil in full sun. Propagation is by division and by seeds sown in May.

Liatris ligulistylis (A. Nelson) K. Schum. (Rocky Mountain Gay-feather). Hardy in all zones; perennial to 1 m. tall.

DESCRIPTION: Perennial, native in moist, low areas, often along roadsides, from Alberta to Wisconsin, south to New Mexico; **leaves** glabrous to densely pubescent, ciliate; basal leaves lanceolate-oblong to oblanceolate, to 15 cm. long, usually petioled; upper leaves lanceolate, reduced upward; **flower** heads to 3 cm. across with 40 to 70 disc flowers, in racemes of 2 to 30 heads, in August and September; involucre broadly campanulate or hemispherical; involucral bracts often purple with scarious, lacerate margins.

USE AND CULTURE: The same as for **Liatris aspera**.

Liatris punctata Hook. (Dotted Gay-feather). Hardy in all zones; perennial to 30 cm. tall.

DESCRIPTION: Glabrous perennial with numerous stems from a crown, native in dry prairies from Alberta to Minnesota, south to New Mexico and Iowa; **leaves** rigid, conspicuously punctate, basal leaves linear, to 10 cm. long, ciliate; upper leaves gradually reduced; **flower** heads 4- to 8-flowered, 2 cm. long, in dense spikes; involucre cylindrical; involucral bracts white-ciliate.

USE AND CULTURE: The sames as for **Liatris aspera**.

Liatris pycnostachya Michx. (Cattail Gay-feather, Kansas Gay-feather). Hardy in all zones; perennial to 1.5 m. tall.

DESCRIPTION: Coarse, upright perennial, native in moist prairies and roadside ditches from South Dakota to Indiana, south to Texas and Florida; **stems** with fleshy, underground corms; **leaves** punctate, glabrous to hairy; lower leaves to 40 cm. long, reduced upward; **flower** heads to 1 cm. across, 5- to 10-flowered, in dense cylindrical spikes to 45 cm. long, in August and September; involucre cylindrical to narrowly turbinate; involucral bracts with spreading tips.

USE AND CULTURE: Plant in flower borders for accent and also in prairie gardens. This is the most widely planted species of Liatris. For propagation, the corms are cut vertically very much as you would cut potatoes, being sure that each piece has a bud. Let the cut surfaces dry for at least an hour before replanting. Seeds are slow to germinate and seelings take 3 years to bloom.

Liatris spicata (L.) Willd. (Spike Gay-feather). Hardy in all zones; perennial to 1.5 m. tall.

DESCRIPTION: Stiff, erect perennial, native in moist soils from Michigan to New York, south to Louisiana and Florida; lower **leaves** linear-lanceolate, to 10 cm. long, reduced upwards; **flower** heads about 1 cm. across, many in spikelike inflorescences to 75 cm. long, in August and September; involucre turbinate-campanulate; involucral bracts often purple with scarious margins.

USE AND CULTURE: The same as for **Liatris aspera**.

Liatris squarrosa (L.) Michx. (Gay-feather). Hardy in all zones; perennial to 1 m. tall.

DESCRIPTION: Stout perennial, native in prairies and roadside ditches from South Dakota to Delaware, south to Texas and Alabama; **stems** several to many, pubescent; **leaves** rigid, punctate, lowest ones to 25 cm. long, shorter above; **flower** heads to 3 cm. across, 20- to 45-flowered, solitary to many in a raceme or panicle, in August and September; involucre cylindrical; involucral bracts with long, tapered, spreading tips.

USE AND CULTURE: The same as for **Liatris aspera**.

Liatris ligulistylis (Rocky Mountain Gay-feather).

In bloom at the Arboretum.

Photograph: Mr. Arvid Lund.

Lithospermum L. (Gromwell, Puccoon)
BORAGINACEAE (Borage Family)
DESCRIPTION: About 45 species of hairy, perennial herbs, native in sunny fields and roadsides, usually in sandy soils on all continents except Australia; **roots** often with a red or purple dye; **leaves** alternate, simple, sessile, entire; **flowers** orange, yellow, or white, in simple or branched scorpioid cymes; calyx and corolla 5-lobed with glands in the throat of the corolla; stamens 5, never exserted; **fruit** of 4 nutlets, usually polished, white.

Lithospermum canescens (Michx.) Lehm. (Indian-paint, Hoary Puccoon). Hardy in all zones; perennial to 45 cm. tall.
DESCRIPTION: Perennial with hoary pubescence, native in sandy soils from North Dakota to Ontario, south to Texas and Georgia; **roots** contain a red dye; **leaves** oblong to linear; **flowers** orange-yellow, 1.4 cm. long, in May and June; corolla lobes entire, with tube glabrous inside; **nutlets** yellow, smooth, and shining.
USE AND CULTURE: Plant in rock gardens or prairie gardens. Plants require full sun and a sandy soil of low fertility. Propagation is by seeds sown as soon as ripe, or by root cuttings. Root cuttings should be about the size of a lead pencil and 5 cm. long. Plant in early spring spacing the plants about 30 cm. apart.

Lithospermum caroliniense (Walt.) MacMill. (Puccoon). Hardy in all zones; perennial to 60 cm. tall.
DESCRIPTION: Perennial, native in upland woods, lake shores, and prairies, usually in sandy soils, from Wyoming to Ontario, south to Texas and Florida; **stems** erect, from a woody root, villous or hirsute; **leaves** linear to lanceolate, to 6 cm. long, rough-hirsute; flowers bright yellow or orange, in leafy-bracted cymes; corolla tube to 1.4 cm. long; **nutlets** ivory-white.
USE AND CULTURE: The same as for **Lithospermum canescens**.

Lobelia L. (Lobelia)
LOBELIACEAE (Lobelia Family)
DESCRIPTION: About 375 species of herbs, shrubs, or trees, native in moist soils, mostly in tropical and warm-temperate regions; **leaves** alternate, simple; **flowers** blue, violet, red, yellow, or white, in bracted racemes; calyx 5-toothed; corolla irregular, mostly 2-lipped, the upper lip 2-lobed, the lower lip 3-cleft, tube slit nearly to base; stamens 5, attached at base of corolla; anthers united into a tube around style; ovary 2-celled; stigma lobes rounded, spreading; **fruit** a capsule.

Lobelia spicata Lam. (Pale-spike Lobelia). Hardy in all zones; biennial to 60 cm. tall.
DESCRIPTION: Biennial, rarely perennial, native in roadside ditches and other disturbed soils from Minnesota to New Brunswick, south to Arkansas and Georgia; **stems** sparsely branched; **leaves** mostly basal, obovate to lanceolate, sessile, serrate; **flowers** bluish-violet, rarely white, in terminal spikes, in June; calyx tube scarcely inflated, about 6 mm. long.
USE AND CULTURE: Plant in flower borders or prairie gardens. Effective in masses. Plants grow well in most soils. Propagation is by seeds sown as soon as ripe. Once established, this species self sows.

Lithospermum canescens (Hoary Puccoon).

In bloom in June 1983.

Liatris pycnostachya (Cattail Gay-feather).

Lupinus L. (Lupine)
LEGUMINOSAE (Pea Family)
DESCRIPTION: About 200 species of annual or perennial herbs or subshrubs, native in sandy or well-drained soils, worldwide but mainly in North America; **leaves** palmately compound, rarely reduced to a single leaflet; stipules united to the petioles; **flowers** showy, pealike, in terminal spikes or racemes; standards erect with reflexed margins; stamens 10, united; **fruit** a legume, often constricted between the seeds.

Lupinus perennis L. (Sundial Lupine, Wild Lupine). Hardy in all zones; perennial to 60 cm. tall.
DESCRIPTION: Pubescent perennial, native in sandy soils along roadsides, waste lands, and pastures from Ontario south to Minnesota and Florida; **leaflets** 7 to 11, blue-green, to 5 cm. long; **flowers** blue, varying to pink or white, in racemes, in May and June; **legumes** pubescent to 4 cm. long.
USE AND CULTURE: Plant in flower borders or prairie gardens. Plants require a well-drained soil that is slightly acid. They need full sun. Plants go dormant in August after the seeds mature. Propagation is by spring division or by seeds. Seeds can be started indoors or seeded directly. Due to the hard seed coat, germination is improved by soaking for 15 minutes in warm water. Seedlings will bloom the second year. Plants self sow once established. The foliage is reported to be poisonous to livestock.

Mentzelia L. (Mentzelia)
LOASACEAE (Loasa Family)
DESCRIPTION: About 60 species of herbs or shrubs with barbed hairs, native in the prairies of North America; **leaves** mostly alternate; **flowers** white, yellow, or orange, often very showy; petals separate; **fruit** a capsule.

Mentzelia decapetala (Pursh) Urb. & Gilg. (Sand Lily, Tenpetal Mentzelia). Hardy in all zones; biennial to 1.2 m. tall.
DESCRIPTION: Biennial or short-lived perennial native in prairies from Alberta to Iowa, south to Mexico and Texas; **leaves** lanceolate to oblong-lanceolate, pinnately lobed; **flowers** white or yellow, to 7.5 cm. across, opening in the evening, fragrant, from July to September; petals 10, stamens many.
USE AND CULTURE: Plant in flower borders or prairie gardens. They require full sun and a well-drained soil. Propagation is by seeds sown as soon as ripe where the plants are to bloom. Seedlings should be thinned to 30 cm. apart.

Monarda L. (Horsemint, Wild Bergamot)
LABIATAE (Mint Family)
DESCRIPTION: About 12 species of annual or perennial aromatic herbs, native in North America; **stems** square; **leaves** opposite, entire or toothed; **flowers** showy, in densely-flowered verticillasters, subtended by leafy bracts; calyx tubular, 15-veined; corolla tube longer than the calyx, with 2-lipped limb; upper lip erect, often emarginate; lower lip spreading, 3-lobed; fertile stamens 2, usually exserted; **fruit** a glabrous nutlet, produced in 4's.

Monarda punctata (Dotted Mint). Along Interstate 90 near Lacrosse, Wisconsin.

Photograph: Bonnie E. Harper Lore.

Monarda punctata L. (Dotted Mint, Dotted Monarda, Horsemint). Hardy in all zones; perennial to 90 cm. tall.
DESCRIPTION: Annual, biennial, or perennial, native in sandy soils from Minnesota to Vermont, south to Texas and Florida; **leaves** lanceolate to oblong, to 8 cm. long, serrate to nearly entire; **flowers** yellow, spotted purple, in several superposed, headlike verticillasters, from July to October; calyx to 1 cm. long with narrow, triangular teeth; corolla to 2 cm. long.
USE AND CULTURE: Plant in flower borders or prairie gardens. They prefer a sandy soil in full sun. Propagation is the same as for **Monarda didyma**.

Oenothera L. (Evening Primrose, Sundrops)
ONAGRACEAE (Evening Primrose Family)
DESCRIPTION: About 80 species of annual, biennial, and perennial herbs, native in sunny areas in North and South America; **stems** erect or lacking; **leaves** basal or alternate, simple, entire to pinnatifid; **flowers** solitary and axillary or in racemes or panicles, 4-merous; calyx tube usually well developed; stamens 8 with versatile anthers; ovary inferior, 4-celled, cylindrical or clavate; **fruit** a capsule.

Oenothera biennis L. (Common Evening Primrose, German Rampion). Hardy in all zones; biennial to 2 m. tall.
DESCRIPTION: Tap-rooted biennial, native in sandy soils in eastern North America; basal **leaves** to 30 cm. long; stem leaves usually lanceolate, to 15 cm. long, with shallow teeth; **flowers** yellow, to 5 cm. across, in spikes or panicles, opening in the evening, from June to September; calyx tube to 5 cm. long; **capsules** tapering upward, to 4 cm. long.
USE AND CULTURE: Plant in prairie gardens. Roots can be eaten as a vegetable and the young shoots used in salads. Plants are easy to grow in any good garden soil. Propagation is by seeds sown either when ripe or in the spring. Plants are coarse and can be weedy if planted in a flower border.

Oenothera missouriensis Sims (Flutter-mills, Glade Lily, Missouri Evening Primrose). Hardy in all zones; perennial to 40 cm. tall.
DESCRIPTION: Low perennial, native in prairies and on rocky hillsides from Nebraska to Missouri, south to Texas; **stems** decumbent to erect, strigose; **leaves** lanceolate, petioled to 10 cm. long, entire; **flowers** yellow, becoming red with age, to 10 cm. across, very showy, opening in the evening; **capsules** woody, 4-winged, to 7.5 cm. long.
USE AND CULTURE: Plant in rock gardens and prairie gardens. Plants prefer a heavy, clay soil in full sun. Propagation is by seeds sown as soon as ripe or in the spring.

Oxalis L. (Lady's Sorrel, Wood Sorrel)
OXALIDACEAE (Oxalis Family)
DESCRIPTION: About 850 species of annual or perennial herbs, native on all continents, especially numerous in Africa and South America; underground **stems** bulbous, tuberous, or rhizomatous; **leaves** alternate, cauline or basal, cloverlike, palmate, 3- to many-foliate, pinnately 3-foliate, or sometimes reduced to 1 or 2 leaflets, often closing at night; **flowers** in most colors except blue, in 1- to several-flowered scapes, umbellate cymes; sepals and petals 5, cohering basally; stamens 10, in 2 series, the outer shorter than the inner, all fertile; **fruit** a capsule.

Oxalis violacea L. (Violet Wood Sorrel). Hardy in all zones; perennial to 25 cm. tall.
DESCRIPTION: Scapose perennial, with brown, scaly bulbs, native in fields and prairies from North Dakota to Maine, south to Colorado and Florida; **leaflets**, 3 obreniform, to 2.5 cm. wide; **flowers** violet to rose-purple, rarely white, in 3- to 10-flowered umbels on peduncles to 25 cm. long.
USE AND CULTURE: Plant in rock gardens or prairie gardens. Plants grow well in any well-drained soil that is slightly acid. Propagation is by seeds or by division of the bulbs. Bulbs should be planted in the fall about 5 cm. deep 15 cm. apart. Plants self sow. There are several introduced species with yellow flowers that can become troublesome weeds.

Oenothera missouriensis (Missouri Evening Primrose).

In bloom in August 1977.

Penstemon gracilis (Slender Beard-tongue).

Penstemon grandiflorus (Shell-leaf Beard-tongue). In bloom

Allison Savanna Preserve, near Bethel, Minnesota.

Photograph: Bonnie E. Harper Lore

Oxytropis DC. (Crazyweed, Locoweed)
LEGUMINOSAE (Pea Family)
DESCRIPTION: About 300 species of low perennial herbs, native in the North Temperate Zone; **leaves** odd-pinnate; leaflets obtuse at base; flowers pealike, in racemes or spikes; keel beaked; stamens 10, 9 united, 1 separate; **fruit** a legume.

Oxytropis campestris (L.) DC. (Locoweed). Hardy in all zones; perennial to 20 cm. tall.
DESCRIPTION: A variable perennial, native near rocks, cliffs, and gravelly lake shores, circumboreal, from British Columbia to Manitoba, south to Colorado and Wisconsin; **leaves** to 15 cm. long, with linear-oblong to oblong-lanceolate leaflets; **flowers** white to yellow, rarely purple, in many-flowered racemes, from May to July; **legumes** thin-walled, to 2 cm. long.
USE AND CULTURE: Plant in flower borders or in prairie gardens. They will grow in any well-drained soil. Propagation is by direct seeding. Plants have a tap root and do not transplant well. Plants are poisonous to livestock when eaten.

Penstemon Mitch. (Beard-tongue)
SCROPHULARIACEAE (Figwort Family)
DESCRIPTION: About 250 species of perennial herbs or rarely shrubs, native mostly in moist rocky soils in full sun chiefly in western North America; **leaves** opposite, rarely in whorls of 3, or upper alternate; **flowers** scarlet, purple, blue, white, or yellow, solitary or in terminal racemes or panicles; calyx 5-parted; corolla tubular, more or less 2-lipped; fertile stamens 4; staminode 1, naked or bearded; **fruit** a capsule.

Penstemon albidus Nutt. (White Beard-tongue). Hardy in all zones; perennial to 40 cm. tall.
DESCRIPTION: Perennial, native in dry prairies from Alberta to Minnesota, south to New Mexico and Iowa; **leaves** lanceolate-oblong, to 8 cm. long, entire or with a few shallow teeth, rounded or truncate at base; **flowers** white, occasionally tinged violet, in May and June; corolla tube to 2 cm. long, gradually dilated upward.
USE AND CULTURE: Plant in rock gardens, flower borders, or prairie gardens. They require a well-drained soil and full sun. Propagation is by division, seeds, or cuttings. Seeds should be sown in the fall or stored in an airtight container at 32 to 40 degrees Fahrenheit for spring planting. Seeds should be covered with screened peat that is kept moist.

Penstemon digitalis Nutt. (Foxglove Penstemon). Hardy in all zones; perennial to 1 m. tall.
DESCRIPTION: Glabrous perennial, native in moist open woods or prairies from South Dakota to Maine, south to Texas; basal **leaves** oblanceolate to elliptic, entire or dentate; stem leaves lanceolate, oblanceolate, or oblong-ovate, to 17 cm. long; **flowers** white or pink, in June and July; corolla to 2.5 cm. long; anthers bearded; staminodes bearded.
USE AND CULTURE: The same as for **Penstemon albidus**.

Penstemon gracilis Nutt. (Slender Beard-tongue). Hardy in all zones; perennial to 60 cm. tall.
DESCRIPTION: Slender perennial, native in sandy or gravelly soils in prairies and in open woods from British Columbia to Ontario, south to New Mexico and Wisconsin; basal **leaves** oblanceolate to elliptic, finely dentate to entire, thin, glabrous; stem leaves linear-lanceolate; **flowers** lilac to white, in June and July; corolla to 2 cm. long, strongly 2-lipped; staminode densely yellow-bearded.
USE AND CULTURE: The same as for **Penstemon albidus**.

Penstemon grandiflorus Nutt. (Shell-leaf Beard-tongue). Hardy in all zones; biennial to 1 m. tall.
DESCRIPTION: Glabrous, glaucous biennial or short-lived perennial, native in dry fields and in prairies from North Dakota to Illinois, south to Wyoming and Texas; **leaves** entire, thick, fleshy; basal leaves ovate; stem leaves elliptic to round-ovate or orbicular,

clasping; **flowers** lilac or blue-lavender, in May and June; corolla to 5 cm. long; staminode hooked, minutely bearded at apex.
USE AND CULTURE: Plant in flower borders or in prairie gardens. The culture is the same as for **Penstemon albidus**.

Petalostemon Michx. (Prairie Clover)
LEGUMINOSAE (Pea Family)
DESCRIPTION: About 50 species of glandular-dotted herbs, native in open prairies in North America; **leaves** alternate, odd-pinnate; **flowers** showy, with 4 petals united basally to the stamen tube and the standard separate, borne in dense heads or spikes; **fruit** a short, indehiscent legume, included in the calyx.

Petalostemon candidum (Willd.) Michx. (White Prairie Clover). Hardy in all zones; perennial to 60 cm. tall.
DESCRIPTION: Perennial, native in low prairies from Saskatchewan south to Arizona and Mississippi; **leaflets** 7 to 9, linear or oblong; **flowers** white, in oblong spikes to 7.5 cm. long, from May to September.
USE AND CULTURE: Plant in prairie gardens. They grow well in any well-drained soil in full sun. Propagation is by seeds sown in early spring. Once established the plants should self sow.

Petalostemon purpureum (Venten.) Rydb. (Purple Prairie Clover). Hardy in all zones; perennial to 60 cm. tall.
DESCRIPTION: Perennial, native in prairies and dry hills from Saskatchewan south to New Mexico and Texas; **leaflets** 3 to 5, linear, to 2 cm. long; **flowers** violet to crimson, in dense spikes to 5 cm. long, from June to September.
USE AND CULTURE: The same as for **Petalostemon candidum**.

Petalostemon villosum Nutt. (Silky Prairie Clover). Hardy in all zones; perennial to 60 cm. tall.
DESCRIPTION: Decumbent or ascending perennial with soft, silky hairs, native on sand dunes and in prairies from Saskatchewan to Michigan, south to Texas; **leaflets** 13 to 19, elliptic to oblong or oblanceolate, to 1.2 cm. long; **flowers** rose-purple, rarely white, in cylindrical spikes to 10 cm. long, from July to September.
USE AND CULTURE: The same as for **Petalostemon candidum**.

Phlox L. (Phlox)
POLEMONIACEAE (Phlox Family)
DESCRIPTION: About 60 species of erect, diffuse, or cespitose annual or perennial herbs, native mostly in North America, one species in Siberia; **leaves** mostly opposite, simple; **flowers** blue, purple, crimson, pink, or white, solitary or in terminal cymes or panicles; calyx 5-cleft; corolla salverform, 5-lobed; stamens 5; **fruit** a 3-valved capsule, rupturing the calyx at maturity.

Petalostemon purpureum (Purple Prairie Clover).

Phlox pilosa (Prairie Phlox).

Photograph: Mr. Arvid Lund.

Physostegia virginiana. In bloom in

Dr. Snyder's garden in September 1982.

Phlox pilosa L. (Prairie Phlox). Hardy in all zones; perennial to 30 cm. tall.
DESCRIPTION: Hairy perennial, native in open upland woods, in dry prairies, and common in roadside ditches from Manitoba to Connecticut, south to Texas and Florida; **leaves** linear to lanceolate, to 7.5 cm. long; **flowers** purple to pink, rarely white, to 2 cm. across, in small clusters, in June.
USE AND CULTURE: Plant in rock gardens and prairie gardens. Plants prefer a slightly acid, sandy loam soil in full sun. Propagation is mainly by seeds since the plants are difficult to divide. Although this phlox usually blooms in late spring, seedlings often bloom the first year in August. Foliage dies down soon after bloom, but under cultivation, this plant can rebloom later in the season.

Physostegia Benth. (False Dragonhead, Lion's-heart,
Obedience, Obedient Plant)
LABIATAE (Mint Family)
DESCRIPTION: About 15 species of glabrous or puberulous perennial herbs, native in North America; **stems** mostly square in cross section; **leaves** opposite, often toothed; **flowers** showy, white, purple, red, or pink, solitary in leaf axils or in panicled, leafless spikes; calyx tubular or campanulate, 10-veined, slightly inflated in fruit; corolla tube longer than the calyx; limb 2-lipped; **fruit** of 4 smooth nutlets.

Physostegia virginiana (L.) Benth. (False Dragonhead, Obedience). Hardy in all zones; perennial to 90 cm. tall.
DESCRIPTION: Stoloniferous, glabrous perennial, native in swampy thickets and wet woods, sometimes in prairies from Minnesota to New Brunswick, south to Oklahoma and South Carolina; **leaves** lanceolate, to 12 cm. long, acute, sharply-serrate; **flowers** showy, rose-purple, in closely flowered spikes clustered in a panicle, from June to September; calyx tubular-campanulate, viscid-glandular, with sharp triangular teeth; corolla to 3 cm. long, inflated at mouth.

Psoralea esculenta (Indian Breadroot). In bloom

in Ottawa, Canada in May 1978.

USE AND CULTURE: Plant in flower borders, wild flower gardens, or prairie gardens. They thrive in any good garden soil. Plants spread rapidly, especially in moist soils. Propagation is mainly by division either in the spring or fall. Plant with the buds near the surface and space the plants 30 cm. apart. Divide plants every third year. Plants grown from seeds sown as soon as ripe will bloom the second year.

Psoralea L. (Scurfy Pea)
LEGUMINOSAE (Pea Family)
DESCRIPTION: About 130 species of scented herbs or shrubs, native in North America and South Africa; **leaves** alternate, odd-pinnate, rarely with 1 leaflet, with translucent dots, with a scurfy surface due to scalelike glands; **flowers** pealike, solitary or in heads, racemes, or spikes; stamens 10, united or separate; **fruit** a short, 1-seeded, indehiscent legume.

Psoralea esculenta Pursh. (Indian Breadroot, Indian Turnip, Pomme Blanche, Prairie Potato). Hardy in all zones; perennial to 40 cm. tall.
DESCRIPTION: Hairy perennial with edible tuberous roots, native in prairies and in dry open woods from Saskatchewan to Wisconsin, south to Texas; **leaflets** 5, oblong to oblanceolate, to 6 cm. long, smooth above, hairy beneath; **flowers** yellow to blue, in dense spikes, to 10 cm. long, from May to July.
USE AND CULTURE: Plant in flower borders or prairie gardens. Roots are edible. Plants require a well-drained soil. Propagation is by seeds. Space plants 45 cm. apart.

Ratibida Raf. (Prairie Coneflower)
COMPOSITAE (Sunflower Family)
Helianthus Tribe
DESCRIPTION: Five species of biennial or perennial rough-hairy herbs, native in prairies of North America; **leaves** alternate, pinnatifid; **flower** heads radiate, solitary; involucral bracts green in one row; receptacle globose to conical, scaly; ray flowers yellow or rarely purple, drooping; disc flowers brown; **fruit** a compressed achene, partially enclosed by a scale; pappus lacking or of 2 awns.

Ratibida columnifera (Nutt.) Woot. & Standl. (Upright Prairie Coneflower). Hardy in all zones; perennial to 1 m. tall.
DESCRIPTION: Short-lived perennial, native in prairies from British Columbia to Minnesota, south to Mexico and Texas; **stems** branching from the base; **leaf** segments linear to narrowly lanceolate, entire; **flower** heads several to many, from June to September; receptacle columnar, to 5 cm. long; ray flowers yellow or purple, to 2 cm. long, drooping; disc flowers brown.
USE AND CULTURE: Plant in flower borders or in prairie gardens. Plants require full sun and a well-drained soil. Propagation is by seeds sown as soon as ripe.

Ratibida pinnata (Venten.) Barnh. (Prairie Coneflower). Hardy in all zones; perennial to 1 m. tall.
DESCRIPTION: Coarse perennial with hairy stems, native in dry, often sandy soils from Minnesota to Ontario, south to Oklahoma and Georgia; **stems** branched above; **leaf** segments narrowly to broadly lanceolate, serrate; **flower** heads solitary or several, from June to August; receptacle ellipsoid to oblong, to 2 cm. long; ray flowers pale yellow, 5 to 10, to 5 cm. long, spreading or reflexed; **achenes** smooth; pappus lacking.
USE AND CULTURE: The same as for **Ratibida columnifera**.

Rudbeckia L. (Coneflower)
COMPOSITAE (Sunflower Family)
Helianthus Tribe
DESCRIPTION: About 25 species of annual, biennial, or perennial herbs throughout North America; **leaves** alternate, simple, pinnatifid or pinnate; **flower** heads radiate, showy, terminal; receptacle hemispherical to columnar, scaly, the scales shorter than or equalling the disc flowers; ray flowers sterile, yellow to reddish-brown; disc flowers perfect; **fruit** a 4-angled achene; pappus a short crown or lacking.

Ratibida pinnata (Prairie Coneflower). In bloom at the McKnight Prairie of Carléton College, Northfield, Minnesota.

Photograph: Bonnie E. Harper Lore.

Rudbeckia hirta L. (Black-eyed Susan). Hardy in all zones; annual, biennial, or perennial to 90 cm. tall.
DESCRIPTION: Hairy annual, biennial, or perennial herb, native in open disturbed soils throughout North America; **leaves** mostly basal, simple, lanceolate, petioled; stem leaves sessile above; **flower** heads showy to 8 cm. across, from June to September; receptacle conical; ray flowers mostly orange-yellow; disc flowers purple-brown; pappus lacking.
USE AND CULTURE: Plant in flower borders or in prairie gardens. Plants grow well in most any well-drained soil in full sun. Propagation is by seeds sown as soon as ripe or started indoors in early April. Plants will bloom the first year if seeds are planted early. By cutting back the flower stalks after bloom, the plants will persist for several years. Plants can self sow. Tetraploid strains of this species are sold as gloriosa daisies.

Rudbeckia laciniata L. (Cutleaf Coneflower). Hardy in all zones; perennial to 3 m. tall.
DESCRIPTION: Tall perennial, native in wet fields, ditches, and ravines from Montana to Quebec, south to Arizona and Florida; **leaves** pinnate, nearly glabrous; leaflets deeply lobed; **flower** heads to 8 cm. across, from July to September; receptacle hemispherical, becoming conic-oblong in age; ray flowers yellow, drooping; disc flowers greenish-yellow.
USE AND CULTURE: The same as for **Rudbeckia hirta**. The cultivar 'Hortensia', called goldenglow, is a double form of this species.

Salvia L. (Ramona, Sage, Salvia)
LABIATAE (Mint Family)
DESCRIPTION: Over 750 species of herbs, subshrubs, and shrubs, native in dry or rocky soils worldwide; **stems** square in cross section; **leaves** opposite, simple to pinnatifid, upper ones reduced to scales; **flowers** in axillary verticillasters; calyx 2-lipped with unequal teeth; corolla 2-lipped; stamens 2; **fruit** of 4 ovoid, 3-angled nutlets.

Salvia azurea Lam. (Azure Salvia, Blue Sage). Hardy in all zones; perennial to 60 cm. tall.
DESCRIPTION: Erect perennial, native in dry prairies from Minnesota to Kentucky, south to Texas; basal **leaves** lanceolate or oblong, to 7.5 cm. long, serrate, tapering at base; upper leaves narrow, often linear; **flowers** deep blue, rarely white, in spikes, in June and July; calyx with upper lip entire; corolla to 2 cm. long.
USE AND CULTURE: Plant in flower borders or prairie gardens. Plants prefer a sunny location and a fertile garden loam. Propagation is by seeds or division. Plant seeds as soon as ripe or in early spring. Seedlings bloom the second year. Plants can be divided either in the spring or fall. Space plants about 20 cm. apart and slightly deeper than they were growing.
VARIETIES: var. **grandiflora** Benth. Flowers larger than in the species. This variety has the same range as the species.

Salvia pitcheri - see **Salvia azurea** var. **grandiflora**

Rudbeckia hirta (Black-eyed Susan).

Rudbeckia laciniata (Cutleaf Coneflower).

Photograph: Mr. Arvid Lund.

Schizachyrium Nees. (Bluestem)
GRAMINEAE (Grass Family)
DESCRIPTION: About 100 species of perennial grasses native around the world; **leaves** elongated, flat; **flowers** similar to **Andropogon** except the racemes are solitary at the ends of the stems and their branches; rachis joints oblique.

Schizachyrium scoparium (Michx.) Nash. (Bluestem, Broom, Broom Beard Grass, Bunchgrass, Little Bluestem, Prairie Beard Grass, Wire Grass). Hardy in all zones; perennial to 1.5 m. tall.
DESCRIPTION: Perennial grass with green or glaucous, sometimes purple stems, native in dry prairies and in open woods from Alberta to Quebec, south to Arizona and Florida; **leaf** sheaths and flat blades commonly glabrous or nearly so; **flowers** in racemes to 6 cm. long on filiform peduncles, wholly or partly included in the sheaths.
USE AND CULTURE: Plant in prairie gardens. The little bluestem can be propagated by division or by seeds.

Sieversia triflorum - see **Geum triflorum**.

Silphium L. (Rosinweed)
COMPOSITAE (Sunflower Family)
Helianthus Tribe
DESCRIPTION: About 25 species of coarse perennial herbs, native in open areas in eastern North America; **stems** sparingly branched, scabrous-hispid; **leaves** opposite below, alternate above, usually scabrous; **flower** heads radiate, in racemes or corymbose panicles; involucre shallowly campanulate; involucral bracts nearly equal, in 2 to several rows; receptacle flat to convex, scaly; ray flowers in 2 to 3 rows, pistillate, yellow or rarely white; disc flowers yellow, sterile; **fruit** a compressed achene with winged edges.

Silphium laciniatum L. (Compass Plant). Hardy in all zones; perennial to 2 m. tall.
DESCRIPTION: Coarse perennial, native in prairies from Minnesota to Ohio, south to Texas and Alabama; **stems** stout, very hispid; **leaves** alternate, deeply pinnatifid, to 50 cm. long; **flower** heads to 12 cm. across, in racemes, from July to September.
USE AND CULTURE: Plant toward the back of flower borders or in prairie gardens. Plants are easy to grow in any well-drained garden soil in full sun. Propagation is by division in early spring or by seeds sown as soon as ripe. Space plants about 30 cm. apart.

Silphium perfoliatum L. (Carpenter Weed, Compass Plant, Cup Plant). Hardy in all zones; perennial to 2.5 m. tall.
DESCRIPTION: Nearly glabrous perennial, native in open fields and open woods from South Dakota to Ontario, south to Oklahoma and Georgia; **stems** 4-angled; **leaves** connate-perfoliate with triangular to ovate blades, to 35 cm. long, coarsely dentate; **flower** heads to 7.5 cm. across, in corymbs, from July to September; ray flowers yellow.
USE AND CULTURE: The same as for **Silphium laciniatum**.

Sisyrinchium L. (Blue-eyed Grass)
IRIDACEAE (Iris Family)
DESCRIPTION: About 75 species of clump-forming herbs, native in sunny locations in the western hemisphere; **rhizomes** very short or none; **leaves** grasslike, linear or cylindrical; **flowers** blue, yellow, or white, in terminal, solitary or fascicled clusters, each cluster subtended by a spathe; perianth rotate or campanulate with 6 segments; stamens 3 with filaments united at the base; style branches 3; **fruit** a 3-valved capsule.

Sisyrinchium albidum Raf. (White Blue-eyed Grass). Hardy in all zones; perennial to 45 cm. tall.
DESCRIPTION: Perennial, native in dry, sandy soils from North Dakota to New York, south to Oklahoma and Georgia; **stems** flattened, slightly winged; **leaves** flat, persisting

Sisyrinchium angustifolium (Blue-eyed Grass).

Photograph: Mr. Arvid Lund.

Sisyrinchium campestre. Flowering in the

McKnight Prairie of Carleton College, Northfield, Minnesota.

Photograph: Bonnie E. Harper Lore.

or withering; **flowers** white or pale violet, to 1.25 cm. across, in May and June; spathe sessile, subtended by an erect leaflike bract.

USE AND CULTURE: Plant in rock gardens, flower borders, and prairie gardens. Plants grow best in a sunny location and in a well-drained sandy loam soil. Propagation is by division or by seeds sown as soon as ripe. Space plants about 20 cm. apart.

Sisyrinchium angustifolium Mill. (Blue-eyed Grass). Hardy in all zones; perennial to 30 cm. tall.
DESCRIPTION: Perennial, native in sunny meadows from North Dakota to New-foundland, south to Texas and Florida; **stems** forked, usually winged; **leaves** mostly basal, grasslike, deep green; **flowers** pale blue or violet, to 1.25 cm. across, from May to July; spathes on stout, flattened, or winged peduncles.
USE AND CULTURE: The same as for **Sisyrinchium albidum**

Sisyrinchium campestre Bickn. Hardy in all zones; perennial to 50 cm. tall.
DESCRIPTION: Perennial, native in dry prairies, meadows, and open woods from Manitoba to Wisconsin, south to Texas and Louisiana; **stems** tufted, slender, flat, winged, glaucous; **leaves** grasslike, to 30 cm. long; **flowers** light blue to white, about 1.25 cm. across, from April to June; spathes sessile, solitary, half as long as the subtending bract.
USE AND CULTURE: The same as for **Sisyrinchium albidum**.

Sisyrinchium montanum Greene. Hardy in all zones; perennial to 60 cm. tall.
DESCRIPTION: Perennial, native in meadows and along lake shores from British Columbia to Quebec, south to Colorado and North Carolina; **stems** simple, flattened, pale green; **leaves** grasslike, shorter than the stem; **flowers** blue-violet on erect pedicels, from May to July; spathes sessile.
USE AND CULTURE: The same as for **Sisyrinchium albidum**.

Solidago L. (Goldenrod)
COMPOSITAE (Sunflower Family)
Aster Tribe
DESCRIPTION: About 150 species of perennial herbs, native mostly in North America, a few in Europe, Asia, and South America; **stems** emerging from rhizomes or a crown; **leaves** alternate, simple, entire or dentate; **flower** heads yellow, radiate, small, often clustered in racemes, corymbs, and panicles; involucral bracts in few rows; involucre nearly cylindrical to campanulate; receptacle flat or convex, naked, pitted; ray flowers pistillate; disc flowers perfect; **fruit** an angled or nearly cylindrical achene; pappus of many capillary bristles.

Solidago canadensis (Canada Goldenrod).

Photograph: Dr. Anne M. Hanchek.

Solidago canadensis L. (Canada Goldenrod). Hardy in all zones; perennial to 1.5 m. tall.
DESCRIPTION: Rhizomatous perennial, native in moist soil in open woods and meadows from Manitoba to Newfoundland, south to Colorado and Virginia; **leaves** numerous, lanceolate-linear to elliptic-lanceolate, to 15 cm. long attenuate, 3-veined, glabrous or scabrous above, pubescent beneath, sharply serrate, losing lower leaves early; **flower** heads in panicles, from July to October.
USE AND CULTURE: Plant in flower borders or prairie gardens. Plants are easy to grow in most soils in full sun. Propagation is by division. Replant only the outer divisions that have young rhizomes. Space plants about 30 cm. apart. Plants often self sow and can spread in fertile soils. This species is but one of many that can be planted. The goldenrods are falsely accused of causing hayfever. Actually, the pollen is sticky and spread by insects. The fluffy panicles possibly can catch ragweed pollen and, when used in flower arrangements, could cause hayfever sufferers to sneeze. In Europe, goldenrods are popular garden flowers.

Sorghastrum Nash. (Indian Grass)
GRAMINEAE (Grass Family)
DESCRIPTION: About 15 species of perennial grasses, native in America and Africa; **leaves** flat with auricled sheaths; **flowers** in narrow panicles made up of 1- to few-jointed racemes; spikelets with one perfect terminal floret above a sterile one; glumes leathery, brown or yellow, the first hairy with the edges overlapping the second; **fruit** a caryopsis.

Sorghastrum avenaceum (Michx.) Nash. (Indian Grass, Wood Grass). Hardy in all zones; perennial to 1.5 m. tall.
DESCRIPTION: Rhizomatous perennial, native in moist or dry prairies or open woods from Manitoba to Quebec, south to Arizona and Florida; **rhizomes** short, scaly; **leaves** narrow, to 1 cm. wide; **flowers** yellow, in dense panicles to 30 cm. long; spikelets to 8 mm. long, lanceolate, hirsute, with bent awns.
USE AND CULTURE: Plant in prairie gardens. Plants are easy to grow in any fertile soil. Propagation is by division of rhizomes or by seeds sown as soon as ripe or in the spring.

Sorghastrum nutans - see **Sorghastrum avenaceum**.

Sphaeralcea St.-Hil. (False Mallow, Globe Mallow)
MALVACEAE (Mallow Family)
DESCRIPTION: About 50 species of annual or perennial herbs or small shrubs, native in dry soils in North and South America; **leaves** linear-lanceolate to orbicular, scarcely 3-lobed to deeply palmately parted or divided, the lobes serrate; **flowers** yellow, orange, lavender, or white, in racemes or panicles; involucral bracts 3, usually early deciduous; corolla cuplike; stamens united in a tubular column; style branches 10 to 20; **fruit** a schizocarp with 10 to 20 mericarps in a single whorl.

Sphaeralcea coccinea (Pursh.) Rydb. (Prairie Mallow, Red False Mallow). Hardy in all zones; perennial to 60 cm. tall.
DESCRIPTION: A decumbent perennial with gray-white pubescence, native in dry prairies from Manitoba, south to Arizona and Texas; root a tap root; **leaves** pedately parted or divided, usually broader than long; **flowers** orange to red, in short racemes, in April and May; involucral bracts absent; **mericarps** 10 or 11, suborbicular.
USE AND CULTURE: Plant in flower borders or prairie gardens. Plants require a well-drained soil and full sun. Due to the tap root, plants are difficult to transplant. Sow seeds as soon as ripe where plants are to grow. Thin plants to about 20 cm. apart.

Tephrosia Pers. (Hoary Pea)
LEGUMINOSAE (Pea Family)
DESCRIPTION: About 400 species of herbs and shrubs, native mostly in the tropics or subtropics; **leaves** alternate, odd-pinnate, **flowers** pealike, in racemes; standard

Solidago canadensis (Canada Goldenrod). Taken along a roadside in Northfield, Minnesota.

Photograph: Bonnie E. Harper Lore.

silky-hairy outside; uppermost stamen separate to the middle or base; **fruit** a flat dehiscent legume.

Tephrosia virginiana (L.) Pers. (Catgut, Goat's Rue, Rabbit's Pea). Hardy in all zones; perennial to 60 cm. tall.
DESCRIPTION: Silky-pubescent perennial, native in sandy prairies from South Dakota to Maine, south to New Mexico and Florida; **leaflets** linear-oblong, to linear-elliptic, in 8-14 pairs, nearly glabrous above with white, silky pubescence beneath; **flowers** pealike, yellow or pinkish-purple, to 2 cm. long in dense terminal racemes, in May; **legumes** to 5 cm. long.
USE AND CULTURE: Plant in prairie gardens. Plants prefer a sandy soil in full sun. Propagation is by direct seeding as soon as the seeds are ripe.

Thermopsis R. Br. (False Lupine, Golden Banner, Golden Pea)
LEGUMINOSAE (Pea Family)
DESCRIPTION: About 20 species of perennial herbs, native in well-drained soils in North America and northeastern Asia; **leaves** palmately compound with 3 leaflets; stipules leaflike; **flowers** pealike, in racemes; stamens 10, separate; **fruit** a narrow flat legume.

Thermopsis caroliniana M.A. Curtis. (Aaron's Rod, Carolina Lupine). Hardy in all zones; perennial to 1 m. tall.
DESCRIPTION: Sparsely branched perennial, native in open woods from Virginia to Georgia; **leaflets** ovate to obovate, to 7.5 cm. long, pubescent and glaucous on under surface; **flowers** yellow, in terminal spikes, in June and July; **legumes** erect, densely hairy, to 5 cm. long.
USE AND CULTURE: Plant in flower borders or in prairie gardens. Plants require a well-drained soil of low fertility. Propagation is by division of dormant plants or by seeds sown as soon as ripe. Seedlings should be transplanted in early spring. Space plants 45 cm. apart. This southern species is hardy and widely planted in our area.

Townsendia Hook. (Easter Daisy)
COMPOSITAE (Sunflower Family)
Aster Tribe.
DESCRIPTION: About 20 species of annual, biennial, or perennial herbs, native mostly in western North America; **leaves** alternate, spatulate to linear, entire; **flower** heads radiate, solitary, sessile or peduncled, many-flowered; ray flowers white, pink, or purple; disc flowers yellow; **fruit** a glabrate or pubescent achene with forked hairs; pappus of bristles.

Townsendia exscapa (Richardson) T.C. Porter. (Stemless Easter Daisy). Hardy in all zones; perennial to 7.5 cm. tall.
DESCRIPTION: Cespitose perennial, native on plains and hills from Manitoba south to Utah and Oklahoma; **leaves** narrowly oblanceolate, to 5 cm. long, strigose-pubescent; **flower** heads sessile or on short peduncles, to 5 cm. across; ray flowers white or pink.

Thermopsis caroliniana (Carolina Lupine).

Photograph: Merv Eisel.

Verbena canadensis (Rose Verbena). In bloom on Padre Island National Seashore in Texas in February 1975.

USE AND CULTURE: Plant in rock gardens or in prairie gardens. Plants require a well-drained soil. Propagation is by seeds sown as soon as ripe or in the spring. Space seedlings about 20 cm. apart.

Verbena L. (Verbena, Vervain)
VERBENACEAE (Verbena Family)
DESCRIPTION: About 200 species of hairy, erect or decumbent, annual or perennial herbs, native in open sunny fields mostly in the tropics and subtropics of the Americas but a few species native in the north; **stems** often 4-angled; **leaves** usually opposite, rarely whorled or alternate, dentate, parted, or dissected, rarely entire; **flowers** of various colors, in spikes or panicles, mostly bracted; calyx 5-toothed, 5-ribbed; corolla salverform or funnelform, sometimes 2-lipped; stamens 4, rarely 2; **fruits** are dry, separating into 4 nutlets at maturity and enclosed by the calyx.

Verbena canadensis (L.) Britt. (Clump Verbena, Creeping Vervain, Rose Verbena, Rose Vervain). Hardy in all zones; perennial to 45 cm. tall.
DESCRIPTION: Branching perennial with creeping stems, native in sandy or rocky prairies from Iowa to Pennsylvania, south to Mexico and Florida, naturalized in Minnesota; **leaves** ovate to ovate-oblong, to 10 cm. long, truncate or broadly cuneate at base, toothed or 3-cleft; **flowers** reddish-purple, lilac, rose, or white, to 1.5 cm. across, in elongated spikes; bracts short.
USE AND CULTURE: Plant as a ground cover in prairie gardens or on slopes. Plants prefer a sandy soil of low fertility. Propagation is by division, cuttings, or seeds. Space plants 60 cm. apart. Plant in the spring for best results. Seedlings will bloom the second year. Other species of native verbenas might be planted, but most are weedy.

Vernonia Schreb. (Ironweed)
COMPOSITAE (Sunflower Family)
Vernonia Tribe
DESCRIPTION: About 1000 species of perennial herbs, subshrubs, shrubs, or rarely trees or woody climbers, native in moist, rich soils in warmer parts of North and South America, Asia, Africa, and Australia; **leaves** alternate, rarely opposite; **flower** heads solitary or in corymbs or panicled cymes; involucre cylindrical, globose, urceolate, campanulate, or turbinate; receptacle flat or convex, naked, pitted; flowers all tubular, perfect; **fruit** a columnar or turbinate, ribbed achene; pappus consisting of 2 rows of bristles.

Vernonia altissima Nutt. (Tall Ironweed). Hardy in all zones; perennial to 2 m. tall.
DESCRIPTION: Perennial, native in lowlands and banks of lakes and streams from Nebraska to New York, south to Louisiana and Georgia; **stems** glabrous, leafy; **leaves** lanceolate to lanceolate-oblong or lanceolate-ovate, to 25 cm. long, long acuminate, glabrous above, thinly hairy below, entire to irregularly serrate; **flower** heads to 1 cm. across in loose cymes; flowers, purple from August to October.
USE AND CULTURE: Plant toward the back of flower borders or plant in prairie gardens. Plants can be grown in most garden soils if kept moist. Propagation is mainly by division in fall or spring. Seedlings take 4 years to bloom.

Vernonia fasciculata Michx. (Western Ironweed). Hardy in all zones; perennial to 2 m. tall.
DESCRIPTION: Perennial, native in low, wet places and in prairies from North Dakota to Ohio, south to Texas and Missouri; **leaves** linear to oblong-lanceolate, acuminate, spinulose-dentate; **flower** heads campanulate in dense cymes; flowers purple, from July to September; **achenes** glabrous, to 3 mm. long.
USE AND CULTURE: The same as for **Vernonia altissima**.

Veronicastrum Fabr. (Culver's-physic, Culver's-root)
SCROPHULARIACEAE (Figwort Family)
DESCRIPTION: Two species of tall, perennial herbs, native in eastern North America and eastern Asia; **leaves** whorled, simple; **flowers** tubular, nearly regular, in spikes;

Vernonia fasciculata (Western Ironweed).

Flowering in the Blackdog Preserve in the

Minnesota River Valley in Burnsville, Minnesota.

Photograph: Bonnie E. Harper Lore.

calyx deeply 4- to 5-parted, the 2 lobes of the lower lip longer than the 2 or 3 lobes of the upper lip; corolla tubular with the lobes shorter than the tube; stamens 2, inserted below the middle of the corolla tube; anther sacs parallel, exserted beyond the corolla tube; **fruit** a capsule opening by 4 short terminal slits.

Veronicastrum virginicum (L.) Farw. (Blackroot, Bowman's-root, Culver's-physic, Culver's-root). Hardy in all zones; perennial to 2 m. tall.
DESCRIPTION: Tall perennial, native in open woods and in prairies from Manitoba to Massachusetts, south to Texas and Florida; **leaves** in whorls of 5, lanceolate to oblong-lanceolate, to 15 cm. long, dentate; **flowers** small, pale blue or white, in tapering terminal racemes to 20 cm. long, from June to September.
USE AND CULTURE: Plant toward the back of flower borders, in prairie gardens, or at the edges of woods. Plants thrive in any good garden soil either in full sun or in partial shade. Propagation is by division or by seeds. Plants can be divided either in the fall or early in the spring. Seeds should be sown as soon as ripe. Space plants 45 cm. apart.

Yucca L. (Yucca)
AGAVACEAE (Agave Family)
DESCRIPTION: About 40 species of stemless or erect woody plants, native in well-drained soils in full sun mostly in warmer parts of North America; **leaves** stiff, sword-shaped or rarely stilettolike; **flowers** white or violet, in racemes or panicles; perianth cup- or saucer-shaped with 6 segments that are separate or partly united; stamens 6; ovary superior, 3-celled; **fruit** a fleshy, indehiscent capsule or sometimes a dry, dehiscent capsule.

Yucca glauca Nutt. ex J. Fraser. (Soapweed, Soapwell). Hardy in all zones; shrub to 1 m. tall.
DESCRIPTION: Shrubs with short, prostrate stems, native in sandy, prairie soils from Montana to South Dakota, south to Arizona and Missouri; **leaves** linear, to 70 cm. long, pale green with white or greenish-white, thread-bearing margins; **flowers** greenish-cream, fragrant, in racemes to 1 m. long, from May to July; perianth segments 6, separate or briefly united at base, to 6 cm. long; style dark green, swollen; **capsules** dry and dehiscent, to 5 cm. long.

Veronicastrum virginicum (Culver's-root).

Photograph: Bonnie E. Harper Lore.

Yucca glauca (Soapweed).

Yucca glauca (Soapweed).

USE AND CULTURE: Plant in rock gardens or in prairie gardens. Plants grow best in a well-drained, sandy soil in full sun. Propagation is by seeds or root cuttings. It takes many years for seedlings to bloom.

Zizia W.D.J. Koch. (Golden Alexanders)
UMBELLIFERAE (Carrot Family)
DESCRIPTION: Four species of perennial herbs, native in moist meadows in North America; **leaves** simple to ternately compound; **flowers** small, yellow, in compound umbels; involucels of few, small bractlets; **fruit** a schizocarp.

Zizia aurea (L.) W.D.J. Koch. (Early Meadow Parsnip, Golden Alexanders). Hardy in all zones; perennial to 75 cm. tall.
DESCRIPTION: Rhizomatous perennial, native in moist meadows from Montana to Newfoundland, south to Texas and Florida; **leaves** ternately compound; leaflets ovate or ovate-lanceolate, dentate, to 5 cm. long; **flowers** yellow, in May and June.
USE AND CULTURE: Plant in moist soils in prairie gardens. Propagation is by seeds sown as soon as ripe or by division. Plants spread rapidly and should not be planted where space is limited.

Zizia aurea (Golden Alexanders). Flowering in the McKnight Prairie, Carleton College, Northfield, Minnesota.
Photograph: Bonnie E. Harper Lore.

FERNS

Matteuccia pensylvanica (Ostrich Fern)

Photograph: Merv Eisel.

Ferns for Shade

Adiantum species
Asplenium species
Athyrium filix-femina
Camptosorus rhizophyllus
Cystopteris species
Dryopteris species
Gymnocarpium dryopteris
Polystichum species
Thelypteris species

Ferns that Are Sun-Tolerant

Athyrium filix-femina
Dennstaedtia punctilobula
Osmunda species
Pellaea atropurpurea
Pteridium aquilinum

Ferns that Are Ground Covers
(usually spread by rhizomes or stolons)

Dennstaedtia species
Gymnocarpium dryopteris
Onoclea sensibilis
Thelypteris phegopteris

Ferns that Tolerate Wet Soils

Dryopteris cristata
Onoclea sensibilis
Osmunda regalis var. spectabilis
Thelypteris palustris

Ferns that Tolerate Drier Soils

Dennstaedtia punctilobula
Pteridium aquilinum

Adiantum L. (Maidenhair Fern).
POLYPODIACEAE (Polypody Family)
DESCRIPTION: About 200 species of dainty ferns, native in moist woods mostly in the tropics with a few in temperate parts of North America; **leaves** thin, delicate, simple or divided into fan-shaped pinnules; petioles slender, shiny, black or purple; **sori** borne at the edges of the pinnules, usually round or oblong, covered by a marginal flap of the pinnule.

Adiantum capillus-veneris L. (Southern Maidenhair, Venus-hair Fern, Dudder Grass). Hardy in sheltered areas in zone 4; fern to 50 cm. tall.
DESCRIPTION: A rhizomatous fern, native on moist, calcareous rocks and along streams from South Dakota to Kentucky, south to the tropics; **rhizomes** slender, covered with dark brown scales; **leaves** thin, 2- to 3-pinnate, ovate to triangular, to 60 cm. long; pinnules to 2.5 cm. wide; stipes equalling the blades in length; **sori** oblong, marginal.

Adiantum pedatum (Maidenhair Fern).

In June 1979 at the Arboretum.

USE AND CULTURE: Ground cover in moist woods. Plant only in sheltered, moist woods on calcareous soil in southern parts of the region. Propagation is by division and by spores. Often found growing under benches in greenhouses.

Adiantum pedatum L. (Maidenhair Fern, American Maidenhair, Five-finger Fern). Hardy in all zones; fern to 45 cm. tall.
DESCRIPTION: A delicate, rhizomatous fern, native in rich, moist woods from Alaska to Quebec, south to California and Georgia; **rhizomes** slender, to 5 mm. in diameter, with brown lance-linear scales; **leaves** nearly orbicular, to 45 cm. across, forked into two spreading branches, each branch bearing 4 to 12 or more narrow 1-pinnate pinnae; pinnules nearly rectangular; petioles smooth, black to purple-brown, longer than the leaf blade; **sori** marginal.
USE AND CULTURE: An excellent plant in a shady portion of a rock garden or as a ground cover in moist, shaded woods. Plant only in a woodsy soil rich in organic matter in shade. Soil must be kept moist at all times. Propagation is by division and by spores.

Asplenium L. (Spleenwort)
POLYPODIACEAE (Polypody Family)
DESCRIPTION: About 700 species of ferns, usually native on calcareous rocks, but also in woods and along moist stream banks, widely distributed; **leaves** usually evergreen, simple, deeply cut, or compound; **sori** oblong or linear, straight or s-shaped, on the veinlets; **indusia** attached along one side, opening toward the apex of the pinnule.

Asplenium platyneuron (L.) Oakes. (Ebony Spleenwort). Hardy in all zones; perennial to 45 cm. tall.
DESCRIPTION: Evergreen fern, native in moist woods, usually on rocks in near neutral soil from Ontario to Quebec, south to Texas and Florida; **leaves** dimorphic, to 40 cm. long, 1-pinnate; pinnae many, oblong-linear, auricled on apical margin, fertile leaves form first, sterile leaves are broader and shorter; petioles purplish-brown; **sori** elongate in a herringbone pattern on opposite sides of the midrib.
USE AND CULTURE: Plant in shaded rock gardens or in wild flower gardens. This fern requires a soil that is near neutral and rich in organic matter. It will tolerate short dry periods. Propagation is by spores. The first year from spores, the leaves spread flat on the ground, while during the second year, they grow upright.

Asplenium trichomanes L. (Maidenhair Spleenwort). Hardy in all zones; fern to 20 cm. tall.
DESCRIPTION: Evergreen fern, native in moist woods and on calcareous rocks, circumboreal, from Alaska to Nova Scotia, south to Arizona and Georgia in North America; **leaves** dimorphic, clustered, to 20 cm. long, 1-pinnate; pinnae round to oblong, cuneate to truncate at base, slightly dentate; sterile leaves appear first and spread horizontally, fertile leaves appear later and are more upright.
USE AND CULTURE: Same as for **Asplenium platyneuron**. It will tolerate short dry periods. This Asplenium needs good drainage.

Athyrium Roth. (Lady Fern)
POLYPODIACEAE (Polypody Family)
DESCRIPTION: About 25 species of ferns native in moist woods, widely distributed in the tropics, a few in north temperate regions; **rhizomes** thick, creeping to suberect; **leaves** pinnate to 3-pinnate, sparingly scaly; veins free, simple or forked, ending in the marginal teeth; **sori** mostly horseshoe-shaped, covered with a lateral indusia.

Athyrium filix-femina (L.) Roth. (Lady Fern). Hardy in all zones; perennial to 90 cm. tall.
DESCRIPTION: Rhizomatous ferns, native in moist woods, meadows, and stream banks, widespread in the northern hemisphere; **leaves** bright green, 2-pinnate, to 90 cm. long; pinnae deeply cut or dentate; **sori** moon-shaped to horseshoe-shaped.
USE AND CULTURE: Plant in wild flower garden. This is one of the easiest ferns to grow, although it thrives best in a woodsy soil high in organic matter. Plant with rhizomes just beneath the surface. Plants multiply rapidly and may require thinning.

Athyrium pycnocarpon - see **Diplazium pycnocarpon**.

Athyrium thelypteroides - see **Diplazium acrostichoides**.

Botrychium Swartz. (Grape Fern, Moonwort)
OPHIOGLOSSACEAE (Adder's-tongue Family)
DESCRIPTION: About 40 species of fleshy ferns, native in cool, moist woods in temperate regions of both hemispheres; **rhizomes** short, each bearing a single leaf; **leaves** with 1- to 3-pinnate sterile blades and an erect, paniclelike fertile blade with several sporangia resembling a cluster of grapes.

Botrychium virginianum (L.) Swartz. (Rattlesnake Fern). Hardy in all zones; fern to 75 cm. tall.
DESCRIPTION: Succulent fern, native in cool, moist woods, circumboreal, from British Columbia to Newfoundland, south to Mexico and Florida; **leaves** deciduous; sterile blades sessile, to 75 cm. tall, broadly triangular, ternately compound; pinnules acutely dentate.
USE AND CULTURE: Plant in wild flower gardens. This fern requires a rich, loose, moist woodland soil that is neutral to slightly acid. Slugs can be a problem so be ready with slug baits. Propagation is by division in early spring or by spores. This is a difficult fern to grow unless you have ideal conditions.

Camptosorus Link. (Walking Fern, Walking Leaf)
POLYPODIACEAE (Polypody Family)
DESCRIPTION: Two species of small, evergreen ferns, native mostly on limestone rocks along streams in North America and northern Asia; **stem** a short, erect, scaly rhizome; **leaves** simple, long-pointed, rooting at the tip where the tip touches the ground; **sori** linear or oblong scattered on veins on the under surface of the leaves; **indusia** scarious, entire, attached on either or both sides of the vein.

Camptosorus rhizophyllus (L.) Link. (Walking Fern, Walking Leaf). Hardy in zone 4; fern to 10 cm. tall.
DESCRIPTION: Evergreen fern, native on calcareous rocks in deep shade from Minnesota to Quebec, south to Oklahoma and Georgia; **leaves** simple, lanceolate, to 22 cm. long, cordate at base, tapering to a long filiform tip; **sori** irregularly arranged along the veins on the under surface of leaves.
USE AND CULTURE: Plant as a low growing ground cover on calcareous rocks in deep shade. Plants require deep shade and a constant supply of moisture. Rocks should be covered with organic matter. Plants root at the tips of the leaves and this is the chief method of propagation. Plants can also be grown from spores. Slugs are fond of this fern so slug baits may be needed.

Cheilanthes Swartz. (Lip Fern)
POLYPODIACEAE (Polypody Family)

Camptosorus rhizophyllus (Walking Fern).

Cystopteris bulbifera. At Queen's Bluff, Winona, Minnesota in May 1978.

DESCRIPTION: About 180 species of small, often hairy, woolly, or scaly ferns native in dry or rocky situations in temperate and tropical regions; **leaves** 1- to 3-pinnate; **sori** produced at the ends of veins, with margins of pinnules folded back to cover them.

Cheilanthes feei T. Moore. (Fee's Lip Fern, Slender Lip Fern). Hardy in all zones; perennial to 30 cm. tall.
DESCRIPTION: Tufted ferns, native on calcareous bluffs and rocks from British Columbia to Wisconsin, south to California and Texas; **leaves** linear-oblong to ovate, 2- to 3-pinnate, hairy above, densely woolly beneath, without scales, to 30 cm. long.
USE AND CULTURE: Plant in rock gardens. Plant in neutral soil near calcareous rocks. Propagation is by division or by spores.

Cystopteris Bernh. (Bladder Fern)
POLYPODIACEAE (Polypody Family)
DESCRIPTION: About 18 species of rock ferns with creeping, scaly rhizomes, native in moist rocky places in shade in the North Temperate Zone; **leaves** delicate, 2- to 4-pinnate; **sori** mostly round, on veins; **indusia** hood-shaped, reflexed, withering early.

Cystopteris bulbifera (L.) Bernh. (Berry Bladder Fern, Bulblet Bladder Fern, Bulblet Fern). Hardy in all zones; perennial to 75 cm. tall.
DESCRIPTION: Delicate fern, native in moist, rocky woods and along streams, often on shaded side of limestone cliffs from Manitoba to Newfoundland, south to Arizona and Georgia; **leaves** linear-lanceolate, 2- to 3-pinnate, to 75 cm. long, tapering toward the tip, bearing green bulblets on lower surfaces; petioles shorter than the blade.
USE AND CULTURE: Plant in moist, shady places in wild flower gardens or in a shady nook in the rock garden. The soil should be high in organic matter and close to neutral. Propagation is by bulblets. These should be just barely covered and kept moist until new plants form.

Cystopteris fragilis (L.) Bernh. (Brittle Fern, Fragile Bladder Fern, Fragile Fern). Hardy in all zones; perennial to 30 cm. tall.
DESCRIPTION: Fragile fern, native in moist, wooded slopes, circumboreal, from Alaska to Labrador, south to California and Pennsylvania in North America; **leaves** ovate-oblong, 2- to 3-pinnate, to 30 cm. long; petioles shorter than the blade; **sori** covered by pale-colored indusia.
USE AND CULTURE: Same as for **Cystopteris bulbifera**.

Dennstaedtia Bernh. (Cup Fern, Hay-scented Fern)
POLYPODIACEAE (Polypody Family)
DESCRIPTION: About 70 species of large or medium-sized ferns, native in open woods and clearings, mostly in the tropics and subtropics, one only native in the north; **rhizomes** creeping, hairy; **leaves** 1- to 3-pinnate; **sori** marginal; **indusia** cup-shaped, open at the top.

Dennstaedtia punctilobula (Hay-scented Fern).

Photograph: Dr. Anne M. Hanchek.

Dennstaedtia punctilobula (Michx.) T. Moore. (Boulder Fern, Hay-scented Fern). Hardy in all zones; perennial to 75 cm. tall.
DESCRIPTION: Rhizomatous, clump-forming fern, native in open woods and clearings, usually in poor, rocky soil from Minnesota to Newfoundland, south to Alabama and Georgia; **rhizomes** slender forming large clumps; **leaves** narrowly triangular to lanceolate, 2-pinnate-pinnatifid, the rachis with gland-tipped hairs; **sori** as described under the genus.
USE AND CULTURE: Plant in wild flower gardens or as a ground cover on slopes. Plants grow best in a slightly acid, moist, woodland soil that is high in organic matter. Propagation is usually by division. Space divisions 30 cm. apart. Slugs can be a problem on this species.

Diplazium Swartz. (Glade Fern, Spleenwort)
POLYPODIACEAE (Polypody Family)
DESCRIPTION: Over 300 species of ferns, native in moist woods, mostly in the tropics or warm temperate regions, two native in the north; **leaves** simple or pinnately compound; **sori** and **indusia** elongate, often double and extending along both sides of the veins.

Diplazium acrostichoides (Swartz) Butters. (Silvery Glade Fern, Silvery Spleenwort). Hardy in all zones; perennial to 90 cm. tall.
DESCRIPTION: Rhizomatous fern, native in rich, moist woods from Ontario to New Brunswick, south to Louisiana and Georgia; **rhizomes** short-creeping; **leaves** tapering at both ends, deeply 2-pinnatifid, to 90 cm. long; pinnae dentate; petioles long, straw-colored; **sori** silvery.
USE AND CULTURE: Plant in wild flower gardens. Plants require a deep, moist soil high in decomposed leaf mold. Propagation is by division or spores.
Diplazium pycnocarpon (K. Spreng.) Broun. (Glade Fern, Narrow-leaved Spleenwort, Silvery Spleenwort). Hardy in all zones; perennial to 75 cm. tall.
DESCRIPTION: Rhizomatous fern, native in cool, moist woods and on hummocks in bogs; **leaves** 1-pinnate, to 75 cm. long; pinnae nearly entire, to 12 cm. long; **sori** elongated with **indusia** attached to veins on one side.
USE AND CULTURE: Sames as for **Diplazium acrostichoides**.

Dryopteris Adans. (Shield Fern, Wood Fern)
POLYPODIACEAE (Polypody Fern)
DESCRIPTION: About 150 species of terrestrial ferns, native in moist woods in temperate and tropical regions; **leaves** 1-pinnate-pinnatifid to compound, glabrous; **sori** round, on under surface; **indusia** reniform.

Dryopteris austriaca (Jacq.) Woyn. (Shield Fern). Hardy in all zones; perennial to 1 m. tall.
DESCRIPTION: Perennial fern, native in swamps, bogs, and rich, moist woods in Europe, Asia, and North America; **leaves** almost evergreen, 2- to 3-pinnate-pinnatifid, abruptly acuminate; pinnules oblong, obtuse, spinulose-toothed; **indusia** glandular.

Dryopteris austriaca var. spinulosa.

Photograph: Dr. Anne M. Hanchek.

USE AND CULTURE: Plant in moist woodland wild flower gardens. The plants require a sheltered, shady location and a soil that is high in organic matter. Propagation is by division in early spring just as new growth is starting and by spores. Requires more water than other species.

VARIETIES: var. **intermedia** (Muhlenb.) C.V. Mort. (Intermediate Shield Fern). Similar to var. **spinulosa** except petioles and **indusia** are glandular.

  var. **spinulosa** (O.F. Mull.) Fiori (Fancy Fern, Florist's Fern, Spinulose Wood Fern). **Leaves** and **indusia** glandless, 2-pinnate-pinnatifid.

Dryopteris clintoniana - see **Dryopteris cristata** var. **clintoniana**

Dryopteris cristata (L.) A. Gray. (Crested Fern, Crested Wood Fern). Hardy in all zones; perennial to 75 cm. tall.

DESCRIPTION: Rhizomatous fern, native in moist woods and on hummocks in bogs from Saskatchewan to Newfoundland, south to Arkansas and North Carolina, also in Europe; **rhizomes** short; **leaves** nearly evergreen, to 75 cm. long, 2-pinnatifid with segments finely dentate.

USE AND CULTURE: Same as for **Dryopteris austriaca**.

VARIETIES: var. **clintoniana** (D.C.Eat.) Underw. (Clinton's Wood Fern). **Leaves** broader than in the species. Distribution is about the same as the species.

Dryopteris filix-mas (L.) Schott. (Male Fern). Hardy in all zones; perennial to 90 cm. tall.

DESCRIPTION: Rhizomatous fern, native in moist woods, rocky shaded hillsides, mostly in calcareous soils, circumboreal in North America and Europe, south to California and Texas; **leaves** deciduous, 2-pinnate, with pinnules dentate or cut.

USE AND CULTURE: Same as for **Dryopteris austriaca**.

Dryopteris goldiana (Hook.) A.Gray. (Goldie's Fern, Goldie's Wood Fern). Hardy in all zones; perennial to 1.2 m. tall.

DESCRIPTION: Large fern, native in moist woods from Minnesota to New Brunswick, south to Iowa and South Carolina; **leaves** nearly evergreen, from large crown, 1.2 m. long and 45 cm. wide, pinnate-pinnatifid; pinnae dentate, dark green, chaffy at base.

USE AND CULTURE: The same as for **Dryopteris austriaca**. This is the largest of the wood ferns. The soil must be kept wet.

Dryopteris hexagonoptera - see **Thelypteris hexagonoptera**

Dryopteris intermedia - see **Dryopteris austriaca** var. **intermedia**

Dryopteris marginalis (L.) A. Gray. (Evergreen Wood Fern, Leather Wood Fern, Marginal Shield Fern). Hardy in all zones; perennial to 75 cm. tall.

DESCRIPTION: Evergreen fern, native in rich, rocky woods from Minnesota to Nova Scotia, south to Oklahoma and Alabama; **leaves** evergreen, dark bluish-green, leathery, 2-pinnate, to 75 cm. long, with scaly rachis; pinnules entire or lobed; **sori** marginal.

USE AND CULTURE: Same as for **Dropteris austriaca**. Fronds are used in flower arrangements.

Dryopteris noveboracensis - see **Thelypteris noveboracensis**

Dryopteris phegopteris - see **Thelypteris phegopteris**

Dryopteris spinulosa - see **Dryopteris austriaca** var. **spinulosa**

Dryopteris thelypteris - see **Thelypteris palustris**

Gymnocarpium Newm. (Oak Fern)
POLYPODIACEAE (Polypody Family)
DESCRIPTION: Two species of delicate ferns, native in moist woods in northern climates; **stems** are slender, creeping rhizomes; **leaves** triangular, to 25 cm. long, 2- to 3-pinnate-pinnatifid, with enlarged basal pinnae; stipes longer than the blade; **sori** submarginal, round or elongate, without indusia.

Gymnocarpium dryopteris (L.) Newm. (Oak Fern). Hardy in all zones; perennial to 25 cm. tall.
DESCRIPTION: Rhizomatous fern, native in cool woods and on talus slopes, circumboreal, south to Arizona and Virginia in North America; **leaves** triangular, to 25 cm. long and as wide, 2-pinnate; pinnae entire or wavy-toothed.
USE AND CULTURE: Plant in wild flower gardens as a ground cover. Oak ferns require a cool, moist, acid soil. Propagation is by division in early spring or by spores.

Gymnocarpium robertianum (Hoffm.) Newm. (Limestone Oak Fern, Limestone Polypody, Northern Oak Fern, Scented Oak Fern). Hardy in all zones; perennial to 20 cm. tall.
DESCRIPTION: Rhizomatous fern, native on limestone rocks, circumboreal, south to Minnesota and Pennsylvania in North America; **leaves** triangular, minutely glandular beneath, 2- to 3-pinnatifid.
USE AND CULTURE: The same as for **Gymnocarpium dryopteris** except the soil should be neutral.

Matteuccia Tod. (Ostrich Fern)
POLYPODIACEAE (Polypody Family)
DESCRIPTION: Three species of large ferns, native in moist woods in temperate parts of North America, Europe, and Asia; **leaves** dimorphic; sterile leaves longer than the fertile ones, forming a vaselike crown surrounding the fertile leaves, deeply 2-pinntifid; fertile leaves with pinnae margins contracted around the **sori**.

Matteuccia pensylvanica (Willd.) Raym. (Ostrich Fern). Hardy in all zones; perennial to 2 m. tall.

Matteuccia pensylvanica (Ostrich Fern).

In full growth and emerging in early spring.

Photographs: Dr. Anne M. Hanchek.

Osmunda cinnamomea (Cinnamon Fern).

At Swarthmore College (Pennsylvania) in 1976.

Photograph: Merv Eisel.

DESCRIPTION: Tall, vase-shaped fern, native in swamps and in moist woods from Alaska to Newfoundland, south to Missouri and Virginia; **leaves** oblong-lanceolate, gradually tapering toward the base, to 2 m. long; pinnules often revolute; petiole 4-angled, to 35 cm. long; fertile fronds brown, to 70 cm. tall, appearing in June or early July.

USE AND CULTURE: Plant in wild flower gardens or along the north side of walls. Plants require some shade and a soil that is kept constantly moist. Propagation is largely by division of clumps. Plant in early spring with the crown at soil level. Space plants about 45 cm. apart. Spores can also be used in propagation, but it takes several years to grow plants large enough to transplant. Fronds die down in late August.

Matteuccia struthiopteris var. **pensylvanica** - see **Matteuccia pensylvanica**.

Onoclea L. (Sensitive Fern)
POLYPODIACEAE (Polypody Family)
DESCRIPTION: One species of terrestrial fern, native in wet soils in the temperate regions of both hemispheres; **rhizomes** creeping and forking, without scales; **leaves** both fertile and sterile.

Onoclea sensibilis L. (Bead Fern, Sensitive Fern). Hardy in all zones; perennial to 1 m. tall.
DESCRIPTION: Rhizomatous ferns, native in moist pastures and swamps from South Dakota to Newfoundland, south to Texas and Florida; sterile **leaves** solitary and scattered, to 1 m. long, deeply pinnatifid, with wavy-margined pinnae; fertile leaves to 75 cm. long, dark brown or black at maturity, 2-pinnate, the pinnules rolled up into beadlike segments which open to shed the spores the following spring.
USE AND CULTURE: Plant in moist soil in wild flower gardens or near pools. This fern is easy to grow in any moist soil. This fern spreads so allow it ample space. The fronds are sensitive to late spring frosts. Propagation is primarily by division of the rhizomes.

Osmunda L. (Flowering Fern)
OSMUNDACEAE (Flowering Fern Family)
DESCRIPTION: About 10 species of attractive, deep-rooted ferns, native in moist woods in temperate and tropical regions of Asia and in North and South America; **leaves** in large crowns, 2-pinnate or pinnatifid; fertile pinnules much contracted, segregated on wholly fertile leaves or at the end or middle of otherwise sterile leaves.

Osmunda cinnamomea L. (Buckhorn, Cinnamon Fern, Fiddleheads). Hardy in all zones; perennial to 1.5 m. tall.
DESCRIPTION: Perennial fern, native in swamps, on stream banks, and other moist areas, usually in acid soil in Asia, South America, and from Minnesota to Labrador, south to New Mexico and Florida in North America; sterile **leaves** to 1.5 m. tall, rusty-tomentose when young, pinnate-pinnatifid, with entire margins and a tuft of hair at the base of each pinnae; petioles to 30 cm. long; fertile leaves in the center of the clumps, 2-pinnate, becoming cinnamon-brown as spores mature, then falling over in early summer.
USE AND CULTURE: Plant in wild flower gardens. Plants prefer a moist, acid soil in partial shade although the plant will grow in full sun. Propagation is by division in early spring and by spores. Young croziers are sometimes eaten like asparagus in early spring.

Osmunda claytoniana L. (Interrupted Fern). Hardy in all zones; perennial to 1.2 m. tall.
DESCRIPTION: Perennial fern, native in open moist woods and the margins of swamps, often along roadsides in slightly acid to neutral, usually sandy soils in Asia, and from Minnesota to Ontario, south to Arkansas and Georgia in North America; **leaves** to 1.2 m. long, pinnate-pinnatifid with nearly entire margins, with no tuft of hair at the base of pinnae; **sporangia** confined to the central pinnae on otherwise sterile leaves.

USE AND CULTURE: The same as for **Osmunda cinnamomea**. Plants thrive in soil that is near neutral in pH.

Osmunda regalis var. **spectabilis** (Willd.) A. Gray. (Flowering Fern, Royal Fern). Hardy in all zones; perennial to 2 m. tall.
DESCRIPTION: Tall fern, native in swamps and moist acid soils from Saskatchewan to Newfoundland, south to Texas and Florida; **leaves** 2-pinnate, to 2 m. long, with leaf margins finely dentate; fertile pinnae toward the apex of the leaf forming a flowerlike terminal panicle; rachis glabrous or nearly so.
USE AND CULTURE: The same as for **Osmunda cinnamomea**.

Pellaea Link. (Cliff Brake)
POLYPODIACEAE (Polypody Family)
DESCRIPTION: About 80 species of small, rock-loving ferns, native on limestone rocks in full sun or partial shade, mostly in temperate and cool tropical regions of North and South America; **leaves** often leathery, 1- to 4-pinnate; **sori** rounded or oblong, often in a marginal band, covered by the reflexed margins of the pinnules.

Pellaea atropurpurea (L.) Link. (Purple Cliff Brake). Hardy in zone 4; perennial to 30 cm. tall.
DESCRIPTION: Leathery fern, native on limestone cliffs from South Dakota to Vermont, south to Arizona and Florida; **leaves** tufted, leathery, 1- to 2-pinnate; pinnae to 5 cm. long; petioles dark purple, to 20 cm. long.
USE AND CULTURE: Plant in rock gardens. They grow best in pockets between limestone rocks that lead to moist, humus-rich soil. Once established, water during prolonged dry periods. Propagation is by division or by spores.

Osmunda regalis var. spectabilis (Royal Fern).
Photographed at Wisley, Surrey, England one of the gardens of the Royal Horticultural Society.
Osmunda claytoniana (Interrupted Fern).
Photographed at Port Wing, Wisconsin in May 1986.

Pellaea atropurpurea (Purple Cliff Brake).

Photographed near Columbia, Missouri in 1974.

Polypodium L. (Polypody)
POLYPODIACEAE (Polypody Family)
DESCRIPTION: A large genus of mostly tropical evergreen ferns; **rhizomes** creeping, branched; **leaves** attached to the rhizomes with a distinct joint, simple or compound; **sori** round, in 1 or more rows on each side of the midrib; indusium absent.

Polypodium virginianum L. (American Wall Fern, Rock Fern). Hardy in all zones; perennial to 25 cm. tall.
DESCRIPTION: Rhizomatous fern, native on cliffs, usually in rock crevices, from Alaska to Newfoundland, south to California and Georgia; **leaves** evergreen to 25 cm. long, usually deeply pinnatifid; pinnae mostly attenuate; **sori** nearly marginal, mixed with glandular hairs.
USE AND CULTURE: Plant in rock or wall gardens. Sometimes planted in wild flower gardens to cover decaying logs. Plants require a soil that is rich in organic matter and kept constantly moist. Propagation is by spores or more commonly by division of the rhizomes. Rhizomes must be firmly pushed into the rock crevices and kept moist until new growth starts.

Polystichum Roth. (Shield Fern)
POLYPODIACEAE (Polypody Family)
DESCRIPTION: About 120 species of terrestrial ferns, native in moist woods throughout the world; **rhizomes** erect; **leaves** elongate, usually pinnatifid to 2-pinnate, with sharp-toothed margins; **sori** round with peltate indusia.

Polystichum acrostichoides (Michx.) Schott. (Canker Brake, Christmas Fern, Dagger Fern, Sword Fern). Hardy in all zones; perennial to 60 cm. tall.
DESCRIPTION: Evergreen fern, native in moist woods and open thickets from Minnesota to Newfoundland, south to Mexico and Florida; **leaves** to 60 cm. long, 1-pinnate; pinnae linear-lanceolate, those bearing sori contracted, with apices bluntly acute to obtuse.
USE AND CULTURE: Plant in wild flower gardens. Especially effective when planted at the base of a stump. Plants are easy to grow in any soil that is rich in organic matter and moist. Propagation is by spores and by division. Set the crown about at soil level.

Polystichum braunii var. **purshii** Fern. (Pursh's Holly Fern). Hardy in all zones; perennial to 60 cm. tall.
DESCRIPTION: Evergreen fern, native in deep, moist woods and on rocky ledges, circumpolar, south to Wisconsin and Pennsylvania; **leaves** 2-pinnate; pinnules broadly oblong, rounded, spine-tipped, covered with hairlike scales.
USE AND CULTURE: The same as for **Polystichum acrostichoides**. Plants should be misted and kept moist in hot, dry weather.

Pteridium aquilinum (Bracken).

Frond photographed at the Arboretum.

Pteridium aquilinum (Bracken).

Photographed at the Arboretum.

Pteridium Gled. (Bracken, Brake)
POLYPODIACEAE (Polypody Family)
DESCRIPTION: A single worldwide species of terrestrial fern; **leaves** triangular, 3- to 4-pinnate; **sori** borne in a marginal line; indusia double.

Pteridium aquilinum (L.) Kuhn. (Brake, Pasture Brake, Hog-pasture Brake, Bracken). Hardy in all zones; perennial to 1.5 m. tall.
DESCRIPTION: Rhizomatous perennial, native worldwide in woods and open fields; **leaves** densely pubescent beneath, 3-pinnate; pinnules oblong or lanceolate; petioles to 1 m. long; **indusia** ciliate.
USE AND CULTURE: These ferns are sometimes planted in naturalistic plantings. Plants thrive in most soils. Propagation is usually by division. Plants can be quite invasive so it is best to limit the use of this fern to large areas.

Struthiopteris - see **Matteuccia**.

Thelypteris Schmidel. (Thelypteris)
POLYPODIACEAE (Polypody Family)
DESCRIPTION: About 500 species of ferns, native in moist woods or swamps mostly in the tropics, a few in the north; **leaves** mostly 1-pinnate-pinnatifid, frequently narrowed at base, with simple or branched hairs; scales on the stipes few; **sori** on the under surface of leaves; indusia absent or reniform.

Thelypteris noveboracensis (L.) Nieuwl. (New York Fern, Tapering Fern). Hardy in all zones; perennial to 60 cm. tall.
DESCRIPTION: Rhizomatous fern, native in mixed woods and at the edges of swamps from Minnesota to Newfoundland, south to Arkansas and Georgia; **leaves** pale green, 1-pinnate, to 60 cm. long; pinnae deeply pinnatifid.
USE AND CULTURE: Plant in wild flower gardens. Plants prefer a moist, humus-rich soil in shade. Plants will grow in the open if the soil is kept moist. Propagation is by division or by spores. Plants should be divided in early spring as soon as growth starts. Leaves tend to turn brown and die down towards fall.

Thelypteris palustris Schott. (Marsh Fern). Hardy in all zones; perennial to 75 cm. tall.
DESCRIPTION: Rhizomatous perennial, native in marshes and bogs around the world, common in eastern North America; **rhizomes** creeping; **leaves** 1-pinnate, to 75 cm. long and 15 cm. wide; pinnae deeply pinnatifid, with revolute margins; **sori** on under surface; indusia glandular-toothed or glandular-ciliate.
USE AND CULTURE: The same as for **Thelypteris noveboracensis**. Excellent fern for wet soils. Plants spread rapidly.

Thelypteris phegopteris (L.) Sloss. (Long Beech Fern, Narrow Beech Fern, Northern Beech Fern). Hardy in all zones; fern to 20 cm. tall.

DESCRIPTION: Rhizomatous fern, native in moist woods, circumpolar, south to Oregon and North Carolina in North America; **leaves** triangular, to 22 cm. long and 20 cm. wide, 1-pinnate; pinnae deeply pinnatifid with ultimate segments entire; **sori** without indusia.

USE AND CULTURE: The same as for **Thelypteris noveboracensis**. It is one of the easiest of ferns to grow.

Woodsia R. Br. (Woodsia)
POLYPODIACEAE (Polypody Family)
DESCRIPTION: About 40 species of small, rock-loving ferns; native in rock crevices, usually in full sun, in temperate regions; plants tufted with leaves growing from compact rhizomes; **leaves** pinnately divided with **sori** on veins; indusia attached beneath and splitting into starlike lobes or slender filiform segments.

Woodsia ilvensis (L.) R. Br. (Fragrant Woodsia, Rusty Cliff Fern, Rusty Woodsia). Hardy in all zones; perennial to 25 cm. tall.
DESCRIPTION: Tufted, perennial ferns, native in rock crevices in exposed sites from Alaska to Greenland, south to British Columbia and North Carolina, also in Europe and Asia; **leaves** lanceolate, to 25 cm. long and 4 cm. wide, 1-pinnate; pinnae pinnatifid into oblong, wavy-toothed pinnules; midrib with rusty chaff beneath; petioles jointed at base, stout, reddish-tan, chaffy.
USE AND CULTURE: Plant in rock or wall gardens. Plants prefer a neutral soil rich in organic matter. Propagation is by division or spores. Plants will survive prolonged dry periods.

Woodsia obtusa (K. Spreng.) Torr. (Blunt-lobed Cliff Fern, Blunt-lobed Woodsia, Common Woodsia, Large Woodsia). Hardy in all zones; perennial to 35 cm. tall.
DESCRIPTION: Tufted fern, native in rock crevices from Minnesota to Nova Scotia, south to Arizona and Florida; **leaves** elliptic-lanceolate to broadly lanceolate, to 35 cm. long and 10 cm. wide, pinnate-pinnatifid to 2-pinnate; pinnae dentate with tiny, white glands on both surfaces giving a grayish appearance; rachis covered with brown scales; **indusia** with broad lobes.
USE AND CULTURE: The same as for **Woodsia ilvensis**.

BOG AND WATER PLANTS

Nymphaea odorata (Fragrant Water Lily). In July 1984

at Wassau Lakes, Wisconsin.

Acorus L. (Sweet Flag)
ARACEAE (Arum Family)
Description: A small genus of two species of perennial herbs native in marshy places in the North Temperate Zone; **leaves** iris or grasslike, emerging from horizontal rhizomes; peduncle and spathe a continuous leaflike structure bearing a green spadix above the middle; **flowers** small, perfect, with a 6-parted perianth.

Acorus calamus L. (Sweet Flag, Calamus, Flagroot, Myrtle Flag). Hardy in all zones; perennial to 2 m. tall.
DESCRIPTION: An aromatic perennial herb, native in wet meadows, bogs, swamps, and shallow water from Oregon to Nova Scotia, south to Texas and Florida; **rhizomes** stout, pink inside, exuding a sweet and aromatic fragrance when cut or bruised; **leaves** irislike to 2 cm. wide with prominent midribs; **flowers** small, on a stout spadix, to 10 cm. long, from May to August.
USE AND CULTURE: Rhizomes are used for making candied sweet flag. Sometimes planted in bog gardens as they like wet locations in full sun. Propagation is by division of the rhizomes.

Alisma L. (Water Plantain)
ALISMATACEAE (Water Plantain Family)
DESCRIPTION: Six species of aquatic, mostly perennial herbs, widespread in the northern hemisphere; **leaves** basal, submerged in water, linear or with broad, cordate blades; petioles basally sheathing; **flowers** white, small, in whorls, in scapose panicles; petals 3, white or rose-tinted; stamens 6; **fruit** a head of achenes.

Alisma plantago-aquatica var. **americanum** Schult. ex Schult. (American Water Plantain, Mad-dog Weed). Hardy in all zones; perennial to 90 cm. tall.
DESCRIPTION: A cormous, aquatic perennial, native in shallow to deep water in swamps and shallow lakes from British Columbia to Nova Scotia, south to Mexico and Florida; **leaves** long-petioled, emersed, lanceolate or elliptic to broadly ovate, mostly to 15 cm. long; **flowers** white, to 1.25 cm. across, ephemeral; **fruiting** heads to 0.5 cm. across.
USE AND CULTURE: Planted in mud at the edge of ponds and streams. Of easy culture in shallow water. Propagation is by seeds or division of corms in fall.

Alisma triviale - see Alisma plantago-aquatica var. **americanum.**

Amorpha L. (Lead Plant, False Indigo)
LEGUMINOSAE (Pea Family)
DESCRIPTION: About 20 species of shrubs, native in North America; **leaves** alternate, odd-pinnate, deciduous, with many leaflets; **flowers** small, blue or white, in dense terminal, often panicled spikes; sepals 5; petals 1, the standard enclosing 10 exserted stamens; **fruit** a short, mostly glabrous, indehiscent legume.

Arethusa bulbosa (Swamp Pink). In flower

at Deer River, Minnesota in July 1971.

Amorpha fruticosa L. (False Indigo, Bastard Indigo, Indigo Bush). Hardy in all zones; shrub to 4 m. tall.
DESCRIPTION: Large shrub, native in moist woods and stream banks from Saskatchewan south to Mexico and Florida; **leaves** green with up to 25 leaflets; leaflets ovate or oblong, to 4 cm. long, obtuse at base, obtuse or slightly mucronate at apex; **flowers** dark purple to pale blue or white, in clustered spikes to 15 cm. long, in May and June; calyx lobes short, obtuse; **fruit** glabrous to 8 mm. long.
USE AND CULTURE: Planted in moist soil along streams or ponds in naturalistic plantings. It is of easy culture when planted in moist soil and in full sun. Propagation is by seeds planted as soon as ripe or in the spring following stratification.

Andromeda L. (Bog Rosemary)
ERICACEAE (Heath Family)
DESCRIPTION: Two species of low, evergreen shrubs, native in North America, Europe, and Asia; **leaves** alternate, simple, with revolute margins, leathery; **flowers** pink to white, nodding, in terminal umbels; sepals 5; corolla urceolate; stamens 10, with awned anthers; ovary superior; **fruit** a capsule.

Andromeda glaucophylla Link. (Bog Rosemary). Hardy in all zones; shrub to 75 cm. tall.
DESCRIPTION: Glaucous evergreen shrub, native in bogs and edges of ponds throughout coniferous forests from Manitoba to Labrador, south to Minnesota and West Virginia; **leaves** linear to oblong, to 6 cm. long, white-puberulent beneath, revolute, green above; **flowers** white, in small umbellike clusters; **fruit** a short, glaucous capsule.
USE AND CULTURE: Used in rock gardens and bog gardens. It requires an acid, peaty soil that is kept moist. Propagation is by seeds sown as soon as ripe or in the spring following stratification, or by softwood cuttings.

Arethusa L. (Arethusa)
ORCHIDACEAE (Orchid Family)
DESCRIPTION: A single species of a low, terrestrial herb, native in eastern North America; **stems** cormlike; **leaves** solitary, grasslike; **flowers** solitary, showy; sepals and petals converging to form a hood; lip reflexed, bearded; **fruit** a capsule.

Arethusa bulbosa L. (Bog Rose, Dragon's-mouth, Swamp Pink, Wild Pink). Hardy in all zones; perennial to 25 cm. tall.
DESCRIPTION: Grasslike perennial, native in acid sphagnum bogs and peaty meadow from Minnesota to Newfoundland, south to Indiana and South Carolina; **stems** cormlike; **leaves** linear, grasslike, developing after the flowers; **flowers** rose-purple, to 5 cm. long; lip white, with 3 fringed ridges and yellow and purple markings.
USE AND CULTURE: Requires an acid soil, high in organic matter, so it is planted in natural or man-made acid bogs. Propagation is by division of corms. This is a protected species and should not be removed from its natural habitat.

Asclepias incarnata (Swamp Milkweed). In seed in September 1970, and in flower at the Arboretum.

Asclepias L. (Butterfly Flower, Milkweed, Silkweed)
ASCLEPIADACEAE (Milkweed Family)
DESCRIPTION: About 200 species of perennial herbs with milky sap, native mostly in North America and Africa; **leaves** opposite or whorled, rarely alternate; **flowers** white, yellow, red, or purple, in terminal or axillary umbellate cymes; corolla rotate, with 5 reflexed lobes; corona present with 5 hoodlike lobes, each with or without a horn; **fruit** a pair of erect follicles; **seed** with a tuft of silky hairs.

Asclepias incarnata L. (Swamp Milkweed). Hardy in all zones; perennial to 1 m. tall.
DESCRIPTION: Upright perennial, native in wet meadows, along streams and lake shores, and in marshes, from Wyoming to Nova Scotia, south to Oklahoma and Florida; **leaves** opposite, linear to ovate-elliptic, to 15 cm. long; **flowers** pink to wine-colored, rarely white, in paired, axillary cymes, in July and August; corolla with short lobes and stalked hoods, each with a curved horn; **follicles** erect, fusiform, to 8 cm. long.
USE AND CULTURE: An excellent plant for the flower border or near a pool. The plants also attract butterflies and the flowers last well in flower arrangements. Although this plant grows in wet soils, it does surprisingly well in ordinary garden soils if kept moist. It prefers a slightly acid soil. Propagation is by division of old crowns in spring or by seeds sown as soon as ripe.

Calla L. (Calla)
ARACEAE (Arum Family)
DESCRIPTION: A single species of perennial herbs, native in wet, boggy places in the North Temperate Zone; **stems** prostrate; **leaves** simple, alternate; **flowers** small, on a fleshy spadix, subtended by an open, short spathe; perianth lacking; **fruit** a red berry.

Calla palustris L. (Water Arum, Water-dragon, Wild Calla). Hardy in all zones; perennial to 25 cm. tall.
DESCRIPTION: A prostrate perennial, native in swamps and lake shores, in slightly acid muck, in Europe and Asia and from Minnesota to New Jersey, south to Indiana in North America; **stems** prostrate; **leaves** leaf blade ovate-cordate, to 15 cm. long on long petioles; **flowers** inconspicuous; spathe green on the outside, white on the inside, about 5 cm. long and 4 cm. wide; spadix short; **fruit** a red berry.
USE AND CULTURE: Plant in wet soil at the edge of a pond. Needs wet, slightly acid soil with rhizomes exposed on the top. Plants spread slowly. The old rhizome dies after flowering and seed production. Propagation is by seeds planted in wet soil as soon as ripe. Stem cuttings can be rooted in a peat-muck mixture in pots submerged in water. A winter mulch is needed unless there is a good snow cover.

Calopogon R. Br. (Grass Pink, Swamp Pink)
ORCHIDACEAE (Orchid Family)
DESCRIPTION: Four species of tuberous, terrestrial, perennial herbs, native in acid sphagnum bogs in North America; **leaves** grasslike; **flowers** in racemes on naked scapes; sepals and petals similar, spreading, with long-clawed lip that is dilated and bearded above; **fruit** a slender capsule.

Calla palustris (Wild Calla). In bloom

at Madeline Island, Wisconsin in September 1985.

Caltha palustris (Cowslip). In bloom at the

Edinburgh Botanic Garden in Scotland in 1979.

Calopogon pulchellus - see **Calopogon tuberosus**.

Calopogon tuberosus (L.) BSP. (Grass Pink). Hardy in all zones; perennial to 45 cm. tall.
DESCRIPTION: Perennial, native in acid bogs, swamps, and wet pine woods from Quebec to Nova Scotia, south to Texas and Florida; **leaves** linear, to 25 cm. long; **flowers** pink to rose-purple, to 4 cm. across, in many-flowered racemes; lip bearded with golden-yellow hairs.
USE AND CULTURE: Plant in artificial or natural acid bogs. This is a protected orchid and should not be dug in the wild. Propagation is by division of the tubers.

Caltha L. (Marsh Marigold)
RANUNCULACEAE (Buttercup Family)
DESCRIPTION: About 20 species of fleshy perennial herbs, native in cold marshes or bogs in North and South Temperate Zones; **leaves** simple, alternate, entire or serrate, long-petioled, dying down in summer after seeds mature; **flowers** showy, yellow, white, or pink, axillary or terminal, on peduncles; sepals 5 to 9, petallike; petals none; stamens many; **fruit** a follicle.

Caltha palustris L. (Cowslip, Kingcup, Marsh Marigold, May-blob, Meadow-bright). Hardy in all zones; perennial to 50 cm. tall.
DESCRIPTION: Branched, fleshy perennial, native in wet meadows, swamps, and shallow water from Alaska to Newfoundland, south to Nebraska and North Carolina, also in Eurasia; **stems** hollow; basal **leaves** with long petioles, shorter above; blades to 18 cm. wide with open basal sinus; **flowers** bright yellow, to 5 cm. across, in May and June; sepals showy, elliptic to obovate.

Caltha palustris (Cowslip). In bloom May 1978.

USE AND CULTURE: Plant along streams, at the edges of ponds, or in wet soils. The leaves are sometimes used as a potherb and the flower buds as a substitute for capers. Plant in early spring with the crown at ground level. Space plants 60 cm. apart. Propagation is by division or by seeds sown as soon as they are ripe. Seedlings may bloom the second year. Since the foliage dies down in summer, plant with a companion plant that retains its foliage such as **Iris pseudacorus**.

Calypso Salisb. (Calypso)
ORCHIDACEAE (Orchid Family)
DESCRIPTION: A single species of terrestrial, perennial herbs, native in cool bogs, circumboreal, **stems** small, cormlike; **leaves** solitary, plicate; **flowers** solitary on a scape with 2 or more basal sheaths; sepals and petals reflexed; lip present, saccate; **fruit** a capsule.

Calypso bulbosa (L.) Oakes. (Calypso, Cytherea, Fairy-slipper, Pink Slipper Orchid). Hardy in all zones; perennial to 20 cm. tall.
DESCRIPTION: Perennial, native in cool forests and bogs across Canada, south to California and New York, also in Europe and Asia; **stem** a bulblike tuber; **leaves** round-ovate, petioled, to 8 cm. long, persisting over winter; **flowers** white to purple, solitary on a scape, to 20 cm. tall, from May to July; sepals and petals narrowly lanceolate, to 2.5 cm. long, purple; lip oblong, about 2.5 cm. long, the sac white to purple and streaked with red to brown stripes.
USE AND CULTURE: Plant in bog gardens. Unless you have ideal conditions, it is best to enjoy this rare wild flower in natural habitats. Propagation is by division of tubers. Collecting wild plants is unlawful.

Decodon J.F. Gmel. (Water Willow)
LYTHRACEAE (Loosestrife Family)
DESCRIPTION: A single species of semi-woody perennials with arching stems, rooting where stem tips touch moist soil, native in swamps and pools throughout the United States; **leaves** willowlike, opposite or whorled; **flowers** purple, in axillary clusters; calyx tube campanulate with 4 to 7 teeth and as many alternating horned appendages; petals 4 to 7; stamens 8 to 10; **fruit** a capsule.

Decodon verticillatus (L.) Elliott. (Swamp Loosestrife, Water Oleander, Water Willow). Hardy in all zones; perennial to 2.5 m. tall.
DESCRIPTION: Perennial with woody base and arching stems, native in wet soils, swamps, and shallow water from Minnesota to Maine, south to Louisiana and Florida.
USE AND CULTURE: Plant in wet soils and shallow water near a pool. Propagation is by seeds or by tip layering.

Drosera L. (Daily-dew, Sundew)
DROSERACEAE (Sundew Family)
DESCRIPTION: About 100 species of perennial, insect-eating herbs, native in wet bogs, worldwide, especially in the southern hemisphere; **stems** short to elongate and climbing; **leaves** alternate, frequently in basal rosettes, covered and fringed with sensitive, gland-tipped green to red hairs capable of slowly changing directions when irritated and when catching and digesting insects; **flowers** small, white, pink, or purple, solitary or several in simple or branched, 1-sided inflorescences; sepals and petals usually 5, sometimes 4 or 8; stamens as many as the petals; styles usually 3, often several times divided; **fruit** a many-seeded capsule.

Drosera rotundifolia L. (Round-leaved Sundew). Hardy in all zones; perennial to 15 cm. tall.
DESCRIPTION: Cespitose perennial, native in acid bogs, circumboreal, from Canada south to California and Florida in North America; **leaves** in basal rosettes, stipuled, with flat petioles; blades orbicular to elliptic, to 1 cm. long; **flowers** white to pink, 1- to 25-flowered on scapes; sepals and petals 5, to 5 mm. long.
USE AND CULTURE: Plant only in an acid bog. The plants require an acid, peaty soil that is kept constantly moist. Unless you have a natural bog, it will be necessary

Drosera rotundifolia (Round-leaved Sundew).

Photograph: Mr. Arvid Lund.

to build an artificial one if you want to grow this interesting insect-eating plant. Propagation is by division or by seeds.

Equisetum L. (Horsetail, Scouring Rush)
EQUISETACEAE (Horsetail Family)
DESCRIPTION: About 35 species of perennial herbs, native in wet sites worldwide; **stems** rhizomatous and upright; **branches** in whorls; upright stems usually hollow and jointed, impregnated with silicon; **leaves** scalelike, marginally united to form a sheath around each node; **sporophylls** produced in terminal, conelike structure.

Equisetum hyemale L. (Common Horsetail, Common Scouring Rush). Hardy in all zones; perennial to 1.2 m. tall.
DESCRIPTION: Upright evergreen perennial, native in sandy, moist banks in North America and Eurasia; **stems** upright, often evergreen, slender, furrowed with 14 to 40 ridges, rough; **leaves** scalelike; **strobiles** terminal, pointed.
USE AND CULTURE: Plant near a pool or on a north facing slope near water. Plants require a moist soil, preferably one that is sandy. Propagation is mainly by division of the rhizomes in early spring.

Equisetum scirpoides Michx. (Dwarf Scouring Rush). Hardy in all zones; perennial to 20 cm. tall.
DESCRIPTION: A low, mat-forming perennial, native in moist, often swampy areas, circumboreal, south to Washington and New York in North America; **stems** evergreen, all alike, erect or ascending, mostly with 3 ridges, solid; **sporophylls** in small, terminal cones.
USE AND CULTURE: Plant as a ground cover in moist areas. The culture is the same as for **Equisetum hyemale**.

Habenaria Willd. (Fringed Orchid, Fringed Orchis,
Rein Orchid, Rein Orchis)
ORCHIDACEAE (Orchid Family)
DESCRIPTION: About 100 species of terrestrial perennial herbs, native in bogs, moist woods, and wet meadows in temperate and tropical areas; **stems** erect, simple, leafy; **leaves** linear to oblanceolate; stem leaves smaller than the basal ones; **flowers** in 1- to many-flowered terminal racemes; petals usually smaller than the sepals; lip entire, lobed, or often fringed, spurred at base; anthers firmly fused to column; **fruit** a capsule.

Habenaria ciliaris (L.) R. Br. (Orange-fringe, Orange-plume, Yellow Fringed Orchid). Hardy in all zones; perennial to 1 m. tall.
DESCRIPTION: Leafy perennial, native in bogs, swamps, meadows, and pine barrens from Ontario to Massachusetts, south to Texas and Florida; **stems** leafy; **leaves** to 30 cm. long; **flowers** bright yellow to deep orange, in racemes to 20 cm. long, from July to September; lip to 1.25 cm. long, copiously ciliate-fringed, with a slender spur.

Equisetum hyemale (Horsetail).

Habenaria psycodes (Butterfly Orchid). In bloom

at Waterrock Knob, North Carolina.

USE AND CULTURE: Plant in wild flower or bog gardens. This fringed orchid requires an acid soil and partial shade. The soil should be kept moist. Propagation is by division. Seed propagation has not been successful. This is one of the easiest of the fringed orchids to grow.

Habenaria fimbriata - see **Habenaria psycodes** var. **grandiflora**.

Habenaria psycodes (L.) K. Spreng. (Butterfly Orchid, Fairy-fringe, Lesser Purple Fringed Orchid, Small Purple Fringed Orchid, Soldier's-plume). Hardy in all zones; perennial to 1 m. tall.
DESCRIPTION: Perennial, native in mossy woods, swamps, and roadside ditches from Alaska to Greenland, south to Wyoming and New York; **stems** leafy; **leaves** several, up to 22 cm. long; **flowers** showy, purple, lilac, or rarely white, in many-flowered racemes, fragrant, from June to August; upper sepal and petals forming a hood; lip 3-lobed, with fringed margins; spur to 2 cm. long.
USE AND CULTURE: The same as for **Habenaria ciliaris**.
VARIETIES: var. **grandiflora** (Bigel.) A. Gray. (Greater Purple Fringed Orchid, Large Butterfly Orchid, Large Purple Fringed Orchid, Plume-royal).
DESCRIPTION: Plants more robust than the species, with flowers twice as large. It has the same range as the species.

Heracleum L. (Cow Parsnip)
UMBELLIFERAE (Carrot Family)
DESCRIPTION: About 60 species of coarse, biennial or perennial herbs, native in Eurasia and North America; **leaves** large, pinnately or ternately compound; **flowers** small, white, pink, green, or yellow, in compound umbels; **fruit** a flattened mericarp.

Heracleum lanatum - see **Heracleum sphondylium** subsp. **montanum**.

Heracleum sphondylium subsp. montanum (Schleich. ex Gaudin) Briq. (American Cow Parsnip, Masterwort). Hardy in all zones; biennial to 3 m. tall.
DESCRIPTION: Coarse biennial, native in moist, usually shaded soils from Alaska to Newfoundland, south to California and Georgia; **leaves** ternately compound; leaflets broadly ovate, lobed and dentate, hairy beneath; **flowers** small, white, in large 15- to 30-rayed umbels, to 20 cm. across, in July; **mericarps** pubescent.
USE AND CULTURE: The cow parsnip is a good plant to grow in moist soils. Propagation is by seeds sown as soon as ripe. Plants self sow.

Iris L. (Flag, Fleur-de-lis, Iris)
IRIDACEAE (Iris Family)

Heracleum sphondylium ssp. montanum (Cow Parsnip).

Photographed in Alaska.

Iris versicolor (Blue Flag).

Photograph: Mr. Arvid Lund.

DESCRIPTION: About 200 species of rhizomatous or bulbous, perennial herbs, native in the North Temperate Zone; **leaves** mostly basal, 2-ranked, linear to sword-shaped; **flowers** showy, in many colors, 1 or more in unbranched or branched inflorescences; perianth segments 6, the outer 3 (falls) narrowed basally, sometimes bearded, the inner 3 (standards) narrowed into a claw, usually erect and arching; stamens 3, born at the base of the falls; style branches 3, bifid or crested, petallike; **fruit** a 3- or 6-angled, leathery capsule.

Iris versicolor L. (Blue Flag, Poison Flag, Wild Iris). Hardy in all zones; perennial to 90 cm. tall.
DESCRIPTION: A tufted, often branched perennial, native in marshes, wet meadows, along lake shores and streams, and in wet roadside ditches from Manitoba to Labrador, south to Arkansas and West Virginia; **stems** often branched; **leaves** firm, linear to sword-shaped, to 90 cm. long, somewhat glaucous; **flowers** in 2- to 3-flowered spathes, in June and July; perianth tube funnelform, to 1.25 cm. long; falls ovate to reniform-ovate, to 7.5 cm. long, lavender, violet, or blue-violet, rarely red-violet or white; standards erect.
USE AND CULTURE: Plant at the edges of pools or in flower borders. This iris can be grown in any fertile garden soil that is kept moist. Bloom is best when grown in full sun. Propagation is by division in late summer or by seeds sown as soon as ripe. Seedlings should bloom the third year.

Ledum L. (Ledum)
ERICACEAE (Heath Family)
DESCRIPTION: Three species of evergreen shrubs, native in sandy or peaty acid soils in the colder parts of North America and Eurasia; **leaves** alternate, simple, entire, leathery; **flowers** white, in dense, terminal umbellike clusters; calyx 5-toothed; corolla with 5 separate petals; stamens 5 to 10; **fruit** a 5-valved capsule.

Ledum groenlandicum Oedr. (Labrador Tea). Hardy in all zones; shrub to 1 m. tall.
DESCRIPTION: Evergreen shrub, native in acid bogs from Alaska to Greenland, south to Washington and Pennsylvania; **leaves** linear-oblong to oblong, to 5 cm. long, rusty-tomentose beneath; **flowers** white, in June; stamens 5 to 7; **capsules** slender, pointed.
USE AND CULTURE: Plant in natural or artificial acid bogs. Plants require an acid soil with a pH of 4.5 with constant moisture. Propagation is by seeds sown as soon as ripe, by cuttings, or layering. Cuttings should be taken in July and rooted in a sand-peat mixture. Native Americans used the leaves of this plant for making a tea.

Menyanthes L. (Bogbean, Buckbean)
GENTIANACEAE (Gentian Family)
DESCRIPTION: A single species of perennial herb, native in wet areas, circumboreal; **leaves** alternate, with 3 long-petioled leaflets; **flowers** regular, 5-merous, in racemes; corolla funnelform, bearded on the whole upper surface; stamens borne on the corolla tube; ovary 1-celled; **fruit** a capsule, bursting irregularly.

Menyanthes trifoliata L. (Bogbean, Buckbean, Marsh Trefoil). Hardy in all zones; perennial to 30 cm. tall.
DESCRIPTION: Perennial with creeping rhizomes, native in bogs, circumboreal, south to Missouri and Virginia in North America; **leaflets** elliptic to obovate, to 10 cm. long, entire to crenate; petiole to 25 cm. long, broadly sheathing at the base; **flowers** white to purple, with a white beard, to 2.5 cm. across, in 10- to 20-flowered racemes on axillary scapes, from May to August; calyx and corolla 5- to 6-merous, cleft nearly to base.
USE AND CULTURE: Plant in bog gardens or at the edges of pools. Plants grow in mud or shallow water. Propagation is by seeds or division of rhizomes. Seeds should be sown as soon as ripe.

Nelumbo Adans. (Lotus, Sacred Bean, Water Lotus)
NYMPHAEACEAE (Waterlily Family)

DESCRIPTION: Two species of large, aquatic herbs with widespreading, horizontal, thickened rhizomes rooted in mud, native in water in Asia and North America; **leaves** orbicular, concave, peltate, usually projecting above the water on long petioles; **flowers** solitary, large, showy, mostly emerging above the leaves; sepals 4 or 5; petals and stamens many, attached at the base of an obconical, flat-topped receptacle in which many 1-ovuled carpels are embedded.

Nelumbo lutea (Willd.) Pers. (American Lotus, Pond Nuts, Water Chinquapin, Wonkapin, Yanquapin, Yellow Nelumbo). Hardy in zone 4; perennial to 2 m. tall.
DESCRIPTION: Aquatic perennial native in rivers, ponds, and lakes from Minnesota to Ontario, south to Texas and Florida; **leaves** circular, mostly above water, to 60 cm. across, entire, bluish-green; **flowers** pale yellow, to 25 cm. across, from July to September.
USE AND CULTURE: Plant in ponds or lakes. Native Americans used the rhizomes for food. They require a muddy bottom in which the rhizomes can become anchored. Propagation is by division of rhizomes or by seeds. Seeds should be embedded in a mud ball and dropped into the pond. Scarification of the hard seeds with a file improves germination.

Nuphar Sm. (Cow Lily, Marsh Collard, Spatterdock,
Water Collard, Yellow Pond Lily)
NYMPHAEACEAE (Water Lily Family)
DESCRIPTION: About 25 species of perennial aquatic herbs with stout, creeping rhizomes, rooting in mud near margins of streams, ponds, and lakes, widespread in the northern hemisphere; **leaves** large, entire, with basal sinus, submerged, floating, or erect above the water; **flowers** solitary, yellow or purple, usually standing above the water surface; sepals 5 to 12, conspicuous, yellow inside; petals and stamens many, small, inserted below the compound ovary; style short; stigma disclike; **fruit** ovoid, many-seeded, maturing above the water.

Nuphar advena (Ait.) Ait.f. (Common Spatterdock). Hardy in all zones; aquatic perennial to 2 m. tall.
DESCRIPTION: Aquatic perennial, native in shallow water in streams and lakes from Minnesota to Maine, south to Mexico and Florida; **leaves** rounded, thick, erect, usually above water surface, sometimes floating, green, glabrous; **flowers** nearly globose, to 4 cm. wide, yellow, from June to October; sepals 6, broad, inner 3 yellow, tipped with green; petals and stamens yellow or tinged red; stigmatic disc 9- to 23-rayed.
USE AND CULTURE: Plant in shallow water in ponds. Propagation is largely by division of rhizomes in early spring. Plant rhizomes in mud.

Nymphaea tuberosa (Tuberous Water Lily).

In bloom in Kenora, Ontario in July 1977.

Nymphaea L. (Water Lily, Water-nymph)
NYMPHAEACEAE (Water Lily Family)
DESCRIPTION: About 35 species of aquatic herbs with horizontal or erect, tuberous rhizomes, native in shallow water in lakes, ponds, and streams, worldwide; **leaves** simple, commonly orbicular, with sinus reaching almost to the attachment of the petiole, floating; petiole long, depending on depth of water; **flowers** showy, floating or standing above the water; sepals 4; petals many, united to the ovary; stamens many; carpels many; **fruit** subglobose, many seeded, depressed and saucerlike at apex, maturing under water.

Nymphaea odorata Ait. (Fragrant Water Lily, Pond Lily, White Water Lily). Hardy in all zones; aquatic perennial.
DESCRIPTION: Aquatic perennial with fleshy rhizomes, native in quiet waters in lakes and streams from Manitoba to Newfoundland, south to Texas and Florida; **leaves** to 25 cm. across, rather thick, entire, dull green above, purplish beneath; **flowers** white, fragrant, to 12 cm. across, opening in the morning for 3 consecutive days, from June to September.
USE AND CULTURE: Plant in ponds and streams. Plants require a deep, fertile mud in slow-running streams or ponds in full sun. The water must be warm for the plants to bloom. Propagation is chiefly by fall division and replanting of the tuberous rhizomes. Plants can also be started by seeds embedded in a mud ball and dropped into the water. Filing the hard seed coat improves the chances of germination.

Nymphaea tetragona Georgi. (Pygmy Water Lily). Hardy in all zones; aquatic perennial.
DESCRIPTION: Aquatic perennial, native in cold ponds and lakes in Siberia, Japan, and in North America south to Minnesota and Maine; **leaves** ovate, brown-blotched, reddish beneath, to 10 cm. across; **flowers** white, to 6 cm. across, open from noon until 5 p.m., from June to September.
USE AND CULTURE: The same as for **Nymphaea odorata**. The water must be cool.

Nymphaea tuberosa Paine. (Magnolia Water Lily, Tuberous Water Lily). Hardy in all zones; aquatic perennial.
DESCRIPTION: Aquatic perennial with horizontal rhizomes with detachable, tuberlike branches, native in quiet waters in streams, lakes, and ponds from Minnesota to Quebec, south to Arkansas and Maryland; **leaves** to 35 cm. across, entire, green beneath; **flowers** pure white, to 20 cm. across, with little or no fragrance, opening in the morning until slightly after noon, from June until September.
USE AND CULTURE: The same as for **Nymphaea odorata**.

Parnassia L. (Bog-stars, Grass-of-Parnassus, White Liverwort)
SAXIFRAGACEAE (Saxifrage Family)
DESCRIPTION: About 10 species of small, perennial herbs, native in damp areas, often in bogs or swamps, on wet cliffs, and in moist meadows, usually in limestone soils in arctic and temperate regions of North America and Eurasia; basal **leaves** long-petioled, entire, stem leaves 1 and sessile; flowers white, solitary; calyx tube short, with 5 lobes; petals 5; stamens 5, fertile; staminodes 5; ovary superior with 4 sessile stigmas; **fruit** a 4-valved capsule.

Parnassia glauca Raf. (Grass-of-Parnassus). Hardy in all zones; perennial to 30 cm. tall.
DESCRIPTION: Perennial native from Saskatchewan to Newfoundland, south to South Dakota and Virginia; **leaves** ovate to orbicular-ovate, to 5 cm. long; stem leaf at or below middle of the stem; **flowers** white, to 4 cm. across, in July and August; petals entire; staminodal scales 3-lobed to below the center, slightly shorter than the stamens.

USE AND CULTURE: Plant in bog gardens or in other wet areas. These plants require a moist soil that is neutral to slightly acid. Propagation is by seeds sown as soon as ripe

in a seedbed of chopped sphagnum. They can also be propagated by fall division. It takes 3 years for seedlings to bloom.

Pogonia Juss. (Pogonia)
ORCHIDACEAE (Orchid Family)
DESCRIPTION: About 10 species of erect, terrestrial herbs, native in moist, shady areas in temperate regions of North America and Asia; **stems** with a single leaf borne about the center; **flowers** 1 to 3 at the tip of the stem; perianth segments separate; lip bearded; column separate, coarsely toothed at apex; **fruit** a capsule.

Pogonia ophioglossoides (L.) Ker-Gawl. (Adder's-tongue-leaved Pogonia, Adder's-mouth, Beardflower, Crested Ettercap, Ettercap, Rose Crest-lip, Rose Pogonia). Hardy in all zones; perennial to 25 cm. tall.
DESCRIPTION: Perennial with brownish-green stems, native in bogs, peaty soils, wet lake shores, and swamps from Minnesota to Newfoundland, south to Texas and Florida; leaves ovate, to 12 cm. long; **flowers** rose to white, fragrant, in June and July; sepals and petals oblong-elliptic, to 2.5 cm. long, lip oblong-spatulate, 2.5 cm. long, lacerate-toothed apically, prominently bearded.
USE AND CULTURE: Plant in bog gardens. The soil must be acid, peaty, and moist. Propagation is by fall division. Purchase plants from a licensed wild flower nursery. A winter mulch is necessary.

Pontederia L. (Pickerel Weed)
PONTEDERIACEAE (Pickerel Weed Family)
DESCRIPTION: A small genus of aquatic perennial herbs, native in shallow water in North and South America; **leaves** thick, parallel-veined, long-petioled; **flowers** blue, in spikes; perianth 6-parted, corollalike; stamens 6; **fruit** a 1-seeded achene.

Pontederia cordata L. (Pickerel Weed). Hardy in all zones; perennial to 1.2 m. tall.
DESCRIPTION: Aquatic perennial with creeping rhizomes, native in quiet water and muddy stream banks from Minnesota to Nova Scotia, south to Texas and Florida; **leaves** mostly ovate, cordate at base, to 15 cm. long; **flowers** deep blue, in spikes, from June to November; upper perianth lobes with 2 yellow spots; stamens 6, 3 long and 3 short.
USE AND CULTURE: Plant in shallow water near the edge of a pool. Plants are easy to grow. Propagation is by division of the rhizomes either in the fall or early spring. Plant rhizomes horizontally in the mud at the bottom of a pond. Water should not be more than 30 cm. deep.

Sagittaria L. (Arrowhead, Swamp Potato)
ALISMATACEAE (Water Plantain Family)
DESCRIPTION: About 20 species of stoloniferous, often tuber-bearing perennial herbs, native in bogs and in shallow water in temperate and tropical America; **leaves** tufted, submerged, and reduced to linear phyllodes or emerged with blades linear to

Pontederia cordata (Pickerel Weed).

Pontederia cordata (Pickerel Weed).

Photograph: close up by Mr. Arvid Lund.

Sarracenia purpurea (Pitcher Plant).

Sagittaria latifolia (Duck Potato).

Photograph: Mr. Arvid Lund.

elliptic, lanceolate, ovate, or sagittate; **flowers** white, in racemes or panicles, monoecious with pistillate flowers below the staminate; sepals 3, green; petals 3, early deciduous; stamens 7 or more; **fruit** a head of flattened, winged, beaked achenes.

Sagittaria latifolia Willd. (Duck Potato, Wapato). Hardy in all zones; perennial to 1.2 m. tall.
DESCRIPTION: Perennial with large tubers, native in shallow water or in mud or wet sand from British Columbia to Nova Scotia, south to Mexico and Florida; **leaves** mostly triangular and sagittate, acute at apex; floral bracts boat-shaped and firm; **flowers** white, to 4 cm. across, from July to September; **achenes** with entire wings.
USE AND CULTURE: Plant in shallow pools or in mud at the edges of pools or streams. Plants are easy to grow in shallow water or wet soils. Propagation is by division of the fleshy tubers either in the fall or early in the spring. This plant is an important food for ducks and other wildlife.

Sarracenia L. (Pitcher Plant)
SARRACENIACEAE (Pitcher Plant Family)
DESCRIPTION: About 8 species of rhizomatous, carnivorous, perennial herbs, native in peaty soils in eastern North America; **leaves** clustered in rosettes, erect, tubular or trumpet-shaped, with a keel or wing on one side and terminating by a lid; **flowers** solitary, nodding or erect, on naked scapes, regular, perfect, in June and July; sepals and petals 5; stamens many; styles expanded at the apex into an umbrellalike cap; ovary 5-celled; **fruit** a capsule.

Sarracenia purpurea L. (Common Pitcher Plant, Huntsman's-cup, Indian-cup, Side-saddle Flower, Southern Pitcher Plant). Hardy in all zones; perennial to 30 cm. tall.
DESCRIPTION: Rhizomatous perennial, native in acid bogs in sun or shade, widely distributed across Canada south to Louisiana and Florida; **leaves** evergreen, decurrent to 30 cm. long, slender below, swollen above, green, variegated or suffused with red-purple, with an erect lid; **flowers** purple or greenish-purple, to 6 cm. across on scapes to 30 cm. long.
USE AND CULTURE: Plant in bog gardens. Plants require a moist, acid peat soil. Propagation is by crown division at any time or by seeds sown as soon as ripe in a sand-peat mixture. Seedlings take from 3 to 5 years to reach a blooming size.

Symplocarpus Salisb. (Skunk Cabbage)
ARACEAE (Arum Family)
DESCRIPTION: A single species of perennial herb with a disagreeable skunklike odor when bruised, native in wet woods and swamps in partial shade in eastern North America and northeastern Asia; **leaves** large, emerging from a stout, vertical rhizome; **flowers** perfect, small, on a spherical spadix, enveloped by an inflated spathe; perianth 4-parted; stamens 4; ovaries 1-celled, **seeds** embedded in the spadix.

Symplocarpus foetidus (L.) Salisb. (Polecat Weed, Skunk Cabbage). Hardy in all zones; perennial to 50 cm. tall.

Symplocarpus foetidus (Skunk Cabbage).

DESCRIPTION: Perennial, native in swampy woods and wet meadows from Manitoba to Quebec, south to Iowa and Georgia; **leaves** ovate-cordate, to 45 cm. long, entire, with petioles to 25 cm. long; **flowers** small, perfect, on stout black spadix to 15 cm. long, partially enclosed by a fleshy spathe that is ovoid, fleshy, to 15 cm. long with pointed tips, purple-brown mottled with greenish-yellow, in April and May.
USE AND CULTURE: Plant near a pond or stream in wet, mucky soil. Plants require a soil that is kept moist by water seeping through the soil. Propagation is by fall division or by seeds sown as soon as ripe in a peaty soil. It takes several years for seedlings to bloom.

Typha L. (Bulrush, Cattail, Cattail Flag)
TYPHACEAE (Cattail Family)
DESCRIPTION: About 15 species of monoecious perennial herbs, native in swamps and wet meadows in North America, Europe, and Asia; **stems** tall, unbranched, from creeping rhizomes; **leaves** long, linear, flat, erect, parallel-veined; **flowers** in dense terminal spikes with staminate flowers above the pistillate; staminate flowers with 2 to 5 stamens; pistillate flowers with a superior ovary and 1 style and 1 stigma; **fruit** an achene subtended by capillary bristles.

Typha angustifolia L. (Narrow-leaved Cattail, Small Bulrush, Soft Flag). Hardy in all zones; perennial to 2 m. tall.
DESCRIPTION: Grasslike perennial, native in swamps, wet meadows, and roadside ditches throughout North America, Asia, and Europe; **leaves** slender, to 8 mm. wide; spikes light brown, to 1.5 cm. in diameter; staminate and pistillate **flowers** separated by a naked axis, from May to July.
USE AND CULTURE: Plant in wet soils where little else will grow. Leaves are used in making baskets. Younger, dried spikes are used in flower arrangements. Young shoots in the spring are edible. Cattails are easy to grow in any moist soil in full sun. Propagation is by seeds or divisions. Seeds can be started in jars of water. Plants can spread and become weedy.

Typha latifolia L. (Bulrush, Common Cattail, Cossack Asparagus, Nail-rod). Hardy in all zones; perennial to 3 m. tall.
DESCRIPTION: Coarse grasslike perennial, native in swamps, wet meadows, and roadside ditches throughout North America, Europe, and Asia; **leaves** linear, to 2.5 cm. wide and 2 m. long; spikes to 2.5 cm. in diameter and 20 cm. long; staminate and pistillate **flowers** not separated.
USE AND CULTURE: The same as for **Typha angustifolia**.

Veronica L. (Brooklime, Speedwell)
SCROPHULARIACEAE (Figwort Family)
DESCRIPTION: About 250 species of annual or perennial herbs, native in the north temperate regions of the world, but mostly in Europe; **stems** erect or prostrate; **leaves** mostly opposite, rarely alternate or whorled near the top of the stem, simple, entire or dentate; **flowers** small, white, rose, purple, or blue, in axillary or terminal spikes,

racemes, or corymbs; calyx 4- to 5-parted; corolla rotate; stamens 2; **fruit** a flattened, notched capsule.

Veronica americana (Raf.) Schweinitz ex Benth. (American Brooklime). Hardy in all zones; perennial to 1 m. tall.
DESCRIPTION: Creeping perennial, native in swamps and marshes, often in shallow water, from Alaska to Newfoundland, south to California and North Carolina, also in Asia; **stems** fleshy, prostrate or ascending; **leaves** elliptic, oblong to suborbicular, serrate to crenate, glabrous; **flowers** violet to blue in loose racemes, from May to August.
USE AND CULTURE: Plant in moist soil near water. Plants must have a continuously moist soil. Propagation is by division or by seeds sown as soon as ripe. Space plants 30 cm. apart.

GLOSSARY

Prunus americana (American Plum).

Photograph: Dr. Anne M. Hanchek.

GLOSSARY

Acaulescent. Apparently without a stem, the leaves and flowers arising near the surface of the ground.

Achene. A dry, indehiscent fruit with a thin wall and a single seed.

Acicular. Needle shaped.

Acuminate. Tapering to a slender point.

Acute. Forming an acute angle at base or apex.

Adnate. Completely or nearly completely united or fused, referring to the union of dissimilar parts or organs, as a filament adnate to the corolla.

Aggregate. A fruit made up of an aggregation of several pistils from the same flower as in the raspberry.

Alternate. Arranged singly at different heights and on different sides of the axis or stem, as leaves on a stem or flowers along an axis.

Androecium. The stamens in a single flower considered collectively.

Angiosperm. A plant that has its seeds enclosed in an ovary. Such structures are found in all flowering plants.

Annual. A plant that grows from seed to maturity and dies in a single growing season.

Annulus. Literally a ring, as the fleshy corona or rim of the corolla in members of the milkweed family.

Anther. The pollen-bearing portion of the stamen, composed of two pollen sacs.

Apex. The tip or distal end (plural, apices).

Apicula. A short, sharp, flexible point.

Apiculate. Terminated by an apicula.

Appressed. Closely pressed against.

Aquatic. Growing in water.

Areole. Spine-bearing sunken or raised spot on the stem of a cactus.

Aril. A usually fleshy appendage of the stalk that attaches the seed to the ovary wall, sometimes partially or completely covering the seed.

Aristate. Bearing a bristlelike awn.

Ascending. Rising up, extending somewhat obliquely or indirectly upward.

Asexual. Without sex.

Asymmetric. Not symmetric, as in flowers in which the petals are not all alike.

Attenuate. Gradually long-tapering, applied to bases or apices of leaves, etc.

Auricle. An ear-shaped lobe or appendage, as the projections at the base of some leaves or petals.

Awn. A slender, terminal bristle.

Axil. The upper angle that a lateral organ such as a leaf petiole forms with the stem.

Axillary. Located in or arising from an axil.

Axis. The main line of development in plants or structures.

Barbate. Bearded.

Basifixed. Attached or fixed by the base, as an ovule or anther that is affixed to its support by its bottom.

Berry. A fleshy fruit developed from a single ovary and usually containing several seeds embedded in a fleshy pulp.

Biennial. Living two years only and blooming and fruiting the second year.

Bifid. Two-cleft at the apex.

Bipinnate. Twice pinnate as in compound leaves.

Bisexual. Having both sexes present in the same flower.

Blade. The expanded terminal part of a flat organ, as a leaf, petal, or sepal, in contrast to the narrowed basal portion.

Bract. A modified leaf from the axil of which a flower or flower cluster arises.

Bractlet. A secondary or very small bract.

Bulb. A short, vertical, underground stem for food storage on which fleshy, modified leaf bases are attached.

Bulbil, bulblet. A small bulb or bulblike structure, usually borne in leaf axils, or among or in place of flowers, or in other unusual places.

Bullate. Blistered or puckered.

Calyx. The outer whorl of modified leaves in a flower, called sepals; usually green.

Campanulate. Bell-shaped, usually descriptive of a corolla or calyx.

Capillary. Hairlike, very slender.

Capitate. Headlike; in a head.

Capsule. A dry, dehiscent fruit formed from a multicarpelled ovary and usually containing many seeds.

Carnivorous. Meat-eating; in plants, usually equivalent of insectivorous.

Carpel. A modified floral leaf that forms a simple pistil or part of a compound pistil.

Caryopsis. An achenelike fruit derived from a superior ovary, with the pericarp united to the seed, as in the grasses.

Catkin. A scaly-bracted, usually flexuous spike or spikelike inflorescence found in the birches, oaks, and willows.

Caudate. Bearing a taillike appendage.

Cauline. Pertaining to or attached to a stem.

Cespitose. Growing in tufts or dense little clumps, forming mats.

Chaff. A thin, dry scale or bract, as in the bracts among the florets of the Compositae.

Chambered. Said of an ovary divided by incomplete partitions.

Chlorotic. Turning yellow, usually due to a lack of available iron.

Ciliate. With marginal hairs.

Ciliolate. Diminutive of ciliate.

Clavate. Club-shaped, gradually increasing diameter toward the summit.

Cleistogamous. Descriptive of a flower that does not open.

Column. The structure formed by the fusion of the style and stamens in the orchid family.

Compound. Referring to leaves made up of two or more leaflets or ovaries made up of two or more carpels.

Cone. A dense and usually elongated collection of sporophylls (cone scales), and usually bracts on a central axis found in the conifers.

Coniferous. Mostly evergreen trees having unisexual flowers in perfect or imperfect cones.

Connate. United or joined; said, in particular, of like or similar structures joined as one body or organ.

Convolute. Rolled up or twisted together lengthwise; said especially of leaves or petals in the bud.

Cordate. Heart-shaped.

Corm. A short, vertical, underground storage or reproductive organ, consisting mainly of a thickened stem portion with scalelike leaves.

Cormel, cormlet. A small corm.

Corolla. The second whorl of leaves in a flower, called petals; usually large and showy.

Corona. A structure in some plants between the corolla and the stamens and often simulating an additional part of the perianth. It may arise from the corolla in the genus **Narcissus** or from the stamens in the genus **Asclepias**.

Corymb. A type of a raceme in which the axis is relatively short and the lower pedicels are relatively long, thus producing a flat-topped inflorescence.

Cotyledon. A seed leaf. In some plants the cotyledons always remain within the seed coats, and in others they emerge above the soil in germination.

Crenate. Leaf margins that are toothed with rounded, shallow teeth.

Crenulate. Diminutive of crenate.

Crown. The base of a plant, where stem and root meet.

Crozier. A hook.

Cucullate. Hooded or hood-shaped.

Culm. The stem of grasses, usually hollow except for the swollen nodes.

Cultivar. A horticultural variety that originated and persisted under cultivation.

Cuneate. Wedge-shaped.

Cuspidate. With a sharp, abrupt, and often rigid point.

Cyathium. A type of inflorescence found in the genus **Euphorbia**. Staminate and pistillate flowers are produced in a cup-shaped involucre.

Cyme. A convex or flat-topped flower cluster in which the central flower opens first.

Cymose. Borne in cymes.

Aster novae-angliae. Corymbose flower.

Deciduous. Falling after the completion of its normal function; refers to leaves and floral parts.

Decompound. Compound, with the divisions once or several times compound.

Decumbent. Reclining or lying down, but with the apex ascending.

Decurrent. Extending down along and adnate to the stem, as in the leaf base of the common mullein.

Deflexed. Reflexed.

Dehiscence. Opening as in an anther to discharge pollen, or in a fruit to discharge seeds.

Dentate. Toothed along the margins, the apex of each tooth sharp and pointed outward.

Dichotomous. Two branches having equal and regular forking.

Dicotyledon. A plant producing seeds with two seed leaves.

Dimorphic. Occuring in two different forms, as the leaves of those ferns in which the fertile fronds or segments have a different form from that of the sterile ones.

Dioecious. Bearing staminate and pistillate flowers on separate plants.

Disc. The central part of the head in the sunflower family.

Discoid. Disc-shaped as in some stigmas, or in members of the sunflower family that have only disc flowers.

Dissected. Deeply divided into many slender segments.

Division. A portion of a plant that is vegetatively divided.

Dormant. A state of rest. Plants that are alive but not actively growing.

Drupe. A fruit with a fleshy exocarp and a hard or bony endocarp that encloses the seed or seeds.

Drupelet. A small drupe.

Ellipsoid. Shaped more or less like a football.

Elliptic. Oblong, but narrowed to rounded ends and widest at or about the middle.

Emarginate. Notched at the apex.

Emersed. Raised above water.

Endocarp. Inner wall of the ovary.

Entire. With a continous unbroken margin.

Ephemeral. Lasting for only a day or less, as in spiderwort flowers.

Epigynous. A flower in which the basal parts of the perianth adhere to the ovary; the perianth and stamens then appear to rise from the summit of the inferior ovary.

Erose. Irregularly jagged, appearing eroded or gnawed; said of apices or margins.

Evergreen. Plants that keep green living leaves all winter.

Exfoliate. To peel off in shreds, thin layers, or plates, as in the bark of a sycamore or birch.

Exocarp. Outer wall of the ovary.

Exserted. Projecting out or beyond; often referring to stamens or styles that project beyond the perianth tube.

Fall. One of the parts of the outer whorl of the perianth in the genus **Iris** and in other related genera, often broader than those of the inner whorl and often drooping or deflexed.

Fascicle. A close bundle or cluster of stems, leaves, flowers, or other organs.

Fertile. Said of stamens bearing pollen, flowers with functional pistils, or fruits with seeds.

Filament. The basal stalklike portion of the stamen below the anthers.

Filiform. Threadlike, long, and very slender.

Fimbriate. Fringed.

Floret. A very small flower, especially when a part of a dense inflorescence such as in the sunflower family.

Follicle. A dry, dehiscent fruit developed from a simple ovary and splitting along a single suture.

Frond. Leaf of a fern.

Fruit. A ripened ovary, together with such parts of the plant that are regularly associated with it.

Funnelform. Having a tube that gradually widens into the limb.

Fusiform. Descriptive of a solid body that is thick in the middle and tapers to both ends.

Geniculate. Abruptly bent, like a knee.

Gibbose. Swollen or protuberant on one side and commonly toward the base.

Fraxinus nigra. Deciduous leaf.

Glabrescent. Becoming glabrous.

Glabrous. Smooth, without pubescence.

Glaucous. Covered with a powdery bloom that is bluish-white or bluish-gray.

Globose. Rounded.

Glume. A small chafflike bract, especially in the spikelets of the inflorescence in grasses; usually two glumes at the base of each spikelet.

Gymnosperm. A plant that bears its seed naked on a sporophyll, not enclosed in an ovary, as in the conifers.

Gynoecium. A pistil or pistils of a single flower considered collectively.

Hastate. Having two divergent basal lobes.

Head. A dense flower cluster, composed of sessile or nearly sessile flowers crowded on a short axis.

Herb. A plant that dies to the ground each fall.

Herbaceous. Dying back to the ground at the end of the growing season; leaflike in color or texture.

Hip. The "fruit" of the rose, consisting of the fleshy, hollow floral cup and the achenes enclosed within it.

Hirsute. Pubescent with spreading hairs.

Hispid. Pubescent with stiff spreading hairs.

Hood. A segment of the corona in the milkweed family. Hooded, as an adjective, indicates an organ with the lateral margins more or less rolled inward and the apex more or less inflexed.

Hypanthium. A ringlike structure where the sepals, petals, and stamens are borne.

Hypogynous. Borne on the receptacle or under the ovary; refers to sepals, petals, and stamens in flowers with a superior ovary.

Imbricate. Overlapping like shingles on a roof.

Imperfect. Flowers that produce either stamens or pistils but not both. Sepals and petals may or may not be present.

Incised. Deeply and irregularly cut.

Indehiscent. Not opening at maturity.

Indusium. A small flap of epidermal tissue that, in most ferns, more or less covers the sorus.

Inferior. Descriptive of an ovary that adheres to the lower part of the perianth and therefore appears to be located below the other floral parts.

Inflated. Blown up, distended.

Inflorescence. A complete flower cluster, including the axis and bracts.

Insectivorous. Literally insect-eating; applied to plants that entrap and digest insects and other small animals.

Involucre. A set of bracts closely associated with each other and subtending an inflorescence.

Involute. Rolled inward so the lower side of the organ is exposed.

Irregular. Descriptive of a flower in which the members of one or more sets of organs differ among themselves in size, shape, or structure.

Keel. A sharp or conspicuous longitudinal ridge; also the two lower united petals in the pea family.

Labellum. The lip of the flower in the orchid family.

Lacerate. Torn, irregularly cleft, or cut.

Laciniate. Deeply cut into narrow segments.

Lanate. Woolly.

Lanceolate. Shaped like a lance head, much longer than wide and widest below the center.

Latex. A colorless or colored fluid, usually white or yellow, produced by the cells of some plants such as the milkweed.

Layering. A form of vegetative propagation in which a portion of the plant is induced to form roots while still attached to the parent plant.

Leaflet. A single segment of a compound leaf.

Legume. A dry, usually dehiscent fruit derived from a simple ovary and usually opening along two sutures.

Lemma. The lower of the two bracts that enclose the flower in the grass family.

Ligule. A strap-shaped organ.

Populus grandidentata. Dentate margin on leaf.

Limb. The upper, more or less widened portion of the corolla or calyx in flowers where the petals or sepals fuse to form a tube.

Linear. Narrow and elongate with nearly parallel sides.

Lip. One of the two divisions (upper and lower) of a bilabiate corolla occurring in the pea, mint, and figwort families; also a highly modified petal in the orchid family.

Loment. A fruit in the pea family in which the fruit is constricted between the seeds, with one-seeded segments separating at maturity.

Lyrate. Pinnately lobed, with the terminal lobe the largest.

Mericarp. One of the segments into which the mature fruits in the carrot and mallow families split at maturity.

-merous. A suffix referring to the number of parts in each circle of floral organs.

Monocotyledon. Plants with a single seed leaf.

Monoecious. A plant bearing both staminate and pistillate flowers on the same plant.

Mucro. A short, sharp, abrupt spur or spiny tip.

Mucronate. Terminated by a mucro.

Nectary. A nectar-secreting gland.

Node. A point on the stem from which leaves or branches arise.

Nut. An indehiscent, one-celled and one-seeded fruit with a hard and bony outer wall; also a drupe with a relatively thin, fleshy covering and a hard inner stony endocarp as in the walnut.

Nutlet. A small nut, differing from an achene in the harder ovary wall.

Ob-. A prefix, signifying a reverse direction.

Obconic, obconical. More or less conical but attached at the narrow end.

Oblanceolate. Inversely lanceolate with the broadest point above the center and tapering toward the base.

Oblanceolate. Inversely lanceolate with the broadest point above the center and tapering toward the base.

Oblate. Nearly spherical but somewhat flattened at the poles.

Oblong. Descriptive of a leaf or fruit that is wider than long with nearly parallel sides.

Obovate. Inversely ovate with the broadest point above the center.

Obovoid. Inversely ovoid with the point of attachment at the narrow end.

Obreniform. Inversely reniform.

Obtuse. Blunt, with a wide angle.

Opposite. Two at a node, on opposite sides of an axis.

Orbicular. Essentially circular.

Ovary. The basal, usually expanded portion of the pistil in which the seeds develop.

Ovate. Descriptive of a flat structure that is broader than lanceolate and widest below the center.

Ovoid. Referring to a solid body that has the shape of a hen's egg, with the point of attachment at the broadest end.

Ovule. A reproductive organ in the ovary that develops into a seed following fertilization.

Palate. An elevated portion of the lower lip of the corolla, wholly or partly closing the throat.

Palea. A small, chaffy bract; the inner of two bracts enclosing the flower in the grasses.

Palmate. With three or more lobes or veins arising from one point.

Panicle. A compound or branched inflorescence that is usually longer than wide.

Papilla. A minute, pimplelike protuberance.

Papillose. Bearing papilla.

Pappus. An outgrowth of hairs, scales, or bristles from the summit of the achene in many species in the sunflower family.

Parthenocarpic. Producing fruits without fertilization of the ovules.

Pectinate. Comblike.

Pedate. Said of a palmately lobed leaf when the two outer side lobes are again divided or cleft.

Pedicel. The stalk of an individual flower.

Peduncle. The portion of the stem that bears a solitary flower or an inflorescence that is leafless.

Peltate. A more or less rounded leaf with the petiole attached near the center of the under surface.

Pendent, pendulous. Drooping or hanging downward.

Viburnum trilobum. Drupe.

Rhus typhina. Pinnate leaf.

Pepo. A fruit of the gourd family with fleshy pulp and a hard rind and containing many seeds.

Perennial. A plant that lives for three or more years.

Perfect. Descriptive of a flower that has both stamens and pistils.

Perfoliate. Descriptive of a sessile leaf or bract, the base of which completely surrounds the stem, the latter seemingly passing through the leaf.

Perianth. The calyx and corolla considered together, or either of them if the other is lacking.

Pericarp. The outer wall of a fruit; sometimes differentiated into an outer layer (exocarp), a middle layer (mesocarp), and an inner layer (endocarp).

Petal. A separate segment of the corolla.

Petaloid. Petallike.

Petiole. The basal, stalklike portion of a leaf.

Petiolule. The stalk of a leaflet of a compound leaf.

pH. Measure of acidity. A pH of 7 is neutral, above 7 is alkaline, and below 7 is acid.

Phyllode. An expanded bladeless petiole.

Pilose. Having distinct, soft hairs.

Pinna. A primary division or primary leaflet of a pinnately compound leaf. If a leaf is decompound, the primary divisions are pinnae, and the ultimate leaflets are pinnules. Terminology used mostly with ferns.

Pinnate. Having branches, lobes, leaflets, or veins on two sides of a rachis.

Pinnatifid. With lobes or divisions pinnately arranged.

Pinnule. See pinna.

Pistil. The central organ of a flower, composed of ovary, style, and stigma.

Pistillate. Having a pistil; usually applied to flowers that lack stamens.

Pith. The soft, spongy, central cylinder in most angiosperm stems; composed of parenchyma cells.

Placenta. A zone of tissue in the ovary where ovules are attached.

Plicate. Folded lengthwise several times (at least in bud).

Plumose. Feathery; usually applied to a style with dense pubescence.

Pod. A dehiscent, dry fruit.

Pollen. Grains borne on anthers, containing the male element.

Polygamodioecious. Essentially dioecious but with a few perfect flowers present.

Polygamous. With both perfect and imperfect flowers on the same plant or on separate plants.

Pome. A fleshy fruit of the apple and other genera in the rose family in which the inferior ovary fuses with the receptacle that grows up around the ovary; the fleshy portion of the fruit is largely stem tissue.

Procumbent. Prostrate or trailing, but not rooting at the nodes.

Prostrate. Lying flat on the ground.

Pseudo-. False.

Puberulent. Minutely pubescent, clothed with small, soft, erect hairs.

Pubescent. Bearing hairs on the surface.

Punctate. Marked with translucent or colored dots, depressions, or pits.

Pungent. Ending in a stiff, sharp point; acrid in taste or odor.

Raceme. A type of inflorescence borne along the axis on short pedicels. The lowest flowers open first.

Rachis. The axis of an inflorescence or a compound leaf.

Radiate. Spreading from a common center; having ray flowers, as in the sunflower family.

Ray. A branch of an umbel or umbellike inflorescence; a corolla of a ray flower in the sunflower family.

Receptacle. The end of a pedicel or peduncle that bears floral organs.

Regular. Describing a flower in which the members of each circle of parts are similar in shape and size.

Reniform. Kidney-shaped; wider than long, rounded in outline, and with a wide basal sinus.

Resinous. Having resin.

Reticulate. Netted, netlike.

Retuse. Notched slightly at a usually obtuse apex.

Revolute. Rolled backward.

Rhizome. An underground stem, usually horizontal and often fleshy, with roots on the under surface.

Rhombic. Shaped like a rhombus, a parallelogram with two opposite acute and two opposite obtuse angles.

Rootstock. Subterranean stem, rhizome.

Rosette. A cluster of basal leaves crowded on short internodes.

Rotate. Wheel-shaped; said of a fused corolla in which a flat, circular limb is at right angles to the corolla tube.

Rugose. Wrinkled.

Sac. Pouchlike part.

Saccate. Pouched.

Sagittate. Arrowheadlike in shape.

Salverform. Said of a gamopetalous corolla with a slender tube.

Samara. An indehiscent winged fruit, as in **Acer**.

Scabrous. Rough to the touch.

Scape. A leafless peduncle arising from the ground.

Scarify. Make incisions in the coats of seeds

Scarious. Thin and dry, often almost translucent.

Schizocarp. A dry, dehiscent fruit that splits into two halves.

Scurfy. Covered with tiny scales.

Sepal. One part of the calyx, usually green.

Serrate. Toothed along the margin, with apex of each tooth pointed and directed forward.

Serrulate. Diminutive of serrate.

Sessile. Without a stalk.

Setose. Beset with bristles.

Sheath. An organ that wholly or partly surrounds another organ at the base, as when the base of a leaf partially surrounds the stem as in the grasses.

Shrub. A woody plant that remains relatively low and has several stems from the base.

Silicle. A short silique.

Silique. A special type of capsule, found in the mustard family, in which the two valves separate from the thin longitudinal partition called a replum.

Simple. Descriptive of a pistil developed from a single carpel or a leaf with the blade in one piece.

Sinuate. Having a wavy margin.

Sinus. An indentation or recess in a margin, between two lobes or divisions of a leaf or other expanded organ.

Solitary. Occurring singly as a solitary flower.

Sorus. A cluster of sporangia in ferns, usually located on the underside of a leaf.

Spadix. A form of spike or head with a thick or fleshy axis, found in the arum family.

Spathe. A large, usually solitary bract subtending and often enclosing an inflorescence.

Spathulate. Shaped like a spatula, maintaining its width or somewhat broadened toward the rounded summit.

Species. The basic unit of classification. Species are combined into genera.

Spike. An elongated inflorescence with sessile or nearly sessile flowers. The oldest flowers are near the base.

Spikelet. A secondary spike; a spicate part of a compound inflorescence as in the grasses.

Spinulose. With small spines.

Sporangia. A sac or body producing spores, as in the ferns.

Spore. A simple reproductive body often used in reference to ferns.

Sporophyll. A leaflike organ which bears spores, as in the ferns.

Stamen. A member of the third set of floral organs, typically composed of the anther and filament.

Staminate. Flowers bearing stamens but no pistils.

Staminode. A sterile structure formed in place of a normal stamen.

Standard. The uppermost petal in flowers of the pea family.

Stellate. Star-shaped; a term usually applied to branched hairs.

Sterile. Nonfunctional, not bearing flowers or producing fruit.

Stigma. The terminal portion of the pistil modified for the reception and germination of pollen.

Lupinus perennis. Raceme flower.

Stipe. The stalk of a pistil or other small organ when axile in origin; also the petiole of a fern leaf.

Stipitate. Borne on a stipe.

Stipule. A pair of small structures at the base of a leaf, varying from minute to leaflike.

Stolon. A horizontal branch arising at or near the base of a plant and taking root and developing new plants at the nodes or at the tip.

Stoloniferous. Producing stolons.

Strigose. With sharp, stiff, appressed hairs, often basally swollen.

Strobile. A conelike structure made up of sporophylls.

Style. The more or less elongated portion of the pistil between the ovary and the stigma.

Sub-. A prefix meaning more or less or somewhat.

Subcordate. Somewhat cordate or heart-shaped.

Suborbicular. Somewhat orbicular.

Subspecies. A major subdivision of a species.

Subtend. To stand below and close to, as a bract just below a flower.

Subulate. Awl-shaped, linear and tapering from the base to a sharp apex.

Succulent. Fleshy and juicy.

Sucker. A shoot coming from the root or an underground stem.

Superior. Above; said of an ovary that arises above the point of attachment of other floral organs.

Syncarp. A compound fruit.

Tendril. A portion of a stem or leaf modified to serve as a holdfast organ.

Tepal. A segment of a perianth.

Ternate. In threes.

Tetraploid. Plant with twice the normal number of chromosomes.

Tomentose. Having tomentum, or dense, woolly hairs.

Tree. A woody plant that produces a single, main trunk and a definite crown.

Truncate. With the base or apex straight or nearly so, as if cut off.

Tuber. A thickened portion of a rhizome used for food storage and also for propagation.

Tubercle. A small, tuberlike structure, usually distinct in color and texture from the organ on which it is borne.

Tuberous. Bearing or producing tubers.

Tunicate. Describing a bulb in which the leaf bases form concentric rings, as in an onion.

Turbinate. Top-shaped.

Umbel. A type of racemose inflorescence with short internodes and long pedicels, usually forming a flat-topped inflorescence.

Undulate. Wavy-margined.

Urceolate. Urn- or pitcher-shaped; ovoid or short tubular and contracted at or just below the mouth, as in the corolla of most species of **Gaultheria** and **Vaccinium**.

Versatile. Attached by the back and freely movable.

Verticillaster. A type of inflorescence found in the mint family where the flowers form in axillary whorls.

Vestigial. Imperfectly developed, said of a part or organ that was fully developed and functional in ancestral forms but is now a degenerate relic, usually smaller and less complex than its prototype.

Villous. With long, soft, shaggy, but not matted hairs.

Viscid. Sticky.

Wing. A thin, dry, or membranous expansion or flat extension or appendage of an organ, as the wing of the samara in **Acer**; also one of the two lateral petals in the flowers of the pea family.

Woolly. With long, soft, and often matted hairs.

BIBLIOGRAPHY

Vaccinium angustifolium.

Books by Dr. Leon Snyder

Snyder, Leon C. **Flowers for Northern Gardens**. Minneapolis: U. of Minnesota Press, 1983.

_____. **Gardening in the Upper Midwest**. Second edition. Minneapolis: U. of Minnesota Press, 1978, 1985.

_____. **Real Radio WCCO and the University of Minnesota Landscape Arboretum Present How Does Your Garden Grow**? Minneapolis: WCCO, 1982.

_____. **Trees and Shrubs for Northern Gardens**. Minneapolis: U. of Minnesota, 1980.

Wild Plant Guides

Gleason, Henry A. **The New Britton and Brown Illustrated Flora of the Northeastern United States and Adjacent Canada**. New York: New York Botanical Garden, 1952. 3 vols.

Gray, Asa. **Manual of Botany; a Handbook of the Flowering Plants and Ferns of the Central and Northeastern United States and Adjacent Canada**. 8th ed. Largely rewritten and expanded by Merritt Lyndon Fernald. New York: American Book Co., 1950.

Great Plains Flora Assoc. **Flora of the Great Plains**. Lawrence: U. Press of Kansas, 1986.

Fassett, Norman F. **Spring Flora of Wisconsin**. 4th. ed. rev. and enl. by Olive S. Thompson. Madison: U. of Wisconsin Press, 1947, 1976.

Lakela, Olga. **A Flora of Northeastern Minnesota**. Minneapolis: U. of Minnesota Press, 1965.

Marotta, Juanita. **Minnesota Wild Flowers of Forest, Field and Wetland**. Minneapolis: author, 1971.

Minnesota's Endangered Flora and Fauna. Edited by Barbara Coffin and Lee Pfannmuller. Minneapolis: U. of Minnesota Press, 1988.

Moyle, John and Evelyn Moyle. **Northland Wild Flowers**. Minneapolis: U. of Minnesota Press, 1977.

National Wildflower Research Center (Midwest Office). **Bibliography for Non-Woody, Native Plants of the Midwest**. Chanhassen MN: author, 1991. (Unpublished bibliography).

Ownbey, Gerald B. and Thomas Morley. **Vascular Plants of Minnesota: a Checklist and Atlas**. Minneapolis: U. of Minnesota Press, 1991.

Newcomb, Lawrence. **Newcomb's Wildflower Guide**. Boston: Little, Brown & Co., 1977.

Niering, William and Nancy Olmstead. **The Audubon Society Field Guide to North American Wildflowers: Eastern Region**. New York: Knopf, 1979.

Peterson, Roger T. and Margaret McKenny. **A Field Guide to Wildflowers of Northeastern and North Central North America**. Boston: Houghton Mifflin, 1968.

Runkel, Sylvan and Alvin Bull. **Wildflowers of Iowa Woodlands**. Ames: Iowa State U. Press, 1987.

Runkel, Sylvan and Dean Roosa. **Wildflowers of the Tallgrass Prairie**. Ames: Iowa State U. Press, 1989.

Van Bruggen, Theodore. **The Vascular Plants of South Dakota**. Ames: Iowa State U. Press, 1976.

_____. **Wildflowers of the Northern Plains and Black Hills**. Interior SD: Badlands Natural History Assoc., 1971.

Vance, F.R., J.R. Jowsey & J.S. McLean. **Wildflowers of the Northern Great Plains**. 2nd. rev. ed. Minneapolis: U. of Minnesota Press, 1984.

Cultural Guides to Wild Plants

Art, Henry. **A Garden of Wildflowers: 101 Native Species and How to Grow Them**. Pownal VT: Storey Communications, 1986.

_____. **The Wildflower Gardener's Guide: Northeast, Mid-Atlantic, Great Lakes, and Eastern Canada**. Pownal VT: Storey Communications, 1987.

Bruce, Hal. **How to Grow Wildflowers and Wild Shrubs and Trees in Your Own Garden**. New York: Knopf, 1976.

Directory to Resources on Wildflower Propagation. Prepared by Gene A. Sullivan and Richard H. Daley. Saint Louis MO: National Council of State Garden Clubs, 1981.

Miles, Bebe. **Wildflower Perennials for Your Garden**. New York: Hawthorne Books, 1976.

National Wildflower Research Center. **The National Wildflower Research Center's Wildflower Handbook**. Austin: Texas Monthly Press, 1989.

Phillips, Harry R.. **Growing and Propagating Wildflowers**. Chapel Hill: U. of North Carolina Press, 1985.

Sperka, Marie. **Growing Wildflowers: A Gardener's Guide**. New York: Harper and Row, 1973.

Steffek, Edwin. **The New Wild Flowers and How to Grow Them**. Enl. and rev. ed. Portland OR: Timber Press, 1983.

United States. Forest Service. **Seeds of Woody Plants in the United States**. Washington: Forest Service, U.S. Dept. of Agriculture/U.S. Govt. Print. Off., 1974. (Agricultural Handbook; No. 450).

Young, James A. and Cheryl Young. **Collecting, Processing and Germinating Seeds of Wildland Plants**. Portland OR: Timber Press, 1986.

Guides to the Landscaping Process

Eckbo, Garrett. **Home Landscape: The Art of Home Landscaping**. Revised and enlarged edition. New York: McGraw-Hill, 1978.

Simonds, John Ormsbee. **Landscape Architecture: A Manual of Site Planning and Design**. Revised edition. New York: McGraw-Hill, 1983.

Smyser, Carol A. **Nature's Design: A Practical Guide to Natural Landscaping**. Emmaus PA: Rodale Press, 1982.

Guides to Sources of Plants

Andersen Horticultural Library's Source List of Plants and Seeds. Edited by Richard T. Isaacson. Chanhassen MN: Andersen Horticultural Library, 1989.

Barton, Barbara J. **Gardening by Mail: a Source Book**. Boston: Houghton Mifflin, 1990.

INDEX

Rejuvenation of a prairie by burning on May 4th

and regrowth by May 27th.

Photographs: Dr. Anne M. Hanchek.